Why Do You Need This New Edition?

If you're wondering why you should buy this new edition of *Patterns of Reflection*, here are five good reasons.

❶ Twenty-nine new selections—almost half of all the readings in the book— offer fresh perspectives in every single chapter.

❷ Six new readings on argument (Ch. 10) look at today's most compelling issues, including the use of torture, how to deal with kids as criminals, and the role of marriage in contemporary America, and two new political cartoons reflect the growing importance of images in our highly visual age.

❸. Five new readings on media (Ch. 5) look particularly at how images pervade our lives and the role television plays in educating our children.

❹ Chapter 1 offers **new guidelines for peer review**, to help you respond to a strategy used more and more often by instructors in composition courses.

❺ **Expanded chapters** offer more models for each rhetorical strategy.

PEARSON
Longman

Patterns of Reflection

A Reader

Seventh Edition

Dorothy U. Seyler

Northern Virginia Community College

PEARSON
Longman

New York San Francisco Boston
London Toronto Sydney Tokyo Singapore Madrid
Mexico City Munich Paris Cape Town Hong Kong Montreal

Senior Sponsoring Editor: Virginia L. Blanford
Senior Marketing Manager: Sandra McGuire
Senior Supplements Editor: Donna Campion
Production Manager: Denise Phillip
Project Coordination, Text Design, and Electronic Page Makeup:
   Electronic Publishing Services Inc., NYC
Cover Designer/Manager: John Callahan
Cover Image: Courtesy of iStockPhoto
Photo Researcher: Rebecca Karamehmedovic
Senior Manufacturing Buyer: Dennis J. Para
Printer and Binder: Courier Corporation / Westford
Cover Printer: Phoenix Color Corporation / Hagerstown

For permission to use copyrighted material, grateful
acknowledgment is made to the copyright holders on pp. 486–491,
which are hereby made part of this copyright page.

Library of Congress Cataloging-in-Publication Data
Patterns of reflection: a reader / [compiled by]
Dorothy U. Seyler.—7th ed.
   p. cm.
Includes bibliographical references and index.
ISBN-13: 978-0-205-64595-4
ISBN-10: 0-205-64595-X
I. Seyler, Dorothy U.
PE1417.P396 2009
808'.0427—dc22
                              2008039880

Visit us at www.pearsonhighered.com

ISBN 13: 978-0-205-64595-4

ISBN 10:   0-205-64595-X

2 3 4 5 6 7 8 9 10—CRW—11 10 09

It is not enough to have a good mind.
The main thing is to use it well.

René Descartes

I like to find
What's not found
at once, but lies
within something of another nature
in repose, distinct.

Denise Levertov

Contents

Preface   **xv**

1. On Reading and Writing   1

The Challenges and Rewards of Writing   1
Good Reasons for Reading   2
Guidelines for Active Reading   4
Guided Reading: *Andrew Sullivan*, "Society Is
   Dead: We Have Retreated into the IWorld"   8
Writing Focus: Using Summary, Analysis,
   and Synthesis   13
Getting Started   17
Richard Wilbur, "The Writer"   17
Gail Godwin, "The Watcher at the Gates"   19
Terry McMillan, "On Reading and Becoming
   a Writer"   23
Kurt Vonnegut, "How to Write with Style"   29
Communicating with Instructors and Peers:
   In Person and Online   34
Participating in Peer Evaluations   35
The 7 Habits of Highly
   Successful Students   36
Making Connections   37
Topics for Writing   38

2.   Using Narration: Growing Up, Growing Wiser   40

When to Use Narration   40
How to Use Narration   41
Writing Focus: Preparing Your Essay for Readers   42
Getting Started: Reflections on Growing Up
   or Growing Wiser   43
N. Scott Momaday, "The End of My Childhood"   44
Luis J. Rodriguez, "Always Running"   47
Sandra Cisneros, "Only Daughter"   51
Mansour al-Nogaidan, "Losing My Jihadism"   55
Bob Kerr, "The Best Story Turned Out to Be No
   Story At All"   60
Gaye Wagner, "Death of an Officer"   66
Jeanne Marie Laskas, "Inconspicuous
   Consumption"   74
Making Connections   77
Topics for Writing   78
A Checklist for Narration Essays   80

3.   Using Description: Reflecting on People and Places   82

When to Use Description   82
How to Use Descriptive Details   83
Writing Focus: It's All About Words   84
Getting Started: Reflections on a Painting
Tracy Kidder, "Mrs. Zajac"   86
Amy Tan, "Lost Lives of Women"   90
   Francisco de Goya y Lucientes, *Third of May,
   1808*; Edgar Degas, *The Dance Class;* Pablo
   Picasso, *The Three Dancers;* Mary Cassatt, *Two
   Women Seated by a Woodland Stream*; Edward
   Hopper, *Room in New York;* Salvador Dali, *The
   Persistence of Memory*
Pat Mora, "Remembering Lobo"   95

Josh Tyrangiel, "Trouble Woman"   100
Lance Morrow, "Africa"   103
David Montgomery, "Snow: A Prism of More
   Than Frozen Water"   110
Jonathan Schell, "Ground Zero"   114
Student Essay—Description: *Alexa Skandar*,
   "Time's Trophy"   119
Making Connections   122
Topics for Writing   123
A Checklist for Description Essays   124

**4. Using Comparison and Contrast:
Ways of Learning   126**

When to Use Comparison and Contrast   126
How to Use Comparison and Contrast   127
Writing Focus: Coherence Is Crucial   129
Getting Started: Reflecting on Expectations
   of College   130
Nancy Masterson Sakamoto, "Conversational
   Ballgames"   131
Judith Viorst, "Boys and Girls: Anatomy
   and Destiny"   136
Amanda Ripley, "Who Says a Woman Can't
   Be Einstein?"   143
David Sadker, "Gender Games"   150
Robin McKie, "Bring Back Stinks
   and Bangs!"   154
Colbert I. King, "Surveying the Damage
   on Campus USA"   160
Linda Pastan, "Marks"   164
Student Essay—Contrast: *Denisse M. Bonilla*,
   "The Faded Stain"   165
Making Connections   170
Topics for Writing   171
A Checklist for Comparison and Contrast
   Essays   172

5. Explaining and Illustrating: Examining Media Images   174

When to Use Examples   174
How to Use Examples   175
Writing Focus: Vary Your Sentences   176
Getting Started: Thinking About
   Advertising   178
Four Ads: Fila, Got Milk?, Council for
   Biotechnology Information, Expedia.com   179
Jack McGarvey, "To Be or Not to Be as Defined
   by TV"   183
Dimitri A. Christakis, "Smarter Kids, Brought
   to You by the Letters T and V"   191
Jonetta Rose Barras, "We Are Our Own
   Worst Imuses"   195
Shelby Steele, "Notes from the Hip-Hop
   Underground"   201
Markus Prior, "The Real Media Divide"   206
Vincent P. Bzdek, "More Powerful Than . . . Ever:
   On-Screen and Off, Superheroes Are a Force to
   Reckon With"   210
Lisa Mundy, "A Date to Remember"   218
Student Essay—Using Examples:
   Michael King, "Rap's Refusal of Injustice"   222
Making Connections   227
Topics for Writing   228
A Checklist for Essays Using Examples   230

6. Using Process Analysis: How We Work and Play   231

When to Use Process Analysis   231
How to Use Process Analysis   232
Writing Focus: Punctuating Properly   233

Getting Started: Reflections on Your
    Favorite Game   235
John P. Aigner, "Putting Your Job Interview
    into Rehearsal"   235
Suzette H. Elgin, "Improving Your Body
    Language Skills"   241
Gail Saltz, "How to Get Unstuck Now!"   251
Jack Welch, "The Five Stages of Crisis
    Management"   257
Carol Krucoff, "Restoring Recess"   263
Ernest Hemingway, "Camping Out"   267
Tiffany Sharples, "Learning to Love"   272
Making Connections   279
Topics for Writing   280
A Checklist for Process Essays   282

7. Using Division and Classification: Understanding Human Connections   284

When to Use Division and Classification   284
How to Use Division and Classification   285
Writing Focus: Words to Live Without!   287
Getting Started: Classifying Recent
    Reading or Viewing   288
Judith Martin, "The Roles of
    Manners"   288
Franklin E. Zimring, "Hot Boxes
    for Ex-Smokers"   295
Curt Suplee, "The Science and Secrets
    of Personal Space"   299
Stephanie Ericsson, "The Ways We Lie"   305
Ralph Whitehead Jr., "Class Acts: America's
    Changing Middle Class"   316
David Brooks, "Psst! Human Capital"   323

Carolyn Foster Segal, "The Dog Ate My Disk and Other Tales of Woe"   326
Student Essay—Division and Classification: *Garrett Berger,* "Buying Time"   331
Making Connections   338
Topics for Writing   339
A Checklist for Division and Classification Essays   341

8.   Using Definition: Explaining Ideas and Values   343

When to Use Definition   343
How to Develop an Extended Definition   344
Writing Focus: Using Metaphors, Avoiding Clichés   345
Getting Started: Reflections on E. B. White's Ideas of Democracy   346
John Ciardi, "Is Everybody Happy?"   347
Robert Keith Miller, "Discrimination Is a Virtue"   352
Andrew Vachss, "The Difference Between 'Sick' and 'Evil'"   356
David Hackett Fischer, "Freedom's Not Just Another Word"   362
Charles Krauthammer, "The Greatness Gap"   368
Robin Givhan, "Glamour, That Certain Something"   371
Alastair Reid, "Curiosity"   375
Student Essay—Definition: *Laura Mullins,* "Paragon or Parasite?"   377
Making Connections   382
Topics for Writing   383
A Checklist for Definition Essays   384

9. **Using Causal Analysis: Analyzing Family and Community Conflicts   386**

When to Use Causal Analysis   386
How to Use Causal Analysis   387
Writing Focus: References to Authors, Works, and the Words of Others   389
Getting Started: Reflections on Why You Are in College   391
Keith Ablow, "When Parents Are Toxic to Children"   391
Linda J. Waite, "Social Science Finds: 'Marriage Matters'"   397
Amitai Etzioni, "Working at McDonald's"   408
Patricia Dalton, "The Don't Blame Me Generation"   414
Ray Fisman, "Cos and Effect"   418
Judith D. Auerbach, "The Overlooked Victims of AIDS"   423
Langston Hughes, "Dream Deferred"   427
Making Connections   428
Topics for Writing   429
A Checklist for Causal Analysis Essays   430

10. **Using Argument and Persuasion: Supporting a Fair and Safe World   432**

The Characteristics of Argument   432
How to Use Argument and Persuasion   434
Writing Focus: Logical Fallacies   436
Getting Started: Reflections on the Challenges Facing Ourselves, Our Society, Our World   438

Jack Ohman, King Cartoon   439
Elizabeth Cady Stanton, "Declaration
   of Sentiments"   440
Linda J. Collier, "Adult Crime, Adult Time"   444
Richard Cohen, "Kids Who Kill Are Still
   Kids"   450
John Borneman and Laurie Kain Hart,
   "An Elastic Institution"   453
Michael Kinsley, "Abolish Marriage"   458
Mark Bowden, "Waterboarding:
   A Clarification"   462
Anne Applebaum, "The Torture Myth"   466
Tom Toles, Cartoon on Global Warming   470
Joel Achenbach, "When Size Really Mattered"   471
Student Essay—Refutation: *David M. Ouellette*,
   "Blame It on the Media and Other Ways to
   Dress a Wolf in Sheep's Clothing"   474
Making Connections   477
Topics for Writing   478
A Checklist for Argument Essays   479

Glossary   481
Credits   486
Index   492

Preface

What This Book Is About

Patterns of Reflection provides engaging selections on personal, social, and community issues, selections that also demonstrate varied uses of the major rhetorical strategies or patterns. The organizing of chapters by both rhetorical patterns and topics or themes makes *Patterns of Reflection* a special text, both a practical guide to the various writing structures and purposes students will use in their college writing and a study of issues generating lively class discussion and personal reflection.

Patterns of Reflection asks writers in its opening chapter to think about the challenges and rewards of reading and writing, both in an honest and helpful introduction and in three essays on such topics as writing anxiety, reading and becoming a writer, and writing style.

Each of the rest of the chapters illustrates one specific pattern or purpose, beginning with those strategies we are most comfortable with and then progressing to the more demanding ones: narration, description, comparison and contrast, explaining and illustrating, process analysis, division and classification, definition, causal analysis, and finally argument and persuasion. At the same time, each chapter's thematic core allows students to begin by reflecting on what is closest to them—their childhood, the people and places they know, the learning process—and then move beyond their immediate lives to our society—the media, working and playing, interpersonal relations, values, and public policy issues. The authors represented throughout the text ask readers to think about how they want to live their lives both as individuals and as part of a social group.

Within the two broad organizational patterns are diverse works appealing to readers of varied backgrounds and interests. Instructors can skip some chapters and order others to meet their needs; students will have their favorite selections at the same time that they can be reminded that we all share so much as individuals who must grow up, learn, and prepare for work and adult relationships. Each chapter gains further diversity by:

- Essays of varied length
- A mix of essays, op-ed columns, and excerpts from longer works
- The addition of a poem or political cartoon
- The inclusion of six annotated student essays.

Patterns of Reflection is both a compact, user-friendly text and a rich storehouse of opportunity.

Although the selections are important, this is not just an anthology. It is a text, providing many aids to learning. Each chapter begins with a clear explanation of the strategy and specific guidelines for writing. Each chapter also contains a different Writing Focus, offering guidance with such topics as punctuation, word choice, and logical fallacies. Then students are encouraged to "get started" by engaging in some reflecting and/or writing activity useful as preparation for reading, as a class activity, or as a basis for journal writing.

Following each reading selection are vocabulary exercises and questions that guide students from understanding to analyzing to responding to their reading. After all of the selections in each chapter comes "Making Connections," a section that helps students stretch their minds beyond one reading. These topics can be used for discussion, research, writing, or all three. Following "Making Connections" are topics for writing based on each chapter's readings. They are designed to provide practice in the chapter's rhetorical strategy. Finally, students will find a helpful checklist for writing that includes specific guidelines for each chapter's strategy.

What's New in the Seventh Edition

The seventh edition includes some changes and additions of value to both instructors and students:

- Twenty-nine new selections out of the 71 total.
- Six new works in Chapter 10 on argument, to keep that chapter updated with current issues for debate.

- Five new selections in Chapter 5, to keep the study of the media current as well. Most chapters have at least two new readings.
- Two political cartoons in Chapter 10, because visual arguments are significant in our highly visual age.
- In Chapter 1, new guidelines for participating in peer reviews of drafts, a strategy many instructors use regularly.
- Additional readings in every chapter, instead of a separate chapter of additional readings found in previous editions.

Acknowledgments

No book of value is written alone. I am happy to acknowledge the help of friends and colleagues in preparing this new edition. Once again I am indebted to my daughter Ruth for her always sound advice on new readings. Thanks are also due, as always, to the library staff at the Annandale Campus of Northern Virginia Community College. I remain grateful to Scott Rubin, Barbara Heinssen, Tim Julet, and Eben Ludlow for their help with the early editions of *Patterns of Reflection*. And I would not be writing the preface to the seventh edition of this text if it were not for the continued support of senior vice president and publisher Joe Opiela and my sponsoring editor Virginia L. Blanford. Since 1992, *Patterns of Reflection* has had a long and fruitful journey from Macmillan to Allyn & Bacon to Pearson Longman.

I also appreciate Assistant Editor Rebecca Gilpin, who works hard to keep me organized, and the many fine suggestions of the following reviewers: Julie D. Dockery, Southwest Tennessee Community College; Anthony Edgington, University of Toledo; Laurie Ferrell, South Dakota State University; Marilyn Patton, De Anza College; Alexandria Piland, Central New Mexico Community College; Peggy Porter, Houston Community College Northwest.

Finally, I want to give a special thank you to the students who gave me permission to use their essays. They were hardworking and thoughtful writers who should be proud of their achievements. I hope they will find the same joy that I have in reaching out to students all over the country.

Dorothy U. Seyler

Annandale, Virginia

On Reading and Writing

You have purchased your texts and are ready to begin another English course. What papers will be assigned, you wonder, perhaps somewhat nervously. And why has this text of readings been assigned? After all, writing is difficult enough; must you read, too? Let's give these questions some reflection, a good beginning for this course.

The Challenges and Rewards of Writing

Many people, of all ages, become nervous about writing; they experience what is called writing anxiety. Some are so anxious, as Gail Godwin observes in this chapter (see pp.19–23), that they dream up all kinds of excuses to put off a writing task. If you have some anxiety about writing, you can take comfort in knowing that others share your nervousness, including professional writers who sometimes go through lengthy periods of writer's block. You can also take some comfort in recognizing the appropriateness of your feelings. When faced with a term of writing compositions, students can expect a degree of anxiety, because writing well is not easy.

Let's consider some realities of the writing process. First, writing is a skill, like dancing or riding a bike or playing tennis. You were not born knowing how to ride a bike. You had to learn, perhaps with some painful bumps and bruises to both bike and ego. To be a competent writer, you must develop your skills the same way tennis players develop a spin serve: good instruction, a strong desire to succeed, and practice, practice, practice. A second fact of writing is that some writers are more talented than others, just as Roger Federer is a more talented tennis player than most. But Federer's ability did not come from a genie in a bottle. The best in any field make their abilities look "like magic." You need to remember, however, that they also spend years of study, self-discipline, and practice to achieve their excellence. This text cannot give you a great tennis game, but it can help you to become, with practice and commitment on your part, a competent writer.

Even for those willing to practice, learning to write well is not easy because writing is a complex skill. Topics to write about, audiences to write for, and reasons to write cannot be completely catalogued, and the ways of choosing and combining words into sentences are infinite in their variety. Still, you can, through instruction and practice in this course, develop some good strategies for planning, organizing, drafting, and revising your writing. In addition, this text will provide opportunities for thinking about issues important to all of us and worthy of exploring through writing.

If learning to write well is difficult, why bother to try to develop your skills? For a good answer to this question, ask any student over twenty-five why he or she is now in college. Many "older" students are training for a second career, but many more want to improve basic skills so that they can advance in their current careers. They will assure you, from their experience in the workplace, that all language skills are essential: reading, speaking, listening, and writing. More immediate and personal goals for writing well can also be noted:

- The more you develop your awareness of the writing process, the better a reader you will become. You will understand, from your own experience, how writers select and organize material to achieve their purpose.
- The more confident a writer you become, the more efficiently you will handle written assignments in your other college courses.
- Since writing is an act of discovery, the more you write, the more you will learn about who you are and what matters to you. After all, how accurately do you see your parents, your friends, your campus? Writing will sharpen your vision of the world around you and your understanding of the world inside you.

Good Reasons for Reading

Good writers make good readers. It is also true that reading well improves writing. The strong connection between reading and writing skills explains why students in reading courses are asked to write and students in writing courses are asked to read. Here are three specific uses of reading in a composition course.

Reading for Models

At times students are assigned readings to illustrate a type of writing: the personal essay, the book review, the scholarly report. Or, the readings may illustrate a strategy or purpose in writing: description, illustration, argument. Chapters 2 through 10 in this text contain readings grouped by a dominant writing pattern or purpose. If you are assigned Tracy Kidder's description of Mrs. Zajac and then asked to write a descriptive essay of someone you know, you have been asked to use Kidder's essay as a model for your assignment.

Readings can also be studied as models of effective writing. They can illustrate clever openings, the use of transitions, varied sentence patterns, and effective metaphors. Read, then, not just for what the work says but for what kind of writing it represents and for what writing techniques it illustrates. Questions on strategies and style following each reading will guide your study of the work's special merits. Remember: In the broadest sense, reading contributes to language development. You learned your first language by imitating the speech you heard around you. Imitate the readings in this text to improve your writing skills.

Reading for Information and Insight

You may also be asked to read for information: for facts, for new ideas, for startling analyses. Even when you are reading for models, you will have the chance to explore many subjects, some new to you. Reading, as syndicated columnist Robert Samuelson has observed, "allows you to explore new places, new ideas and new emotions." In this text when you read, you can travel with Lance Morrow to Africa, understand with Linda Waite the ways that marriage improves people's lives, and contemplate with John Ciardi the meaning of happiness. When preparing reading assignments, be sure to think about the questions asking for your reactions. Approach each reading assignment as an opportunity to grow in knowledge, understanding, and imagination.

Reading for Writing

One of the interesting effects of reading is that it produces writing, more works to read and react to in a never-ending chain reaction. A columnist writes about assault weapons. A reader responds with a letter to the editor opposing the banning of such guns. A student, to complete an argument assignment, writes a refutation of the letter. At times writing assignments in this course may call for a response to reading. You may be asked to summarize an essay, analyze a writer's use of details, or contrast writers' differing views on a subject. When writing about reading, you will need to show both skill in writing and understanding of the reading, a challenging task.

Guidelines for Active Reading

When first looking over library materials or texts for courses, you are wise to begin by skimming to see how the material is put together and what, in general, it is about. But, once you become engaged in a particular work that you need to know well, accuracy—not speed—is your goal. You can improve your reading skills by becoming an active, engaged reader who follows a clear three-step reading strategy: prepare, read actively, respond.

Prepare

1. *Prepare to become a part of the writer's audience.* Not all writers write with each one of us in mind. Some writers prepare scholarly reports for other specialists. Some scholars, such as Linda Waite (see page 397–408), present the results of research to a more generally educated audience. Writers of the past wrote for readers in their time, readers who may be expected to know their times or other works with which you may be unfamiliar. So, prepare yourself to join the writer's audience by learning as much as you can about each of the following:

   - the writer
   - the time in which the work was written
   - the kind of work it is (a textbook chapter, a newspaper editorial, a personal narrative)
   - the writer's anticipated audience.

For writings in this book, you will be aided in this step by introductory notes. Be sure to study them. *Never start to read words on a page without first knowing what you are reading!*

2. *Prepare to read with an open mind.* Good readers seek new knowledge and ideas. They do not "rewrite" a work to suit themselves. Keep in mind that not all who write will share your views or express themselves as you do. Read what is on the page, giving the writer a fair chance to develop ideas, giving yourself the thoughtful reflection needed to understand those ideas. Remember: You are in a college course to learn, not to be entertained. So, stick to the task of reading with understanding, not complaining that you didn't "like" this work or that the assignment was "boring." If the reading is difficult for you, look up words or references you do not know and be prepared to read a second time to really learn the material.

3. *Prepare by prereading.* To be prepared to read with understanding, you need to skim the selection to see what kind of work you are about to read (#1 above), to get some idea of the author's subject, and to start thinking about what you already know on that topic. Follow these steps:

   - Read all introductory or biographical notes.
   - Consider the title. What clues in the title reveal the work's subject and perhaps the writer's approach to or attitude about that subject?
   - Read the opening paragraph and then skim the rest of the work, noting in particular any subheadings and/or graphics.
   - Ask yourself: "What do I already know about this subject?" and "What do I expect to learn—and what will I need to know—from reading this work?"
   - From your prereading, raise two or three questions about the subject that you hope to find answers to by reading the work.

Read Actively

4. *Read with concentration.* Your goal is understanding, not completing an assignment as quickly as possible, so read as slowly as necessary to achieve comprehension. Maintain concentration. Avoid reading a page and then gazing out the window or getting a snack. You will have to go back to the beginning to really know what you have read if you

keep interrupting the reading process. Read an entire essay, story, poem, or chapter at one time.

5. *Use strategies for understanding words and references.* Reading a work containing words you do not know is like trying to play tennis with some of the strings missing from your racket. When you come to a word you do not know, begin by studying the sentence in which it appears. You may be able to guess the word's meaning from its context. If context clues do not help, study the parts that make up the word. Many words are combinations of words or word parts that appear in other words that you do know. For example, take the word *autobiography*. This is made up of *auto*, a root meaning "self" (*auto*mobile), *bio*, a root meaning "life" (*bio*logy), and *graph*, a root meaning "writing" (auto*graph*). You can understand many longer words if you think about their parts. Often these strategies will allow you to keep reading. But, be sure to look up words that you cannot figure out. You should also use a dictionary or encyclopedia to learn about writers an author refers to. Understanding references to people, places, and other written works is essential for full comprehension.

6. *Be alert to the use of figurative language and other writing strategies.* Figures of speech such as metaphors, irony, and understatement help shape a writer's tone and convey a writer's attitude toward his or her topic. Use the Glossary if necessary to check the definitions of these terms.

7. *Annotate or make notes as you read.* Studies have demonstrated that students who *annotate* (underline key passages and make notes in the margin) their texts get higher grades than those who do not annotate. So, to be a successful student, develop the habit of reading with pen in hand. As you read, underline key sentences such as each paragraph's topic sentence and the writer's thesis, if stated. When you look up a definition or reference, write what you learn in the margin so that you can reread that section with understanding. When you underline a writer's thesis, note in the margin that this is the main idea. When you see a series of examples or a list, label it as examples (exs) or

list and then number each one in the margin. If you read that there are *three* reasons for this or *four* ways of doing that, be sure to find all three or all four in the passage and label each one. Put a question mark next to a difficult passage—and then ask about it in class. Pay attention to transition words and phrases; these are designed to show you how the parts of the work fit together. Become engaged with the text, as illustrated by the sample annotation in Figure 1.

8. *As you read and annotate, think about the writer's primary purpose in writing and the structures or strategies being used.* Keep in mind the strategies examined in Chapters 2 through 10 and identify the primary strategy that gives the work its

---

Johnson?
Descartes?   "I write, therefore I am," wrote Samuel Johnson, altering   1
Descartes' famous dictum: "I think, therefore I am."

Thesis   When writing in my journal, I feel keenly alive and some-   2
how get a glimpse of what Johnson meant.

advantages   My journal is a storehouse, a treasury for everything in my   3   ①
of journal   daily life: the stories I hear, the people I meet, the quotations I
writing   like, and even the subtle signs and symbols I encounter that
speak to me indirectly. Unless I capture these things in writing,
I lose them.

All writers are such collectors, whether they keep a journal   4
or not; they see life clearly, a vision we only recognize when
Thoreau   reading their books. Thoreau exemplifies the best in journal
example of   writing—his celebrated *Walden* grew out of his journal entries.
journal   By writing in my own journal, I often make discoveries. I see   5   ②
writer   connections and conclusions that otherwise would not appear
obvious to me. I become a craftsman, like a potter or a carpen-
interesting   ter who makes a vase or a wooden stoop out of parts. Writing
simile   is a source of pleasure when it involves such invention and
creation.   *meaning?*
I want to work on my writing, too, hone it into clear, read-   6   ③
able prose, and where better to practice my writing than in my
journal. Writing, I'm told, is a skill and improves with practice.
I secretly harbor this hope. So my journal becomes the arena
where I do battle with the written word.

Figure 1. Sample annotation of first six paragraphs of Joseph Reynolds's "I Think (and Write in a Journal), Therefore I Am."

structure and/or purpose. Consider, as well, if the writer's primary purpose is to share feelings and experiences, to inform readers, or to argue for a claim. However, also keep in mind that writers can—and usually do—mix strategies and may have more than one purpose. For example, a writer using a contrast pattern can develop the points of contrast by providing examples.

9. *Keep a reading journal.* You may want to develop the habit of writing regularly in a journal. A reading journal records your responses to reading assignments but is more informal and personal than class notes. Keeping a journal gives you the chance to list impressions and feelings in addition to ideas that you may use in your next paper. Develop the habit of writing regularly and often. Chances are that both your reading and writing skills will improve.

Respond

10. *Review your reading.* To aid memory, review your reading immediately and then periodically. After finishing an assignment in this text, you can review by answering the questions following each selection. Then, look over your annotations and your reading journal shortly before class discussion of the assigned selection. *Warning: When you are called on, the instructor does not want to hear that you read the selection but cannot remember enough to answer the question!*

11. *Reflect.* In addition to reviewing to check comprehension, reflect on your reading and connect it to other parts of the course and other parts of your life. Remember that reading is not "drill." It is one of the most important ways that we gain new knowledge and new insights into ourselves and our world.

Guided Reading

Read the following article, practicing all the guidelines for active reading. Remember to prepare, to read actively, and then to respond to your reading. Use the questions to the right of the article to guide your reading and thinking. Add your own annotations as well.

Society Is Dead: We Have Retreated into the IWorld

ANDREW SULLIVAN

Born in England, Andrew Sullivan has a doctorate in political science from Harvard. He contributes essays to the *Atlantic Monthly, Time*, and the *Sunday Times* of London, in addition to managing his blog, Andrewsullivan.com. He is a frequent commentator on radio and television, examining a wide range of political and cultural issues. The following essay appeared February 20, 2005, on *Times Online*.

I was visiting New York last week and noticed something I'd never thought I'd say about the city. Yes, nightlife is pretty much dead (and I'm in no way the first to notice that). But daylife— that insane mishmash of yells, chatter, clatter, hustle and chutzpah that makes New York the urban equivalent of methamphetamine—was also a little different. It was quieter. **1** *How has Manhattan changed?*

Manhattan's downtown is now a Disney-like string of malls, riverside parks and pretty upper-middle-class villages. But there was something else. And as I looked across the throngs on the pavements, I began to see why. **2**

There were little white wires hanging down from their ears, or tucked into pockets, purses or jackets. The eyes were a little vacant. Each was in his or her own musical world, walking to their soundtrack, stars in their own music video, almost oblivious to the world around them. These are the iPod people. **3**

Even without the white wires you can tell who they are. They walk down the street in their own MP3 cocoon, bumping into others, deaf to small social cues, shutting out anyone not in their bubble. **4**

5   Every now and again some start unconsciously emitting strange tuneless squawks, like
a badly tuned radio, and their fingers snap or
their arms twitch to some strange soundless
rhythm. When others say "Excuse me" there's no
response. "Hi," ditto. It's strange to be among so
many people and hear so little. Except that each
one is hearing so much.

6   Yes, I might as well own up. I'm one of them.   *What "cult"*
I witnessed the glazed New York looks through   *has Sullivan*
my own glazed pupils, my white wires peeping   *joined?*
out of my ears. I joined the cult a few years ago:
the sect of the little white box worshippers.

7   Every now and again I go to church—those
huge, luminous Apple stores, pews in the rear,
the clerics in their monastic uniforms all bustling
around or sitting behind the "Genius Bars," like
priests waiting to hear confessions.

8   Others began, as I did, with a Walkman—and
then a kind of clunkier MP3 player. But the sleek-
ness of the iPod won me over. Unlike other models it gave me my entire music collection to
rearrange as I saw fit—on the fly, in my pocket.

9   What was once an occasional musical diversion became a compulsive obsession. Now I have
my iTunes in my iMac for my iPod in my iWorld.
It's Narcissus heaven: we've finally put the "i"
into Me.

10   And, like all addictive cults, it's spreading.
There are now 22m iPod owners in the United
States and Apple is becoming a mass-market
company for the first time.

11   Walk through any airport in the United States
these days and you will see person after person
gliding through the social ether as if on autopilot.
Get on a subway and you're surrounded by a
bunch of Stepford commuters staring into mid-
space as if anaesthetized by technology. Don't
ask, don't tell, don't overhear, don't observe. Just
tune in and tune out.

It wouldn't be so worrying if it weren't part of 12
something even bigger. Americans are beginning
to narrow their lives.

You get your news from your favourite blogs, 13
the ones that won't challenge your view of the
world. You tune into a satellite radio service that
also aims directly at a small market—for new age
fanatics, liberal talk or Christian rock. Television
is all cable. Culture is all subculture. Your cell
phones can receive e-mail feeds of your favourite
blogger's latest thoughts—seconds after he has
posted them—or get sports scores for your team
or stock quotes of your portfolio.

Technology has given us a universe entirely 14
for ourselves—where the serendipity of meeting
a new stranger, hearing a piece of music we
would never choose for ourselves or an opinion
that might force us to change our mind about
something are all effectively banished.

*How has the
iPod changed
society?*

Atomisation by little white boxes and cell 15
phones. Society without the social. Others who
are chosen—not met at random. Human beings
have never lived like this before. Yes, we have
always had homes, retreats or places where we
went to relax, unwind or shut out the world.

But we didn't walk around the world like 16
hermit crabs with our isolation surgically
attached.

Music was once the preserve of the living 17
room or the concert hall. It was sometimes solitary but it was primarily a shared experience,
something that brought people together, gave
them the comfort of knowing that others too
understood the pleasure of a Brahms symphony
or that Beatles album.

But music is as atomised now as living is. And 18
it's secret. That bloke next to you on the bus
could be listening to heavy metal or a Gregorian
chant. You'll never know. And so, bit by bit,
you'll never really know him. And by his white

wires, he is indicating he doesn't really want to know you.

19   What do we get from this? The awareness of more music, more often. The chance to slip away for a while from everydayness, to give our lives its own soundtrack, to still the monotony of the commute, to listen more closely and carefully to music that can lift you up and keep you going.

What are the advantages of iPods?

20   We become masters of our own interests, more connected to people like us over the internet, more instantly in touch with anything we want, need or think we want and think we need. Ever tried a Stairmaster in silence? But what are we missing? That hilarious shard of an overheard conversation that stays with you all day; the child whose chatter on the pavement takes you back to your early memories; birdsong; weather; accents; the laughter of others. And those thoughts that come not by filling your head with selected diversion, but by allowing your mind to wander aimlessly through the regular background noise of human and mechanical life.

What do we lose when we turn into our own world?

21   External stimulation can crowd out the interior mind. Even the boredom that we flee has its uses. We are forced to find our own means to overcome it.

22   And so we enrich our life from within, rather than from white wires. It's hard to give up, though, isn't it.

23   Not so long ago I was on a trip and realised I had left my iPod behind. Panic. But then something else. I noticed the rhythms of others again, the sound of the airplane, the opinions of the taxi driver, the small social cues that had been obscured before. I noticed how others related to each other. And I felt just a little bit connected again and a little more aware.

24   Try it. There's a world out there. And it has a soundtrack all its own.

WRITING FOCUS
USING SUMMARY, ANALYSIS, AND SYNTHESIS

You will have many occasions, in your composition class, in other classes, and in the workplace, to write using summary, analysis, and synthesis. The book review, for example, combines all three.

Summary

Whether it is paragraph length or a few pages, a *summary* is a condensed, nonevaluative restatement of a writer's main ideas.

To prepare a good summary, read carefully and then follow these guidelines for writing:

1. Maintain a direct, objective style without using overly simplistic sentences.
2. Begin with the author's thesis and then present additional key points.
3. Exclude all specific examples, illustrations, or background sections. However, you may want to indicate the kinds of evidence or methods of development used.
4. Combine main ideas into fewer sentences than were used in the original article or book.
5. Select precise, accurate verbs (*asserts, argues, concludes*) rather than vague verbs (*says, talks about*) that provide only a list of ideas. Pay attention to word choice to avoid such judging words as "Jones then develops the *silly* idea that . . ."

With these guidelines in mind, read the following summary of Andrew Sullivan's "Society Is Dead" (pp. 9–12) and consider why it needs revision.

Summary #1

In "Society Is Dead," Andrew Sullivan talks about people plugged into their iPods. He says that Manhattan is quiet. Sullivan goes to church—but it really is an Apple store. He also listens to music on his iPod. Except when he forgot it on a trip and had to talk to the taxi driver.

We can agree that the writer of this summary has read Sullivan's essay, but we can also assert that the summary lacks focus and is actually misleading. The writer has gone through the essay, picked out some ideas, and strung them together. One result is no clear statement of Sullivan's main idea. Another is that the ending misrepresents Sullivan's thesis. Now read the second summary and be able to explain why it is better.

Summary #2

In "Society Is Dead," Andrew Sullivan observes that Manhattan is much quieter because so many people are plugged into their iPods. Retreating into their own worlds, individuals can choose their own music and Internet sites, easing boring commutes. However, they miss, Sullivan argues, the rhythms of the world around them and the opportunities to interact with, or at least watch, strangers. They also miss chances to develop a meaningful inner life.

Analysis

You will find chapters on process analysis and causal analysis in this text. The process of comparison (or contrast) is also analysis. To establish some guidelines for writing analysis, let's consider one paragraph in an essay that analyzes a writer's style.

Suppose your thesis is that the writer uses connotative words, clever metaphors, and ironic understatement to convey her attitude. You will need a paragraph on each element of style: word choice, metaphors, irony, and understatement. Follow these guidelines for each paragraph.

1. Have a *topic sentence* that conveys the paragraph's subject and ties the paragraph to the essay's thesis.
2. Quote or paraphrase to present *examples* of the element of style, at least three examples taken from throughout the work.
3. *Explain* how the examples support the paragraph's topic sentence and hence your thesis. This is your analysis, the "glue" that holds the paragraph together and makes your point.

4. Use the correct tense. Analyze style in the *present tense.*

Here is one paragraph from student Alan Peterson's style analysis of an essay by Ellen Goodman.

Sample Analysis

Perhaps the most prevalent element of style present in Goodman's article, and a dominant characteristic of her essay style, is her use of metaphors. From the opening sentences through to the end, this article is full of metaphors. Keeping with the general focus of the piece (the essay appeared on Thanksgiving day), many of the metaphors liken food to family. Her references include "a cornucopia of family," "chicken-sized households" and "a turkey-sized family," people who "feast on the sounds as well as the tastes," and voices that "add relish to a story." She imparts that a politician can use the word "family" like "gravy poured over the entire plate." Going to the airport to pick up members of these disjointed American families has become "a holiday ritual as common as pumpkin pie." Goodman draws parallels between the process of "choosing" people to be with us and the simple ritual of passing seconds at the table. Indeed, the essay's mood emphasizes the comparison of and inextricable bond between food and family.

Synthesis

There are many reasons for drawing on two or more sources to develop your own piece of writing, and there is more than one way to acknowledge sources to readers. But what you must do, whether with a formal pattern of documentation or informally including details of author and title in your essay, is *always* let readers know where ideas and information not original with you have been found. Follow these general guidelines for creating synthesis.

1. Have a clear topic sentence in each paragraph. Material from sources is used to support an idea; it is not just "filler."

2. Combine information/ideas from several sources. If you devote each paragraph to only one source, you are writing a series of summaries. You are not synthesizing.
3. Put most of the borrowed material in your own words. When necessary, use brief quotations.
4. Make the sources of your borrowed material absolutely clear throughout. Use signal phrases to guide your reader through the material.
5. Explain and discuss the material. Do not just dump material from sources on your reader. The result is a list, not a synthesis.

The following paragraph, part of a documented report on theories of dinosaur warm-bloodedness, illustrates one student's command of synthesis. (The essay concludes with a "works cited" page that includes the sources cited after the paragraph.)

Sample Synthesis

The body weight of a dinosaur provides one of the arguments supporting the assertion that some dinosaurs were endotherms. Don Lessem reports that one reason for paleontologists' change of thinking arose in 1964 from Dr. John Ostrom's discovery of *Deinonchyus*, "terrible claw," in central Montana (43). Christopher Lampton argues that since *Deinonchyus* had large claws on its feet and was only as tall as a human, it must have been endothermic to remain active enough to flee from larger predators and to attack its own prey with its terrible claw (90). Lampton quotes Ostrom in further support of *Deinonchyus's* endothermy: "'It does not surprise us to see a hawk slash with its talons. . . . Reptiles are just not capable of such intricate maneuvers, such delicate balance'" (88–89). Lampton concludes that *Deinonchyus* could not have been cold-blooded and still remain an aggressive predator that actively hunted by slashing with the claws on its feet (89). The evidence suggests that at least this one dinosaur was warm-blooded.

Works Cited

Lampton, Christopher. *New Theories on Dinosaurs*. New York:
    Watts, 1989.
Lessem, Don. *Dinosaurs Rediscovered: New Findings Which Are
    Revolutionizing Dinosaur Science*. New York: Simon, 1992.

Getting Started

Read the following poem by Richard Wilbur; it is not a difficult
poem to read, I promise! Enjoy his images and metaphors as
you picture the scene he re-creates. Then think about what
Wilbur has to say about the writing process. Use these questions to guide your reading and thinking:

1. What is his daughter doing in her room? Why are there
   silences in between the periods of typing?
2. Five stanzas are about a bird trapped in his daughter's
   room. What does this story have to do with his daughter's
   current activity?
3. What does he wish for his daughter? Why, at the end of the
   poem, does he wish her the same thing—but harder?
4. What would you say is the basic meaning or point of the
   poem?
5. Why has this poem been included in this chapter?

Did you like this poem? If so, do you think you can use it as a
useful reminder or as a guide through this writing course? If
not, why not? You may want to answer these questions in a
journal entry or have answers ready for class discussion.

The Writer

RICHARD WILBUR

Born in New York City, Richard Wilbur attended Amherst College and fought in World War II. He then taught at several colleges, including Harvard and Smith. He has published poetry,
literary criticism, and children's books. His books have led to
two Pulitzer Prizes and a National Book Award. The following
poem is from his collection *The Mind Reader* (1971).

In her room at the prow of the house
Where light breaks, and the windows are tossed with linden,
My daughter is writing a story.

I pause in the stairwell, hearing
5   From her shut door a commotion of typewriter-keys
Like a chain hauled over a gunwale.*

Young as she is, the stuff
Of her life is a great cargo, and some of it heavy:
I wish her a lucky passage.

10   But now it is she who pauses,
As if to reject my thought and its easy figure.
A stillness greatens, in which

The whole house seems to be thinking,
And then she is at it again with a bunched clamor
15   Of strokes, and again is silent.

I remember the dazed starling
Which was trapped in that very room, two years ago;
How we stole in, lifted a sash

And retreated, not to affright it,
20   And how for a helpless hour, through the crack of the door,
We watched the sleek, wild, dark

And iridescent creature
Batter against the brilliance, drop like a glove
To the hard floor, or the desk-top,

25   And wait then, humped and bloody,
For the wits to try it again; and how our spirits
Rose when, suddenly sure,

It lifted off from a chair-back,
Beating a smooth course for the right window
30   And clearing the sill of the world.

It is always a matter, my darling.
Of life or death, as I had forgotten. I wish
What I wished you before, but harder.

*Upper edge of the side of a boat, pronounced gün' əl—Ed.

The Watcher at the Gates

GAIL GODWIN

With degrees from the Universities of North Carolina and Iowa, Gail Godwin began her career as a journalist and English instructor before becoming primarily a fiction writer. She has published a collection of short stories and several novels, including her 1982 best-seller *A Woman and Two Daughters*. In the following essay, published in 1977 in the *New York Times Book Review*, Godwin examines the sources of writer's block and offers some solutions to the problem.

Questions to Guide Your Reading and Reflection

1. What two unpleasant traits do most "Watchers" have?
2. What advice do you have for students who have trouble getting started on a writing assignment?

I first realized I was not the only writer who had a restrain- 1
ing critic who lived inside me and sapped the juice from green inspirations when I was leafing through Freud's *Interpretation of Dreams* a few years ago. Ironically, it was my "inner critic" who had sent me to Freud. I was writing a novel, and my heroine was in the middle of a dream, and then I lost faith in my own invention and rushed to "an authority" to check whether she could have such a dream. In the chapter on dream interpretation, I came upon the following passage that has helped me free myself, in some measure, from my critic and has led to many pleasant and interesting exchanges with other writers.

Freud quotes Schiller, who is writing a letter to a friend. The 2
friend complains of his lack of creative power. Schiller replies with an allegory. He says it is not good if the intellect examines too closely the ideas pouring in at the gates. "In isolation, an idea may be quite insignificant, and venturesome in the extreme, but it may acquire importance from an idea which follows it. . . . In the case of a creative mind, it seems to me, the intellect has withdrawn its watchers from the gates, and the ideas rush in pell-mell, and only then does it review and

inspect the multitude. You are ashamed or afraid of the momentary and passing madness which is found in all real creators, the longer or shorter duration of which distinguishes the thinking artist from the dreamer . . . you reject too soon and discriminate too severely."

3   So that's what I had: a Watcher at the Gates. I decided to get to know him better. I discussed him with other writers, who told me some of the quirks and habits of their Watchers, each of whom was as individual as his host, and all of whom seemed passionately dedicated to one goal: rejecting too soon and discriminating too severely.

4   It is amazing the lengths a Watcher will go to keep you from pursuing the flow of your imagination. Watchers are notorious pencil sharpeners, ribbon changers, plant waterers, home repairers and abhorrers of messy rooms or messy pages. They are compulsive looker-uppers. They are superstitious scaredy-cats. They cultivate self-important eccentricities they think are suitable for "writers." And they'd rather die (and kill your inspiration with them) than risk making a fool of themselves.

5   My Watcher has a wasteful penchant for 20-pound bond paper above and below the carbon of the first draft. "What's the good of writing out a whole page," he whispers begrudgingly, "if you just have to write it over again later? Get it perfect the first time!" My Watcher adores stopping in the middle of a morning's work to drive down to the library to check on the name of a flower or a World War II battle or a line of metaphysical poetry. "You can't possibly go on till you've got this right" he admonishes. I go and get the car keys.

6   Other Watchers have informed their writers that:

7   "Whenever you get a really good sentence you should stop in the middle of it and go on tomorrow. Otherwise you might run dry."

8   "Don't try and continue with your book till your dental appointment is over. When you're worried about your teeth, you can't think about art."

9   Another Watcher makes his owner pin his finished pages to a clothesline and read them through binoculars "to see how they look from a distance." Countless other Watchers demand "bribes" for taking the day off: lethal doses of caffeine, alcoholic doses of Scotch or vodka or wine.

There are various ways to outsmart, pacify or coexist with 10
your Watcher. Here are some I have tried, or my writer friends
have tried, with success:

Look for situations when he's likely to be off guard. Write 11
too fast for him in an unexpected place, at an unexpected time.
(Virginia Woolf captured the "diamonds in the dustheap" by
writing at a "rapid haphazard gallop" in her diary.) Write when
very tired. Write in purple ink on the back of a Master Charge
statement. Write whatever comes into your mind while the
kettle is boiling and make the steam whistle your deadline.
(Deadlines are a great way to outdistance the Watcher.)

Disguise what you are writing. If your Watcher refuses to let 12
you get on with your story or novel, write a "letter" instead,
telling your "correspondent" what you are going to write in
your story or next chapter. Dash off a "review" of your own
unfinished opus. It will stand up like a bully to your Watcher
the next time he throws more obstacles in your path. If you
write yourself a good one.

Get to know your Watcher. He's yours. Do a drawing of him 13
(or her). Pin it to the wall of your study and turn it gently to
the wall when necessary. Let your Watcher feel needed. Watchers are excellent critics after inspiration has been captured; they
are dependable, sharp-eyed readers of things already set
down. Keep your Watcher in shape and he'll have less time to
keep you from shaping. If he's really ruining your whole working day sit down, as Jung did with his personal demons, and
write him a letter. On a very bad day I once wrote my Watcher
a letter. "Dear Watcher," I wrote, "What is it you're so afraid I'll
do?" Then I held his pen for him, and he replied instantly with
a candor that has kept me from truly despising him.

"Fail," he wrote back.   14

Expanding Vocabulary

1. In her essay Godwin refers to four people and one work. She does
   not identify them because she expects her readers to know them.
   Find the people and book and identify each one in a sentence.
   Use your dictionary or a biographical dictionary in your library
   or online.
2. Match each word in column A with its definition in column B.
   When in doubt, first find the word in the essay and look for

context clues to aid your understanding of the word's meaning. Then, if necessary, use your dictionary to complete the matching exercise. The number in parentheses is the number of the paragraph in which the word appears.

Column A	*Column B*
restraining (1)	note differences
sapped (1)	those who strongly dislike
allegory (2)	deadly
duration (2)	liking
discriminate (2)	holding back
severely (2)	symbolic story
notorious (4)	work
abhorrers (4)	frankness
eccentricities (4)	weakened or cut off
penchant (5)	calm down
begrudgingly (5)	reluctantly
admonishes (5)	length of time in an activity
lethal (9)	famous in a negative way
pacify (10)	warns
opus (12)	seriously or harshly
candor (13)	oddities

Understanding Content

1. Where did Godwin find the idea of a Watcher at the Gates?
2. What are some of the tricks Watchers use to keep us from writing?
3. What do Watchers fear? Why do many writers have a Watcher at the Gates problem?
4. What are some ways writers can outsmart their Watchers?

Drawing Inferences about Thesis and Purpose

1. What is a Watcher at the Gates? That is, what problem does the Watcher stand for?
2. What is Godwin's primary purpose in writing? To develop the idea of the Watcher? To offer some understanding of writing anxiety? To explain ways to get rid of writing anxiety?

Analyzing Strategies and Style

1. What strategy does Godwin use when she calls a restraining critic a Watcher at the Gates and suggests that writers get to know him or her? What is effective about this strategy, this approach to her subject?

2. Godwin opens with a metaphor: "sapped the juice from green inspirations." Explain the metaphor.
3. Godwin's piece is a good example of a personal essay. On the basis of your study of this essay, list the characteristics of a personal essay.

Thinking Critically

1. Follow Godwin's suggestion about getting to know your Watcher. Begin by drawing, as best you can, a picture of your Watcher. Then write a brief description of this person or thing.
2. What are some of your favorite excuses for avoiding writing? Now pretend that you are Gail Godwin; how might she tell you to get around these excuses and go on to write?

On Reading and Becoming a Writer

TERRY MCMILLAN

Terry McMillan has published several novels, including *Waiting to Exhale* (1992), *How Stella Got Her Groove Back* (1996), and *The Interruption of Everything* (2005). An instructor in writing at the University of Arizona, McMillan has also edited *Five for Five: The Films of Spike Lee* (1991) and *Breaking Ice: An Anthology of Contemporary African-American Fiction* (1990). The following excerpt, from the introduction to *Breaking Ice*, recounts McMillan's exciting discovery of black writers and her development as a writer.

Questions to Guide Your Reading and Reflection

1. What did McMillan learn from her college course in African-American literature?
2. What advice do you have for someone who wants to be a writer?

As a child, I didn't know that African-American people 1
wrote books. I grew up in a small town in northern Michigan, where the only books I came across were the Bible and required reading for school. I did not read for pleasure, and it wasn't until I was sixteen when I got a job shelving books at the public library that I got lost in a book. It was a biography of Louisa

May Alcott. I was excited because I had not really read about poor white folks before; her father was so eccentric and idealistic that at the time I just thought he was crazy. I related to Louisa because she had to help support her family at a young age, which was what I was doing at the library.

2   Then one day I went to put a book away, and saw James Baldwin's face staring up at me. "Who in the world is this?" I wondered. I remember feeling embarrassed and did not read his book because I was too afraid. I couldn't imagine that he'd have anything better or different to say than Thomas Mann, Henry Thoreau, Ralph Waldo Emerson, Nathaniel Hawthorne, Ernest Hemingway, William Faulkner, etc. and a horde of other mostly white male writers that I'd been introduced to in Literature 101 in high school. I mean, not only had there not been any African-American authors included in any of those textbooks, but I'd never been given a clue that if we did have anything important to say that somebody would actually publish it. Needless to say, I was not just naïve, but had not yet acquired an ounce of black pride. I never once questioned why there were no representative works by us in any of those textbooks. After all, I had never heard of any African-American writers, and no one I knew hardly read *any* books.

3   And then things changed.

4   It wasn't until after Malcolm X had been assassinated that I found out who he was. I know I should be embarrassed about this, but I'm not. I read Alex Haley's biography of him and it literally changed my life. First and foremost, I realized that there was no reason to be ashamed of being black, that it was ridiculous. That we had a history, and much to be proud of. I began to notice how we had actually been treated as less than human; began to see our strength as a people whereas I'd only been made aware of our inferiorities. I started thinking about my role in the world and not just on my street. I started *thinking*. Thinking about things I'd never thought about before, and the thinking turned into questions. But I had more questions than answers.

5   So I went to college. When I looked through the catalog and saw a class called Afro-American Literature, I signed up and couldn't wait for the first day of class. Did *we* really have enough writers to warrant an entire class? I remember the textbook was called *Dark Symphony: Negro Literature in America*

because I still have it. I couldn't believe the rush I felt over and over once I discovered Countee Cullen, Langston Hughes, Ann Petry, Zora Neale Hurston, Ralph Ellison, Jean Toomer, Richard Wright, and rediscovered and read James Baldwin, to name just a few. I'm surprised I didn't need glasses by the end of the semester. My world opened up. I accumulated and gained a totally new insight about, and perception of, our lives as "black" people, as if I had been an outsider and was finally let in. To discover that our lives held as much significance and importance as our white counterparts was more than gratifying, it was exhilarating. Not only had we lived diverse, interesting, provocative, and relentless lives, but during, through, and as a result of all these painful experiences, some folks had taken the time to write it down.

Not once, throughout my entire four years as an undergraduate, did it occur to me that I might one day *be* a writer. I mean, these folks had genuine knowledge and insight. They also had a fascination with the truth. They had something to write about. Their work was bold, not flamboyant. They learned how to exploit the language so that readers would be affected by what they said and how they said it. And they had talent. 6

I never considered myself to be in possession of much of the above, and yet when I was twenty years old, the first man I fell in love with broke my heart. I was so devastated and felt so helpless that my reaction manifested itself in a poem. I did not sit down and say, "I'm going to write a poem about this." It was more like magic. I didn't even know I was writing a poem until I had written it. Afterward, I felt lighter, as if something had happened to lessen the pain. And when I read this "thing" I was shocked because I didn't know where the words came from. I was scared, to say the least, about what I had just experienced, because I didn't understand what had happened. 7

For the next few days, I read that poem over and over in disbelief because *I* had written it. One day, a colleague saw it lying on the kitchen table and read it. I was embarrassed and shocked when he said he liked it, then went on to tell me that he had just started a black literary magazine at the college and he wanted to publish it. Publish it! He was serious and it found its way onto a typeset page. Seeing my name in print excited me. And from that point on, if a leaf moved on a tree, I wrote a poem about it. If a crack in the sidewalk glistened, surely 8 there was a poem in that. Some of these verbose things actually got published in various campus newspapers that were obviously desperate to fill up space. I did not call myself a poet; I told people I wrote poems.

9   Years passed.

10   Those poems started turning into sentences and I started getting nervous. What the hell did I think I was doing? Writing these little go-nowhere vignettes. All these beginnings. And who did I think I was, trying to tell a story? And who cared? Even though I had no idea what I was doing, all I knew was that I was beginning to realize that a lot of things mattered to me, things disturbed me, things that I couldn't change. Writing became an outlet for my dissatisfactions, distaste, and my way of trying to make sense of what I saw happening around me. It was my way of trying to fix what I thought was broken. It later became the only way to explore personally what I didn't understand. The problem, however, was that I was writing more about ideas than people. Everything was so "large," and eventually I had to find a common denominator. I ended up asking myself what I really cared about: it was people, and particularly African-American people.

11   The whole idea of taking myself seriously as a writer was terrifying. I didn't know any writers. Didn't know how you knew if you "had" it or not. Didn't know if I was or would ever be good enough. I didn't know how you went about the business of writing, and besides, I sincerely wanted to make a decent living. (I had read the horror stories of how so few writers were able to live off of their writing alone, many having lived like bohemians.) At first, I thought being a social worker was the right thing to do, since I was bent on saving the world (I was an idealistic twenty-two years old), but when I found out I couldn't do it that way, I had to figure out another way to make an impact on folks. A positive impact. I ended up majoring in journalism because writing was "easy" for me, but it didn't take long for me to learn that I did not like answering the "who, what, when, where, and why" of anything. I then— upon the urging of my mother and friends who had graduated and gotten "normal" jobs—decided to try something that would still allow me to "express myself" but was relatively safer, though still risky: I went to film school. Of course what

was inherent in my quest to find my "spot" in the world was this whole notion of affecting people on some grand scale. Malcolm and Martin caused me to think like this. Writing for me, as it's turned out, is philanthropy. It didn't take years for me to realize the impact that other writers' work had had on me, and if I was going to write, I did not want to write inconsequential, mediocre stories that didn't conjure up or arouse much in a reader. So I had to start by exciting myself and paying special attention to what I cared about, what mattered to me.

Film school didn't work out. Besides, I never could stop   12 writing, which ultimately forced me to stop fighting it. It took even longer to realize that writing was not something you aspired to, it was something you did because you had to . . . .

I've been teaching writing on the university level now for   13 three years, and much to my dismay, rarely have I ever had an African-American student. I wish there were more ways to encourage young people to give writing a shot. Many of them still seem to be intimidated by the English language, and think of writing as "hard"—as in Composition 101–hard. So many of them are set on "making it" (solely in material terms) that we find many of our students majoring in the "guaranteed" professions: the biological sciences, law, engineering, business, etc. If I can make an appeal to those who will read this anthology, I would like to say this to them: If for whatever reason you do not derive a genuine sense of excitement or satisfaction from your chosen field, if you are majoring in these disciplines because of a parent's insistence, if you are dissatisfied with the world to any extent and find yourself "secretly" jotting it down whenever or wherever you can; if you don't understand why people (yourself included) do the things that they do and it plagues you like an itch—consider taking a fiction writing course. Find out if there are African-American writing groups or *any* workshops that are available in your area. Then write. Read as much "serious" fiction as you can—and not just African-American authors. Then, keep writing. "Push it," says Annie Dillard. "Examine all things intensely and relentlessly. Probe and search . . . do not leave it, do not course over it, as if it were understood, but instead follow it down until you see it in the mystery of its own specificity and strength."

Persist.   14

Expanding Vocabulary

Determine the meaning of each of the following words either from its context in this essay or from studying your dictionary. Then select five of the words and use each one in a separate sentence of your own. The number in parentheses is the number of the paragraph in which the word appears.

eccentric (1)   bohemians (11)
exhilarating (5)   philanthropy (11)
provocative (5)   inconsequential (11)
flamboyant (6)   mediocre (11)
verbose (8)   conjure (11)
vignettes (10)   specificity (13)

Understanding Content

1. In what way did the author identify with Louisa May Alcott?
2. What writers was McMillan introduced to in high school? What writers were not part of her required reading?
3. How did McMillan come to write and publish her first poem? Why did she not want to call herself a poet? What seems to have been her attitude toward writers and writing?
4. What were her reasons for writing fiction? How did she narrow and focus her writing?
5. Why did she go to film school? What was the result?
6. What dismays McMillan as a college teacher? What reasons does she offer for students' not taking a fiction writing course? What advice does she give to potential African-American writers?

Drawing Inferences about Thesis and Purpose

1. What is McMillan's purpose in writing?
2. From your reading of this essay, what sort of person do you imagine McMillan to be? Describe her personality.

Analyzing Strategies and Style

1. How would you characterize the style in which this essay is written? (Style is shaped from word choice and sentence structure.) List examples of McMillan's word choice and sentence patterns that help to create the essay's style.
2. What is McMillan's tone? That is, what voice do you hear? How does she create that tone?

Thinking Critically

1. McMillan presents a list of writers in paragraph 2 and another list in paragraph 5. How many writers from the first list do you know? How many from the second list? From your own survey (or the class's as a whole), would you conclude that students today are more familiar than McMillan was with African-American authors, or has the situation not changed much?
2. McMillan believes that students think of fiction writing as "hard" in the same way that freshman composition is hard. Which course do you think would be harder for you? Why?
3. The author concludes with advice directed to the expected audience for *Breaking Ice*, African-American students, some of whom may possibly become writers. How can her advice be applied to composition writers as well as to fiction writers? Explain.

How to Write with Style

KURT VONNEGUT

Kurt Vonnegut has been one of our most popular contemporary novelists. A former employee of General Electric in public relations, Vonnegut is now famous for such novels as *Cat's Cradle* (1963), *Slaughterhouse Five* (1969), and, most recently, *Timequake* (1993). The following advice on style was published by International Paper Company as one of a series of articles used as ads on the "Power of the Printed Word."

Questions to Guide Your Reading and Reflection

1. What will happen when you break rules, give new meanings to words, or try to create an avant-garde style?
2. What do you think is the most important element in a writer's style?

Newspaper reporters and technical writers are trained to   1
reveal almost nothing about themselves in their writings. This makes them freaks in the world of writers, since almost all of the other ink-stained wretches in that world reveal a lot about themselves to readers. We call these revelations, accidental and intentional, elements of style.

2   These revelations tell us as readers what sort of person it is with whom we are spending time. Does the writer sound ignorant or informed, stupid or bright, crooked or honest, humorless or playful—? And on and on.

3   Why should you examine your writing style with the idea of improving it? Do so as a mark of respect for your readers, whatever you're writing. If you scribble your thoughts any which way, your readers will surely feel that you care nothing about them. They will mark you down as an egomaniac or a chowderhead—or worse, they will stop reading you.

4   The most damning revelation you can make about yourself is that you do not know what is interesting and what is not. Don't you yourself like or dislike writers mainly for what they choose to show you or make you think about? Did you ever admire an empty-headed writer for his or her mastery of the language? No.

5   So your own winning style must begin with ideas in your head.

1. Find a Subject You Care About

6   Find a subject you care about and which you in your heart feel others should care about. It is this genuine caring, and not your games with language, which will be the most compelling and seductive element in your style.

7   I am not urging you to write a novel, by the way—although I would not be sorry if you wrote one, provided you genuinely cared about something. A petition to the mayor about a pothole in front of your house or a love letter to the girl next door will do.

2. Do Not Ramble, Though

8   I won't ramble on about that.

3. Keep It Simple

9   As for your use of language: Remember that two great masters of language, William Shakespeare and James Joyce, wrote sentences which were almost childlike when their subjects were most profound. "To be or not to be?" asks Shakespeare's Hamlet. The longest word is three letters long. Joyce, when he

was frisky, could put together a sentence as intricate and as glittering as a necklace for Cleopatra, but my favorite sentence in his short story "Eveline" is this one: "She was tired." At that point in the story, no other words could break the heart of a reader as those three words do.

Simplicity of language is not only reputable, but perhaps 10 even sacred. The *Bible* opens with a sentence well within the writing skills of a lively fourteen-year-old: "In the beginning God created the heaven and the earth."

4. Have the Guts to Cut

It may be that you, too, are capable of making necklaces for 11 Cleopatra, so to speak. But your eloquence should be the servant of the ideas in your head. Your rule might be this: If a sentence, no matter how excellent, does not illuminate your subject in some new and useful way, scratch it out.

5. Sound Like Yourself

The writing style which is most natural for you is bound to 12 echo the speech you heard when a child. English was the novelist Joseph Conrad's third language, and much that seems piquant in his use of English was no doubt colored by his first language, which was Polish. And lucky indeed is the writer who has grown up in Ireland, for the English spoken there is so amusing and musical. I myself grew up in Indianapolis, where common speech sounds like a band saw cutting galvanized tin, and employs a vocabulary as unornamental as a monkey wrench.

In some of the more remote hollows of Appalachia, children 13 still grow up hearing songs and locutions of Elizabethan times. Yes, and many Americans grow up hearing a language other than English, or an English dialect a majority of Americans cannot understand.

All these varieties of speech are beautiful, just as the vari- 14 eties of butterflies are beautiful. No matter what your first language, you should treasure it all your life. If it happens not to be standard English, and if it shows itself when you write standard English, the result is usually delightful, like a very pretty girl with one eye that is green and one that is blue.

15   I myself find that I trust my own writing most, and others seem to trust it most, too, when I sound most like a person from Indianapolis, which is what I am. What alternatives do I have? The one most vehemently recommended by teachers has no doubt been pressed on you, as well: to write like cultivated Englishmen of a century or more ago.

6. Say What You Mean to Say

16   I used to be exasperated by such teachers, but am no more. I understand now that all those antique essays and stories with which I was to compare my own work were not magnificent for their datedness or foreignness, but for saying precisely what their authors meant them to say. My teachers wished me to write accurately, always selecting the most effective words, and relating the words to one another unambiguously, rigidly, like parts of a machine. The teachers did not want to turn me into an Englishman after all. They hoped that I would become understandable—and therefore understood. And there went my dream of doing with words what Pablo Picasso did with paint or what any number of jazz idols did with music. If I broke all the rules of punctuation, had words mean whatever I wanted them to mean, and strung them together higgledy-piggledy, I would simply not be understood. So you, too, had better avoid Picasso-style or jazz-style writing, if you have something worth saying and wish to be understood.

17   Readers want our pages to look very much like pages they have seen before. Why? This is because they themselves have a tough job to do, and they need all the help they can get from us.

7. Pity the Readers

18   They have to identify thousands of little marks on paper, and make sense of them immediately. They have to *read*, an art so difficult that most people don't really master it even after having studied it all through grade school and high school—twelve long years.

19   So this discussion must finally acknowledge that our stylistic options as writers are neither numerous nor glamorous, since our readers are bound to be such imperfect artists. Our audience requires us to be sympathetic and patient teachers,

even willing to simplify and clarify—whereas we would rather
soar high above the crowd, singing like nightingales.

That is the bad news. The good news is that we Americans   20
are governed under a unique Constitution, which allows us to
write whatever we please without fear of punishment. So the
most meaningful aspect of our styles, which is what we choose
to write about, is utterly unlimited.

8. For Really Detailed Advice

For a discussion of literary style in a narrower sense, in a   21
more technical sense, I commend to your attention *The Elements
of Style*, by William Strunk, Jr., and E. B. White (Allyn & Bacon,
2000). E. B. White is, of course, one of the most admirable literary stylists this country has so far produced.

You should realize, too, that no one would care how well or   22
badly Mr. White expressed himself, if he did not have perfectly
enchanting things to say.

Expanding Vocabulary

Match each word in column A with its definition in column B. When
in doubt, first find the word in the essay and look for context clues
to aid your understanding of the word's meaning. Then, if necessary, use your dictionary to complete the matching exercise. The
number in parentheses is the number of the paragraph in which the
word appears.

Column A	Column B
egomaniac (3)	having many complexly arranged parts
chowderhead (3)	moving, expressive language use
intricate (9)	iron or steel with zinc coating
reputable (10)	appealingly provocative
eloquence (11)	one who is pretty dense, like
piquant (12)	a soup
galvanized (12)	particular style of speaking
locutions (13)	angrily impatient
exasperated (16)	one who has an obsessive focus on
higgledy-piggledy (16)	the self
	in utter disorder
	esteemed, of good reputation

Understanding Content

1. How will readers respond to you if you "scribble your thoughts any which way"?
2. A winning style begins with what?
3. List the specific guidelines Vonnegut provides, each in a separate sentence, in your own words.
4. Explain Vonnegut's rule for cutting text.
5. Why is it best to sound like yourself?

Drawing Inferences about Thesis and Purpose

1. What is Vonnegut's purpose?
2. More than anything else, what does your style tell readers?
3. What, for Vonnegut, is the most important "element of style"?

Analyzing Strategies and Style

1. The author has little to say about his second point. What does he gain by his brevity?
2. Find some examples of clever word choice or metaphors. Explain why they are effective.

Thinking Critically

1. Which of Vonnegut's points do you think is most important for writers? Why? Which point is most important for *you* to focus on as you work on your writing? Why?
2. Vonnegut writes that simplicity is "perhaps even sacred." Explain how simple language can be called sacred. Is this a new idea for you? Does it make sense?
3. Vonnegut begins and ends emphasizing the importance of having something to say. Do you agree with him that this is the most important element of style? Why or why not?

COMMUNICATING WITH INSTRUCTORS AND PEERS: IN PERSON AND ONLINE

During your college experience, you will be communicating with both faculty and students—in your classes, in the instructor's office, and, increasingly, electronically. Here are some suggestions for effective communication.

1. In general, err on the side of formality. Do not assume that instructors will accept a first-name relationship. Use Professor, Doctor, or Mr./Ms. until asked to do otherwise.
2. Speak politely to classmates, even when disagreeing in class discussions. Most faculty will not accept obscenities or name calling in class, in their offices, or in online discussion forums.
3. Do not write personal messages in online discussion boards. Keep your postings focused on the assignment.
4. If your college provides e-mail addresses for students, use that address when communicating with your instructors. If you use a private account, make sure that your address does not appear to be spam—or is not blocked as spam. (You may need to give up that sexy handle you chose some years ago. It will be blocked or some faculty will delete your message without reading it.)
5. You can find lists of netiquette rules online, or follow the basic ones provided here.
   a. Always use a basic letter format—a salutation, body of the message, in paragraphs if it is long, and your name at the end.
   b. Never send unsigned e-mails to faculty or classmates.
   c. Never send an e-mail without a clear subject heading.
   d. Never write in all capitals. This is the equivalent of shouting.
   e. Never write in all lowercase letters. This appears childish to many, and is difficult to read. Capitalize those "I's."
   f. Do not use a variety of symbols. Not everyone knows what they represent.
   g. Take the time to reread your message—and to use spell check—before you send it. When rereading, pay close attention to the tone of the message.

PARTICIPATING IN PEER EVALUATIONS

Peer reviews of drafts are a frequent part of the revision process in composition classes. Follow these guidelines when you participate in peer reviews, whether in class or online, keeping in mind as you work what feedback *you* would like to receive from your classmates.

1. Keep your language and tone courteous and supportive when you are suggesting changes.
2. Begin by addressing the "big" elements. Be precise in your comments on each of these elements.
   a. Does the draft respond to the assignment? (Consider topic selection, approach, and length.)
   b. Does the draft show an awareness of audience? (Consider word choice and tone.)
   c. Is there a clear thesis? (Can you state it with confidence?)
   d. Is there a clear and appropriate organization to develop the thesis? (Can you see *what* the writer is doing, *how* the essay develops?)
3. Next, evaluate each paragraph.
   a. Is each paragraph unified? (Identify any paragraphs in trouble.)
   b. Is each paragraph adequately developed? (Identify any needing expansion.)
   c. Are coherence strategies used effectively? (Point out places in need of help.)
   d. Unless your instructor requires analysis at the level of the sentence, your task is completed. Resist correcting grammar and mechanics while ignoring specific suggestions for the big elements.
   e. Follow your instructor's guidelines precisely.

THE 7 HABITS OF HIGHLY SUCCESSFUL STUDENTS

In 1989 Stephen Covey wrote a best-selling book titled *The 7 Habits of Highly Effective People*. With a nod to his title, we can compile here seven guidelines for success both in college and the workplace.

1. ***Successful students come early.*** Successful business people do not arrive on time for important meetings; they arrive *ahead* of the meeting time to be organized and prepared. Get to your class meetings early, have books and notebooks open, and be ready to learn.
2. ***Successful students come prepared.*** Students who have completed readings or other assignments will get the most

learning from each class. The point of class is to learn, not to "show up" to avoid an absence.

3. *Successful students mark their texts.* Reading actively requires reading with pen in hand, ready to underline key passages and write notes in the margins. Studies have shown that students who mark their texts get higher grades. So get with the program!

4. *Successful students participate.* It is easier to learn "as you go" than to cram for tests. Smart students have figured this out! Shyness is not an excuse. The more you participate, the more at ease you will become.

5. *Successful students submit work on time.* To get ahead in the workplace you need to meet deadlines. The college classroom is your workplace at this time. Develop the habit now of staying on top of assignments to be a success in college and then later in your career.

6. *Successful students show respect for their co-workers— both classmates and faculty.* Do not nap or chat. Turn off all electronics. Do not rattle papers or get up in the middle of a lecture or class discussion. Remember that you are only one person in a group, and that group has work to do together, whether or not you feel like participating.

7. *Successful students understand that image matters.* Dress for the workplace, not the beach or a bar. Submit work that is professional looking and follows your instructor's guidelines in every detail. Always copy everything instructors put on the board or show electronically. Look alert—and you will be alert.

MAKING CONNECTIONS

---

 1. Several writers in this chapter refer to other writers in their essays. Select a writer referred to about whom you know little and read about that writer in at least two sources. Select sources either from your library or online. (Your library will own several biographical indexes, both in paper and electronic formats. You can also "Google" your writer to see what the Internet offers.) Prepare a short biography (that includes a list of the author's main works) for your class.

2. Alternatively, keep a journal for several days. Include in your entries your thoughts and reflections on the writer whose life you learned about.

3. Godwin, Vonnegut, and McMillan are all authors of novels. After becoming acquainted with each of these writers through their essays in this chapter, which one's novels do you most want to read? Be prepared to defend your choice. Alternatively, read a novel by the writer of your choice and prepare a two-page summary and evaluation of the novel for your class.

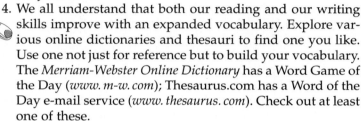

4. We all understand that both our reading and our writing skills improve with an expanded vocabulary. Explore various online dictionaries and thesauri to find one you like. Use one not just for reference but to build your vocabulary. The *Merriam-Webster Online Dictionary* has a Word Game of the Day (*www. m-w. com*); Thesaurus.com has a Word of the Day e-mail service (*www. thesaurus. com*). Check out at least one of these.

TOPICS FOR WRITING

---

1. Terry McMillan offers some insight into how she creates her literature. How do you get started on a piece of writing? How do ideas come to you? What strategies do you use? In an essay explain the ways you get started on a piece of writing. Your purpose in writing should be either to offer your strategies as a useful way to get started or to offer your approach as something to avoid because, on reflection, you have decided that your approach is not effective.

2. How have you learned to fool your "Watcher at the Gates" (see Godwin, pp. 19–23)? In an essay give your advice to anxious writers for avoiding writer's block, based on techniques that have worked for you. Think of your essay as possibly a feature article in your college paper. (Remember: If you use the term "Watcher at the Gates," give Godwin credit.)

3. What kind of reading do you enjoy most? Do you like science fiction, romance novels, the newspaper, magazines devoted to a special interest or hobby? In an essay explain why you

enjoy the kind of material you usually read. Illustrate your reasons with specific examples from your reading.

4. Terry McMillan advises future writers to read as much fiction as they can. What are good reasons for reading? In an essay explain and support reasons for encouraging college students to read more.

5. This chapter's introduction offers some reasons for writing. Why should adults become competent writers? Why should an engineer, a banker, or a teacher be able to write? In an essay answer these questions. Focus either on the practical considerations of a particular job or on more philosophical reasons having to do with personal growth and discovery or general career needs. Remember to explain and illustrate each reason.

2

Using Narration

Growing Up, Growing Wiser

"Once upon a time there lived a princess"—so the fairy tale begins. A story, or narrative, relates a series of events in time sequence. If the narrative relates events that are made up out of the writer's imagination, then the narrative is *fiction*. If the narrative relates events that have taken place, it is *nonfiction*. Nonfiction narratives are found in histories, biographies, newspaper articles, and essays that use narration as a development strategy.

In some writing, distinction between fiction and nonfiction blurs. The historical novel, for example, is fiction bound by the author's research of a particular time and place. Many feature articles in newspapers and magazines reveal the use of such story elements as conflict and point of view. Luis Rodriguez's "Always Running" is a good example of nonfiction that reads very much like a story.

When to Use Narration

Your instructor may ask you to write a story, a narrative account drawn, perhaps, from some incident in your life, complete with characters and dialogue. More likely, you will be asked to draw on incidents from your life to develop a narrative essay. This means that narration will be used as a technique for developing a main idea or thesis. Your purpose in writing may be to share experiences or inform readers of a different time, place, or culture, or some blending of both purposes. (In other classes, you may use narrative to answer test questions, especially in history classes.) However you see your primary purpose in writing, the incidents you select, the way you tell about them, and the reflective comments you include will add up to a statement (or strong implication) of the main point you want to make.

How to Use Narration

Purpose and Thesis

The fewer observations you make about the significance of the events you narrate, the more you need to rely on the telling of the events to carry your meaning. Rodriguez, for example, tells his story with only a few sentences of comment about the sense of always being on the run. Gaye Wagner, on the other hand, reflects on the events she narrates, observing in paragraph 4, "With the death of a comrade, I understood that I was inside the fence." Only you can decide just how much comment you want in a given narrative essay and where those comments should be placed to greatest effect. But first, and most important, have a clear sense of purpose and thesis. An unfocused retelling of some event in your life does not become a polished essay.

When thinking about experiences you might use in a narrative essay, reflect on your purpose and subject as a way to decide on a thesis. Ask, "Why do I want to tell readers about a particular incident?" "What insights into human life do I find in the incident?" Try analyzing your experiences as potential stories shaped by a central conflict that is resolved in some way. But remember that resolution does not necessarily mean a happy ending. Often the only resolution to some experiences is a lesson, bitterly learned. Growing up seems, all too often, to be filled with such painful lessons. Fortunately, they can become the topics of good stories and essays.

Organization and Details

After selecting your topic and deciding on a tentative thesis, think about the shape of your essay. The good narrative essay does not include every stray telephone call that you received the day of the big game. Select the details that are truly significant, that will carry the meaning of the experience for readers. Make your writing vivid through the use of concrete details, but be sure that they are details that contribute to the support of your thesis.

Usually narratives are presented in chronological order, but you may want to consider beginning at the end of the event and then going back to recount the events leading up to the key moment. For example, Gaye Wagner begins with her feelings after an officer's death and then goes back in time to recount his death and funeral before going forward to tell of the event after his death that altered her thinking. Varying time sequence requires careful attention to verb tenses and transition words and phrases so that readers can follow the shifts in time. Some transition words you may need to use include *first, next, then, after, the following day (week, etc.), meanwhile, at the same time.* You will find other examples in the essays in this chapter and in Chapter 5's *Writing Focus* that lists many transition words.

Another choice you must make is the perspective or point of view from which the incident will be told. Most narrative essays are told in the first person. Some writers prefer to use the third person (he, she, they) even though they are writing about their own experiences. Another choice to make is the vantage point of the narrator or essayist. Do you want to take your reader into the event at the time it occurred in your life? That is, should you tell it as if it is occurring as you write? Or, should you select the distance of the adult voice reflecting back on a childhood experience?

Keep in mind these several issues when planning your narrative essay. We all have stories to tell, experiences worth sharing with others. The key is to shape those experiences into a composition that brings readers into our lives and makes them want to know us and understand us, and thereby to understand better what they share with us.

WRITING FOCUS
PREPARING YOUR ESSAY FOR READERS

Your instructor has probably emphasized the writing process early in your course. You may have reviewed invention strategies, ways to state a good thesis, and tips for revising and editing drafts. These steps are important, but also important is preparing your essay to meet the expectations of readers. Here are basic guidelines that will usually work. List in the margin any variations required by your instructor.

1. Always type (keyboard) papers not written in class.
2. Double-space throughout, with 1-inch margins.
3. Use a 12-point font and a standard form of type, such as Times New Roman or Courier. Never use unusual type or a script type; these are hard to read.
4. Indent paragraphs five spaces. Do not quadruple space between paragraphs.
5. Modern Language Association style guidelines call for placing your name, the date, and course information (e.g., English 111) in the upper left of your paper. Starting at the left margin on the first line, place your name. Put the date and course information on separate lines following your name.
6. Center your title and capitalize appropriately. (Capitalize first and last words and all other words except articles, conjunctions, and prepositions of five letters or less.) Do not underline the title or put it in quotation marks. *Remember:* Every essay has a title. "Essay #1" is not an effective title. Make your title clever if you can—but not "cutesy." Clear and direct are always good goals for titles.
7. Refer to Chapter 9's *Writing Focus* (pp. 389–401) for handling references to people and titles and for handling direct quotations.

Getting Started: Reflections on Growing Up or Growing Wiser

Think back over your growing-up years. What periods in your life, particular events, or individuals come to mind as having had an impact on you, perhaps moving you closer to adulthood, to a clearer understanding of yourself and of life? What, on reflection, was an important period in your life? What was an event that changed you in some way? Who was an influential person? Why was he or she important? Write some of your reflections on these questions in a journal entry. Keep your reflections in mind as you read the essays in this chapter, thinking as you read about ways you might use your experiences in an effective narrative essay.

The End of My Childhood

N. SCOTT MOMADAY

For many years an English professor at the University of Arizona, N. Scott Momaday is an artist, poet (*The Gourd Dancer*), Pulitzer Prize–winning novelist (*House Made of Dawn*), and author of a much-praised autobiography, *The Names: A Memoir*, published in 1976. Momaday, whose father was a Kiowa, explores this heritage in his memoir, capturing the American Indian's sense of harmony with the Earth. The following excerpt from *The Names* recounts Momaday's loss of childhood innocence.

Questions to Guide Your Reading

1. What is Momaday's point of view, the perspective from which the event is presented to readers?
2. Think about your most frightening experience. How did you feel then? What do you think about it now?

1   At Jemez I came to the end of my childhood. There were no schools within easy reach. I had to go nearly thirty miles to school at Bernalillo, and one year I lived away in Albuquerque. My mother and father wanted me to have the benefit of a sound preparation for college, and so we read through many high school catalogues. After long deliberation we decided that I should spend my last year of high school at a military academy in Virginia.

2   The day before I was to leave I went walking across the river to the red mesa, where many times before I had gone to be alone with my thoughts. And I had climbed several times to the top of the mesa and looked among the old ruins there for pottery. This time I chose to climb the north end, perhaps because I had not gone that way before and wanted to see what it was. It was a difficult climb, and when I got to the top I was spent. I lingered among the ruins for more than an hour, I judge, waiting for my strength to return. From there I could see the whole valley

below, the fields, the river, and the village. It was all very beautiful, and the sight of it filled me with longing.

I looked for an easier way to come down, and at length I   3
found a broad, smooth runway of rock, a shallow groove wind-
ing out like a stream. It appeared to be safe enough, and I
started to follow it. There were steps along the way, a stairway,
in effect. But the steps became deeper and deeper, and at last I
had to drop down the length of my body and more. Still it
seemed convenient to follow in the groove of rock. I was more
than halfway down when I came upon a deep, funnel-shaped
formation in my path. And there I had to make a decision. The
slope on either side was extremely steep and forbidding, and
yet I thought that I could work my way down on either side.
The formation at my feet was something else. It was perhaps
ten or twelve feet deep, wide at the top and narrow at the bottom, where there appeared to be a level ledge. If I could get
down through the funnel to the ledge, I should be all right;
surely the rest of the way down was negotiable. But I realized
that there could be no turning back. Once I was down in that
rocky chute I could not get up again, for the round wall which
nearly encircled the space there was too high and sheer. I
elected to go down into it, to try for the ledge directly below.
I eased myself down the smooth, nearly vertical wall on my
back, pressing my arms and legs outward against the sides.
After what seemed a long time I was trapped in the rock. The
ledge was no longer there below me; it had been an optical illusion. Now, in this angle of vision, there was nothing but the
ground, far, far below, and jagged boulders set there like teeth.
I remember that my arms were scraped and bleeding, stretched
out against the walls with all the pressure that I could exert.
When once I looked down I saw that my legs, also spread out
and pressed hard against the walls, were shaking violently. I
was in an impossible situation: I could not move in any direction, save downward in a fall, and I could not stay beyond
another minute where I was. I believed then that I would die
there, and I saw with a terrible clarity the things of the valley
below. They were not the less beautiful to me. It seemed to me
that I grew suddenly very calm in view of that beloved world.
And I remember nothing else of that moment. I passed out of
my mind, and the next thing I knew I was sitting down on the

ground, very cold in the shadows, and looking up at the rock where I had been within an eyelash of eternity. That was a strange thing in my life, and I think of it as the end of an age. I should never again see the world as I saw it on the other side of that moment, in the bright reflection of time lost. There are such reflections, and for some of them I have the names.

Expanding Vocabulary

Examine the following words in their contexts in the essay and then write a brief definition or synonym for each one. (Do not use a dictionary; try to guess the word's meaning from its context.) The number in parentheses is the number of the paragraph in which the word appears.

mesa (2)
negotiable (3)
chute (3)
optical illusion (3)

Understanding Content

1. What were the circumstances that led Momaday to the event at Jemez?
2. Momaday presents dramatic details of the incident. Where was he climbing? What could he see at the top of his climb? How did the view make him feel?
3. Why did Momaday choose to come down a different way? After starting down, what decision did he have to make?
4. How did that decision turn out to be critical? What situation did it lead to?
5. When stretched across the rocky chute, what does Momaday think about initially? Then what happens to him?

Drawing Inferences about Thesis and Purpose

1. Momaday says that this experience marked "the end of an age." Why? Why will he "never again see the world as I [he] saw it on the other side of that moment"? What did Momaday have to face on the rocky chute?
2. What is Momaday's thesis?

Analyzing Strategies and Style

1. Analyze Momaday's style of writing. Is his word choice mostly informal or formal, concrete or abstract? Are his sentences

mostly simple or complex, short or long, straightforward or highly qualified? Do the choices seem right for the telling of this narrative? What does he gain by his choice of style?

2. Momaday uses an effective metaphor in the middle of paragraph 3: "jagged boulders set there like teeth." Explain the comparison and its emotional effect.

Thinking Critically

1. Momaday took his climb "to be alone with my [his] thoughts" before his move to a new state and school. Why is it good to take time for reflection before major changes in our lives? Do you take time for reflection, for time alone, on a regular basis? Why or why not?
2. Many people like to test themselves physically, believing that such activities build character as well as muscles. Do you enjoy some strenuous physical activity? If so, what are your reasons for the activity? What do you think you have gained?

Always Running

LUIS J. RODRIGUEZ

Luis Rodriguez (b. 1954), a poet, journalist, and community activist, grew up poor in Los Angeles, struggled with drugs and gangs, and held many odd jobs before and during his years at East Los Angeles College, Berkeley, and UCLA. He has served as a facilitator for various writing workshops and has published two books of poems, *Poems Across the Pavement* (1989) and *The Concrete River* (1991). In the following (an excerpt from Chapter 2 of Rodriguez's memoir *Always Running* [1993]), observe how the author combines descriptive details and dialogue—and uses restraint effectively.

Questions to Guide Your Reading and Reflection

1. Why does Rodriguez begin with the "barrio" quotation? What does it contribute to the essay?
2. What is your response to the quotation below?

"If you ain't from no barrio, then you ain't born."

—a 10-year-old boy from South San Gabriel

1   One evening dusk came early in South San Gabriel, with wind and cold spinning to earth. People who had been sitting on porches or on metal chairs near fold-up tables topped with cards and beer bottles collected their things to go inside. Others put on sweaters or jackets. A storm gathered beyond the trees.

2   Tino and I strolled past the stucco and wood-frame homes of the neighborhood consisting mostly of Mexicans with a sprinkling of poor white families (usually from Oklahoma, Arkansas and Texas). *Ranchera* music did battle with Country & Western songs as we continued toward the local elementary school, an oil-and-grime stained basketball under my arm.

3   We stopped in front of a chain-link fence which surrounded the school. An old brick building cast elongated shadows over a basketball court of concrete on the other side of the fence. Leaves and paper swirled in tiny tornadoes.

4   "Let's go over," Tino proposed.

5   I looked up and across the fence. A sign above us read: NO ONE ALLOWED AFTER 4:30 PM, BY ORDER OF THE LOS ANGELES COUNTY SHERIFF'S DEPARTMENT. Tino turned toward me, shrugged his shoulders and gave me a who-cares look.

6   "Help me up, man, then throw the ball over."

7   I cupped my hands and lifted Tino up while the boy scaled the fence, jumped over and landed on sneakered feet.

8   "Come on, Luis, let's go," Tino shouted from the other side.

9   I threw over the basketball, walked back a ways, then ran and jumped on the fence, only to fall back. Although we were both 10 years old, I cut a shorter shadow.

10   "Forget you, man," Tino said. "I'm going to play without you."

11   "Wait!" I yelled, while walking further back. I crouched low to the ground, then took off, jumped up and placed torn sneakers in the steel mesh. I made it over with a big thud.

12   Wiping the grass and dirt from my pants, I casually walked up to the ball on the ground, picked it up, and continued past Tino toward the courts.

13   "Hey Tino, what are you waiting for?"

14   The gusts proved no obstacle for a half-court game of B-ball, even as dark clouds smothered the sky.

Boy voices interspersed with ball cracking on asphalt. Tino's   15
lanky figure seemed to float across the court, as if he had wings
under his thin arms. Just then, a black-and-white squad car
cruised down the street. A searchlight sprayed across the
school yard. The vehicle slowed to a halt. The light shone
toward the courts and caught Tino in mid-flight of a lay-up.

The dribbling and laughter stopped.   16

"All right, this is the sheriff's," a voice commanded. Two   17
deputies stood by the fence, batons and flashlights in hand.

"Let's get out of here," Tino responded.   18

"What do you mean?" I countered. "Why don't we just stay   19
here?"

"You nuts! We trespassing, man," Tino replied. "When they   20
get a hold of us, they going to beat the crap out of us."

"Are you sure?"   21

"I know, believe me, I know."   22

"So where do we go?"   23

By then one of the deputies shouted back: "You boys get   24
over here by the fence—now!"

But Tino dropped the ball and ran. I heard the deputies yell   25
for Tino to stop. One of them began climbing the fence. I
decided to take off too.

It never stopped, this running. We were constant prey, and   26
the hunters soon became big blurs: the police, the gangs, the
junkies, the dudes on Garvey Boulevard who took our money,
all smudged into one. Sometimes they were teachers who
jumped on us Mexicans as if we were born with a hideous
stain. We were always afraid. Always running.

Tino and I raced toward the dark boxes called class-   27
rooms. The rooms lay there, hauntingly still without the
voices of children, the commands of irate teachers or the
clapping sounds of books as they were closed. The rooms
were empty, forbidden places at night. We scurried around
the structures toward a courtyard filled with benches next
to the cafeteria building.

Tino hopped on a bench, then pulled himself over a high   28
fence. He walked a foot or two on top of it, stopped, and pro-
ceeded to climb over to the cafeteria's rooftop. I looked over
my shoulder. The deputies weren't far behind, their guns
drawn. I grabbed hold of the fence on the side of the cafeteria.

I looked up and saw Tino's perspiring face over the roof's edge, his arm extended down toward me.

29   I tried to climb up, my feet dangling. But then a firm hand seized a foot and pulled at it.

30   "They got me!" I yelled.

31   Tino looked below. A deputy spied the boy and called out: "Get down here . . . you *greaser!*"

32   Tino straightened up and disappeared. I heard a flood of footsteps on the roof—then a crash. Soon an awful calm covered us.

33   "Tino!" I cried out.

34   A deputy restrained me as the other one climbed onto the roof. He stopped at a skylight, jagged edges on one of its sides. Shining a flashlight inside the building, the officer spotted Tino's misshapen body on the floor, sprinkled over with shards of glass.

Expanding Vocabulary

Study the contexts in which the following words are used, or study their definitions in your dictionary, and then use each word in a separate sentence. The number in parentheses is the number of the paragraph in which the word appears.

elongated (3)	smudged (26)
scaled (7)	hauntingly (27)
obstacle (14)	irate (27)
interspersed (15)	scurried (27)

Understanding Content

1. Briefly summarize the situation of the narrative by answering the reporter's questions: who, what, where, when.
2. What happens to Tino?

Drawing Inferences about Thesis and Purpose

1. Although both Tino and Luis are ten years old, their relationship does not seem quite equal. Which one seems to be the leader? How do you know?
2. Since Tino is already on the court, why does Luis say, in paragraph 13, "What are you waiting for?" What does he want to accomplish?
3. What is Rodriguez's purpose in writing? What is his thesis?

Analyzing Strategies and Style

1. Examine the author's opening three paragraphs. What do we learn about the narrator from the opening? What tone do the paragraphs establish?
2. Rodriguez includes several metaphors and images in his writing. Find three and explain each one's meaning and contribution.

Thinking Critically

1. Are you surprised by Tino's assertion that the police will beat the boys if they are caught? Do you think that he overstates and over-reacts? If you think so, how would you explain your views to Rodriguez? If you agree with Rodriguez, do you have evidence to support your views?
2. Rodriguez writes that the many "hunters" blur into one. Included are teachers "who jumped on us Mexicans." Does this statement surprise you? Why or why not?
3. What are some strategies young people can use to try to cope with gangs, with drug dealers, and with prejudiced teachers?

Only Daughter

SANDRA CISNEROS

Born in Chicago to a Mexican-American mother and Mexican father, and the only daughter in a family of seven children, Sandra Cisneros not surprisingly turned to books in her childhood when her brothers would not play with her. She attended the University of Iowa's Writing Workshop and earned a master's degree in creative writing. Her most famous novel is *The House on Mango Street* (1983), her most recent, *Caramelo* (2002). Cisneros has also published short stories and poetry. This essay, published in 1990 in *Glamour*, explores the challenge of winning a father's respect as a woman and a writer.

Questions to Guide Your Reading and Reflection

1. What did Cisneros gain from her family situation?
2. Do you have memories of problems with parents or siblings while growing up? If so, were you able to turn any of these into a positive outcome?

1   Once, several years ago, when I was just starting out my writing career, I was asked to write my own contributor's note for an anthology I was part of. I wrote: "I am the only daughter in a family of six sons. *That* explains everything."

2   Well, I've thought about that ever since, and yes, it explains a lot to me, but for the reader's sake I should have written: "I am the only daughter in a *Mexican* family of six sons." Or even: "I am the only daughter of a Mexican father and a Mexican-American mother." Or: "I am the only daughter of a working-class family of nine." All of these had everything to do with who I am today.

3   I was/am the only daughter and *only* a daughter. Being an only daughter in a family of six sons forced me by circumstance to spend a lot of time by myself because my brothers felt it beneath them to play with a *girl* in public. But that aloneness, that loneliness, was good for a would-be writer—it allowed me time to think and think, to imagine, to read and prepare myself.

4   Being only a daughter for my father meant my destiny would lead me to become someone's wife. That's what he believed. But when I was in the fifth grade and shared my plans for college with him, I was sure he understood. I remember my father saying, "*Que bueno, ni'ja*, that's good." That meant a lot to me, especially since my brothers thought the idea hilarious. What I didn't realize was that my father thought college was good for girls—good for finding a husband. After four years in college and two more in graduate school, and still no husband, my father shakes his head even now and says I wasted all that education.

5   In retrospect, I'm lucky my father believed daughters were meant for husbands. It meant it didn't matter if I majored in something silly like English. After all, I'd find a nice professional eventually, right? This allowed me the liberty to putter about embroidering my little poems and stories without my father interrupting with so much as a "What's that you're writing?"

6   But the truth is, I wanted him to interrupt. I wanted my father to understand what it was I was scribbling, to introduce me as "My only daughter the writer." Not as "This is only my daughter. She teaches." *Es maestra*—teacher. Not even *profesora*.

7   In a sense, everything I have ever written has been for him, to win his approval even though I know my father can't read English words, even though my father's only reading includes

the brown-ink *Esto* sports magazines from Mexico City and the bloody *¡Alarma!* magazines that feature yet another sighting of *La Virgen de Guadalupe* on a tortilla or a wife's revenge on her philandering husband by bashing his skull in with a *molcajete* (a kitchen mortar made of volcanic rock). Or the *fotonovelas*, the little picture paperbacks with tragedy and trauma erupting from the characters' mouths in bubbles.

My father represents, then, the public majority. A public   8
who is uninterested in reading, and yet one whom I am writing about and for, and privately trying to woo.

When we were growing up in Chicago, we moved a lot   9
because of my father. He suffered bouts of nostalgia. Then we'd have to let go of our flat, store the furniture with mother's relatives, load the station wagon with baggage and bologna sandwiches, and head south. To Mexico City.

We came back, of course. To yet another Chicago flat,   10
another Chicago neighborhood, another Catholic school. Each time, my father would seek out the parish priest in order to get a tuition break, and complain or boast: "I have seven sons."

He meant *siete hijos*, seven children, but he translated it as   11
"sons." "I have seven sons." To anyone who would listen. The Sears Roebuck employee who sold us the washing machine. The short-order cook where my father ate his ham-and-eggs breakfasts. "I have seven sons." As if he deserved a medal from the state.

My papa. He didn't mean anything by that mistranslation,   12
I'm sure. But somehow I could feel myself being erased. I'd tug my father's sleeve and whisper: "Not seven sons. Six! and *one daughter.*"

When my oldest brother graduated from medical school, he   13
fulfilled my father's dream that we study hard and use this— our heads, instead of this—our hands. Even now my father's hands are thick and yellow, stubbed by a history of hammer and nails and twine and coils and springs. "Use this," my father said, tapping his head, "and not this," showing us those hands. He always looked tired when he said it.

Wasn't college an investment? And hadn't I spent all those   14
years in college? And if I didn't marry, what was it all for? Why would anyone go to college and then choose to be poor? Especially someone who had always been poor.

Last year, after ten years of writing professionally, the financial   15
rewards started to trickle in. My second National Endowment for

the Arts Fellowship. A guest professorship at the University of California, Berkeley. My book, which sold to a major New York publishing house.

16   At Christmas, I flew home to Chicago. The house was throbbing, same as always; hot *tamales* and sweet *tamales* hissing in my mother's pressure cooker, and everybody—my mother, six brothers, wives, babies, aunts, cousins—talking too loud and at the same time, like in a Fellini film, because that's just how we are.

17   I went upstairs to my father's room. One of my stories had just been translated into Spanish and published in an anthology of Chicano writing, and I wanted to show it to him. Ever since he recovered from a stroke two years ago, my father likes to spend his leisure hours horizontally. And that's how I found him, watching a Pedro Infante movie on Galavision and eating rice pudding.

18   There was a glass filmed with milk on the bedside table. There were several vials of pills and balled Kleenex. And on the floor, one black sock and a plastic urinal that I didn't want to look at but looked at anyway. Pedro Infante was about to burst into song, and my father was laughing.

19   I'm not sure if it was because my story was translated into Spanish, or because it was published in Mexico, or perhaps because the story dealt with Tepeyac, the *colonia* my father was raised in and the house he grew up in, but at any rate, my father punched the mute button on his remote control and read my story.

20   I sat on the bed next to my father and waited. He read it very slowly. As if he were reading each line over and over. He laughed at all the right places and read lines he liked out loud. He pointed and asked questions: "Is this So-and-so?" "Yes," I said. He kept reading.

21   When he was finally finished, after what seemed like hours, my father looked up and asked: "Where can we get more copies of this for the relatives?"

22   Of all the wonderful things that happened to me last year, that was the most wonderful.

Expanding Vocabulary

Examine the following words in their contexts in the essay and then write a brief definition or synonym for each one. (Do not use a dictionary; try to guess the word's meaning from its context.) The number in parentheses is the number of the paragraph in which the word appears.

destiny (4)   erupting (7)
philandering (7)   vials (18)

Understanding Content

1. Why did the author's father think college was good for his daughter?
2. How did Cisneros feel about her father's not interrupting her while she wrote?
3. How did her father describe his family to others?
4. What piece of Cisneros's writing pleased her father?

Drawing Inferences about Thesis and Purpose

1. When her father asked for copies for the relatives, why was that the most wonderful thing that had happened to the author?
2. What seems to be the author's purpose in writing? What does she want readers to take from her family experiences?

Analyzing Strategies and Style

1. The author uses Spanish words in several places. What does she accomplish by this?
2. Cisneros provides many details about her father. Examine them and draw some conclusions about him.

Thinking Critically

1. Cisneros asserts that she wrote only to get her father's approval. Does this surprise you? How important is approval from parents?
2. How common today is the preference for boys in a family? Are we still a sexist society? If so, what can we/should we do to change this discrimination?

Losing My Jihadism

MANSOUR AL-NOGAIDAN

In his thirties now, Mansour al-Nogaidan has altered his thinking —and his life. Formerly a radical imam, al-Nogaidan now speaks out against the training of terrorists in schools and mosques in the Islamic world—putting his safety at risk. He has been published in U.S. newspapers and writes for the Bahraini paper *al-Waqt*. "Losing My Jihadism" appeared in the *Washington Post* on July 22, 2007.

Questions to Guide Your Reading and Reflection

1. What does *jihad* mean? If you are not sure, look it up before reading the essay.
2. What can we learn from another person's spiritual struggles?

---

1   BURAIDAH, Saudi Arabia

Islam needs a Reformation. It needs someone with the courage of Martin Luther.

2   This is the belief I've arrived at after a long and painful spiritual journey. It's not a popular conviction—it has attracted angry criticism, including death threats, from many sides. But it was reinforced by Sept. 11, 2001, and in the years since. I've only become more convinced that it is critical to Islam's future.

3   Muslims are too rigid in our adherence to old, literal interpretations of the Koran. It's time for many verses—especially those having to do with relations between Islam and other religions—to be reinterpreted in favor of a more modern Islam. It's time to accept that God loves the faithful of all religions. It's time for Muslims to question our leaders and their strict teachings, to reach our own understanding of the prophet's words and to call for a bold renewal of our faith as a faith of goodwill, of peace and of light.

4   I didn't always think this way. Once, I was one of the extremists who clung to literal interpretations of Islam and tried to force them on others. I was a jihadist.

5   I grew up in Saudi Arabia. When I was 16, I found myself assailed by doubts about the existence of God. I prayed to God to give me the strength to overcome them. I made a deal with Him: I would give up everything, devote myself to Him and live the way the prophet Muhammad and his companions had lived 1,400 years ago if He would rid me of my doubts.

6   I joined a hard-line Salafi group. I abandoned modern life and lived in a mud hut, apart from my family. Viewing modern education as corrupt and immoral, I joined a circle of scholars who

taught the Islamic sciences in the classical way, just as they had been taught 1,200 years ago. My involvement with this group led me to violence, and landed me in prison. In 1991, I took part in firebombing video stores in Riyadh and a women's center in my home town of Buraidah, seeing them as symbols of sin in a society that was marching rapidly toward modernization.

Yet all the while, my doubts remained. Was the Koran really   7 the word of God? Had it really been revealed to Muhammad, or did he create it himself? But I never shared these doubts with anyone, because doubting Islam or the prophet is not tolerated in the Muslim society of my country.

By the time I turned 26, much of the turmoil in me had   8 abated, and I made my peace with God. At the same time, my eyes were opened to the hypocrisy of so many who held themselves out as Muslim role models. I saw Islamic judges ignoring the marks of torture borne by my prison comrades. I learned of Islamic teachers who molested their students. I heard devout Muslims who never missed the five daily prayers lying with ease to people who did not share their extremist beliefs.

In 1999, when I was working as an imam at a Riyadh   9 mosque, I happened upon two books that had a profound influence on me. One, written by a Palestinian scholar, was about the struggle between those who deal pragmatically with the Koran and those who take it and the hadith literally. The other was a book by a Moroccan philosopher about the formation of the Arab Muslim way of thinking.

The books inspired me to write an article for a Saudi news-   10 paper arguing that Muslims have the right to question and criticize our religious leaders and not to take everything they tell us for granted. We owe it to ourselves, I wrote, to think pragmatically if our religion is to survive and thrive.

That article landed me in the center of a storm. Some men in   11 my mosque refused to greet me. Others would no longer pray behind me. Under this pressure, I left the mosque.

I moved to the southern city of Abba, where I took a job as   12 a writer and editor with a newly established newspaper. I went back to leading prayers at the paper's small mosque and to writing about my evolving philosophy. After I wrote articles stressing our right as Muslims to question our Saudi clerics and their interpretations and to come up with our own, officials from the kingdom's powerful religious establishment complained, and I was banned from writing.

13   The attacks of Sept. 11, 2001, gave new life to what I had been saying. I went back to criticizing the rote manner in which we Muslims are fed our religion. I criticized al-Qaeda's school of thought, which considers everyone who isn't a Salafi Muslim the enemy. I pointed to examples from Islamic history that stressed the need to get along with other religions. I tried to give a new interpretation to the verses that call for enmity between Muslims and Christians and Jews. I wrote that they do not apply to us today and that Islam calls for friendship among all faiths.

14   I lost a lot of friends after that. My old companions from the jihad felt obliged to declare themselves either with me or against me. Some preferred to cut their links to me silently, but others fought me publicly, issuing statements filled with curses and lies. Once again, the paper came under great pressure to ban my writing. And I became a favorite target on the Internet, where my writings were lambasted and labeled blasphemous.

15   Eventually I was fired. But by then, I had started to develop a different relationship with God. I felt that He was moving me toward another kind of belief, where all that matters is that we pray to God from the heart. I continued to pray, but I started to avoid the verses that contain violence or enmity and only used the ones that speak of God's mercy and grace and greatness. I remembered an incident in the Koran when the prophet told a Bedouin who did not know how to pray to let go of the verses and get closer to God by repeating. "God is good, God is great." Don't sweat the details, the prophet said.

16   I felt at peace, and no longer doubted His existence.

17   In December 2002, in a Web site interview, I criticized al-Qaeda and declared that some of the Friday sermons were loathsome because of their attacks against non-Muslims. Within days, a fatwa was posted online, calling me an infidel and saying that I should be killed. Once again, I felt despair at the ways of the Muslim world. Two years later, I told al-Arabiya television that I thought God loves all faithful people of different religions. That earned me a fatwa from the mufti of Saudi Arabia declaring my infidelity.

18   But one evening not long after that, I heard a radio broadcast of the verse of light. Even though I had memorized the Koran at 15, I felt as though I was hearing this verse for the first time.

God is light, it says, the universe is illuminated by His light. I felt the verse was speaking directly to me, sending me a message. This God of light, I thought, how could He be against any human? The God of light would not be happy to see people suffer, even if they had sinned and made mistakes along the way.

I had found my Islam. And I believe that others can find it, too. 19 But first we need a Reformation similar to the Protestant Reformation that Martin Luther led against the Roman Catholic Church.

In the late 14th century, Islam had its own sort of Martin 20 Luther. Ibn Taymiyya was an Islamic scholar from a hard-line Salafi sect who went through a spiritual crisis and came to believe that in time, God would close the gates of hell and grant all humans, regardless of their religion, entry to his everlasting paradise. Unlike Luther, however, Ibn Taymiyya never openly declared this revolutionary belief; he shared it only with a small, trusted circle of students.

Nevertheless, I find myself inspired by Luther's courageous 21 uprising. I see what Islam needs—a strong, charismatic personality who will lead us toward reform, and scholars who can convince Islamic communities of the need for a bold new interpretation of Islamic texts, to reconcile us with the wider world.

Expanding Vocabulary

Match each word in column A with its definition in column B. When in doubt, first find the word in the essay and look for context clues to aid your understanding of the word's meaning. Then, if necessary, use your dictionary to complete the matching exercise. The number in parentheses is the number of the paragraph in which the word appears.

Column A	Column B
adherence (3)	hateful
assailed (5)	commitment to
abated (8)	deep hatred
imam (9)	judges
hadith (9)	berated
enmity (13)	Islamic religious leader
lambasted (14)	attacked
blasphemous (14)	eased
loathsome (17)	religious edict
fatwa (17)	speaking irreverently
mufti (17)	Islamic oral teachings

Understanding Content

1. How does the author want Islam to change its thinking and teaching?
2. Briefly summarize al-Nogaidan's spiritual journey.
3. What were the reactions of Islamic leaders to the author's speaking and writing about his views?

Drawing Inference about Thesis and Purpose

1. What contrast does the author suggest between his view of what the Koran teaches and what he has experienced from Muslims?
2. What does al-Nogaidan want readers to learn from his retelling of his spiritual journey? What are the larger implications of this personal narrative?

Analyzing Strategies and Style

1. Describe the author's style. Are his sentences mostly short or long? How does he gain intensity in his narrative?
2. What two conflicts are developed throughout the narrative? How do they intersect?
3. When al-Nogaidan calls for an Islamic Martin Luther, what type of change does he want to encourage? What did Luther do for the Christian Church?

Thinking Critically

1. Are you more drawn to the author's personal story of change or to the call for broader political/religious change? Why? Analyze your response.
2. Are there any solutions to the world's religious conflicts? Reflect on this critical question.

The Best Story Turned Out to Be No Story At All

BOB KERR

A graduate of Hamilton College, Bob Kerr served two years of his Marine Corps stint as a combat correspondent in Vietnam. After several years of developing his journalism career, Kerr came to the *Providence Journal*. He has been a local columnist there since 1994. In the following article, published in the *Providence Sunday Journal* on April 3, 2000, Kerr revisits an event from his Vietnam experience, reexamining what he learned as a young correspondent for an unpopular war.

___

Questions to Guide Your Reading and Reflection

1. What do you know about attitudes toward the Vietnam War, especially about the reporting of the war?
2. What role do our assumptions play in our perceptions of reality?

___

The man was a North Vietnamese soldier. He sat on a pile of   1
ammunition crates on a brutal day in September of 1968, an enigmatic smile playing across his face as he waited to be taken away. He seemed to be wondering if he had done the right thing.

He was the centerpiece of the best war story I was ever a   2
part of. I was a Marine combat correspondent. As much as anyone, that man summed up the experience of reporting on Vietnam while having to ignore its casualties.

I have written about him before, and on this quarter-century   3
anniversary of the dreary, defeated end of the war, he seems the most enduring image to pull from that incredible jumble of images that make up the Vietnam scrapbook. He came to stand for the separate truth we were often issued, along with the salt tablets and bush hats.

They revisit us now and then, these people who were part   4
of a time when we were taken as far from old comforts and beliefs as we could ever get. A smell, a sound, a passing face or stupid comment can be enough to connect us to a small but lasting piece of ourselves.

Sometimes, there is a feeling that we should make it all   5
mean something—find out the role Vietnam plays in making us the people we've become. But most of the time, I think, there is a simple gratitude that we were able to survive the great adventure of our generation, hold on to the memories, and enjoy that slightly crazy edge we've all been granted by historians, moviemakers, and standup comics.

The memories are dark and cruel, funny and drunken. I was   6
given a wonderful window on Vietnam when the Marine Corps made me a combat correspondent and allowed me to

move about with a freedom some generals didn't enjoy. I was able to stop and watch and listen sometimes.

7   Every Christmas now, somewhere in the giving frenzy, I think about the beautiful little girl in Cam Lo village, near Quang Tri. She had great big eyes and a joyous laugh, and we couldn't help watching her as she waited by the side of a Marine truck for her turn to reach up and receive one of the brightly wrapped packages sent by Americans to children in Vietnam. She carried her package to the shade of a tree, tore it open, and took out . . . a pair of white figure skates. She held them up, clearly mystified by the metal blades stuck to what appeared a perfectly good pair of shoes. She dragged them along the dirt street. A Navy corpsman who was treating villagers in a makeshift clinic looked over and said, "Don't those bozos back in the world know anything about this place?"

8   In a Montagnard village, where a Marine sergeant was living and working with the villagers, we sat in a low-roofed hut around the body of a man who had died after a long life and before the war had reached him. Rice wine was passed in small shells as the men of the village talked in low voices. I wasn't sure if we Marines were welcome there, or merely tolerated. There was always in Vietnam the question of whether a deep distrust or hatred of Americans was hidden behind a forced show of friendship.

9   On a fire-support base in I Corps, the northernmost section of South Vietnam, Viet Cong sappers worked their way through perimeter wire at night by flashing tiny flashlights on and off, to blend in with the ever-present fireflies. They moved from bunker to bunker, throwing in satchel charges. The next morning, we carried a body onto a relief helicopter. It had no face and was being taken back for dental identification. As we rode away, the people lined up along the sides of the helicopter studiously avoided looking at the body that lay between us.

10   At Cua Viet, on the South China Sea, a bunch of kids we had picked up in Quang Tri swam and ran on the beach and waited for us to throw them over our mighty Marine shoulders and into the ocean. A friend said it could have been a Sunday afternoon at the beach back home. And for a few hours, it almost seemed like it. Simple contact like that always made the most sense.

11   At the Vandegrift Combat Base, not far from Khe Sanh, North Vietnamese soldiers fished in the river by dropping in grenades, then skimming the dead fish off the top of the water.

There were times on operations when there was no contact   12
with the enemy, and we would sit on a hillside and look out at
the most beautiful place many of us had ever seen.

There were other times when there was contact and 18- and   13
19-year-olds would react magnificently in the middle of the
madness. Say what you will about the Marine Corps, it has
great job training.

In August of 1969, shortly before coming home, I was made a   14
"brig chaser" and told to escort another 19-year-old to the brig in
Da Nang. He had been convicted of being an accessory to murder for having held open a hooch door while another Marine
threw in a fragmentation grenade and killed their company commander. It was a time when "fragging" had become a new and
frightening threat on the U.S. bases. The kid was facing 25 years
in prison at Leavenworth. As we sat by the side of the airstrip
waiting for a helicopter, he pleaded with me to look the other
way and let him escape. I reminded him that we were in Vietnam
and his options were limited. We never did get a helicopter that
day, and I was relieved of having to take him to the brig. If he later
went on to serve his full sentence, he would have gotten out in
the mid-90s.

I tell people I had a good year in Vietnam. It sounds strange,   15
considering how twisted and twisting the experience is supposed
to have been. But I did get to see a lot of country that was a long,
long way from Grosse Pointe, Mich.—and, on the best days, learn
things about that country that had nothing to do with the war.

I had some of the best times of my life in Vietnam, with some   16
of the best people I've ever known.

But there was, of course, that day when I saw that North   17
Vietnamese soldier sitting on the ammunition crates, and reality
shifted.

It was the same day on which I had scrambled to find my   18
helmet during a mortar barrage, only to discover that I was sitting on it. It was the day, too, when I had looked out from a
descending helicopter, saw men lying on ponchos in the landing zone, and wondered how they could be sleeping in the
middle of the action. I was new "in country."

I heard about the two Marines who had taken the North   19
Vietnamese soldier prisoner. I was told he had a weapon, and
they didn't. It sounded like a story to me. My news instincts
were just beginning to take shape.

20   I found the prisoner and his captors. The two Marines were eager to tell me the story:

21   As Marines will do, they had taken the canteens from their entire squad and headed for a nearby stream to fill them. They carried the canteens on a wire held between them. They didn't carry their M-16s.

22   The North Vietnamese soldier stepped out from the side of the trail and pointed his AK-47 at them. The Marines thought they were dead—could feel their bodies giving in to the paralyzing fear of it.

23   But instead of dying, they took the man prisoner. They were young and excited, and told the story with rich detail. They told of how they had used their four or five words of Vietnamese and some careful gestures to negotiate for their lives.

24   "I saw the barrel of his rifle start to lower just a little bit," said one of them.

25   They said they had talked of "beer," making drinking motions to indicate that there was some cold brew waiting if the soldier decided to go the American way.

26   They took an unlikely prisoner. The story—of unarmed Marines taking an armed enemy soldier prisoner—spread quickly through the Marines on the parched hillside. I took it all down in the plastic-wrapped notebook pulled from the side pocket of my camouflage trousers.

27   I couldn't talk to the prisoner. He was going to be put on a helicopter and taken somewhere to be questioned—I could make no demands about my right to get his side of the story. I was a Marine combat correspondent, a "military journalist"; there were restrictions. It is something I think about now, as I do my newspaper job with a freedom I didn't have then.

28   I wrote the story about the capture after I got back to Dong Ha. I thought it was great testimony to Marine ingenuity.

29   It was sent off in the daily news packet to the American military press center in Da Nang, where all our stories were reviewed before being sent to divisional newspapers, *Stars and Stripes*, sometimes stateside newspapers.

30   It came back a couple of days later with the words "Marines would not go for water without their weapons" written across the top.

So it hadn't happened. I had been out there, seen the pris- 31
oner, and talked to the two Marines, and I was pretty sure that
it had happened.

But in that year, when the truth of things was starting to get 32
skewed on almost every level, my story of Marines drawing on
incredible reserves to save their lives was declared inappropriate and inoperative.

A sergeant told me it was good that this lesson in Marine reality 33
happened early in my tour. It would guide me in the future, he said.

And it did. From then on, I knew that the bad stuff— 34
Marines with their faces missing, Marines tossing grenades at
their own officers—would be something for the civilian press
to uncover. But not me. I was upbeat. Under orders, I could
turn a flat-out rout into a strategic retreat.

It invited a play on that old, salty bit of Marine wisdom that 35
if the Marine Corps had wanted you to have something, the
Corps would have issued it. Including, apparently, the truth.

Expanding Vocabulary

Study definitions of any of the following words that are unfamiliar
to you. Then use each one of the words in a separate sentence. The
number in parentheses is the number of the paragraph in which the
word appears.

bozos (7)	fragging (14)
sappers (9)	ingenuity (28)
hooch (14)	skewed (32)

Understanding Content

1. What are some of the positive memories of Vietnam held by Kerr?
   What are some of the unpleasant memories?
2. What is "the story" that the author wrote that was not published?
3. Why was this story not published?

Drawing Inferences about Thesis and Purpose

1. Kerr does not write an angry or cynical essay about Vietnam, and
   he admits to some good memories as well as gruesome ones.
   What, then, is his purpose in writing?
2. What was the lesson Kerr learned about journalism in the hands
   of the Marine Corps?

Analyzing Strategies and Style

1. Examine Kerr's organization. What does he gain by starting with the image of the captured soldier and then not giving the rest of the story until the end of his essay?
2. Kerr writes of a young girl getting ice skates as a Christmas gift from Americans. Why does he include this incident?
3. Study the contrasts in the details in paragraphs 9 through 11. What is clever about the combining of details in these paragraphs?

Thinking Critically

1. When Kerr was new to Vietnam he saw, from a helicopter, "men lying on ponchos in the landing zone," and he wondered why they were asleep in the midst of a war. What inference are we to draw about the men on the ponchos? How does this incident demonstrate just how *new* Kerr was to war?
2. What did the author have to learn about being a military correspondent in a war?
3. Is the military the only organization that tries to shape reality through its control of reporting? Can distortions of the truth be found even in a "free" press?

Death of an Officer

GAYE WAGNER

Gaye Wagner is a detective with the child abuse unit in the San Diego Police Department. She holds a master's degree and previously worked in children and youth services in New Hampshire. "Death of an Officer" was first published in *The American Enterprise* magazine in May 1995. Through narration Wagner examines issues of a police officer's commitment and perspective and shows us how we can learn and grow through reflection on telling moments in our lives, regardless of our age.

Questions to Guide Your Reading and Reflection

1. How did Officer Wagner feel after Officer Davis's death? What was the difference between her training experience and this experience?

2. Reflect on a time you cried in front of others. How did you
feel then? What are your reflections on the incident now?

When Officer Ron Davis was shot in the dark, foggy 1
predawn of September 17, 1991, I momentarily lost my perspective on why I've chosen to do what I'm doing. For a time,
I focused on just one dimension of my job as a police officer:
the possibility of a violent death, for me or people I care about.

Despite the graphic slides and blow-by-blow descriptions of 2
on-duty deaths that we sat through in the Academy, I still must
have believed deep down that I, and those alongside me, were
invincible. Then the faceless gloom of mortality took the face of
a fallen comrade. The streets became an evil, threatening place.

Before I felt the blow of a co-worker's death, I looked on 3
each shooting, stabbing, and act of violence as any rubber-
necker would—with a certain detachment. I was living the ulti-
mate student experience: Social Wildlife 101. What better way
to understand problems of crime and justice than to immerse
yourself in the 'hood. I was there, but I was still an onlooker
peering inside some kind of fence. I watched, probed each
tragic or bizarre incident with curiosity, and pondered the
problems I faced.

With the death of a comrade, I understood that I was inside 4
the fence. I'm no longer an outsider looking in. The shadow of
death stalks all of us who walk in the valley of drugs, guns,
alcohol, hopelessness, and hate. Police, addicts, hustlers, parents trying to build futures for their children, good people
struggling—we all risk falling into the firing line of desperation, apathy, or corruption.

For a while, my response to the new threats I saw around me 5
was to treat all people like they were the enemy. Since an "us"
and "them" mentality can be a self-fulfilling prophecy, some of
my contacts with people were a little bumpy. Normally my
approach is courteous, in one of several variations: either as
sympathizer, "just the facts, Bud" chronicler, or all-ears naive
airhead who can hardly believe that you, yes you, could do a
dastardly deed . . . ("how did this all happen my friend?").

But suddenly I just wasn't as enamored with this job as I had 6
been. Let's face it, a sense of contributing to society, the excitement of racing cars with lights and sirens, helping folks, and

the drama of never knowing what's next place a poor second to living long enough to count grey hairs and collect Social Security.

7   I had trouble getting an impersonal all-units bulletin about someone I knew out of my head. I read these bulletins every day, but the words now stung: "187 Suspect . . . Arrest in Public for 187 P.C.—Homicide of a Police Officer . . . Suspect Description: Castillo, Arno . . . On September 17, 1991, at 05:15 hours, Castillo was contacted by two officers in regard to a domestic violence call. As the officers approached, Castillo opened fire with a .45 cal. automatic weapon, fatally wounding one officer."

8   It was a routine incident that any one of us could have gone to, in an apartment complex that we've all been to. A victim mired in her own problems—a broken collar bone and a life crushing down around her—forgot to tell officers that her crazed, abusive boyfriend had fled with a gun. What followed happened fast. Thick fog and darkness shrouded the complex parking lot where Davis and his partner stopped to contact a driver backing out of the lot.

9   Ron took a bullet in the neck as he stepped out of his passenger side door. The bullet bled him faster than any resuscitating efforts could counteract. He died while his partner hopelessly tried to breathe life back into his bloody, weakening body. Medics said that even if they'd been there when it happened, there would have been nothing they could do to save his life.

10   The next week brought a crush of support for our division. The chief, the field operations commander, psychological services counselors, and peer support counselors all came to our lineups to say we're here man, and we know it doesn't feel good. The lineup room looked like a wake with its display of food, flowers, and cards that showered in from other divisions, other departments, and the citizens of our division.

11   Ron's squad was placed on leave, so officers came from other divisions to help us cover manpower shortages. And on the day of the funeral, officers volunteered from all over the city to cover our beats so that everyone in our division could go to the service.

12   The funeral procession filled the three miles from Jack Murphy Stadium to the church with bumper-to-bumper police units flashing red and blue overhead lights. Police cars came from San

Diego, the Border Patrol, the U.S. Marshals, El Cajon, La Mesa, Chula Vista, National City, Riverside, Los Angeles, seemingly everywhere. The sight we made sent chills up my spine.

For the breadth of that three-mile procession, for a few min- 13 utes at least, drivers couldn't keep racing in their usual preoccupied frenzy. Traffic had to stop. In those frozen freeway moments, a tiny corner of the world had to take time out to notice our mourning at the passing of Ronald W. Davis, age 24, husband, father of two, San Diego police officer. The citizens held captive by the procession responded with heart. There was no angry beeping, there were no cars nosing down breakdown lanes. Drivers turned off ignitions in anticipation of a long wait and watched patiently. Many got out of their cars and waved or yelled words of sympathy.

The pastor's words at the funeral have stayed with me, 14 because he began stretching my perspective back to a more fruitful, hopeful size. "Life is not defined by the quantity of years that we are on this earth, but by the quality of the time that we spend here."

I never cried at the funeral. I cried three weeks later in front 15 of a second grade class.

Staring at the bulletin board one day drinking my coffee, 16 I noticed a sheaf of papers with big, just-learned-to-write letters on them. The papers were letters to the Officers of Southeastern from Ms. Matthews's second grade class at Boone Elementary:

Dear Friends of Officer Davis,

We hope this letter will make you feel better. We feel sad about what happened to Officer Davis. We know he was a nice man and a good cop. We thank you for protecting our neighborhood. We know you try to protect every one of us. We know Officer Davis was a good father. We're sorry.

Your friend, Jeffrey

Dear Friends of Officer Davis,

We feel sorry about Officer Davis. I know you feel sorry for what happened when the bad guy killed your friend, Officer Davis. Thank you for protecting us. I know that he's dead and I know you feel sorry about it. I'm glad you got the bad guy.

Do you think this would happen again? I'm sure not. Please protect yourself.

Your friend,

Henry

P.S. I live in Meadowbrook apartments.

Thank you.

Dear Friends of Officer Davis,

We feel sad about Officer Davis being killed. The man that killed Officer Davis got killed right behind our house. We live in front of Meadowbrook apartments. It is really sad that Officer Davis got killed. Last year when my brother was in sixth grade and he was playing basketball with his friends, two kids came and took the ball away. They broke his basketball hoop. Officers helped find the two kids. We are thankful you are trying to protect us.

Your friend,

Travis

Dear Friends,

I hope you will feel better. I know how you feel, sad. Was Officer Davis your friend? Well, he was my friend, too. When I saw the news I felt very sad for him. When I grow up, I might be a police officer. I'll never forget Officer Davis. I know how losing a friend is. When you lose a friend you feel very sad. I know how losing a friend is cause my best friend moved away to Virginia. They wrote to me once and I still miss her and I miss Officer Davis, too.

Your Friend,

Jennifer L.

Dear Officers,

I hope you feel a little better with my letter. We feel sorry that Officer Davis was killed. I heard that he got shot on his neck when he was just getting out of his car. I also heard that Officer Davis was an officer for two years and that he has two children.

That one is one years old and the other five years old. I want to say thank you for protecting us and for helping us. We all wish that Officer Davis was still alive.

Your friend always,

Arlene

Dear Officers,

We were so sad that your friend Officer Davis died. Last night on 9-17-91 I couldn't sleep because I was thinking all about your friend Officer Davis. When I heard about Officer Davis getting shot I was so sad. I know how it feels when a friend is gone. I wish that Officer Davis could hear this but he can't right now. Officer Davis and the rest of the force do a great job.

Sincerely,

Jasper

Those letters brought feelings up from my gut. The next day   17
I visited Room B-17 to deliver thank you notes to the authors. Ms. Matthews was so excited with my visit that she asked me to speak to the class. She explained that the letters were a class exercise to help the students deal with fears they had expressed to her after the shooting. Because many of her students lived in the apartments where Ron was shot, the shooting was very personal to them. Some couldn't sleep, others were afraid to walk to school, and some were shocked at the realization that the "good guys" get killed too.

I hadn't expected to give a speech, and wasn't really ready   18
to give one on this particular topic. When I faced the class, I saw 32 sets of Filipino, Latino, white, and African-American eyes fixed on me. Their hands all sat respectfully in their laps. In those young faces, I saw an innocence and trust that I didn't want to shake. I thought of the sympathy in their letters; I pictured them passing by the large, dark stain of Officer Davis's blood that still scarred the parking lot pavement; and I wondered what young minds must think when a force of blacked-out SWAT officers sweeps through nearby homes in search of the "bad guy" who shot the "good guy."

19   I wondered how many of the children had been home looking out their windows when the suspect, Arnanda Castillo, was shot by a volley of officers' gunfire as he sprung out of his hiding place in the late afternoon of September 17. I couldn't imagine what these children must be thinking, because a second grader growing up in rural New Hampshire in 1962 didn't witness such events. I could only think that second graders of any generation in any place in the world shouldn't have to witness or ponder the senselessness of human violence.

20   When I finally opened my mouth to speak, my eyes watered and no words would come out. I could say nothing. Each time I tried to push my voice, my eyes watered more. I looked helplessly at Ms. Matthews and the vice principal, who had come to listen to me. Ms. Matthews came to my rescue by starting to talk to the class about strong feelings and the importance of letting feelings out so we don't trap sadness inside ourselves. "Even police officers know that crying can be a strong thing to do." Her reassurances to them reassured me and made me smile at the image of myself, "the big, brave cop" choked up by a second grade class.

21   We talked for a time about the shooting, about having someone to talk to about scary things, and about how important their thoughtful letters had been in a time of sadness. By the time I left, they were more enchanted with my handcuffs and nunchakus than they were concerned by death. Ahhh, the lure for us kids of all ages conjured up by cops and robbers, catching bad guys, rescuing good guys, and having a belt full of cop toys. Through Ron's death, I grew to have a more mature, realistic view of my job.

22   Through the eyes of the pastor at the funeral and Ms. Matthews's second grade class, I recovered perspective and belief in the value of what I do. It's important for me to live my life doing something I believe is important for this thing we call humanity. And I believe that what I do is important because of people like Henry, Jasper, Jennifer L., Jeffrey, Travis, Arlene, Ms. Matthews, and all of the kids in Room B-17.

Expanding Vocabulary

Examine the following words in their contexts in the essay and then write a brief definition or synonym for each one. (Do not use a dictionary; try to guess the word's meaning from its context.) The number in parentheses is the number of the paragraph in which the word appears.

invincible (2)	shrouded (8)
rubbernecker (3)	resuscitating (9)
bizarre (3)	nunchakus (21)
dastardly (5)	conjured (21)
enamored (6)	

Understanding Content

1. Where does the author work, and what does she do?
2. What was her initial response to Officer Davis's death?
3. What did she do in response to reading the students' letters? Then what happened?

Drawing Inferences about Thesis and Purpose

1. What did the author receive from the young students? How did they help her change her thinking?
2. What is Wagner's thesis?

Analyzing Strategies and Style

1. Describe Wagner's chronology. How could the order be altered? What does Wagner gain with her chronology?
2. Near the end, Wagner writes that the students seem most interested in her "cop toys." What does she gain by including this detail?

Thinking Critically

1. Have you experienced violence in your family, neighborhood, or school? If so, how did the experience make you feel? If not, can you describe how you think the second graders from the neighborhood where Officer Davis was shot may have felt?
2. Has it occurred to you that police officers may doubt their commitment or fear for their safety? Should officers express their feelings as Wagner has? Why or why not?
3. Is it fair to say that there are some truths we have to "learn" several times before we really understand? Is there any age limit to learning tough truths? How hard is it to learn, to gain perspective, to grow wiser? Be prepared to discuss your answers to these questions.

Inconspicuous Consumption

JEANNE MARIE LASKAS

On the faculty of the University of Pittsburgh, Jeanne Marie Laskas is the author of three nonfiction books, including *Fifty Acres and a Poodle* (2000). A widely published feature writer for magazines and newspapers, she writes a regular *Washington Post Magazine* column, "Significant Others," and has appeared on half a dozen TV shows. "Inconspicuous Consumption," a "Significant Others" column from January 20, 2008, recounts her heroic replacement of a broken shoelace.

Questions to Guide Your Reading and Reflection

1. From the title of this essay, what do you expect to read about? Why "inconspicuous" consumption?
2. Do you usually repair items or replace them? Can you defend your preference?

1   WHEN THE SHOELACE on my left boot snapped (it had been weakened in an incident last winter with a cat), an observant college student in one of the classes I teach said with a smile, "Looks like it's time for some new boots."

2   I looked down. There was nothing wrong with the boot itself. "It's a shoelace," I said, and made a remark about buying a pair of new laces.

3   "At, like, a sewing store?" the young woman said, perplexed about where one might go to buy such an item. Others joined in the discussion, the sort of small talk you make as you gather books and put on coats after class.

4   "Oh, just Google the brand, and you can probably order direct from the company," offered one young man. "It's a *shoelace!*" I said. An utterly average, plain, brown shoelace. Somehow, the fact that my shoelace was no longer intact opened the door to a discussion of history, of cobblers and grandparents, junkyards and TV repair shops.

5   "Back in those days," one student said, "people tried to fix everything. It was a much better way to live."

6   "*It's a shoelace!*" I said. "You would give up on a shoe because of a broken lace?"

"Probably not an athletic shoe," one said with a shrug, an   7
offering.

On my drive home, I decided not to get depressed about liv-   8
ing in a society so quick to dispose, decided not to think about
how, back in my day, parents didn't just buy you every new
thing you thought you needed. For that matter, I decided not
to think about how, back in my day, your teacher did not have
to tell you to turn off the iPhone you got for Christmas even
though you already had a perfectly functioning Razr V$_3$. No, I
decided I would not go to any of those places cranky adults go.
I would just stop at the store and get me some shoelaces.

I pulled into the shopping area most conveniently located   9
off the highway and scanned my choices: Costco, Best Buy,
Target, Toyota, Home Depot, Pier 1, RadioShack, Blockbuster,
Sprint, PetSmart, Sears.

I weighed Sears versus Target and opted for Target, and out   10
of habit got a cart and went wheeling through the store in the
direction of the pharmacy. I imagined foot care products, insoles
and bunion cushions, and just figured, stupidly, that shoelaces
would be found in the . . . foot department. The pharmacist
assured me I was wrong, and said, woman to woman, "Shoes?"

"Shoes!" I said, thanking her, and went wheeling confi-   11
dently forth, cutting through electronics, where a mother and
a son were arguing about how virtually killing people should
or should not be considered a sport, and then through appliances,
where a man stopped me and asked me if I worked there.
When I said no, he sighed, and so I slowed down out of a kind
of politeness, and he asked me if I thought his wife would like
a vacuum cleaner for her birthday. I winced. "Not even a
Dyson?" he said. I just kept . . . wincing.

When I found the shoelaces, it felt like a victory. They were on   12
sale for 48 cents. They were brown, 45 in/114 cm, Fashion Laces,
Women's Low Cut 5–6 Pair Eyelets. Nothing more on the packaging. No promises of better tying power or advanced
microfiber technology, nothing organic, nothing green, no information about animal testing associated with or without the making of the laces, no Web site listed for further lace information.

Just: 48 cents. A pair of laces. End of story.   13

There was something fantastically satisfying about the   14
purity of this moment. It put me in a better place. I was Laura
Ingalls on the prairie. I was a girl with a penny in her sweaty

palm, just enough for a gum ball. I was lifted up and out of the world I have come to know too well. I put the laces in my cart, went wheeling forth. It was ridiculous to wheel a pair of shoelaces around that big store in that big cart, and I could feel all the old instincts flirting with me, all the urges to fill that cart, to not stop until I had about $100 worth of items in that cart, which would inevitably turn out to actually be $240 worth of items, which I would marvel at with the clerk, who would have just marveled about the same thing with the last customer.

15   But I didn't need anything except the shoelaces. Not one thing. If I thought long enough, I could have come up with plenty of things. But I decided not to think long enough. I wheeled my laces up to the register. The clerk was about my age. She had a fashionable slanted bob cut and a clip in her bangs. "It seems . . . wrong, doesn't it?" I said, holding up my puny purchase.

16   She smiled. "It's definitely a first for me," she said. With tax, my total came to 51 cents. "It's harder to buy less now than it is to buy more," she said. "Isn't that weird?"

17   I smiled smugly, a hero, an accidental champion of some vital human cause, and decided not to spoil things by mentioning the urge I suddenly felt, an actual craving, to stop at Best Buy and look at the plasmas.

Expanding Vocabulary

Examine the following words in their contexts in the essay. Then write a brief definition or synonym for each one. (Do not use a dictionary; try to guess the word's meaning from its context.) The number in parentheses is the number of the paragraph in which the word appears.

intact (4)	bunion (10)
cobblers (4)	puny (15)
opted (10)	plasmas (17)

Understanding Content

1. What has happened to the author that gives her the subject of this essay?
2. What—in general—is the response of Laskas's students?
3. What does the author do to solve her immediate problem? How does she feel about her success?

Drawing Inferences about Thesis and Purpose

1. What is Laskas's subject? Do not answer "new shoelaces"! Think about her purpose in recounting the broken shoelace event.
2. What, then, is her thesis? What does she want readers to reflect on, to understand about our society?

Analyzing Strategies and Style

1. Twice in the opening paragraphs, Laskas puts her response to students in italics. Why? What does she think that young people fail to understand?
2. Look again at paragraph 12. Why does she emphasize the specifics of cost and dimensions of the shoelaces? And what is *not* found on the package?
3. How does the author describe her march through Target and her purchase there? What does she feel that she is accomplishing?

Thinking Critically

1. Laskas implies that young people—her students—in particular are today's conspicuous consumers. Do you agree with her view? Why or why not?
2. What are the advantages of our throwaway culture? What are the disadvantages?

MAKING CONNECTIONS

---

1. How important are names? Do names help to shape our characters? Do you know people whose names do not seem to fit them? Do you think that your name fits you? Be prepared for a class discussion on the topic of "names."
2. Luis Rodriguez and N. Scott Momaday write of dangerous experiences that led to greater awareness and a loss of innocence. Most of us, though, do not face such dramatic moments. We need to learn and grow from being made to feel different (Cisneros), from experiences on the job (al-Nogaidan), or when we travel (Kerr). Reflect on how we gain insight and mature from seemingly insignificant encounters with life. Why do some young people seem

more grown up than others? What is required of us to grow from our experiences? What do the authors suggest on this subject? What can you add from your experience and reflection?

3. Luis Rodriguez and N. Scott Momaday have written autobiographies and Sandra Cisneros has written an autobiographical novel. Select one from your library and read it. Think about what more you learn about the writer's life from your reading. Prepare a two-page summary of the book.

4. Mentors can help young people enormously. Would you like to be a mentor, to help a younger person? What mentoring programs are available on your campus or in your community? Schools and churches often provide mentoring opportunities. There is also the national Big Brother/Big Sister program. You can learn more about them online at *http://www.bbbsa.org*.

TOPICS FOR WRITING

---

1. Several authors in this chapter write of dangerous experiences. Have you ever experienced a situation of physical danger? If so, what were your thoughts and feelings at the time? What were your reactions to the experience after the danger had passed? Did the experience change you in any way? Select the important details of your experience, decide on a point of view, and write a narrative essay in which you let the details of the experience reveal much, if not all, of the effect of the experience on you.

2. Parents and peers are great influences on us, especially when we are young and trying to find our way through adolescence. Do you have a story to tell about the influence of either parents or a social group or clique in your school or community? If so, select one narrative moment to retell to show the influence on—or pressure to influence—you. Your essay can reveal how you resisted the influence and the consequences or how you were influenced and the consequences.

3. Think of a situation, or period in your life, in which you felt unattractive or physically different from others in

some way. (For example, you were big for your age, or short for your age, or had to wear braces.) How did the situation affect you at the time? Later? Reflect on what you might share from that time with readers and then plan your narrative essay to develop and support those reflections.

4. Think of your years in school. Was there a special teacher who made a difference in your attitude toward education or about yourself? If so, reflect on the incidents involving that teacher and then select either several important moments in that teacher's class or one particular event to serve as a narrative basis for your reflections. Decide whether you want to take your reader back to that time to present only your understanding then, or whether you want to blend your emerging awareness at the time with your greater understanding as an adult.

5. If you came to America as a young person or were born here of parents who were recent immigrants, think of the stories you might tell of growing up in the midst of two cultures. Did you experience discrimination in any way? Did you experience feeling torn between two cultures? How did these situations make you feel then? Now? If you maintained elements of your family's culture, how has that benefited you? If you rejected your family's culture, what, from your perspective now, do you think you have lost? Reflect on these questions as a way to select your essay's subject and thesis. Resist the urge to write in general about your childhood. Rather, focus on one incident or short period.

6. Can you recall an incident in which one of your parents embarrassed you, or in which you embarrassed your parent? If you have experienced either one of these situations, think about your feelings both at the time and now. If you were embarrassed by a parent, do you think, on reflection, that you should have felt embarrassment? If you embarrassed a parent, were you aware of it at the time or only on looking back? What insights into the parent/child relationship or into the problems of growing up have you gained from reflecting on these incidents? Those insights can serve as the thesis of your narrative essay. Focus your

retelling only on the important elements of the incident, those parts that will guide your reader to the insight you have gained.

7. Recall an event in your life from which you learned a lesson, perhaps a painful one. What was the lesson? How much did you understand at the time? Did you try to deny the lesson, or did you accept it? Construct your narrative so that your retelling carries your point. Offer some reflection but avoid stating the lesson as a simple moral, such as "I learned that one shouldn't steal."

8. Recall a particular event or period in your life that resulted in your losing some of your innocence, in your rather suddenly becoming much more grown up. What romantic or naive view of life did you lose? What more adult view was forced on you? You will probably want to place your reader back in that time of your growing up. Use chronological order and focus your attention on the key stages in the event that moved you from innocence to awareness.

A CHECKLIST FOR NARRATION ESSAYS

Inventing

☐ Have I selected a topic and approach consistent with the instructor's guidelines for this assignment?

☐ Have I chosen, among the possible topics, one that fits with my experiences?

☐ Have I reflected on that experience and the assignment to create a tentative thesis that is clear, focused, and interesting to others?

☐ Have I chosen an effective perspective, a position in time from which to best present my experience?

☐ Have I recognized and selected the key incidents and rejected those that will distract from advancing my thesis?

Drafting

☐ Have I succeeded in completing a first draft at one sitting so that I can "see" the whole?

☐ Do I have enough—enough to meet assignment demands and enough to develop and support my thesis? If not, do I need new paragraphs or more details or reflection in existing paragraphs?

☐ Does the order work? If not, what needs to be moved—and where?

☐ Am I satisfied with the way I have expressed the insights to be gained? Do the details or incidents carry my point? Have I been too heavy-handed with a message?

Revising

☐ Have I made any needed additions, deletions, or changes in order based on answering the questions above about my draft?

☐ Have I revised my draft to produce coherent paragraphs, using transition words, especially time words, to guide readers?

Polishing

☐ Have I eliminated wordiness and clichés?

☐ Have I avoided or removed any discriminatory language?

☐ Have I used my word processor's spell check and proofread a printed copy with great care?

☐ Do I have an appropriate and interesting title?

3

Using Description
Reflecting on People and Places

Good writing is concrete writing. Good writers *show* readers what they mean; they do not just tell them. Vague and abstract words may be confusing and often fail to engage readers. "The tawny-colored cocker spaniel with big, floppy ears" has our attention in ways that "The dog" will never achieve. We can see the "spaniel"; what "dog" are we to imagine? Thus, descriptive details are a part of all good writing, whatever its primary purpose or form.

When to Use Description

Sometimes writers use description to make the general concrete and to engage readers. But sometimes a writer's primary purpose is to describe—to show us—what a particular person, place, or thing looks like. Many instructors like to assign descriptive essays both because they are fun to write and because they provide good practice for using concrete language in other essays.

The descriptive essay can be viewed as a painting in words. (Not surprisingly, you will find some paintings reproduced in this chapter.) Like the artist who draws or paints, the artist working with words must be a perceptive observer. Some people actually see more than others. Can you close your eyes and "see" your writing classroom? The college library? Your history instructor? How carefully have you looked at the world around you? Some people go to a restaurant because they are hungry. The food critic goes to a restaurant not just to have dinner but to observe the color of the walls, the politeness of the waiters, the taste of the food. The food critic does not want to write, in her Sunday column, that the service was "okay."

She needs to decide whether the waiters were formally polite, chatty, intrusive, uninformed. To generate details for good essays you will need to see more of the world around you and to store those visual impressions in your memory.

How to Use Descriptive Details

Descriptive Language

Really seeing what you want to describe is the necessary first step to writing a good descriptive essay. But, just as the artist must transfer impressions into forms and colors on canvas, so you must transfer your impressions into words. To help your reader see what you see, you need to choose words that are accurate, concrete, and vivid. If you are describing your backyard, for example, you want descriptive details so precise that a reader could easily draw a picture of your yard. If you were to write that you have "a large yard that goes to a creek," you would not be helping your reader to see much. How large is large? To an apartment dweller, the fifteen-by-twelve-foot deck of a townhouse might seem large. Better to describe your backyard as "gently sloping seventy feet from the screened-in back porch to a narrow creek that marks the property line." Now we can begin to see—really to see—your yard.

Take time to search for just the right word. The food critic will soon lose her column if she writes that the walls of a restaurant are "a kind of beige with pink." She needs to write, instead, that they are "salmon-colored." Do not settle for describing a lake as "bluish green." Is the water aquamarine? Or a deeper turquoise? Is its surface mirror-like or opaque? You might notice that some of these examples are actually metaphors: "salmon-colored" and "mirror-like." Fresh, vivid comparisons (not worn-out clichés) will help readers see your world and will leave a lasting impression on them. Lance Morrow, describing an East African wildlife preserve, writes that "a herd of elephants moves like a dense gray cloud . . . a mirage of floating boulders" and "a lion prowls in lion-colored grasses."

Finding Unity

When your primary purpose is to write a description, one way to get started is to list all the details that come to mind. However, to shape those details into a unified essay, you will eventually want to eliminate some and develop others. Remember that a list of details, no matter how vivid, does not make an essay. First, select the *telling details*, the specifics that really work to reveal your subject. Second, be sure that your essay has a thesis. Select the details that, taken together, create a unified impression, that make a point. In an essay on her father, Nobel prize winning novelist Doris Lessing wanted to show that war kills the spirit if not the body of those who have to fight. To support her thesis, she first draws the portrait of her father as a vigorous young man, full of life, and then presents the unpleasant details of the angry, sick, shattered man whom she knew after the war.

Organization

Remember to organize details according to some principle so that readers can follow the developing picture. You need to decide on a perspective from which the details will be "seen" by the reader. In describing a classroom, for example, you could create the impression of someone standing at the door by presenting details in the order in which the person's eyes move around the room. Spatial patterns are numerous. You can move from foreground to background, from the center out, from left to right. Descriptions of people are sometimes more challenging to organize, because in addition to physical details you need possessions, activities, and ways of speaking—the telling details of character. You could take the perspective of a new acquaintance, presenting what one would see first and then what details of personality emerge as a relationship develops. Whatever pattern you choose, develop it consistently and use connecting words (e.g., *from* the left, *below* the penetrating eyes, *next* to the rose bushes) to guide your reader. It's your canvas; get to know your subject well, select your colors with care, and pay close attention to each brushstroke.

WRITING FOCUS
IT'S ALL ABOUT WORDS

As we have noted, good writing is concrete and specific. In addition to taking time to search for vivid language, though, you need to be sure to select the *right* word.

There are many simple, frequently used words that writers confuse. Learn to use the following words correctly. Consult a handbook for a longer list of words in each category.

Possessive Pronouns	*Contractions*
its (Its message is clear.)	it's (it is)
their (*Their books are on the table.*)	they're (*they are*)
whose (*Whose jacket is this?*)	who's (*who is*)
your (Your time is up.)	you're (you are)

Homonyms (Words that sound alike but are spelled differently and have different meanings.)

which (*one of a group*)	witch (*female sorcerer*)
roll (*move by turning over; bread*)	role (*part played*)
aisle (*passage between rows*)	isle (*island*)
bare (*naked*)	bear (*to carry; an animal*)
course (*path; part of a meal*)	coarse (*rough*)
cite (*refer to*)	sight (*vision*)
	site (*a place*)
capital (*major city; wealth*)	capitol (*government building*)
principal (*first; school head*)	principle (*basic truth/belief*)
stationery (*paper*)	stationary (*not moving*)
weather (*climatic condition*)	whether (*if*)

Pseudohomonyms (words that are similar in sound and often confused)

accept (*to receive*)	except (*other than*)
affect (*to influence*)	effect (*result; to bring into existence*)
then (*at that time; next*)	than (*in comparison with*)
allusion (*indirect reference*)	illusion (*misleading image, idea*)
conscience (*sense of right behavior*)	conscious (*aware; awake*)
loose (*not tight*)	lose (*to misplace*)
sense (*perception*)	since (*from then until now*)

Getting Started: Reflections on a Painting

In this chapter, following page 94, you will find reprints of six paintings representing a range of time, styles, and subjects. Examine them, reflect on them, and then select the one you find most appealing or most startling. Write briefly (in your journal or class notebook), explaining what attracted you to the particular painting you selected. Then read at least one biographical entry about the painter (in an encyclopedia or art book—including online) and add a paragraph on the painter to your journal or notes. Your paragraph should include information that goes beyond the brief details included with the painting. Be prepared to share your information about the painter and your reactions to the work with classmates.

Mrs. Zajac

TRACY KIDDER

In his Pulitzer Prize–winning book *The Soul of a New Machine* (1981), Tracy Kidder makes complex technical material about computers clear and interesting. He perfected his talent for clarity by writing articles on a variety of complex topics for the *Atlantic*, where he has served as a contributing editor. In 2003 Kidder published the *New York Times* best-selling *Mountains Beyond Mountains*. Kidder's portrait of Mrs. Zajac comes from his best-seller, *Among Schoolchildren* (1988), a compassionate study of a year in Mrs. Zajac's fifth-grade classroom. As you read, pay close attention to Kidder's telling details, the details that reveal character.

Questions to Guide Your Reading and Reflection

1. What is the italic print of the opening paragraph designed to represent? What is effective about beginning this way?
2. Close your eyes and visualize a favorite teacher. What telling details of appearance and character do you "see"?

---

1   *Mrs. Zajac wasn't born yesterday. She knows you didn't do your best work on this paper, Clarence. Don't you remember Mrs. Zajac*

saying that if you didn't do your best, she'd make you do it over? As for you, Claude, God forbid that you should ever need brain surgery. But Mrs. Zajac hopes that if you do, the doctor won't open up your head and walk off saying he's almost *done, as you just said when Mrs. Zajac asked you for your penmanship, which, by the way, looks like who did it and ran. Felipe, the reason you have hiccups is, your mouth is always open and the wind rushes in. You're in fifth grade now. So, Felipe, put a lock on it. Zip it up. Then go get a drink of water. Mrs. Zajac means business, Robert. The sooner you realize she never said everybody in the room has to do the work except for* Robert, *the sooner you'll get along with her. And . . . Clarence. Mrs. Zajac knows you didn't try. You don't just hand in junk to Mrs. Zajac. She's been teaching an awful lot of years. She didn't fall off the turnip cart yesterday. She told you she was an old-lady teacher.*

She was thirty-four. She wore a white skirt and yellow   2
sweater and a thin gold necklace, which she held in her fingers, as if holding her own reins, while waiting for children to answer. Her hair was black with a hint of Irish red. It was cut short to the tops of her ears, and swept back like a pair of folded wings. She had a delicately cleft chin, and she was short—the children's chairs would have fit her. Although her voice sounded conversational, it had projection. She had never acted. She had found this voice in classrooms.

Mrs. Zajac seemed to have a frightening amount of energy.   3
She strode across the room, her arms swinging high and her hands in small fists. Taking her stand in front of the green chalkboard, discussing the rules with her new class, she repeated sentences, and her lips held the shapes of certain words, such as "home-work," after she had said them. Her hands kept very busy. They sliced the air and made karate chops to mark off boundaries. They extended straight out like a traffic cop's, halting illegal maneuvers yet to be perpetrated. When they rested momentarily on her hips, her hands looked as if they were in holsters. She told the children, "One thing Mrs. Zajac expects from each of you is that you do *your* best." She said, "Mrs. Zajac gives homework. I'm sure you've all heard. The old meanie gives homework." *Mrs. Zajac.* It was in part a role. She worked her way into it every September.

At home on late summer days like these, Chris Zajac wore   4
shorts or blue jeans. Although there was no dress code for

teachers here at Kelly School, she always went to work in skirts or dresses. She dressed as if she were applying for a job, and hoped in the back of her mind that someday, heading for job interviews, her students would remember her example. Outside school, she wept easily over small and large catastrophes and at sentimental movies, but she never cried in front of students, except once a few years ago when the news came over the intercom that the Space Shuttle had exploded and Christa McAuliffe had died—and then she saw in her students' faces that the sight of Mrs. Zajac crying had frightened them, and she made herself stop and then explained.

5   At home, Chris laughed at the antics of her infant daughter and egged the child on. She and her first-grade son would sneak up to the radio when her husband wasn't looking and change the station from classical to rock-and-roll music. "You're regressing, Chris," her husband would say. But especially on the first few days of school, she didn't let her students get away with much. She was not amused when, for instance, on the first day, two of the boys started dueling with their rulers. On nights before the school year started, Chris used to have bad dreams: her principal would come to observe her, and her students would choose that moment to climb up on their desks and give her the finger, or they would simply wander out the door. But a child in her classroom would never know that Mrs. Zajac had the slightest doubt that students would obey her.

6   The first day, after going over all the school rules, Chris spoke to them about effort. "If you put your name on a paper, you should be proud of it," she said. "You should think, This is the best I can do and I'm proud of it and I want to hand this in." Then she asked, "If it isn't your best, what's Zajac going to do?"

7   Many voices, most of them female, answered softly in unison, "Make us do it over."

8   *"Make you do it over,"* Chris repeated. It sounded like a chant.

9   "Does anyone know anything about Lisette?" she asked when no one answered to that name.

10   Felipe—small, with glossy black hair—threw up his hand.

11   "Felipe?"

12   "She isn't here!" said Felipe. He wasn't being fresh. On those first few days of school, whenever Mrs. Zajac put the sound of

a question in her voice, and sometimes before she got the question out, Felipe's hand shot up.

In contrast, there was the very chubby girl who sat nearly 13 motionless at her desk, covering the lower half of her face with her hands. As usual, most of their voices sounded timid the first day, and came out of hiding gradually. There were twenty children. About half were Puerto Rican. Almost two-thirds of the twenty needed the forms to obtain free lunches. There was a lot of long and curly hair. Some boys wore little rattails. The eyes the children lifted up to her as she went over the rules—a few eyes were blue and many more were brown—looked so solemn and so wide that Chris felt like dropping all pretense and laughing. Their faces ranged from dark brown to gold, to pink, to pasty white, the color that Chris associated with sunless tenements and too much TV. The boys wore polo shirts and T-shirts and new white sneakers with the ends of the laces untied and tucked behind the tongues. Some girls wore lacy ribbons in their hair, and some wore pants and others skirts, a rough but not infallible indication of religion—-the daughters of Jehovah's Witnesses and Pentecostals do not wear pants. There was a lot of prettiness in the room, and all of the children looked cute to Chris.

Expanding Vocabulary

Examine the following words in their contexts in the essay. Then write a brief definition or synonym for each one. (Do not use a dictionary; try to guess the word's meaning from its context.) The number in parentheses is the number of the paragraph in which the word appears.

projection (2)	egged . . . on (5)
karate (3)	unison (7)
maneuvers (3)	pretense (13)
perpetrated (3)	infallible (13)
holsters (3)	

Understanding Content

1. The excerpt you have read comes from the first four pages of Kidder's book. Why does Kidder begin his study in this way? What, exactly, does he accomplish in these opening pages?
2. What specific details do we get about Mrs. Zajac? List them. (Consider age, physical appearance, personality traits, values.)

3. Why does Mrs. Zajac go to school in a skirt or dress?
4. What details do we get about the children? List them.

Drawing Inferences about Thesis and Purpose

1. What is effective about Kidder's last sentence? What does it tell us about Mrs. Zajac's attitude toward teaching?
2. What can you conclude about the Kelly School neighborhood from details about the children?
3. What is the author's attitude toward his subject? Does he present Mrs. Zajac in a positive or negative way? As a good or bad teacher?

Analyzing Strategies and Style

1. Kidder offers some contrasts between Mrs. Zajac's classroom behavior and her behavior at home and with her children. How do these contrasts help us to understand Mrs. Zajac?
2. Can you find any sentences that contain general or abstract ideas?
3. What does your answer to question 2 tell you about Kidder's style of writing? Is his writing primarily general or specific? Abstract or concrete?

Thinking Critically

1. Would you have enjoyed being in Mrs. Zajac's fifth-grade class? Why or why not?
2. Mrs. Zajac emphasizes being proud of work you sign your name to. Is it ever too early to teach this idea? Is it ever too late?
3. Are you usually proud of the work you hand in? If not, why do you hand it in that way?
4. Mrs. Zajac believes in dressing properly for her job. Should students have a dress code or wear uniforms? How can clothes make a difference in the classroom or on the job?

Lost Lives of Women

AMY TAN

Amy Tan was born in California shortly after her parents immigrated to the United States from China. Tan started a career in consulting on programs for disabled children and then turned to writing short stories, some of which became part of her first and

best-selling novel *The Joy Luck Club*. She has since published two
books for children and three novels. In the following article,
which appeared in the April 1991 issue of *Life* magazine, Tan cap-
tures the stories of several women, relatives of hers, grouped in
an old photo.

Questions to Guide Your Reading and Reflection

1. Tan tells us in paragraph 5 that the women in the photo
   "were not peasant women but big city people, very modern."
   Why does she include this comment? Why is this a telling
   detail?
2. If you were going to take a family photograph, who would
   you include and how would you arrange them?

When I first saw this photo as a child, I thought it was exotic   1
and remote, of a faraway time and place, with people who had
no connection to my American life. Look at their bound feet!
Look at that funny lady with the plucked forehead!

The solemn little girl is, in fact, my mother. And leaning   2
against the rock is my grandmother, Jingmei. "She called me
Baobei," my mother told me. "It means Treasure."

The picture was taken in Hangzhou, and my mother believes   3
the year was 1922, possibly spring or fall, judging by the clothes.
At first glance, it appears the women are on a pleasure outing.

But see the white bands on their skirts? The white shoes?   4
They are in mourning. My mother's grandmother, known to
the others as Divong, "The Replacement Wife," has recently
died. The women have come to this place, a Buddhist retreat,
to perform yet another ceremony for Divong. Monks hired for
the occasion have chanted the proper words. And the women
and little girl have walked in circles clutching smoky sticks of
incense. They knelt and prayed, then burned a huge pile of
spirit money so that Divong might ascend to a higher position
in her new world.

This is also a picture of secrets and tragedies, the reasons   5
that warnings have been passed along in our family like heir-
looms. Each of these women suffered a terrible fate, my mother
said. And they were not peasant women but big city people,
very modern. They went to dance halls and wore stylish
clothes. They were supposed to be the lucky ones.

6   Look at the pretty woman with her finger on her cheek. She is my mother's second cousin, Nunu Aiyi, "Precious Auntie." You cannot see this, but Nunu Aiyi's entire face was scarred from smallpox. Lucky for her, a year or so after this picture was taken, she received marriage proposals from two families. She turned down a lawyer and married another man. Later she divorced her husband, a daring thing for a woman to do. But then, finding no means to support herself or her young daughter, Nunu eventually accepted the lawyer's second proposal—to become his number two concubine. "Where else could she go?" my mother asked. "Some people said she was lucky the lawyer still wanted her."

7   Now look at the small woman with a sour face *(third from left).* There's a reason that Jyou Ma, "Uncle's Wife," looks this way. Her husband, my great-uncle, often complained that his family had chosen an ugly woman for his wife. To show his displeasure, he often insulted Jyou Ma's cooking. One time Great-Uncle tipped over a pot of boiling soup, which fell all over his niece's four-year-old neck and nearly killed her. My mother was the little niece, and she still has that soup scar on her neck. Great-Uncle's family eventually chose a pretty woman for his second wife. But the complaints about Jyou Ma's cooking did not stop.

Doomma, "Big Mother," is the regal-looking woman seated   8
on a rock. (The woman with the plucked forehead, far left, is a
servant, remembered only as someone who cleaned but did not
cook.) Doomma was the daughter of my great-grandfather and
Nu-pei, "The Original Wife." She was shunned by Divong,
"The Replacement Wife," for being "too strong," and loved by
Divong's daughter, my grandmother. Doomma's first daughter
was born with a hunchback—a sign, some said, of Doomma's
own crooked nature. Why else did she remarry, disobeying her
family's orders to remain a widow forever? And why did
Doomma later kill herself, using some mysterious means that
caused her to die slowly over three days? "Doomma died the
same way she lived," my mother said, "strong, suffering lots."

Jingmei, my own grandmother, lived only a few more years   9
after this picture was taken. She was the widow of a poor
scholar, a man who had the misfortune of dying from influenza
when he was about to be appointed a vice-magistrate. In 1924
or so, a rich man, who liked to collect pretty women, raped my
grandmother and thereby forced her into becoming one of his
concubines. My grandmother, now an outcast, took her young
daughter to live with her on an island outside of Shanghai. She
left her son behind, to save his face. After she gave birth to
another son she killed herself by swallowing raw opium buried
in the New Year's rice cakes. The young daughter who wept at
her deathbed was my mother.

At my grandmother's funeral, monks tied chains to my   10
mother's ankles so she would not fly away with her mother's
ghost. "I tried to take them off," my mother said. "I was her
treasure. I was her life."

My mother could never talk about any of this, even with her   11
closest friends. "Don't tell anyone," she once said to me. "People don't understand. A concubine was like some kind of pros-
titute. My mother was a good woman, high-class. She had no
choice."

I told her I understood.   12

"How can you understand?" she said, suddenly angry. "You   13
did not live in China then. You do not know what it's like to
have no position in life. I was her daughter. We had no face! We
belonged to nobody! This is a shame I can never push off my
back." By the end of the outburst, she was crying.

14   On a recent trip with my mother to Beijing, I learned that my uncle found a way to push the shame off his back. He was the son my grandmother left behind. In 1936 he joined the Communist party—in large part, he told me, to overthrow the society that forced his mother into concubinage. He published a story about his mother. I told him I had written about my grandmother in a book of fiction. We agreed that my grandmother is the source of strength running through our family. My mother cried to hear this.

15   My mother believes my grandmother is also my muse, that she helps me write. "Does she still visit you often?" she asked while I was writing my second book. And then she added shyly, "Does she say anything about me?"

16   "Yes," I told her. "She has lots to say. I am writing it down."

17   This is the picture I see when I write. These are the secrets I was supposed to keep. These are the women who never let me forget why stories need to be told.

Expanding Vocabulary

Define each of the following words and then use each one in a sentence. The number in parentheses is the number of the paragraph in which the word appears.

    exotic (1)
    heirlooms (5)
    concubine (6)
    shunned (8)
    muse (15)

Understanding Content

1. When and where was the picture taken?
2. Who are the women in the photo? That is, what is their relationship to the author?
3. Why are the women together? What have they gathered to do?
4. What was the author's initial reaction to the photo?

Drawing Inferences about Thesis and Purpose

1. What reaction does Tan want readers to have after they read her descriptions of the women? What do the women share, other than family connections?

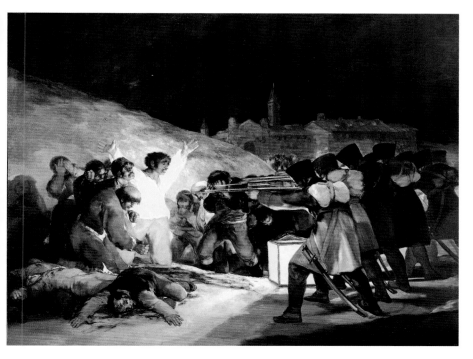

Francisco de Goya y Lucientes, *Third of May, 1808*, 1814. Approximately 8′ 8″ × 11′ 3″. Museo del Prado, Madrid, Spain. Copyright Erich Lessing/Art Resource.

A Spaniard, Goya (1746–1828) lived and painted at the Spanish court of Charles II. His paintings reveal an unsentimental, tough-minded observation of human life.

Edgar Degas, *The Dance Class*, c. 1873–1876. Oil on canvas, 85 × 75 cm. Musée d'Orsay, Paris, France. Copyright Rénunion des Musées Nationaux/Art Resource.

One of the best known of the French Impressionists, Degas (1834–1917) is famous for his skill in capturing movement, a skill that led to many studies of dancers and racehorses.

Pablo Picasso, *The Three Dancers*, 1925. Copyright Tate Gallery, London, Great Britain/Art Resource.

Perhaps the best-known of twentieth-century painters, Picasso (1881–1973) was born in Spain but lived most of his life in France. His many canvases provide lessons in modern art's movements from Impressionism to Expressionism.

Mary Cassatt, *Two Women Seated by a Woodland Stream*, 1869.
Copyright Giraudon/Art Resource.

*Mary Cassatt (1844–1926) is an American painter who settled in
Paris and exhibited her work with the French Impressionists. She contributed to the success of the Impressionists by promoting their work
in the United States.*

Edward Hopper, *Room in New York*, 1932. Copyright courtesy Chicago Art Institute.

One of the most important American painters of the twentieth century, Edward Hopper (1882–1967) painted rural landscapes, small towns, and the city, usually incorporating the sharp lines and angles of houses and roads. City scenes often make us spectators of lives somewhat lost amid concrete and glass.

Salvador Dali, *The Persistence of Memory* [*Persistance de la mémoire*], 1931. Oil on canvas, 9-1/2" × 13" (24.1 × 33 cm). Copyright the Museum of Modern Art/Licensed by SCALA/Art Resource.

Salvador Dali (1904–1989), a native of the Spanish province of Catalan, drew on dream imagery to create his surrealist canvases.

2. Explain the last line of the essay.
3. What is Tan's thesis?

Analyzing Strategies and Style

1. What details do you consider to be especially important? Why do you select them?
2. Tan gives each woman's Chinese name and then its meaning in English. What does she gain from this strategy?
3. Tan uses a metaphor in paragraph 5. Explain the metaphor.

Thinking Critically

1. Do you have stories to tell about your family? If you have a family album, find a picture in it that you think holds a secret or tells a story, and write that story in your journal.
2. Why is it important to write the stories of these women? What does Tan gain for herself? For others?
3. Why is it important for humans generally to tell stories? What does each culture, each age, gain from making stories?

Remembering Lobo

PAT MORA

Educated at Texas Western College and the University of Texas at El Paso, Pat Mora has published several children's books, volumes of poetry and a memoir, *House of Houses* (1997). Her essays have been collected in *Nepantla: Essays from the Land in the Middle* (1993), from which "Remembering Lobo" comes. Look for the telling details that Mora presents to develop and reveal the character of her aunt.

Questions to Guide Your Reading and Reflection

1. What is Mora's purpose in writing? What does she want to share with readers?
2. If you were going to write a descriptive essay about someone in your family, who would you choose? Why?

We called her *Lobo*. The word means "wolf" in Spanish, an   1
odd name for a generous and loving aunt. Like all names it

became synonymous with her, and to this day returns me to my childself. Although the name seemed perfectly natural to us and to our friends, it did cause frowns from strangers throughout the years. I particularly remember one hot afternoon when on a crowded streetcar between the border cities of El Paso and Juarez, I momentarily lost sight of her. "Lobo! Lobo!" I cried in panic. Annoyed faces peered at me, disappointed at such disrespect to a white-haired woman.

2   Actually the fault was hers. She lived with us for years, and when she arrived home from work in the evening, she'd knock on our front door and ask, "*¿Dónde están mis lobitos?*" "Where are my little wolves?"

3   Gradually she became our *lobo*, a spinster aunt who gathered the four of us around her, tying us to her for life by giving us all she had. Sometimes to tease her we would call her by her real name. "*¿Dónde está Ignacia?*" we would ask. Lobo would laugh and say, "She is a ghost."

4   To all of us in nuclear families today, the notion of an extended family under one roof seems archaic, complicated. We treasure our private space. I will always marvel at the generosity of my parents, who opened their door to both my grandmother and Lobo. No doubt I am drawn to the elderly because I grew up with two entirely different white-haired women who worried about me, tucked me in at night, made me tomato soup or hot *hierbabuena* (mint tea) when I was ill.

5   Lobo grew up in Mexico, the daughter of a circuit judge, my grandfather. She was a wonderful storyteller and over and over told us about the night her father, a widower, brought his grown daughters on a flatbed truck across the Rio Grande at the time of the Mexican Revolution. All their possessions were left in Mexico. Lobo had not been wealthy, but she had probably never expected to have to find a job and learn English.

6   When she lived with us, she worked in the linens section of a local department store. Her area was called "piece goods and bedding." Lobo never sewed, but she would talk about materials she sold, using words I never completely understood, such as *pique* and *broadcloth*. Sometimes I still whisper such words just to remind myself of her. I'll always savor the way she would order "sweet milk" at restaurants. The precision of a speaker new to the language.

Lobo saved her money to take us out to dinner and a movie,   7
to take us to Los Angeles in the summer, to buy us shiny black
shoes for Christmas. Though she never married and never bore
children, Lobo taught me much about one of our greatest challenges as human beings: loving well. I don't think she ever discussed the subject with me, but through the years she lived her
love, and I was privileged to watch.

She died at ninety-four. She was no sweet, docile Mexican   8
woman dying with perfect resignation. Some of her last words
before drifting into semiconsciousness were loud words of
annoyance at the incompetence of nurses and doctors.

"*No sirven.*" "They're worthless," she'd say to me in Spanish.   9

"They don't know what they're doing. My throat is hurting   10
and they're taking X rays. Tell them to take care of my throat
first."

I was busy striving for my cherished middle-class polite-   11
ness. "Shh, shh," I'd say. "They're doing the best they can."

"Well, it's not good enough," she'd say, sitting up in anger.   12

Lobo was a woman of fierce feelings, of strong opinions. She   13
was a woman who literally whistled while she worked. The
best way to cheer her when she'd visit my young children was
to ask for her help. Ask her to make a bed, fold laundry, set the
table or dry dishes, and the whistling would begin as she
moved about her task. Like all of us, she loved being needed.
Understandable, then, that she muttered in annoyance when
her body began to fail her. She was a woman who found self-
definition and joy in visibly showing her family her love for us
by bringing us hot *té de canela* (cinnamon tea) in the middle of
the night to ease a cough, by bringing us comics and candy
whenever she returned home. A life of giving.

One of my last memories of her is a visit I made to her on   14
November 2, *El Día de los Muertos*, or All Souls' Day. She was
sitting in her rocking chair, smiling wistfully. The source of the
smile may seem a bit bizarre to a U.S. audience. She was fondly
remembering past visits to the local cemetery on this religious
feast day.

"What a silly old woman I have become," she said. "Here   15
I sit in my rocking chair all day on All Souls' Day, sitting when
I should be out there. At the cemetery. Taking good care of *mis
muertos*, my dead ones.

16 "What a time I used to have. I'd wake while it was still dark outside. I'd hear the first morning birds, and my fingers would almost itch to begin. By six I'd be having a hot bath, dressing carefully in black, wanting *mis muertos* to be proud of me, proud to have me looking respectable and proud to have their graves taken care of. I'd have my black coffee and plenty of toast. You know the way I like it. Well browned and well buttered. I wanted to be ready to work hard.

17 "The bus ride to the other side of town was a long one, but I'd say a rosary and plan my day. I'd hope that my perfume wasn't too strong and yet would remind others that I was a lady.

18 "The air at the cemetery gates was full of chrysanthemums: that strong, sharp, fall smell. I'd buy tin cans full of the gold and wine flowers. How I liked seeing aunts and uncles who were also there to care for the graves of their loved ones. We'd hug. Happy together.

19 "Then it was time to begin. The smell of chrysanthemums was like a whiff of pure energy. I'd pull the heavy hose and wash the gravestones over and over, listening to the water pelting away the desert sand. I always brought newspaper. I'd kneel on the few patches of grass, and I'd scrub and scrub, shining the gray stones, leaning back on my knees to rest for a bit and then scrubbing again. Finally a relative from nearby would say, '*Ya, ya, Nacha,*' and laugh. Enough. I'd stop, blink my eyes to return from my trance. Slightly dazed, I'd stand slowly, place a can of chrysanthemums before each grave.

20 "Sometimes I would just stand there in the desert sun and listen. I'd hear the quiet crying of people visiting new graves; I'd hear families exchanging gossip while they worked.

21 "One time I heard my aunt scolding her dead husband. She'd sweep his gravestone and say, '*¿Porqué?* Why did you do this, you thoughtless man? Why did you go and leave me like this? You know I don't like to be alone. Why did you stop living?' Such a sight to see my aunt with her proper black hat and her fine dress and her carefully polished shoes muttering away for all to hear.

22 "To stifle my laughter, I had to cover my mouth with my hands."

Expanding Vocabulary

Examine the following words in their contexts in the essay. Then write a brief definition or synonym for each one. (Do not use a dictionary; try to guess each word's meaning from its context.) The number in parentheses is the number of the paragraph in which the word appears.

synonymous (1)	semiconsciousness (8)
spinster (3)	bizarre (14)
nuclear (4)	pelting (19)
archaic (4)	trance (19)
precision (6)	

Understanding Content

1. How did the author know her "Lobo"?
2. What are some of the telling details of Lobo's character? What activities or moments in her life reveal these character traits?

Drawing Inferences about Thesis and Purpose

1. When the author and her siblings called Lobo by her real name, Lobo answered that "she is a ghost." Why did she say that to the children?
2. What does Mora mean by "loving well"? What can we infer to be the characteristics of a person who loves well?

Analyzing Strategies and Style

1. Several times Mora uses Spanish words or phrases, which she then translates into English. What does she gain by including the Spanish?
2. Mora ends with Lobo's own account of visiting family graves. What does the author accomplish by ending with Lobo's own words?

Thinking Critically

1. Do you live in an extended family? If so, do you have an older family member whom you especially care for? What do we gain from extended families? What do we lose? Do the advantages outweigh the disadvantages?
2. What do you think are the marks of a meaningful life?
3. Without having read this essay, would you have included "loving well" as a mark of a meaningful life? Do you think it should be on everyone's list? Why or why not?

Trouble Woman

JOSH TYRANGIEL

A journalist with a master's degree in American Studies from Yale University, Josh Tyrangiel is editor of Time.com and assistant managing editor of *Time* magazine. He joined *Time* in 1999 as a staff writer and music critic. His essay on Grammy nominee Amy Winehouse, published in *Time* on February 4, 2008, reveals his music critic expertise.

Questions to Guide Your Reading and Reflecting

1. What do you know about Amy Winehouse? If you do not know this singer, do an Internet search to have some knowledge before you read this essay.
2. Who are your favorite musicians? Why do you prefer them?

1   On her best days, Any Winehouse is a mess. The 24-year-old wears her hair in a beehive so large and teetering that it could hide the chorus of middle-aged black women that seems to materialize at the back of her throat whenever she sings. Having once thought herself overweight, Winehouse now keeps her body little-girl tiny and covered with enough tattoos to earn her cred at a medium-security prison. Onstage, she's known to favor poodle skirts. It's an aesthetic that takes some getting used to.

2   On her worst days—and there have been plenty of late— Winehouse looks a safe bet for an early grave. After a 2007 full of well-chronicled erratic behavior ranging from mumbled concert performances to a drug arrest in Norway, her in-laws pleaded for a public boycott of her music so that she and her equally troubled husband, Blake Fielder-Civil—currently in jail for attempting to bribe a bartender he allegedly assaulted to drop the charges—might be deprived of the income they spend getting wasted. One day in December, Winehouse wobbled out of her London home at 6 a.m. wearing only jeans, a red bra and a look of complete befuddlement. On Tuesday video of her (now blond) snorting and smoking various substances hit the Internet.

Nothing inspires scorn like wasted fame—or kills nuance   3
like a fire-engine-red bra. But to dismiss Winehouse as just
another train wreck is to presume that she has no idea she's
off the rails, and this distinction matters when considering
how to feel about her. Winehouse's *Back to Black* is up for six
Grammy Awards on Feb. 10, including one for Album of the
Year. While the Grammys are notorious for their grandfa-
therly taste (she'll be competing against Herbie Hancock,
among others), they're spot-on about Winehouse. On *Back to
Black* she sounds like Dusty Springfield teleported into the
hip-hop era. The songs—all of which move with the economy
of old 45s and all of which Winehouse had a hand in writing—tell tight, complicated stories, but more important, they
tell her stories.

From the first line of the album—"They tried to make me   4
go to rehab/I said 'No, no, no'"—Winehouse is in complete
control of her out-of-control tale. "You know that I'm no
good," she sings with remarkable power and sinew in another
song, and it's not a boast, though her put-downs of the men
who would take advantage of her certainly are. Throughout,
she's mouthy, funny, sultry and quite possibly crazy, yet
unlike Britney Spears or a dozen other pop idiot savants,
Winehouse not only knows who she is but is able to express it
in a way that's often beautiful and meaningful to others. Traditionally, we call that art.

The last time pop music was dealt this card, it went by the   5
name Kurt Cobain, another lower-middle-class kid for whom
being messed up was a source of creativity and, eventually, the
killer of it too. Cobain told his few high school friends that he
had "suicide genes," and there's a dangerous echo of that
infatuation with doom in Winehouse's fetish for ill-fated soul
singers. No matter how true her music feels, it's hard to tell the
difference between pain and performance and impossible to
guess how approval reinforces her self-perception.

Still, boycotts and scorn are the wrong response. For one   6
thing, they're not likely to work. For another, we're supposed
to encourage people who feel doomed to share it in words and
know that others can relate. The law can take care of their
actions, and in Winehouse's case, it already has: she's likely to
miss her Grammy moment because of the visa issues that go

along with being a danger to yourself. But that doesn't mean
you shouldn't root for her.

Expanding Vocabulary

Match each word in column A with its definition in column B. When
in doubt, first find the word in the essay and look for context clues to
aid your understanding of the word's meaning. Then, if necessary, use
your dictionary to complete the matching exercise. The number in
parentheses is the number of the paragraph in which the word
appears.

cred (1)	protest by not buying or dealing with
aesthetic (1)	well known but not admired
erratic (2)	subtlety
boycott (2)	hot and sensual
nuance (3)	concept of beauty
notorious (3)	people who know/do one thing well but
sinew (4)	are clueless about the rest of life
sultry (4)	obsessive attachment
idiot savants (4)	worth, credibility
fetish (5)	vigorous strength
	unconventional, inconsistent

Understanding Content

1. What specific event is the occasion for Tyrangiel's study of
   Winehouse?
2. What physical details reveal elements of character?
3. What behavior problems are part of the singer's character?
4. How does the author describe Winehouse's singing?

Drawing Inferences about Thesis and Purpose

1. What do you consider the *telling* details in this portrait of Winehouse? Why?
2. What is Tyrangiel's thesis? How does he want readers to see
   Winehouse?

Analyzing Strategies and Style

1. Describe the parallel structure and repetition the author uses at the
   beginning of paragraphs 1 and 2; what does he gain by this strategy?
2. The author contrasts Winehouse with Britney Spears. What does
   that contrast tell us about Winehouse?

Thinking Critically

1. If Amy Winehouse is a mess, even on her good days, does it really matter that she knows this? Why does Tyrangiel think it matters? Do you agree?
2. So many celebrities, from music to sports to Hollywood, have messed-up lives. Any thoughts on why?

Africa

LANCE MORROW

After joining *Time* in 1965, journalist Lance Morrow became a senior writer at *Time* and contributor to cover stories and the *Time* essay section. Morrow has also written several books, including *The Chief: A Memoir of Fathers and Sons* (1985), a study of the author's relationship with his famous journalist father Hugh Morrow, and *Evil: An Investigation* (2004). In 1981, Morrow received the National Magazine Award for his *Time* essays. He is now a professor of journalism at Boston University. In "Africa," published in the February 23, 1987, issue of *Time*, Morrow re-creates in words what he saw, felt, and reflected about while on safari in East Africa.

Questions to Guide Your Reading and Reflection

1. Morrow uses many images of light and dark—"blinding clarities" and "shadows." How do these images help him portray the landscape and its animal inhabitants?
2. What is your favorite wild animal? Why?

The animals stand motionless in gold-white grasses—zebras   1
and impala, Thomson's gazelles and Cape buffalo and harte-
beests and waterbuck and giraffes, and wildebeests by the
thousands, all fixed in art naïf, in a smiting equatorial light.
They stand in the shadowless clarity of creation.

Now across the immense African landscape, from the dis-   2
tant escarpment, a gray-purple rainstorm blows. It encroaches
upon the sunlight, moving through the air like a dark idea. East
Africa has a genius for such moments. Wildlife and landscape

here have about them a force of melodrama and annunciation. They are the *Book of Genesis* enacted as an afternoon dream.

3   In Amboseli,[1] under the snow-covered dome of Mount Kilimanjaro, a herd of elephants moves like a dense gray cloud, slow motion, in lumbering solidity: a mirage of floating boulders. Around them dust devils rise spontaneously out of the desert, like tornadoes that swirl up on the thermals and go jittering and rushing among the animals like evil spirits busy in the primal garden.

4   Later, in the sweet last light of the afternoon, a lion prowls in lion-colored grasses and vanishes into the perfect camouflage—setting off for the hunt, alert, indolent and somehow abstracted, as cats are. A rhinoceros disappears: the eye loses it among gray boulders and thorn trees. . . .

5   To the human eye, the animals so often seem mirages: now you see them, now you don't. Later, just after dusk, Abyssinian nightjars discover the magic wash of the headlight beams. The birds flit in and out of the barrels of light, like dolphins frisking before a boat's prow. The Land Cruiser jostles, in four-wheel drive, across black volcanic stones toward the camp, the driver steering by the distant light-speck of the cooking fire.

6   And then the African night, which, more than elsewhere, seems an abnegation of the conscious world. MMBA, "miles and miles of bloody Africa," and it all falls into black magic void.

7   The world stills, for the longest time. Then, at the edge of sleep, hyenas come to giggle and whoop. Peering from the tent flap, one catches in the shadows their sidelong criminal slouch. Their eyes shine like evil flashlight bulbs, a disembodied horror-movie yellow, phosphorescent, glowing like the children of the damned. In the morning, one finds their droppings: white dung, like a photographic negative. Hyenas not only eat the meat of animals but grind up and digest the bones. The hyenas' dung is white with the calcium of powdered bones.

8   Africa has its blinding clarities and its shadows. The clarities proclaim something primal, the first days of life. The shadows lie at the other extreme of time: in the premonition of last days, of extinction. Now you see the animals. Soon, perhaps, you won't.

---

[1] A game reserve in Kenya—Ed.

Africa is comprehensive: great birth, great death, the beginning   9
and the end. The themes are drawn, like the vivid, abstract hide
of the zebra, in patterns of the absolute.

The first question to ask is whether the wildlife of Africa can   10
survive.

The second question is this: If the wild animals of Africa vanish   11
from the face of the earth, what, exactly, will have been lost?

The Africa of the animals is a sort of dream kingdom. Carl   12
Jung traveled to East Africa in 1925 and wrote of a "most
intense sentiment of returning to the land of my youth," of a
"recognition of the immemorially known." Africa, he said, has
"the stillness of the eternal beginning."

Earliest man lived in these landscapes, among such animals,   13
among these splendid trees that have personalities as distinct
as those of the animals: the aristocratic flat-topped acacia, the
gnarled and magisterial baobab. Possibly scenes from that
infancy are lodged in some layer of human memory, in the brilliant but preconscious morning. . . .

It is easy to fall in love not only with the shapes and colors of   14
the animals but with their motions, their curving and infinitely
varied gaits. The zebra moves with a strong, short-muscled
stride. It is a sleek, erotic beast with vigorous bearing. The zebra's
self-possession is a likable trait. It is human habit to sort the animals almost immediately into orders of preference. The animals
are arranged in people's minds as a popularity contest. Some animals are endearing, and some repulsive. One wants to see the
lion first, and then the elephant and after that the leopard, then
rhino . . . and so on. One wants to see some animals because they
are fierce, and some because they are lovable and soft. It is hard
to explain the attractions and preferences. It is possible that
human feelings about wild animals reflect the complexities of
sexual attractions. Certain animals are admired for their majestic
aggressions, and others for softer qualities. The lion is a sleek
piece of violence, the waterbuck a sweet piece of grace.

Some of the animals move in deep slow motion, as if tra-   15
versing another medium, previous to air, and thicker—an
Atlantis of time. The elephant goes sleeping that way across the
spaces. The medium through which it moves can be seen as
time itself, a thicker, slower time than humans inhabit, a pre-
historic metabolism. The giraffe goes with undulous slow

motion, a long waving that starts with the head and proceeds dreamily, curving down the endless spine. The giraffe is motion as process through time. It is delicate, intelligent and eccentric, and as Karen Blixen said, so much a lady. Each of the animals has its distinct gait. The Grant's gazelle's tail never stops switching, like a nervous windshield wiper. The hartebeest moves off, when startled, in an undulous hallumph.

16   For days in Masai Mara,[2] the visitor watched the wildebeests. Ungainly and pewter colored, they are subject to sudden electric jolts of panic, to adrenal bursts of motion that can make them seem half crazed as a tribe. Now they were engaged not so much in migration as in vagrancy, wandering across the plain on strange but idiotically determined vectors. Wildebeests smell monsters on the afternoon breeze, take sudden fear and bolt for Tanzania or Uganda or the Indian Ocean, anywhere to get away.

17   Sometimes, of course, the monsters are there. The veldt is littered with the corpses that the lion or cheetah has killed and dined on. But sometimes the herding wildebeests seem to be caught in a collective shallow madness. A fantasy of terror shoots through a herd, and all the beasts are gone: hysteria of hooves. The wildebeests thunder by the thousands across rivers and plains, moving like a barbarian invasion. They follow their instinct for the rains, for better grass. And they mow the grass before them. If they know where rain is, the wildebeests are relentless. Otherwise, they march with an undirected rigor, without destination, like cadets on punishment, beating a trail in the parade ground. The wildebeest's bisonlike head is too large for its body, its legs too thin and ungainly. It looks like a middle-aged hypochondriac, paltry in the loins and given to terrible anxiety attacks, the sort of creature whose hands (if it had hands) would always be clammy. God's genius for design may have faltered with the wildebeest.

18   In Masai Mara, vultures wheel dreamily in the air, like a slow motion tornado of birds. Below the swirling funnel, a cheetah has brought down a baby wildebeest. The cheetah, loner and fleet aristocrat, the upper-class version of the hyena, has opened up the wildebeest and devoured the internal

[2]A game reserve in Kenya.—Ed.

organs. The cheetah's belly is swollen and its mouth is ringed with blood as it breathes heavily from the exertion of gorging. A dozen vultures flap down to take their turn. They wait 20 yards away, then waddle in a little toward the kill to test the cheetah. The cheetah, in a burst, rushes the vultures to drive them off, and then returns to the baby wildebeest. The vultures grump and readjust their feathers and wait their turn, the surly lumpen-carrion class.

The skeleton of an elephant lies out in the grasses near a   19
baobab tree and a scattering of black volcanic stones. The thick-trunked, gnarled baobab gesticulates with its branches, as if trying to summon help. There are no tusks lying among the bones, of course; ivory vanishes quickly in East Africa. The elephant is three weeks dead. Poachers. Not far away, a baby elephant walks alone. That is unusual. Elephants are careful mothers and do not leave their young unattended. The skeleton is the mother, and the baby is an orphan. . . .

The wild animals fetch back at least 2 million years. They   20
represent, we imagine, the first order of creation, and they are vividly marked with God's eccentric genius of design: life poured into pure forms, life unmitigated by complexities of consciousness, language, ethics, treachery, revulsion, reason, religion, premeditation or free will. A wild animal does not contradict its own nature, does not thwart itself, as man endlessly does. A wild animal never plays for the other side. The wild animals are a holiday from deliberation. They are sheer life. To behold a bright being that lives without thought is, to the complex, cross-grained human mind, profoundly liberating. And even if they had no effect upon the human mind, still the wild animals are life—other life.

John Donne asked, "Was not the first man, by the desire of   21
knowledge, corrupted even in the whitest integrity of nature?" The animals are a last glimpse of that shadowless life, previous to time and thought. They are a pure connection to the imagination of God.

Expanding Vocabulary

1. Match each word in column A with its definition in column B. When in doubt, first find the word in the essay and look for context clues to aid your understanding of the word's meaning.

Then, if necessary, use your dictionary to complete the matching exercise. The number in parentheses is the number of the paragraph in which the word appears.

Column A	Column B
naïf (1)	original
escarpment (2)	sensual
annunciation (2)	irregular
thermals (3)	luminous
primal (3)	directions
abnegation (6)	open grassland
phosphorescent (7)	excessively worried about
premonition (8)	health
gnarled (13)	current of warm air
magisterial (13)	unqualified or unaffected
erotic (14)	natural simplicity
Atlantis (15)	authoritative
metabolism (15)	meager
undulous (15)	forewarning
eccentric (15)	expresses through gestures
adrenal (16)	twisted and knotty
vectors (16)	mythical island
veldt (17)	worthless
hypochondriac (17)	religious significance
paltry (17)	process of generating energy in an
lumpen-carrion (18)	organism
gesticulates (19)	sudden charge of energy
unmitigated (20)	rejection
	clifflike ridge of land or rock
	wavelike

2. Morrow mentions three people he expects his readers to know. After checking a dictionary or encyclopedia (in print or online), add a one-sentence biographical statement to your text for Carl Jung, Karen Blixen, and John Donne.

Understanding Content

1. In the first thirteen paragraphs, Morrow "paints" the East Africa game preserve landscape. What are the predominant colors of this landscape? What does the land look like?
2. Morrow devotes paragraph 7 to the hyenas. What image of this animal emerges? How does the detail of the hyenas romping in the darkness help to create Morrow's view of the hyenas?

3. In paragraphs 14 through 19 Morrow describes the animals' movements. Read these paragraphs again, picturing each animal's movements as Morrow presents them. Which animals would you want to see first? Why?

4. Morrow notes what others have also experienced when on safari in a group: members of the group have animal favorites. Morrow suggests that preferences may be connected to sexual attractions. Is this a new idea for you? Does it seem to make sense?

5. Morrow ends the section on movement with nonmovement: a dead elephant and lonely baby elephant. How does this detail contribute to the image of East Africa that he seeks to develop? If the animals become extinct, what will we have lost?

Drawing Inferences about Thesis and Purpose

1. Is there one sentence in the essay that could stand as Morrow's thesis? If you don't think so, then state the essay's thesis in your own words.

2. After several paragraphs about the wildebeests, Morrow concludes that "God's genius . . . may have faltered." Why? What details lead to this conclusion?

3. Why, in Morrow's view, are the animals "pure forms" and "sheer life"? How do they differ from humans? What do they represent in the development of life forms?

Analyzing Strategies and Style

1. Look at Morrow's opening paragraphs. What does the first paragraph accomplish? As the camera rolls on, what is added in paragraph 2? How do these two scenes announce the complex world of the game preserve that Morrow develops in the rest of the essay?

2. Examine Morrow's organization. Is it appropriate to say that Morrow first shows us photographs of his trip and then a videotape? Why?

3. How many paragraphs at the beginning of the essay give us photographs? How many separate photos are needed? What is the organizing principle of the photos?

4. Morrow presents some details as contrasts, almost contradictions. Find some examples. Is a landscape of contrasts simple or complex? Boring or awesome? What sense of this world does the author give us?

5. Morrow uses some striking metaphors to develop his description. Find three that you particularly like and explain why they are effective.

Thinking Critically

1. Has Morrow rekindled, or awakened, in you an interest in the wildlife of East Africa? If so, but you cannot afford to go on safari, what can you do to see these animals and learn more about them? List as many sources of information and experience as you can.
2. On the basis of Morrow's description—or your experiences—which of the big game is your favorite animal? Why? What attracts you to that animal? List the characteristics that you find appealing.
3. Closer to home, what domestic animal is or would be your favorite pet? Why? List the characteristics that you find appealing.
4. Should we be concerned about the possible extinction of the African elephant or rhino, the two most seriously threatened species of the big game in East Africa? What can you learn about the problem online?

Snow: A Prism of More Than Frozen Water

DAVID MONTGOMERY

Journalist David Montgomery is a graduate of Princeton University and the University of Michigan, from which he obtained a master's degree in American culture. A reporter and feature writer at the *Washington Post* for fifteen years, he now writes features for the Style section, including writing about the Latino community. His description of Washington's first snow-fall of the winter was published on December 6, 2007.

Questions to Guide Your Reading and Reflection

1. What are snow's traits and qualities—beyond its primary nature of frozen water?
2. How often do you examine closely, and reflect on, small details of the natural world? What can we gain from such studies and then reflection?

1   How come snow never is what it is? It's always something else: magic, hassle, politics. The first snow of the year, especially, refuses to just lie there.

Early in the morning, everybody rushes to the window. "It's   2
coming down strong!" says Iris, 3, who has nothing in her conscious memory with which to compare it. "It's everywhere."

She spies the Weber grill, a symmetrical black dome with a   3
white pile in the middle on top, which, to any adult with the
standard appreciation for doom that comes with age, resembles a black widow spider.

"The grill looks like a ladybug!" Iris says.   4

The first snow can turn a black-and-white landscape under   5
an ashen sky into Technicolor. Metaphorically speaking.

Later, a class of preschoolers and their teachers hold   6
mittened hands two-by-two and step down the sidewalk with
snowflakes in their eyelashes, like fairy wings.

The adults at the window, what are they thinking? They   7
remember the snows of yesteryear, a memory that stirs just once
every year, and then—blink!—they're thinking about black ice.

So much nostalgia and meaning invested in what is, after all,   8
nothing more than water crystallized, hexagonally, around bits
of dust. Too much dread, too. Is there any other substance less
metaphorically stable? Red wine, perhaps, or a split atom.

Snow begins as paranoid prophecy in Washington, ripe for   9
selffulfillment, beyond parody. Snow tracks on the highway in
Prince William! Snow beginning to stick in Rockville!

At the Long Branch Community Center in Silver Spring, the   10
county's two mobile medical vans arrive a little bit late to see
patients. They were delayed, stuck in all the Beltway traffic,
which is stuck behind he/she up there who did something
stupid. Why?

We know why. It's the first snowfall, and *other people* need to   11
get a grip. Snow is a test of competence, of carrying on, and
many falter while the Minnesotans and Mainers among us har-
rumph. (Was campaigning halted these past few days in New
Hampshire and Iowa? No, it was not.)

But sometimes, snow pushes people to achieve! Flotillas of   12
buses from all the area's public schools set forth bravely. Even
in Montgomery County!

Which is why snow is also politics. A poor showing can cost   13
the job of a public works director, undermine a superintendent,
hurt a mayor's reelection chances. As a consequence, for the
authorities, snow becomes a kind of competition. The first

No Two Are Alike...

Though unique, a snow crystal falls into a category of shapes: here, examples of the type "stellar plates."

snow is a chance at regional bragging rights, the real deal after all those snow-plow regattas around orange cones in summer. The District crows on the radio about spiking the snowmelt marinade with beet juice.

14   Snow is also Wite-Out, correcting flaws in the landscape and the look of the city. A little bit of snow on sills and sidewalks is all the street wreaths and holiday windows in town need to look a little less contrived. Snow is a fresh reason to buy presents.

15   Snow hides litter, trims the new roofline of the Georgetown library, banishing the memory of the catastrophic fire. Those red-and-white snow-emergency route signs that taunt us in August stand straight with purpose.

16   Yet snow also is a pitiless highlighter, exposing the incongruous, the ironic, the problematic. Is there anything more jarring than snow on bamboo thickets? Those yellow pansies and pink begonias still alive in sidewalk gardens are drifted in white: It is past time for them to die. The first snow scolds tardy municipal leaf collectors, for now those remaining piles of leaves in the gutter look like badly frosted gingerbread cookies.

17   Ask those who have never experienced snow before to describe it, and they reach for metaphors, similes. "It's like

cotton, it's like frozen cotton," says Lester Martinez, 27, who arrived a few months ago from Honduras.

"It's like sand," says Francois Kemgang, 40, who arrived 18 from Cameroon a month ago. "But it's strong, and sand is not strong. It's something that is falling like rain, but it is not like water. . . . It makes the place become white and covers all the place."

Kemgang says the first picture he will take in this country 19 will be of the snow.

The snow falls on all, and the snow falls for all. Some peo- 20 ple want to jog among the frosted trees in Rock Creek Park. They inhale gulps of snowflake-laden air, like cold fairy dust. When they look up, the flakes dust their faces. The flakes are big, seeming to materialize out of nothing, shreds of ashen sky descending. When they fall into the creek, they vanish—a million kisses lightly rippling the water.

Under the sun, later today, the season's first snow will be 21 memory.

Expanding Vocabulary

Write a definition for each of the following words. Then select five of the words and use each one of those in a separate sentence of your own. The number in parentheses is the number of the paragraph in which the word appears.

ashen (5)	regattas (13)
paranoid (9)	incongruous (16)
parody (9)	ironic (16)
flotillas (12)	

Understanding Content

1. What is snow—actually?
2. What other attributes does Montgomery give to snow? List them in his order.

Drawing Inferences about Thesis and Purpose

1. When you read in paragraph 1 that "snow never is what it is," what do you expect the essay to do with snow?
2. We know the author's subject; what is his thesis? What does he want readers to know when they see snow?

Analyzing Strategies and Style

1. Examine Montgomery's sentence style. Are his sentences mostly long or short? Simple or complex? What makes his sentences effective?
2. Montgomery uses many metaphors in this essay. First, see how many you can locate and underline. Then select three that you like and be prepared to explain why.

Thinking Critically

1. What are your reactions to snow? Is it beautiful; is it fun; is it a hassle? Can you account for your reactions?
2. Has Montgomery given you some new ways of seeing snow? Why or why not?
3. What larger points can we take from this essay? (Consider the various responses to snow supplied by the author, but also consider what this entire chapter is about.)

Ground Zero

JONATHAN SCHELL

Jonathan Schell has taught at Princeton University, New York University, and Wesleyan University and has been a writer and editor of *The New Yorker*. He is the author of many articles and books; among his books are *The Fate of the Earth* (1982), a look at the potential horrors of nuclear war, and *The Unconquerable World* (2003). He is currently the Harold Willens Peace Fellow at the Nation Institute and author of a column in *The Nation*, "Letter from Ground Zero," from October 15, 2001, to March 6, 2006, to explore and comment on issues that have arisen as a result of the Twin Towers attacks. The following is part of his first "Letter."

Questions to Guide Your Reading and Reflection

1. What did we learn from the 9/11 attacks?
2. Many people have visited the site in lower Manhattan. Have you? If so, what was your reaction? If not, what do you think your reaction might be?

Of course there can be no such thing as a literal letter from   1
ground zero—neither from the ground zeros of September 11
nor from the potential nuclear ground zero that is the origin of
the expression. There are no letters from the beyond. (By now,
"zero" has the double meaning of zero distance from the bom-
bardier's assigned coordinates and the nothingness that's left
when his work is done.) As it happens, though, I live six blocks
from the ruins of the north tower of the World Trade Center,
which is about as close as you can be to ground zero without
having been silenced. My specific neighborhood was violated,
mutilated. As I write these words, the acrid, dank, rancid
stink—it is the smell of death—of the still-smoking site is in my
nostrils. Not that these things confer any great distinction—
they are merely the local embodiment of the circumstance, felt
more or less keenly by everyone in the world in the aftermath
of the attack, that in our age of weapons of mass destruction
every square foot of our globe can become such a ground zero
in a twinkling. We have long known this intellectually, but now
we know it viscerally, as a nausea in the pit of the stomach that
is unlikely to go away. What to do to change this condition, it
seems to me, is the most important of the practical tasks that
the crisis requires us to perform.

It takes time for the human reality of the losses to sink in.   2
The eye is quick but the heart is slow. I had two experiences
this week that helped me along. It occurred to me that I would
be a very bad journalist and maybe a worse neighbor if, living just a few blocks from the catastrophe, I did not manage
to get through the various checkpoints to visit the site. A
press pass was useless; it got me no closer than my own
home. A hole in the storm-fence circling the site worked better. I found myself in the midst of a huge peaceable army of
helpers in a thousand uniforms—military and civilian. I was
somehow unprepared by television for what I saw when I
arrived at ground zero. Television had seemed to show
mostly a low hillock of rubble from which the famous bucket
brigade of rescuers was passing out pieces of debris. This
proved to be a keyhole vision of the site. In fact, it was a
gigantic, varied, panoramic landscape of destruction, an Alps
of concrete, plastic and twisted metal, rising tier upon tier in
the smoky distance. Around the perimeter and in the

surrounding streets, a cornucopia of food, drinks (thousands of crates of spring water, Gatorade, etc.) and other provisions contributed by well-wishers from around the country was heaped up, as if some main of consumer goods on its way to the Trade Center had burst and disgorged its flood upon the sidewalks. The surrounding buildings, smashed but still standing, looked down eyelessly on their pulverized brethren. The pieces of the facade of the towers that are often shown in photographs—gigantic forks, or bent spatulas— loomed surprisingly high over the scene with dread majesty. Entry into the ruins by the rescue workers was being accomplished by a cage, or gondola, suspended by a crane, as if in some infernal ski resort. When I arrived at the southern rim, the rescuers were all standing silent watching one of these cages being lifted out of the ruins. Shortly, a small pile of something not shaped like a human being but covered by an American flag was brought out in an open buggy. It was the remains, a solemn nurse told me, of one of the firemen who had given his life for the people in the building. And then the slow work began again. Although the site was more terrible even than I had imagined, seeing was somehow reassuring. Unvisited, the site, so near my home, had preyed on my imagination.

3   A few days later—one week after the catastrophe—I took my dog for a walk in the evening in Riverside Park, on the upper West Side. Soft orange clouds drifted over the Hudson River and the New Jersey shore. In the dim, cavernous green of the park, normal things were occurring—people were out for walks or jogging, children were playing in a playground. To the south, a slender moon hung in the sky. I found myself experiencing an instant of surprise: So it was still there! It had not dropped out of the sky. That was good. After all, our local southern mountain peaks—the twin towers—had fallen. The world seemed to steady around the surviving moon. "Peace" became more than a word. It was the world of difference between the bottom half of Manhattan and the top. It was the persistence of all the wonderful, ordinary things before my eyes.

4   Curiously, it was only after this moment of return to confidence in the continuity of life that the shape and size of the

change that had been wrought in the world a week before began to come into view. The very immensity of that change— and, what was something different, the news coverage of that change—was itself a prime fact of the new situation. In an instant and without warning on a fine fall morning, the known world had been jerked aside like a mere slide in a projector, and a new world had been rammed into its place. I have before me the *New York Times* of September 11, which went to press, of course, the night before the attack. It is news from Atlantis.[1] "Key Leaders," were talking of "Possible Deals to Revive Economy," a headline said, but who was paying attention now? Were "School Dress Codes" still in a struggle with "A Sea of Bare Flesh"? Yes, but it was hard to give the matter much thought. Was "Morning TV" still a "Hot Market" in "a Nation of Early Risers"? It was, but not for the reasons given in the article. Only one headline—"Nuclear Booty: More Smugglers Use Asia Route"—seemed fit for the day's events.

Has the eye of the world ever shifted more abruptly or com-   5 pletely than it did on September 11? The destruction of Hiroshima of course comes to mind. It, too, was prepared in secrecy and fell like a thunderbolt upon the world. But it came after years of a world war and ended the war, whereas the September 11 attack came in a time of peace and—so our President has said—started a war. The assassination of Archduke Ferdinand on June 28, 1914, starting the First World War, is another candidate. Yet the possibility of war among the great powers had long been discussed, and many previous crises—in the Far East, in the Mediterranean, in the Balkans—had threatened war. It was not the event but the aftermath (we are still living in it)—the war's ferocity and duration and the war-born horrors that sprang out of it to afflict the entire twentieth century— that changed the world. Also, whereas the guns of August touched off a chain of events—the invocation of a web of treaty agreements, the predetermined mobilization schedules of great armies—that statesmanship and diplomacy seemed powerless to prevent, today little seems predetermined, and the latitude of choice, ranging from international police work to multifront major war, seems exceptionally wide.

[1]A legendary island—Ed.

Expanding Vocabulary

Match each word in column A with its definition in column B. When in doubt, first find the word in the essay and look for context clues to aid your understanding of the word's meaning. Then, if necessary, use your dictionary to complete the matching exercise. The number in parentheses is the number of the paragraph in which the word appears.

Column A	Column B
acrid (1)	unbroken view
embodiment (1)	that which gives shape to
viscerally (1)	a small hill
hillock (2)	reduced to dust
panoramic (2)	spewed out
cornucopia (2)	appeal to
pulverized (2)	unpleasantly sharp
disgorged (2)	abundance
invocation (5)	emotionally, instinctively

Understanding Content

1. What is the author's relationship to the "ground zero" of the 9/11 site?
2. Why did he feel compelled to visit the site?
3. How did the site affect him before he visited? How did visiting make him feel?
4. What did Schell do a week after the attacks? How did this activity make him feel?

Drawing Inferences about Thesis and Purpose

1. Schell's opening and concluding paragraphs suggest that his primary purpose is something more than description. What is his purpose in writing?
2. Is there a sentence (or two) in paragraph 1 that serve(s) as a thesis? If yes, underline it (them); if no, write a thesis statement for the essay.

Analyzing Strategies and Style

1. Reread Schell's description of ground zero. What details strike you as most vivid, most effective? Why?
2. Schell uses a number of metaphors. Select two and explain each one.
3. What do the historical details of paragraph 5 contribute to the essay?

Thinking Critically

1. In paragraph 4, the author lists headlines from a newspaper published the morning of 9/11. Why does he include these details? What point does he want to make?
2. What is the connection between the details in paragraph 3 and those in paragraph 2? Why does Schell include the details in paragraph 3?
3. How did 9/11 affect you initially? Are there ways in which it continues to affect you? In what ways has the country been affected by that day?

STUDENT ESSAY—DESCRIPTION

TIME'S TROPHY
Alexa Skandar

There is something timeless and comforting about an old face. The face of my grandmother is built of a thousand weathered wrinkles. She doesn't smile too often anymore. On those rare occasions when we are lucky enough to catch her smile, her eyes seem to completely disappear behind the folds of time, yet somehow they still radiate that light that always attracted everyone to her.

Subject introduced through details of aging.

My grandmother smells of rose oil and lettuce cream. She keeps her yellowed white hair permed and short and slicks it back with water every so often. Her skin is like the leather of her brown sandals, and her hands reveal the years of toil she has survived. Veins show like ancient

Subject is now identified—her grandmother.

Good use of metaphors to describe physical details.

flowing rivers through her aged skin. The index finger of her right hand is curved. "It's from years of crocheting," her daughter once explained to me in whispers. Her small, frail body, bent like her finger by the hands of time, seems to reflect pain and hardship in her past.

Celuta Quiroga de Skandar wears black every day, black to mourn her dead husband. Every day she prays for him. Every day her cloudy hazel eyes show her grief that has been there since he passed away close to thirty years ago. She used to go to church every day and to visit his grave every Sunday, but she has grown too old for that now. Instead she sits in a chair in the corner, rosary beads in hand, eyes partially closed, pupils rolled back, whispering her "Hail Mary's" as she rocks herself back and forth. Senile though she is, sometimes she gets serious, and her eyes become clear, as if she has broken out of some kind of trance for a moment, and she admits that she prays every day for God to take her to be with her husband. Then her eyes cloud over and her words become meaningless again.

Grandmother's name and widowed state revealed.

My grandmother is very old now. Little matters to her anymore. She has stopped living on the same plane of existence as the rest of us. She sits down to tell us the same stories over and over. She goes to bed at eight in the evening only to wake up a few hours later, make her bed, and get dressed. She often makes her way to the kitchen and is fixing breakfast before she is found and told gently, "Abuelita, it's still nighttime. Time to sleep. Let's put you back to bed." A confused look comes over her face, but she obliges, often just to get back up and repeat the morning routine a few hours later.

She used to be a strong and active woman. "Dona Celu," as they called her in her small village, was a mother, a nurse, a midwife, a farmer, a cook, and a storyteller. People who remember how she used to be tell stories of her greatness, making me proud to be her granddaughter. They recount how she organized the building of the first swimming pool in the valley in which she lived and how she saved the lives of new mothers and their infants from the complications of small-town childbirth. They tell of how she took in the neighbors' orphaned children when they had nowhere else to turn, and raised them as her own. Now her feeble attempts to sneak out of the house and stumble to

Example of her senility.

Details given to reveal the person she once was.

church inspire pity in all of us. She has become a mere shadow of the strong and determined woman she once was. But, there is a certain strength in the lines that time has etched in her face, a kind of beauty that she has attained as a trophy for all she has been through in her years of existence. For one, a wonderful grand-mother.

Thesis stated at end.

MAKING CONNECTIONS

1. Degas and Picasso both depict dancers in their paintings. (See reproductions following p. 96.) How do their paintings differ? How do the differences in presentation change the viewer's "picture" of dancers? Can one painting be said to be more realistic than the other? If so, what is meant by *realistic*?
2. Study the essays of Kidder and Mora. What conclusions can you draw about effective strategies for presenting telling details of character?
3. Pat Mora (pp. 95–98) and Amy Tan in this chapter (pp. 91–94) were influenced by growing up as minorities in American culture. Think about what these writers say—imply—about the shaping of personality. Reflect: What are the strongest forces in the molding of character?

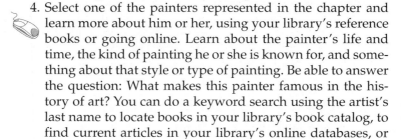

4. Select one of the painters represented in the chapter and learn more about him or her, using your library's reference books or going online. Learn about the painter's life and time, the kind of painting he or she is known for, and something about that style or type of painting. Be able to answer the question: What makes this painter famous in the history of art? You can do a keyword search using the artist's last name to locate books in your library's book catalog, to find current articles in your library's online databases, or to locate information online.

5. What place in the world would you like to visit for the first time? Go online and see what you can learn about your choice. Find out how you can get there and what you can see and do there. Be prepared to share your information with classmates.

TOPICS FOR WRITING

1. Describe a place you know well and that has a special significance for you. (Possibilities include your backyard, the path you walked to school, a favorite park, playground, vacation spot, city street.) Give the details that will let your reader see this place clearly. But also provide the telling details that will let your reader understand why this place has (or had) significance for you, why it is (or was) special.
2. Describe a place you have visited that produced a strong reaction in you, a place that you fell in love with (e.g., Fifth Avenue in New York City the week before Christmas), heartily disliked (e.g., Los Angeles in heavy smog), found incredibly beautiful or awe-inspiring or special in some way (e.g., the Florida Everglades, Niagara Falls, the green hills of Vermont). Give enough details to let readers who have not been there see the place, but concentrate on presenting those details so that readers will want to visit—or never visit—depending on your thesis.
3. Have you been in an earthquake or hurricane or seen a tornado? If so, re-create the event in words so that readers can see it and feel the accompanying human emotions. Do not write a narrative account; rather select a moment or two and describe that time vividly.
4. Describe a specific scene during one of the seasons. Possibilities include your garden in autumn, a city park in summer, a city center at holiday time, your campus in the spring.
5. Describe a room on your campus to develop and support the thesis that the room fulfills—or fails to fulfill—its purpose or function. Possibilities include a classroom, science lab, learning lab, writing center, cafeteria, or library. If your library is a large and separate building, select one section

of it, such as the periodicals room. Resist the urge to describe a large building, such as the entire student center. Instead, focus on one place and present details to support your thesis.

6. Lance Morrow offers readers some detailed and moving descriptions of animals he saw in the East Africa game preserves. If you enjoy wildlife, either in the wild or in a nearby zoo, take some time to watch one of your favorite animals. Or, if you have a pet, reflect on that animal. Then write a description of the animal you have selected, giving many details but also the telling details that will support a thesis about the animal. Reflect on what is central to the animal's way of life or personality to arrive at your thesis. Is the animal funny? Endearing? Inspiring? Mean? Intelligent or clever?

7. How well do you see someone close to you—a family member, friend, colleague, teacher? Select telling physical and biographical details to create an interesting and thoughtful portrait of the person you select. Pay close attention to the details that shape personality.

8. Select one of the paintings reproduced in this text or find a color reproduction of a favorite painting in your library's art book collection. Explain how the details in the painting work to create the painting's dominant effect. You will need to reflect on the painting's effect, or the artist's attitude toward the subject. Then ask yourself: How is that effect achieved by the details—the objects, composition, color, and brushwork—that make up the painting?

A CHECKLIST FOR DESCRIPTION ESSAYS

Inventing

☐ Have I selected a topic and approach consistent with the instructor's guidelines for this assignment?

☐ Have I chosen, among the possible topics, one that fits my knowledge?

☐ Have I reflected on my knowledge of person or place or painting to create a tentative thesis that is clear, focused, and interesting to others?

☐ Have I recognized, from my reflection, the *telling details* that will best reveal my subject?

☐ Do I have an order for my descriptive details—spatial or by type of detail?

Drafting

☐ Have I succeeded in completing a first draft at one sitting so that I can "see" the whole?

☐ Do I have enough—enough to meet assignment demands and enough to develop and support my thesis? If not, do I need new paragraphs or more details or reflection in existing paragraphs?

☐ Does the order work? If not, what needs to be moved—and where?

☐ Am I satisfied with the way I have expressed the insights to be gained? Do the details carry my point? Have I been too heavy-handed with a message?

Revising

☐ Have I made any needed additions, deletions, or changes in order based on answering the questions about my draft?

☐ Have I revised my draft to produce coherent paragraphs, using transition words, including spatial terms if I am writing about a place or painting, to guide readers?

Polishing

☐ Have I eliminated wordiness and clichés?

☐ Have I avoided or removed any discriminatory language?

☐ Have I used my word processor's spell check and proofread a printed copy with great care?

☐ Do I have an appropriate and interesting title?

4

Using Comparison and Contrast
Ways of Learning

When we compare we examine similarities; when we contrast we examine differences. These are strategies frequently used—whether in thinking for ourselves or communicating with others—to organize information or ideas about two (or more) similar subjects. When you think about why you like your biology course more than your chemistry course, you begin to note points of difference between them. You begin to use contrast. When shopping for a stereo system, you might read a consumer guide or gather information from friends so that you can contrast several models for cost, reliability, and sound.

When to Use Comparison and Contrast

Let's see what we have said about thinking comparatively. First, it is a strategy for organizing information and ideas. You may be able to think more clearly about problems in your chemistry course if you contrast those problems with your successes in biology. Second, you have a reason to examine similarities or differences between subjects. Your goal, in our example, is to understand why you are doing better in biology than in chemistry. Perhaps you came to college thinking that you would major in chemistry. Rethinking career goals may be aided by a careful listing of specific differences in your study of chemistry and biology. (One difference is the amount of math needed in the study of chemistry. Could that be the problem?) Third, we compare or contrast items that are similar.

There seems to be little purpose in contrasting your chemistry course with doing your laundry. We compare or contrast two cities, two schools, two jobs, two dorms. We probably do not contrast living in Louisville with living in a frat house because there is no point to such a contrast. (You might have good reason, though, to contrast living at home with living away at school.) Finally, a useful comparison or contrast focuses on important similarities or differences. If you have plenty of space for your new stereo, then contrasting the sizes of different systems is unimportant. But unless you have unlimited funds, the cost of each unit is quite important for your goal of choosing the best stereo for you.

Remember that an organizing principle such as comparison or contrast does not supply a purpose for writing. Rather it is a strategy that needs to grow logically out of your topic and purpose. Nancy Sakamoto contrasts American and Japanese conversations to show why sometimes Japanese and Americans have trouble communicating or being comfortable in conversation with one another. Her contrast structure is a strategy, not an end in itself.

How to Use Comparison and Contrast

Sometimes writers combine comparison and contrast, but more often their goal is to show either similarities or differences. Thus the student who asserts that there are good reasons for parents to move their children from McLean to Langley High School has a thesis that announces a contrast purpose. Although the schools certainly have some similarities—both are high schools in northern Virginia—readers will expect to learn about the significant differences between the two schools.

Organization

How should points of difference between two high schools (or any two items) be organized in an essay? You have two basic plans from which to choose. Suppose you want to show differences in the two buildings, in the courses offered, and in the extracurricular activities. If we assign "A" to McLean and "B"

to Langley and number the points of difference 1, 2, and 3, we
can diagram the two patterns as follows:

Whole by Whole	*Part by Part*
A. McLean	A. Physical Plant
1. McLean Physical Plant	1. McLean
2. McLean Courses	2. Langley
3. McLean Activities	B. Courses
B. Langley	1. McLean
1. Langley Physical Plant	2. Langley
2. Langley Courses	C. Activities
3. Langley Activities	1. McLean
	2. Langley

Observe that the whole-by-whole pattern organizes the essay
first by school and then by points of difference, whereas the
part-by-part pattern organizes the paper by the three (in this
example) points of difference.

As you will see in the essays in this chapter, professional
writers do not always strictly follow one plan or the other. Your
instructor, however, may want you to practice using either the
whole-by-whole or part-by-part structure. In fact, many
instructors believe that, for most contrast topics, the part-
by-part pattern is the best choice because it keeps writers
focused on the business of explaining points of difference.

Transitions

When you read articles that have a comparison or contrast purpose, you may want to label the two subjects A and B and then,
in the margin of your book, assign a number to each point of
similarity or difference as you read. When you are writing a
contrast essay, remember that you want your reader to be able
to recognize the parts of your contrast structure. This means
that you will need to use appropriate transitions to mark those
parts. Consider these possibilities and other similar expressions
to guide your reader:

by contrast	on the other hand
another difference	a third similarity

Metaphors and Analogies

When we think about the strategies of comparison and contrast, two related terms come to mind: metaphor (or simile) and analogy. We have said that we compare or contrast similar items: two schools, two courses, and so on. A *metaphor* (or a *simile*) differs in that it compares two items that are essentially unalike. When the poet writes the simile: "My love is like a red, red rose," he asks us to consider the ways that love (a feeling) can be like a rose (a flower). (To express the idea as a metaphor, the poet can write: "My love blooms.") In either case, we understand that a feeling isn't really like a flower. This is why a metaphor or a simile is called a *figure of speech*—we are speaking figuratively, not literally. The cleverness of a fresh metaphor delights us, sometimes surprises us, and affects us emotionally. You will find the essayist E. B. White using metaphors effectively to express feelings about his subjects.

In Linda Pastan's poem at the end of this chapter, she has a grading system to comment on family relationships. She uses, in other words, the same figurative idea throughout the poem. In an essay, the use of an extended metaphor is called an *analogy*. Think of an analogy as fanciful (like a metaphor) but developing a number of points of similarity or difference to support a thesis. Both metaphors and analogies, when original and thoughtful, enrich our writing. Some of this chapter's exercises will give you a chance to practice both strategies.

WRITING FOCUS
COHERENCE IS CRUCIAL

Transition words are essential to guide readers through a contrast essay. But writers need to use *coherence strategies* in all of their writing, not just to show contrast. Think of each body paragraph (excluding the opening and concluding paragraphs) as a "mini" essay; each one needs both *unity* and *coherence*. *Unity* means that all sentences in each paragraph are on that paragraph's topic. *Coherence* means using strategies that *show* readers how each body paragraph holds together. Make a point to use coherence strategies. They are illustrated and labeled in the following sample paragraph and then listed for you.

Paragraph's topic sentence

Repetition of subject or key words

Transition words/phrases

Clear structure of material—air, sea, land

> During the Cretaceous Period (about 160 million to 65 million years ago) in North America, you would have found some familiar plants—for example, ferns, palm trees, and redwoods—and you would have been surprised by the mix of animals. At that time you would have found many birds, including giant flying pterosaurs. In the sea, you would have seen an interesting mix; for example, sharks and turtles along with giant marine lizards and fishlike ichthyosaurs. On land there were insects and small, furry mammals, but also the dinosaurs. Although some dinosaurs were already extinct, others still roamed North America; for instance, duck-bills, *Triceratops*, and the famous *Tryannosaurus rex*.

Coherence Strategies

1. Clear organization (e.g., air, sea, land)
2. Repetition of key words (e.g., "North America," "mix")
3. Use of transition worlds (e.g., "at that time," "also")
4. Consistent person (e.g., "*you* would")

Getting Started:
Reflecting on Expectations of College

Although you may not have been at college for long, still you have probably had some experiences that were not what you expected. Reflect on what you expected college to be like and how your experiences have, in part, differed from those expectations. In your journal or class notebook make two columns— one of expectations and one of what you have actually experienced. Have most of your expectations been met? Only some of them? Is there one important difference that is bothering you? You may want to write about that difference in another journal entry, or perhaps in an essay.

Conversational Ballgames

NANCY MASTERSON SAKAMOTO

American-born Sakamoto (b. 1931) lived with her Japanese husband in Osaka and taught English to Japanese students. She
then became a professor at Shitennoji Gakuen University in
Hawaii. "Conversational Ballgames" is a chapter from her textbook on conversational English, *Polite Fictions*, published in
1982. Her contrasts of English and Japanese styles of conversation and her strategy for developing that contrast make us
aware of the effect of cultural conditioning on the ways we learn
to use language.

Questions to Guide Your Reading and Reflection

1. What differences between American culture and Japanese
   culture are suggested in Sakamoto's discussion of conversation?
2. How would you characterize conversation in a language
   other than English or Japanese? Or, how would you describe
   the conversation of young children and their parents?

After I was married and had lived in Japan for a while, my   1
Japanese gradually improved to the point where I could take
part in simple conversations with my husband and his friends
and family. And I began to notice that often, when I joined in,
the others would look startled, and the conversational topic
would come to a halt. After this happened several times, it
became clear to me that I was doing something wrong. But for
a long time, I didn't know what it was.

Finally, after listening carefully to many Japanese conversa-   2
tions, I discovered what my problem was. Even though I was
speaking Japanese, I was handling the conversation in a
western way.

Japanese-style conversations develop quite differently from   3
western-style conversations. And the difference isn't only in the
languages. I realized that just as I kept trying to hold western-
style conversations even when I was speaking Japanese, so my
English students kept trying to hold Japanese-style conversations

even when they were speaking English. We were unconsciously playing entirely different conversational ballgames.

4   A western-style conversation between two people is like a game of tennis. If I introduce a topic, a conversational ball, I expect you to hit it back. If you agree with me, I don't expect you simply to agree and do nothing more. I expect you to add something—a reason for agreeing, another example, or an elaboration to carry the idea further. But I don't expect you always to agree. I am just as happy if you question me, or challenge me, or completely disagree with me. Whether you agree or disagree, your response will return the ball to me.

5   And then it is my turn again. I don't serve a new ball from my original starting line. I hit your ball back again from where it has bounced. I carry your idea further, or answer your questions or objections, or challenge or question you. And so the ball goes back and forth, with each of us doing our best to give it a new twist, an original spin, or a powerful smash.

6   And the more vigorous the action, the more interesting and exciting the game. Of course, if one of us gets angry, it spoils the conversation, just as it spoils a tennis game. But getting excited is not at all the same as getting angry. After all, we are not trying to hit each other. We are trying to hit the ball. So long as we attack only each other's opinions, and do not attack each other personally, we don't expect anyone to get hurt. A good conversation is supposed to be interesting and exciting.

7   If there are more than two people in the conversation, then it is like doubles in tennis, or like volleyball. There's no waiting in line. Whoever is nearest and quickest hits the ball, and if you step back, someone else will hit it. No one stops the game to give you a turn. You're responsible for taking your own turn.

8   But whether it's two players or a group, everyone does his best to keep the ball going, and no one person has the ball for very long.

9   A Japanese-style conversation, however, is not at all like tennis or volleyball. It's like bowling. You wait for your turn. And you always know your place in line. It depends on such things as whether you are older or younger, a close friend or a relative stranger to the previous speaker, in a senior or junior position, and so on.

When your turn comes, you step up to the starting line with your bowling ball, and carefully bowl it. Everyone else stands back and watches politely, murmuring encouragement. Everyone waits until the ball has reached the end of the alley, and watches to see if it knocks down all the pins, or only some of them, or none of them. There is a pause, while everyone registers your score.

Then, after everyone is sure that you have completely finished your turn, the next person in line steps up to the same starting line, with a different ball. He doesn't return your ball, and he does not begin from where your ball stopped. There is no back and forth at all. All the balls run parallel. And there is always a suitable pause between turns. There is no rush, no excitement, no scramble for the ball.

No wonder everyone looked startled when I took part in Japanese conversations. I paid no attention to whose turn it was, and kept snatching the ball halfway down the alley and throwing it back at the bowler. Of course the conversation died. I was playing the wrong game.

This explains why it is almost impossible to get a western-style conversation or discussion going with English students in Japan. I used to think that the problem was their lack of English language ability. But I finally came to realize that the biggest problem is that they, too, are playing the wrong game.

Whenever I serve a volleyball, everyone just stands back and watches it fall, with occasional murmurs of encouragement. No one hits it back. Everyone waits until I call on someone to take a turn. And when that person speaks, he doesn't hit my ball back. He serves a new ball. Again, everyone just watches it fall.

So I call on someone else. This person does not refer to what the previous speaker has said. He also serves a new ball. Nobody seems to have paid any attention to what anyone else has said. Everyone begins again from the same starting line, and all the balls run parallel. There is never any back and forth. Everyone is trying to bowl with a volleyball.

And if I try a simpler conversation, with only two of us, then the other person tries to bowl with my tennis ball. No wonder foreign English teachers in Japan get discouraged.

Now that you know about the difference in the conversational ballgames, you may think that all your troubles are over.

But if you have been trained all your life to play one game, it is no simple matter to switch to another, even if you know the rules. Knowing the rules is not at all the same thing as playing the game.

18   Even now, during a conversation in Japanese I will notice a startled reaction, and belatedly realize that once again I have rudely interrupted by instinctively trying to hit back the other person's bowling ball. It is no easier for me to "just listen" during a conversation than it is for my Japanese students to "just relax" when speaking with foreigners. Now I can truly sympathize with how hard they must find it to try to carry on a western-style conversation.

19   If I have not yet learned to do conversational bowling in Japanese, at least I have figured out one thing that puzzled me for a long time. After his first trip to America, my husband complained that Americans asked him so many questions and made him talk so much at the dinner table that he never had a chance to eat. When I asked him why he couldn't talk and eat at the same time, he said that Japanese do not customarily think that dinner, especially on fairly formal occasions, is a suitable time for extended conversation.

20   Since westerners think that conversation is an indispensable part of dining, and indeed would consider it impolite not to converse with one's dinner partner, I found this Japanese custom rather strange. Still, I could accept it as a cultural difference even though I didn't really understand it. But when my husband added, in explanation, that Japanese consider it extremely rude to talk with one's mouth full, I got confused. Talking with one's mouth full is certainly not an American custom. We think it very rude, too. Yet we still manage to talk a lot and eat at the same time. How do we do it?

21   For a long time, I couldn't explain it, and it bothered me. But after I discovered the conversational ballgames, I finally found the answer. Of course! In a western-style conversation, you hit the ball, and while someone else is hitting it back, you take a bite, chew, and swallow. Then you hit the ball again, and then eat some more. The more people there are in the conversation, the more chances you have to eat. But even with only two of you talking, you still have plenty of chances to eat.

Maybe that's why polite conversation at the dinner table has   22
never been a traditional part of Japanese etiquette. Your turn to
talk would last so long without interruption that you'd never
get a chance to eat.

Expanding Vocabulary

Study definitions of each of the following words and then use each
one in a separate sentence. The number in parentheses is the number
of the paragraph in which the word appears.

elaboration (4)	belatedly (18)
murmuring (10)	customarily (19)
registers (10)	etiquette (22)

Understanding Content

1. When Sakamoto first participated in Japanese conversations,
   what happened? What was the cause of her problem?
2. What are the characteristics of an American-style conversation?
3. What are the characteristics of a Japanese-style conversation?
4. How do the Japanese feel about conversing during dinner? How
   do Americans feel about dinner conversation?

Drawing Inferences about Thesis and Purpose

1. How hard is it to converse in another language after one has
   "learned" the language?
2. What is Sakamoto's thesis? Where is it stated?

Analyzing Strategies and Style

1. What strategy does Sakamoto use as an opening? What makes it
   effective?
2. Explain each analogy. How is American-style conversation like a
   tennis game, and how is Japanese-style conversation like bowling? What other game comparison does the author use?
3. Who is Sakamoto's primary audience? (Be sure to read the head-
   note.) What makes her writing style appropriate for her audience
   and purpose?

Thinking Critically

1. Did the author's analogies help you to see the differences
   between American and Japanese conversational styles? If not,
   why not? If the analogies did help you, can you explain why?

2. Had you thought before about the way we carry on conversations? After reflection, do you agree with the author's description of American conversation patterns? Why or why not?
3. What might we conclude about the relationship between language and cultural traits and values? What else do we learn when, as children, we learn our primary language?

Boys and Girls: Anatomy and Destiny

JUDITH VIORST

Judith Viorst is a poet, journalist, and author of books for both children and adults. She has published several volumes of poetry and more than a dozen books. Viorst may be best known as a contributing editor to *Redbook* magazine; she has received several awards for her *Redbook* columns. Her book *Necessary Losses* (1986) is an important book about coping with the changes we experience at different times in our lives. The following is an excerpt from *Necessary Losses*.

Questions to Guide Your Reading and Reflection

1. What are the incorrect beliefs about males and females, according to Maccoby and Jacklin?
2. Make a list of what you think are differences between males and females (other than anatomy) and compare your list to Viorst's.

1   It is argued that sex-linked limits have been culturally produced. It is argued that sex-linked limits are innate. What gender-identity studies seem to strongly suggest, however, is that—from the moment of birth—both boys and girls are so clearly treated as boys or as girls that even very early displays of "masculine" or "feminine" behavior cannot be detached from environmental influences.

2   For parents make a distinction between boys and girls.

3   They have different ways of holding boys and girls.

4   They have different expectations for boys and girls.

And as their children imitate and identify with their atti-   5
tudes and activities, they encourage or discourage them,
depending on whether or not they are boys or girls.

Are there, in actual fact, *real* sex-linked limits? Is there an   6
inborn male or female psychology? And is there any possible
way of exploring such tricky questions unbiased by culture,
upbringing or sexual politics? . . .

Sigmund Freud . . . went on record as saying that women are   7
more masochistic, narcissistic, jealous and envious than men,
and also less moral. He saw these qualities as the inevitable
consequences of the anatomical differences between the
sexes—the result of the fact (fact?) that the original sexuality of
the little girl is masculine in character, that her clitoris is merely
an undeveloped penis and that she correctly perceives herself
as nothing more than a defective boy. It is the girl's perception
of herself as a mutilated male that irrevocably damages her
self-esteem, leading to resentments and attempts at reparation
which produce all the subsequent defects in her character.

Well, as his friends say, who can be right about everything?   8

For in the years since this was written, science has estab-   9
lished that while genetic sex is determined at fertilization by
our chromosomes (XX for girls; XY for boys), all mammals,
including humans, *regardless of their genetic sex*, start out female
in nature and in structure. This female state persists until the
production, some time later in fetal life, of male hormones. It is
only with the appearance of these hormones, at the right time
and in the right amount, that anatomical maleness and postnatal
masculinity become possible.

While this may not tell us much about the psychology of   10
femaleness and maleness, it does put a permanent crimp in
Freud's phallocentricity. For, far from little girls starting out as
incomplete little boys, in the beginning all human beings are
female.

Despite his phallocentricity, however, Freud was smart   11
enough to note at the time that his comments on the nature of
women were "certainly incomplete and fragmentary."

He also said: "If you want to know more about femininity,   12
enquire from your own experiences of life, or turn to the poets,
or wait until science can give you deeper and more coherent
information."

13   Two Stanford psychologists have tried to do just that in a highly regarded book called *The Psychology of Sex Differences*. Surveying and evaluating a broad range of psychological studies, authors Eleanor Maccoby and Carol Jacklin conclude that there are several widely held but dead-wrong beliefs regarding the ways in which males and females differ:

14   That girls are more "social" and more "suggestible" than boys. That girls have lower self-esteem. That girls are better at rote learning and simple repetitive tasks and boys more "analytic." That girls are more affected by heredity and boys by environment. That girls are auditory and boys are visual. And that girls lack achievement motivation.

15   Not true, say authors Maccoby and Jacklin. These are myths.

16   Some myths, however—or are they myths?—have not yet been dispelled. Some sexual mysteries remain unsolved:

17   Are girls more timid? Are they more fearful? More anxious?

18   Are boys more active, competitive and dominant?

19   And is it a female quality—in contrast to a male quality—to be nurturing and compliant and maternal?

20   The evidence, the authors say, is either too ambiguous or too thin. These tantalizing questions are still open.

21   There are, however, four differences which they believe to be fairly well established: That girls have greater verbal ability. That boys have greater math ability. That boys excel in visual-spatial ability. And that verbally and physically, boys are more aggressive.

22   Are these innate differences, or are they learned? Maccoby and Jacklin reject this distinction. They prefer to talk in terms of biological predispositions to learn a particular skill or kind of behavior. And talking in these terms, they designate only two sexual differences as clearly built upon biological factors.

23   One is boys' better visual-spatial ability, for which there is evidence of a recessive sex-linked gene.

24   The other is the relationship that exists between male hormones and the readiness of males to behave aggressively.

25   However, even that has been disputed. Endocrinologist Estelle Ramey, professor of physiology and biophysics at Georgetown Medical School, told me:

26   "I think hormones are great little things and that no home should be without them. But I also think that virtually all the

differences in male and female behavior are culturally, not hormonally, determined. It's certainly true that *in utero* sex hormones play a vital role in distinguishing male from female babies. But soon after birth the human brain takes over and overrides *all* systems, including the endocrine system. It is said, for instance, that men are innately more aggressive than women. But conditioning, not sex hormones, makes them that way. Anyone seeing women at a bargain-basement sale—where aggression is viewed as appropriate, even endearing—sees aggression that would make Attila the Hun turn pale."

Although Maccoby and Jacklin's survey also concludes that 27 little girls are no more dependent than boys, the female-dependency issue will not go away. A few years ago Colette Dowling's best-selling book *The Cinderella Complex* struck a responsive chord in women everywhere with its theme of a female fear of independence.

> Here it was—the Cinderella Complex. It used to hit girls of sixteen or seventeen, preventing them, often, from going to college, hastening them into early marriages. Now it tends to hit women after college—after they've been out in the world a while. When the first thrill of freedom subsides and anxiety rises to take its place, they begin to be tugged by that old yearning for safety: the wish to be saved.

Dowling argues that women, in contrast to men, have a deep 28 desire to be taken care of and that they are unwilling to accept the adult reality that they alone are responsible for their lives. This tendency toward dependency, Dowling maintains, is bred into them by the training of early childhood, which teaches boys that they're on their own in this difficult, challenging world and which teaches girls that they need and must seek protection.

Girls are trained *into* dependency, says Dowling. 29

Boys are trained *out* of it. 30

Even in the mid-1980s, at an Eastern liberal-elite private 31 school where the mothers of students are doctors and lawyers and government officials and the students themselves are full of feminist rhetoric, there are echoes of the Cinderella Complex. One of the teachers, who gives a course in human behavior to the high school seniors, told me that he has asked them, for the last several years, where they expect to see themselves at age thirty. The answers, he said, are consistently the same. Both boys and girls expect that the girls will be bearing and rearing children, while also engaged in some interesting *part-time* work. And although the boys express a desire to have a great deal of freedom at that age, the girls routinely place the boys in successful *full-time* jobs, supporting their families.

32   Now it surely is true that a great many women live with a someday-my-prince-will-take-care-of-me fantasy. It is true that the way girls are raised may help explain why. But we also need to consider that the source of female dependence may run deeper than the customs of early child care. And we also need to remember that dependence isn't always a dirty word.

33   For female dependence appears to be less a wish to be protected than a wish to be part of a web of human relationships, a wish not only to get—but to give—loving care. To need other people to help and console you, to share the good times and bad, to say "I understand," to be on your side—*and also to need the reverse, to need to be needed*—may lie at the heart of women's very identity. Dependence on such connections might be described as "mature dependence." It also means, however, that identity—for women—has more to do with intimacy than with separateness.

34   In a series of elegant studies, psychologist Carol Gilligan found that while male self-definitions emphasized individual achievement over attachment, women repeatedly defined themselves within a context of responsible caring relationships. Indeed, she notes that "male and female voices typically speak of the importance of different truths, the former of the role of separation as it defines and empowers the self, the latter of the ongoing process of attachment that creates and sustains the human community." It is only because we live in a world where maturity is equated with autonomy, argues Gilligan, that women's concern with relationships appears to be a weakness instead of a strength.

35   Perhaps it is both.

36   Claire, an aspiring physician, finds essential meaning in attachment. "By yourself, there is little sense to things," she says. "It is like the sound of one hand clapping. . . . You have to love someone else, because while you may not like them, you are inseparable from them. In a way, it is like loving your

right hand. *They are part of you*; that other person is part of that giant collection of people that you are connected to."

But then there is Helen who, talking about the end of a rela- 37
tionship, reveals the risks inherent in intimacy. "What I had to learn . . .," she says, "wasn't only that I had a Self that could survive it when Tony and I broke up; but that I had a Self *at all!* I wasn't honestly sure that, when we two were separate, there would be anything there that *was me*."

Freud once observed that "we are never so defenseless 38
against suffering as when we love, never so helplessly unhappy as when we have lost our loved object or its love." Women will find these words particularly true. For women, far more often than men, succumb to that suffering known as depression when important love relationships are through. The logic thus seems to be that women's dependence on intimacy makes them, if not the weaker sex, the more vulnerable one.

Expanding Vocabulary

Match each word in column A with its definition in column B. When in doubt, first find the word in the essay and look for context clues to aid your understanding of the word's meaning. Then, if necessary, use your dictionary to complete the matching exercise. The number in parentheses is the number of the paragraph in which the word appears.

Column A	*Column B*
masochistic (7)	impossible to retract or change
narcissistic (7)	held together, logically connected
mutilated (7)	to have a hampering effect on
irrevocably (7)	idea of the central role of the
reparation (7)	penis—or lack of one—in
crimp (10)	shaping one's psychology
phallocentricity (10)	tending to yield to others
coherent (12)	independence, self-direction
auditory (14)	getting pleasure from being
compliant (19)	dominated or abused
predispositions (22)	submit or yield to something
autonomy (34)	overwhelming
inherent (37)	easily affected
succumb (38)	deprived of a limb or essential part
	existing as an essential characteristic

vulnerable (38)   process of making amends
advance inclinations to something
having excessive love of oneself
related to sense of hearing

Understanding Content

1. What do gender-identity studies suggest about how we become masculine or feminine?
2. How did Freud explain the "defects" in women's characters?
3. How do all mammals begin their development?
4. For what myths about males and females is there still inadequate evidence?
5. What is the "Cinderella Complex"?
6. How can dependency be seen as a strength? What seems to matter more to women than to men?

Drawing Inferences about Thesis and Purpose

1. What is Viorst's subject? What is her purpose in writing?
2. What is her position on differences between males and females and on the source(s) of those differences?

Analyzing Strategies and Style

1. Examine Viorst's opening. How does it both establish her subject and get reader interest?
2. The author uses many brief paragraphs. When does she use them? What does she gain by using them?

Thinking Critically

1. How many of the myths about male and female differences have you believed? Has Viorst convinced you that most are unsupported by evidence? Why or why not?
2. Observe how the author introduces the specialists on whom she draws. Are you prepared to accept them as reliable sources? Can they be reliable and still leave readers with questions and concerns? If so, why?
3. Do you see female "dependence" or desire for close relationships as a weakness or strength? Explain your views.
4. Why do we have so much trouble sorting out similarities and differences among males and females? What are some of the issues that get in the way?

Who Says a Woman Can't Be Einstein?

AMANDA RIPLEY

Amanda Ripley is a reporter for *Time* magazine. The following article, slightly condensed, was the cover story on March 7, 2005, probably in response to the issue raised by Harvard President Larry Summers over possible reasons for so few women pursuing careers in math, science, and engineering.

Questions to Guide Your Reading and Reflection

1. What does the title suggest to you about the article's subject matter? What does the title suggest about the writer's attitude toward the subject?
2. What may be some of the reasons why women do not choose careers in the sciences in the same numbers as men?

Now that scientists are finally starting to map the brain with   1
some accuracy, the challenge is figuring out what to do with that knowledge. The possibilities for applying it to the classroom, workplace and doctor's office are tantalizing. "If something is genetic, it means it must be biological. If we can figure out the biology, then we should be able to tweak the biology," says Richard Haier, a psychology professor who studies intelligence at the University of California at Irvine. . . .

Lesson 1: Function Over Form

Scientists have been looking for sex differences in the brain since   2
they have been looking at the brain. Many bold decrees have been issued. In the 19th century, the corpus callosum, a bundle of nerve fibers that connects the two hemispheres of the brain, was considered key to intellectual development. Accordingly, it was said to have a greater surface area in men. Then, in the 1980s, we were told that no, it is larger in women—and that explains why the emotional right side of women's brains is more in touch with the analytical left side. Aha. That theory has since been discredited, and scientists remain at odds over who has the biggest and what it might mean. Stay tuned for more breaking news.

3   But most studies agree that men's brains are about 10% bigger than women's brains overall. Even when the comparison is adjusted for the fact that men are, on average, 8% taller than women, men's brains are still slightly bigger. But size does not predict intellectual performance, as was once thought. Men and women perform similarly on IQ tests. And most scientists still cannot tell male and female brains apart just by looking at them.

4   Recently, scientists have begun to move away from the obsession with size. Thanks to new brain-imaging technology, researchers can get a good look at the living brain as it functions and grows. Earlier studies relied on autopsies or X-rays— and no one wanted to expose children or women, who might be pregnant, to regular doses of radiation.

5   The deeper you probe, the more interesting the differences. Women appear to have more connections between the two brain hemispheres. In certain regions, their brain is more densely packed with neurons. And women tend to use more parts of their brain to accomplish certain tasks. That might explain why they often recover better from a stroke, since the healthy parts of their mind compensate for the injured regions. Men do their thinking in more focused regions of the brain, whether they are solving a math problem, reading a book or feeling a wave of anger or sadness.

6   Indeed, men and women seem to handle emotions quite differently. While both sexes use a part of the brain called the amygdala, which is located deep within the organ, women seem to have stronger connections between the amygdala and regions of the brain that handle language and other higher-level functions. That may explain why women are, on average, more likely to talk about their emotions and men tend to compartmentalize their worries and carry on. Or, of course, it may not.

7   "Men and women have different brain architectures, and we don't know what they mean," says Haier. By administering IQ tests to a group of college students and then analyzing scans of their brain structure, Haier's team recently discovered that the parts of the brain that are related to intelligence are different in men and women. "That is in some ways a major observation, because one of the assumptions of psychology has been that all human brains pretty much work the same way," he says. Now that we know they don't, we can try to understand why some

brains react differently to, say, Alzheimer's, many medications and even teaching techniques, Haier says.

Even more interesting than the brain's adult anatomy might 8 be the journey it takes to get there. For 13 years, psychiatrist Jay Giedd has been compiling one of the world's largest libraries of brain growth. Every Tuesday evening, from 5 o'clock until midnight, a string of children files into the National Institutes of Health outside Washington to have their brains scanned. Giedd and his team ease the kids through the MRI procedure, and then he gives them a brain tour of their pictures—gently pointing out the spinal cord and the corpus callosum, before offering them a copy to take to show-and-tell.

Most of the kids are all business. Rowena Avery, 6, of Sparks, 9 Nev., arrived last week with a stuffed animal named Sidewalk and stoically disappeared into the machine while her mom, dad and little sister watched. In preparation, she had practiced at home by lying very still in the bathtub. Her picture came out crystal clear. "The youngest ones are the best at lying still. It's kind of surprising," Giedd says. "It must be because they are used to hiding in kitchen cabinets and things like that."

Among the girls in Giedd's study, brain size peaks around 10 age 11/12. For the boys, the peak comes three years later. "For kids, that's a long time," Giedd says. His research shows that most parts of the brain mature faster in girls. But in a 1999 study of 508 boys and girls, Virginia Tech researcher Harriet Hanlon found that some areas mature faster in boys. Specifically, some of the regions involved in mechanical reasoning, visual targeting and spatial reasoning appeared to mature four to eight years earlier in boys. The parts that handle verbal fluency, handwriting and recognizing familiar faces matured several years earlier in girls. . . .

Lesson 2: The Segregation of the Senses

So how do we explain why, in study after study, boys and 11 men are still on average better at rotating 3-D objects in their minds? As for girls and women, how do we explain why they tend to have better verbal skills and social sensitivities?

The most surprising differences may be outside the brain. "If 12 you have a man and a woman looking at the same landscape, they see totally different things," asserts Leonard Sax, a physician and psychologist whose book *Why Gender Matters* came out last month. "Women can see colors and textures that men cannot see. They hear things men cannot hear, and they smell things men cannot smell." Since the eyes, ears and nose are portals to the brain, they directly affect brain development from birth on.

13   In rats, for example, we know that the male retina has more cells designed to detect motion. In females, the retina has more cells built to gather information on color and texture. If the same is true in humans, as Sax suspects, that may explain why, in an experiment in England four years ago, newborn boys were much more likely than girls to stare at a mobile turning above their cribs. It may also help explain why boys prefer to play with moving toys like trucks while girls favor richly textured dolls and tend to draw with a wider range of colors, Sax says.

14   Likewise, women's ears are more sensitive to some noises. Baby girls hear certain ranges of sound better. And the divergence gets even bigger in adults. As for smell, a study published in the journal *Nature Neuroscience* in 2002 showed that women of childbearing age were many times more sensitive than men to several smells upon repeated exposure. (Another study has found that heterosexual women have the most sensitive smell and homosexual men have the least.)

15   Rest assured, Sax says: none of that means women are, overall, better than men at perception. It just means the species is internally diverse, making it more likely to survive. "The female will remember the color and texture of a particular plant and be able to warn people if it's poisonous. A man looking at the same thing will be more alert to what is moving in the periphery," he says. "Which is better? You need both."

Lesson 3: Never Underestimate the Brain

16   Until recently, there have been two groups of people: those who argue sex differences are innate and should be embraced and those who insist that they are learned and should be eliminated by changing the environment. Sax is one of the few in the middle—convinced that boys and girls are innately different and that we must change the environment so differences don't become limitations.

17   At a restaurant near his practice in Montgomery County, Md., Sax spreads out dozens of papers and meticulously

makes his case. He is a fanatic, but a smart, patient one. In the early 1990s, he says, he grew alarmed by the "parade" of parents coming into his office wondering whether their sons had attention-deficit/hyperactivity disorder. Sax evaluated them and found that, indeed, the boys were not paying attention in school. But the more he studied brain differences, the more he became convinced that the problem was with the schools. Sometimes the solution was simple: some of the boys didn't hear as well as the girls and so needed to be moved into the front row. Other times, the solution was more complex.

Eventually, Sax concluded that very young boys and girls would be better off in separate classrooms altogether. "[Previously], as far as I was concerned, single-sex education was an old-fashioned leftover. I thought of boys wearing suits and talking with British accents," he says. But coed schools do more harm than good, he decided, when they teach boys and girls as if their brains mature at the same time. "If you ask a child to do something not developmentally appropriate for him, he will, No. 1, fail. No. 2, he will develop an aversion to the subject," he says. "By age 12, you will have girls who don't like science and boys who don't like reading." And they won't ever go back, he says. "The reason women are underrepresented in computer science and engineering is not because they can't do it. It's because of the way they're taught." 18

So far, studies about girls' and boys' achievements in same-sex grammar schools are inconclusive. But if it turns out that targeting sex differences through education is helpful, there are certainly many ways to carry it out. Says Giedd: "The ability for change is phenomenal. That's what the brain does best." A small but charming 2004 study published in *Nature* found that people who learned how to juggle increased the gray matter in their brains in certain locations. When they stopped juggling, the new gray matter vanished. A similar structural change appears to occur in people who learn a second language. . . . 19

In a recent experiment with humans at Temple University, women showed substantial progress in spatial reasoning after spending a couple of hours a week for 10 weeks playing *Tetris*, of all things. The males improved with weeks of practice too, says Nora Newcombe, a Temple psychologist who specializes 20 in spatial cognition, and so the gender gap remained. But the improvement for both sexes was "massively greater" than the gender difference. "This means that if the males didn't train, the females would outstrip them," she says.

21   Of course, we already manipulate the brain through drugs— many of which, doctors now realize, have dramatically different effects on different brains. Drugs for improving intelligence are in the works, says Haier, in the quest to find medication for Alzheimer's. "We're going to get a lot better at manipulating genetic biology. We may even be better at manipulating genetic biology than manipulating the environment."

22   Until then, one solution to overcoming biological tendencies is to consciously override them, to say to yourself, "O.K., I may have a hard time with this task, but I'm going to will myself to conquer it." Some experiments show that baby girls, when faced with failure, tend to give up and cry relatively quickly, while baby boys get angry and persist, says Witelson at Ontario's Michael G. DeGroote School of Medicine at McMaster University. "What we don't know is whether that pattern persists into adulthood," she says. But in her experience in academia, she says she knows of at least a couple of brilliant women who never realized their potential in science because they stopped trying when they didn't get grants or encountered some other obstacle. "It's much better," she says, "for people to understand what the differences are, act on their advantages and be prepared for their disadvantages."

Lesson 4: Expectations Matter

23   We have a tendency to make too much of test-score differences between the sexes (which are actually very small compared with the differences between, say, poor and affluent students). And regardless of what happens in school, personality and discipline can better predict success when it comes to highly competitive jobs.

24   One thing we know about the brain is that it is vulnerable to the power of suggestion. There is plenty of evidence that when young women are motivated and encouraged, they excel at science. For most of the 1800s, for example, physics, astronomy, chemistry and botany were considered gender-appropriate

subjects for middle-and upper-class American girls. By the 1890s, girls outnumbered boys in public high school science courses across the country, according to *The Science Education of American Girls*, a 2003 book by Kim Tolley. Records from top schools in Boston show that girls outperformed boys in physics in the mid-19th century. Latin and Greek, meanwhile, were considered the province of gentlemen—until the 20th century, when lucrative opportunities began to open up in the sciences.

Today, in Iceland and Sweden, girls consistently outperform 25 boys in math and physics. In Sweden the gap is widest in the remote regions in the north. That may be because women want to move to the big cities farther south, where they would need to compete in high-tech economies, while men are focused on local hunting, fishing and forestry opportunities, says Niels Egelund, a professor of educational psychology at the Danish University of Education. The phenomenon even has a name, the Jokkmokk effect, a reference to an isolated town in Swedish Lapland.

Back in the States, the achievement gap in the sciences is 26 closing, albeit slowly. Female professors have been catching up with male professors in their publishing output. Today half of chemistry and almost 60% of biology bachelor of science degrees go to females. Patience is required.

Expanding Vocabulary

Examine the following words in their contexts in the essay and then write a brief definition or synonym for each one. (Do not use a dictionary; try to guess the word's meaning from its context.)

meticulously (17)	vulnerable (24)
fanatic (17)	lucrative (24)
cognition (20)	albeit (26)

Understanding Content

1. How do the brains of men and women differ in size overall? Is this difference considered significant?
2. What are the key differences in brain functioning? What inferences are drawn from these differences? How confident are researchers about these inferences?
3. What are the differences in brain development?
4. What differences has Sax found among men's and women's senses?

5. What do studies suggest about the effect of teaching?
6. What roles do motivation and social expectations play?

Drawing Inferences about Thesis and Purpose

1. This cover article on gender differences and the brain was motivated by some politically unwise statements made by then president of Harvard Lawrence Summers. How does this article address the question of why more men than women excel in the sciences?
2. What seems to be Ripley's primary purpose in writing, her primary focus?
3. Write a thesis statement for the article.

Analyzing Strategies and Style

1. In paragraph 2, Ripley provides a brief history of brain size studies and their conclusions. After studies revealed that women's hemisphere connections were larger, a new inference was drawn. Why does Ripley write "Aha" after providing this information? What does she imply?
2. How has Ripley organized her material? Look at the four headings in the article. What unites each section? What is significant about the order of information and discussion through the four lessons?

Thinking Critically

1. Did you find new ideas and information here? If so, what new idea or fact seems most important to you? Why?
2. What information is most important for parents to know? For teachers to know? For everyone—society—to know? Why?

Gender Games

DAVID SADKER

A professor of education at American University, David Sadker has written extensively on educational issues, especially on the treatment of girls in the classroom. He is the co-author, with his wife Myra, of *Failing at Fairness: How Our Schools Cheat Girls* (1995) and the co-author of a successful introductory teacher education textbook. "Gender Games" appeared in the *Washington Post* on July 31, 2000.

Questions to Guide Your Reading and Reflection

1. Why does Sadker use the word *games* in his title?
2. Did you ever feel, in any of your classes, that your teacher gave more attention to the boys? Or to the girls? If so, reflect on possible reasons for this.

Remember when your elementary school teacher would 1
announce the teams for the weekly spelling bee? "Boys against the girls!" There was nothing like a gender showdown to liven things up. Apparently, some writers never left this elementary level of intrigue. A spate of recent books and articles takes us back to the "boys versus girls" fray but this time, with much higher stakes.

May's *Atlantic Monthly* cover story, "Girls Rule," is a case in 2
point. The magazine published an excerpt from *The War Against Boys* by Christina Hoff Sommers, a book advancing the notion that boys are the real victims of gender bias while girls are soaring in school.

Sommers and her supporters are correct in saying that girls 3
and women have made significant educational progress in the past two decades. Females today make up more than 40 percent of medical and law school students, and more than half of college students. Girls continue to read sooner and write better than boys. And for as long as anyone can remember, girls have received higher grades than boys.

But there is more to these selected statistics than meets the 4
eye. Although girls continue to receive higher report card grades than boys, their grades do not translate into higher test scores. The same girls who beat boys in the spelling bees score below boys on the tests that matter: the PSATs crucial for scholarships, the SATs and the ACTs needed for college acceptances, the GREs for graduate school and even the admission tests for law, business and medical schools.

Many believe that girls' higher grades may be more a reflec- 5
tion of their manageable classroom behavior than their intellectual accomplishment. Test scores are not influenced by quieter classroom behavior. Girls may in fact be trading their

initiative and independence for peer approval and good grades, a trade-off that can have costly personal and economic consequences.

6   The increase in female college enrollment catches headlines because it heralds the first time that females have outnumbered males on college campuses. But even these enrollment figures are misleading. The female presence increases as the status of the college decreases. Female students are more likely to dominate two-year schools than the Ivy League. And wherever they are, they find themselves segregated and channeled into the least prestigious and least costly majors.

7   In today's world of e-success, more than 60 percent of computer science and business majors are male, about 70 percent of physics majors are males, and more than 80 percent of engineering students are male. But peek into language, psychology, nursing and humanities classrooms, and you will find a sea of female faces.

8   Higher female enrollment figures mask the "glass walls" that separate the sexes and channel females and males into very different careers, with very different paychecks. Today, despite all the progress, the five leading occupations of employed women are secretary, receptionist, bookkeeper, registered nurse and hairdresser/cosmetologist.

9   Add this to the "glass ceiling" (about 3 percent of Fortune 500 top managers are women) and the persistence of a gender wage gap (women with advanced degrees still lag well behind their less-educated male counterparts) and the crippling impact of workplace and college stereotyping becomes evident.

10   Even within schools, where female teachers greatly outnumber male teachers, school management figures remind us that if there is a war on boys, women are not the generals. More than 85 percent of junior and senior high school principals are male, while 88 percent of school superintendents are male.

11   Despite sparkling advances of females on the athletic fields, two-thirds of athletic scholarships still go to males. In some areas, women have actually lost ground. When Title IX was enacted in 1972, women coached more than 90 percent of intercollegiate women's teams. Today women coach only 48 percent of women's teams and only 1 percent of men's teams.

If some adults are persuaded by the rhetoric in such books   12
as *The War Against Boys*, be assured that children know the
score. When more than 1,000 Michigan elementary school students were asked to describe what life would be like if they
were born a member of the opposite sex, more than 40 percent
of the girls saw positive advantages to being a boy: better jobs,
more money and definitely more respect. Ninety-five percent
of the boys saw no advantage to being a female.

The War Against Boys attempts to persuade the public to aban-   13
don support for educational initiatives designed to help girls
and boys avoid crippling stereotypes. I hope the public and Congress will not be taken in by the book's misrepresentations. We
have no time to wage a war on either our boys or our girls.

Expanding Vocabulary

Define each of the following words and then use each one in a separate sentence. The number in parentheses is the number of the paragraph in which the word appears.

spate (1)	prestigious (6)
fray (1)	initiatives (13)

Understanding Content

1. What is the occasion for Sadker's essay? What is the argument
   made by the work he challenges?
2. What facts about girls are accurate?
3. What facts show a gender gap in education, sports, and work?

Drawing Inferences about Thesis and Purpose

1. What is the author's thesis—what does he assert about girls?
2. What is Sadker's view of books such as Sommers's? How do you
   know?

Analyzing Strategies and Style

1. Sadker begins with a reminder to readers of their school days
   with spelling bees. What makes his opening paragraph effective?
2. The author refers to the common phrase "the glass ceiling." What is
   effective about his play on this phrase with the phrase "glass walls"?
3. Find 2 or 3 other cleverly worded sentences. What makes them
   effective?

Thinking Critically

1. What statistic is most startling to you? Why?
2. Do you agree that the author's evidence shows significant differences between girls and boys in education, sports, and work? If you agree, what do you think we should do about this situation? If you disagree, how would you challenge his evidence and argument?

Bring Back Stinks and Bangs!

ROBIN McKIE

Science editor of the London newspaper the *Observer* since 1982, Robin McKie is author or co-author of several science books, including *The Book of Man: The Quest to Discover Our Genetic Heritage* (1994), with Sir Walter Bodmer; *African Exodus: The Origins of Modern Humanity* (1996); and *Face of Britain: How Our Genes Reveal the History of Britain* (2006), the book that accompanied a British television series on this subject. The following essay, published in the *New Statesman* on April 18, 2005, draws on his experiences to contrast with today's version of science education.

Questions to Guide Your Reading and Reflection

1. Given the essay's title and what you know about the author, what do you think the essay will be about?
2. As a child did you enjoy exploring the natural world? Were you encouraged to do so? If you liked learning about nature, did your interest continue in science classes? Why or why not? If you did not explore much on your own, do you now regret that? Why or why not?

1   The blast that wrecked my family's Sunday morning 40 years ago remains my most spectacular, and certainly most memorable, involvement in chemical research. At around 8 A.M., as the first weak rays of Glaswegian sunshine stole across my room and illuminated the walk-in cupboard that acted as my laboratory, there was a detonation of Verdun-like

proportions. A cloud of ammonia-rich chemicals whipped across my room, spraying out pieces of laboratory glassware. My mother shrieked across the hall; my father raced into my room, cursing with unsuspected fluency; and I leapt from my bed as glittering garments tinkled around me.

"Tri-nitrogen iodide," I gabbled. "I was drying it out and   2
sunlight must have ignited it. It's used as a detonating agent, you know." I could tell that my father was unimpressed with this information, because he merely repeated a number of quite specific threats to my physical well-being before he returned, muttering, to his bed.

My chemical "shenanigans" were well known, and were   3
usually indulged, both at home and school. At the end of term, my friends and I would set off magnesium-weedkiller fire-crackers; dump potassium permanganate into the school's hot-water tank so that purple solutions would emerge, rather satisfyingly, from main-block toilet taps; or drop pieces of sodium metal—bought from a local chemicals warehouse—into drains, thus generating clouds of hydrogen that would ignite and send geysers of steam and water across the playground. Our teachers were amused, and occasionally impressed.

We were mere energetic amateur chemists, of course—   4
though no one, ourselves included, was ever harmed by our antics. We also learned a great deal, because chemistry not only lets youthful practitioners make stinks and bangs, it lets them test things and record conclusions with instant—usually gratifying—results. It satisfies youthful inquisitiveness in a spectacular manner.

Or at least it used to, for thanks to a host of health and safety   5
measures that have been introduced over the past decade, the nation's youth is now denied such stimulation. It has become taboo to allow young people access to anything more harmful than a piece of litmus paper: the chemist who sold us sodium would be jailed and the teacher who turned a blind eye to our petty pilfering of his stock would be sacked. And jolly good, too, you might think. Can't have our kids blowing themselves up. It's common sense, isn't it?

Well no, it isn't, a point that has been made recently by a   6
growing number of researchers—such as Sir Alec Jeffreys, the Leicester geneticist who discovered DNA fingerprinting. "I am

a scientist today only because I was allowed to go through a period of significant danger to myself," he says. "I had to grow a beard in later life because I burned my face with acid while mucking about with chemicals as a lad. But it was a risk I was willing to take. Doing these things let me satisfy my interest in the world around me. Children simply cannot do that now."

7   Nor is the problem confined to chemistry. Take that great college perennial: the geology field trip. Students used to hike into the wilderness, armed only with a hammer (for breaking up samples) and a tent. Then it was decreed they must wear hard hats. "So we set off with some building-site helmets in our minibus," says the geologist Ted Nield, a lecturer at University College Swansea at the time the decree was imposed. "Then the bus went round a bend, and the helmets fell off their rack and gashed three students' heads. We hadn't had an injury until then."

8   Or consider an article I wrote recently for the *Observer* about preparations to celebrate Einstein Year by sending students to this summer's Glastonbury Festival, where they plan, among other things, to set off rockets powered by Alka-Seltzer. (Mix them with water and use the power of the fizz. Simple.) I was deluged with e-mails from local officials demanding to know more about possible missile hazards to festival-goers. I was stunned. I had been writing about the Glastonbury Festival, home of drugs and rockers, yet these officials were worrying about the dangers of an exploding Alka-Seltzer.

9   In fact, the list of inane illustrations is almost endless, particularly those from school science classrooms, where it seems the problem is particularly insidious. They include: refusing to demonstrate small steam engines in case they should blow up; avoiding doing fractional distillation of crude oil (to show its different components) because of the dangers of causing cancer; and a ban on burning peanuts (to show their high calorific content) because someone might suffer a nut-allergy reaction. These are all real examples, though health officials say they do not seek such bans; it's just nervous teachers who are over-zealously interpreting the safety rule book. Such experiments are not officially forbidden, they insist.

10   And true enough, the *Safeguards in the School Laboratory* manual does not actually forbid laboratory antics, but equally it

does nothing to encourage them. Indeed, it goes to great pains to stress the dangers of everything from working with detergent enzymes to the taking of samples of breath, which could cause "dizziness or fainting from forced breathing". And in the case of the peanut burning experiments, teachers are warned that the consequences of a student suffering a nut-allergy reaction "could be severe".

Small wonder that teachers don't bother. Who needs a lawsuit on top of crap pay and lousy working conditions? And in any case, does it matter? Young people today may not have the fun we had when studying science, but our generation didn't have the Discovery Channel and the internet. So it all balances out, you could argue.   11

But it doesn't. Take the issue of technical training. The government places great stress on Britain developing powerful knowledge-based industries, for which it will need a cadre of well-trained scientists. But where are they supposed to come from? Not our schools or university, it would appear. "We get graduates coming into our laboratories who do not know how to weigh chemicals, measure liquids or take samples," says Tim Hunt, the Cancer Research UK scientist and joint winner of the 2001 Nobel Prize for Medicine. "They should have been taught these techniques in school but haven't because they are not allowed to go near chemicals, because of all the safety paranoia. So we have to teach them." Thus many hours have to be taken from valuable postgraduate teaching to inculcate learning that should have passed on a decade earlier. This is scarcely the way to raise a generation of experts in white-hot UK technology.   12

The problem goes even deeper, however. In the past, when pupils asked "what happens if . . . ?" during a science lesson, they might have been allowed to find out for themselves by being guided through an experiment. Today, their teacher will, at best, scribble a brief explanation on a blackboard before returning to the rigours of the class's strictly delineated coursework. The chance of them indulging their natural curiosity is blocked and the opportunity to think freely and independently stymied. Thus intellectual curiosity is stifled by fear of health and safety legislation and court action, a point stressed by Jeffreys. "I am quite prepared to stick out my neck and let kids   13 experiment with stinks and bangs. If a couple get maimed or even killed, that will be the price we have to pay for stimulating an interest in science and in getting young people to think for themselves."

14   That will doubtless infuriate many. However, I suspect that most researchers support Jeffreys and share his concerns—particularly in the light of a recent national survey which revealed that only four out of ten British people consider themselves informed, in any way, about science. In other words, almost two-thirds of the population now say they know nothing about science, despite many acknowledging its importance to the country. Worse still the gulf between the "knows" and the "don't knows" is growing all the time—because people are being disenfranchised from involvement in scientific activities. It's all too mysterious and dangerous for the likes of you, they are told. From this perspective, the prospects of creating a new generation of freethinking, technically minded researchers and academics do not look encouraging.

15   The trouble, as David Brooks has pointed out in the *New York Times*, is that we are living in the age of the lily-livered, where everything is a pallid parody of itself, from salt-free pretzels to the schooling of children amid foam-corner protectors and flame-retardant paper. Or in the case of the science lab, to the distant and anaesthetized demonstration.

16   Most critics stress the physical problems that we face as we raise a generation unexposed to risk. I would argue, along with Jeffreys, Hunt and the rest, that the real danger is the one posed to our intellectual well-being. Thinking and testing the world is a dangerous business and we should not shirk from it. My father would doubtless have been one of those who would disagree with me. To fail to think and test, however, will be much more damaging.

Expanding Vocabulary

Match each word in column A with its definition in column B. When in doubt, first find the word in the essay and look for context clues to aid your understanding of the word's meaning. Then, if necessary, use your dictionary to complete the matching exercise. The number in parentheses is the number of the paragraph in which the word appears.

Column A	Column B
detonation (1)	ban based on custom or belief
Verdun-like (1)	fired
geysers (3)	spreading in a subtle way
taboo (5)	thwarted, crushed
pilfering (5)	similar to a terrible World War I battle
sacked (5)	delusions
perennial (7)	lacking sense, silly
deluged (8)	satirical imitation
inane (9)	stealing
insidious (9)	instill in, teach
cadre (12)	pale, dull
paranoia (12)	regularly occurring
inculcate (12)	lacking sensation, dulled
delineated (13)	explosion
stymied (13)	inundated, overwhelmed with
pallid (15)	spelled out
parody (15)	natural hot springs that spray water
anaesthetized (15)	in the air
	nucleus, core group

Understanding Content

1. What was McKie allowed to do when he was growing up?
2. What are the restrictions on scientific learning today?
3. What, in McKie's view, are the consequences of the change?

Drawing Inferences about Thesis and Purpose

1. What, specifically, is McKie's subject? State it as a contrast.
2. What, then, is his thesis? What does he want readers to understand through his contrast?

Analyzing Strategies and Style

1. In his opening four paragraphs, the author reports on his youthful chemistry experiences. What do these details accomplish? How do they create an effective opening?
2. Look at the end of paragraph 5 and the beginning of paragraph 6. What does the author do here? What gives power to his opening words in paragraph 6?
3. Find a similar shift from one paragraph to the next as examined in the question above. What makes this writing strategy effective?

Thinking Critically

1. McKie refers to *New York Times* columnist David Brooks (see Ch. 7), who describes our times as "lily-livered." McKie clearly agrees with Brooks; has he convinced you? Have we become too much of a "nanny state"? Explain and support your views.
2. The author fears that today's "safe" teaching of science will lead to fewer scientists. Are we educating fewer scientists than in the past? See what you can find online to respond to this question.
3. McKie also worries about an increasing gap between those who "know science" and those who do not. Is this a realistic concern in the United States as well as in Britain? Are you scientifically knowledgeable? What about your classmates? Take a class survey and then discuss this issue.

Surveying the Damage on Campus USA

COLBERT I. KING

Deputy Editor of the Editorial page of the *Washington Post* and a syndicated columnist, Colbert King is also a regular on the political talk show *Inside Washington*. The following column appeared in the *Post* on November 30, 2002.

Questions to Guide Your Reading and Reflection

1. Contemporary American college students are compared to two other groups: what are they?
2. If you were a college president, how would you handle your students' destruction of property, both on campus and in the neighborhood?

1   It's sad to see what prompts student unrest on American university campuses these days. On recent weekends, we've seen glasses and bottles flying in Pullman, Wash., and students arrested in Berkeley, Calif.—and in Raleigh, N.C., too. A woman and a cop were hurt in Clemson, S.C., and cars were set afire, furniture was burned and dozens were arrested in Columbus, Ohio. Then there are the student riots last year in College Park.

And what is causing America's future leaders to abandon   2
civility, embrace violence and convert their campuses into war
zones? What injustice has moved them so?

Suppression of student rights? Incursions on speech, assem-   3
bly, academic freedom? Nah. On American campuses, students
are fistfighting and smashing and burning over what else?
Sports. Yep. They're socking it to the town over football and
basketball. (In Gainesville, Fla., the University of Florida stations a German shepherd at each corner of the football field.)
In stadiums across America, the frenzy to win is driving
responsibility out the window. The fear of losing is trumping
respect. And indulgence in personal excess is the ruling ethic.

Contrast that kind of campus behavior with the university   4
scene in Iran. Thousands of Iranian students have been bravely
taking on their country's oppressive Islamic regime, openly
criticizing the supreme leader Ayatollah Ali Khamenei and
other hard-line Muslim clerics for standing in the way of social
and political reforms. Unlike the drunken hooliganism on the
grounds of American academe, students in Iran have been seriously and soberly engaged in a power struggle against Islamic
hard-liners. And it's no weekend affair.

It's not cost-free either. Unlike their American counterparts,   5
Iranian students aren't waging their battle with credit cards in
their pockets and with protective and indulging school admin-
istrations covering their backsides. In Iran, student demonstrators and their courageous professors are up against the
country's police, Islamic courts and militiamen—armed foes
who will break their heads at the order of the conservative
Islamic regime.

America's students riot over the defeat of a legendary rival.   6
Iranian students are in the streets over the sentencing to death
of a history lecturer, Hashem Aghajari, who had the nerve to
criticize the regime in a speech. The American collegiate sports
fans erupt in rowdyism in pursuit of fun. The Iranian students
put it on the line in the name of democracy.

They are a different breed. The supreme religious leader   7
denounced their protests as the work of the devil. He ordered
the movement suppressed and student leaders arrested.
They responded to the crackdown by announcing a symbolic
referendum on the Islamic regime to be held next week

among students attending more than a dozen universities in Tehran. Now they are in even deeper trouble with the conservative hard-liners, who are mobilizing thousands of their supporters and paramilitary units to stare down and frighten off the pro-reformers.

8   Ah, but who can think of stuff like that in Iran when here at home there are beers to be drunk, goal posts to be torn down, fires to be started, and sofas and chairs to be burned. Today is a far cry from that time in America when students built shantytowns on their campuses and marched on their administration buildings to demand that their schools cut ties with companies that invested in apartheid South Africa. Then students were all about raising consciousness about South Africa's oppression. Today it's all about losing consciousness in a fog of alcohol on Saturday night.

9   And when the football team isn't so hot, there are other fun ways to pass the time at school. How about a party? A dress-up party? A party where fraternity guys and sorority gals can paint their faces black like they used to do in minstrel shows back in the good ol' days. Where you can dress in tennis outfits and come in blackface as Venus and Serena Williams, the two African American tennis champions. Or, if you have a patriotic bent, you can dress as Uncle Sam, of course with black makeup. That's the way they did it last month at a fraternity-sponsored Halloween party at the University of Virginia.

10   What do they know? What do they care about college students who sat at lunch counters, conducted read-ins in public libraries, kneel-ins in churches, stand-ins at movie theaters, wade-ins in public swimming pools, because, as they said in the '60s, "Education without freedom is useless"? Are they even fazed by a movement started by African American students that was joined by hundreds of white students from across the country, which saw 1,700 student demonstrators standing trial in 1960 alone?

11   That was then. Nowadays, for some in America's next generation of leaders, when it comes to sheer emotional fulfillment, nothing quite matches the act of tearing up the campus or coloring the skin and lips to exaggerate black features.

12   Welcome to American college daze, 2002.

Expanding Vocabulary

Write a definition for each of the following words. Then use each word in a separate sentence of your own. The number in parentheses is the number of the paragraph in which the word appears.

incursions (3)   hooliganism (4)
frenzy (3)   rowdyism (6)
indulgence (3)   apartheid (8)

Understanding Content

1. What are contemporary college students in the United States making headlines for doing? How does King evaluate their actions?
2. What are Iranian students doing? How does King evaluate their cause?
3. What did American students do in the 1960s? How are their actions evaluated by King?

Drawing Inferences about Thesis and Purpose

1. What is King's purpose? What does he want to accomplish through his contrasts?
2. Write a thesis statement for the essay that reveals the contrast structure.

Analyzing Strategies and Style

1. What does King want to underscore when he describes the American students as "America's future leaders"?
2. How are we to understand paragraph 11? What writing strategy for emphasis does King use in this paragraph?
3. What play on words does King employ in his final sentence? What is its effect?

Thinking Critically

1. Which of the two kinds of actions of American students do you think is the less excusable: rioting after games or dressing to look like black personalities at parties? Why? Explain your reasoning.
2. King, in rhetorical questions in paragraph 10, suggests that today's American students neither know nor care about the demonstrations for change of students from the past. Is he right? Do you know about student actions of the 1960s? Do you think those actions were significant? What about your fellow students?

Marks

LINDA PASTAN

A graduate of Radcliffe College and Brandeis University, Linda Pastan (b. 1932) is the author of eight books of poetry. Many of her poems, such as the one that follows from *The Five Stages of Grief Poems* (1978), examine the complexity and problems of family life.

Questions to Guide Your Reading and Reflection

1. Who is speaking—or more accurately thinking—the words of the poem? What relationships does the speaker refer to in the poem?
2. How would you grade your relationships with your parents?

My husband gives me an A
for last night's supper,
an incomplete for my ironing,
a B plus in bed.
5 My son says I am average,
an average mother, but if
I put my mind to it
I could improve.
My daughter believes
10 in Pass/Fail and tells me
I pass. Wait 'til they learn
I'm dropping out.

Understanding Content and Strategies

1. What marks does the speaker receive? For what activities? Who does the speaker's son sound like when he says that she "could improve" if she put her "mind to it"?
2. The poem is organized and developed, then, by using what extended metaphor? The speaker is being compared to what?
3. What is the speaker's attitude toward her situation? What lines reveal her attitude?

Drawing Inferences about Theme

1. Whose perspective on family responsibilities and chores are we given in the poem?
2. What observations about family life is Pastan making?

Thinking Critically

1. Do you think the views of family life expressed here are fairly widespread? What evidence do you have for your opinions?
2. Have you ever felt as though you were being graded by family members or rated on a scale from 1 to 10? If so, how did that make you feel?
3. Try your hand at a short, free-verse poem similar to Pastan's. In your poem create a speaker who is a teenager being "graded" by other family members.

STUDENT ESSAY—CONTRAST

THE FADED STAIN
Denisse M. Bonilla

"The plantain stain on a 'jíbaros' back can never be erased," says an old Puerto Rican proverb. "Jíbaros," or Puerto Rican peasants, is what my compatriots fondly call each other. The proverb is most commonly used to illustrate their feeling that, regardless of where a Puerto Rican lives, a Puerto Rican always remains a Puerto Rican. But reflecting on my own experiences, I have read a different meaning into the old proverb. My compatriots could be saying that once a Puerto Rican has lived on the

Student uses a proverb as an attention-getting opening.

island, she or he can never forget it. However, in saying this, one must ponder what happens to the stain itself. Does it look like a plantain for the rest of the jíbaros' life, or does it change over time? Perhaps it starts resembling a banana, looking similar but not exactly the same.

Coming back to Puerto Rico as an adult, I found a place quite different from the one I thought I had left behind. The memories I had were those of a child who had never lived outside the island. Because I lived in Puerto Rico as an insular child, I had the memories of such a child. Youth had shaped my perception when I lived there; then time further confused my memory, neutralizing the colors of the countryside, creating indistinguishable Puerto Rican cities, sharpening the soft accent of the people. When I came back as an adult, what I saw was not what I expected to see.

Thesis stated: What I saw on a return visit to Puerto Rico was different from my youthful memories. The thesis clearly emphasizes contrast.

I remembered the trip from San Juan to Ponce, a trip crossing the island from north to south, as an incredibly long and painful ordeal. Impatient to get to my grandmother's house in Ponce, I would look out the car window, sometimes noticing the small towns or the way the sea peeked

First difference: the trip to Ponce was not as long or unpleasant as it seemed in her memories.

out from in-between the mountains. The mountains that I saw during the beginning of the trip were green, seeming to remain in the landscape for hours. I would anxiously await the golden mountains to the south, which to me were an indication of the end of our trip.

When I returned as an adult, I remembered and expected the same grueling and unexciting trip, but was happily disappointed. The trip south was not as long as I remembered; it was over in two hours. Perhaps it did not seem as long as it did in my youth because I had become accustomed to driving longer distances in the large North American continent. But I accredited my newfound tolerance to the enchanting beauty of the Caribbean countryside! The vegetation in the north was a lush shade of green, growing profusely and becoming a tangle of startling color. The houses on the outskirts of the small towns we passed seemed to blossom out of the foliage, their old-fashioned charm reminiscent of a bygone time when the Puerto Rican economy was more dependent on agriculture. In what seemed like a short distance, the mountains changed to golden hues and a softer green. The Caribbean Sea appeared

Student analyzes causes for the differences between youthful memories and adult realities.

to be a watercolor painting framed by the dry southern mountains. The beauty of the trip bewildered me, causing me to recollect in disbelief the impatience I had felt as a young girl. Had I been color-blind when I was young?

The Puerto Rican cities I remembered from my youth were <u>also different</u> when viewed through my adult eyes. I remembered Old San Juan as a beautiful old city, <u>comparing</u> it in my memory to places such as Old Town Alexandria. I <u>also</u> saw generic streets in my recollections, remembering how as a young girl I used to imagine that the bigger roads looked exactly like the ones in the United States. <u>But in contrast to my recollections</u>, neither Old San Juan nor the streets of the other cities were similar to those in the U.S. Taking a stroll down the narrow, cobblestoned streets of Old San Juan, I often discovered hidden parks and nicely shaded plazas in which old gentlemen sat to chat, play dominoes, or feed doves. Wooden fruit stands brimming with delectable tropical fruits stood on many corners. The pastel-colored ambiance of Old San Juan, bespeaking Spanish ancestry and Caribbean sensibility, <u>could not be compared</u> to the somber

Second difference: cities and streets were different than remembered.

Observe transition words and phrases.

ambiance of the old American cities in the north. As for my recollections of Puerto Rican streets that looked exactly like the ones in the United States, to my eyes accustomed to the large, smooth highways of North America, the streets of Puerto Rico looked humble and in need of repair.

The people of Puerto Rico proved to be equally changed to my adult eyes and ears. In the memories of a young insular child, Puerto Rican manners were just like American manners and Puerto Rican Spanish was bland, without any distinguishable accent. In contrast, I found my people to be more physically demonstrative than Americans. Their faces and bodies would remain mobile through an entire conversation, allowing someone standing a few feet away to guess what they were talking about. They spoke Spanish with a funny melodic sound, characterized by relaxed pronunciation. The Puerto Rican people were more flamboyant than I had noticed as a child.

Third difference: the people—and their way of speaking Spanish—are different than remembered.

Although the plantain stain on my back faded after I left my country, the experience of rediscovering its many hues left me with an even bigger impression. To notice the essence of a country, one

Conclusion refers again to the proverb and extends the thesis to suggest that one's country is best understood when one spends time away from it.

must spend time outside it. My recollections were bland when compared to what I
later saw. What I saw when I came back
to Puerto Rico left a moist, green, ripe
plantain stain on my back, a stain that
will never fade.

MAKING CONNECTIONS

1. Viorst and Ripley examine gender differences. Ripley provides updates of studies and Viorst gives some explanations of behavioral differences. Study both articles and see
   if you find any connections between the two discussions.
   Make a list of all connections you find.
2. Sakamoto discusses differences in American and Japanese
   conversational styles. What are some of the ways that cultural and class differences may affect students in the classroom? What are some ways that instructors and students
   can ease some of the problems created by cultural and class
   differences?
3. Ripley raises the issues of motivation and expectations in
   education. How important are effort and desire to succeed?
   How important is intellectual curiosity? How much difference can facilities and dedicated teachers make if students
   are unmotivated to learn? If parents and society do not
   place a high value on education?
4. Ripley writes in response to remarks by then Harvard
   president Summers; King writes about American students in the 1960s and Iranian students in 2002. Select
   one of these references to the past and get the facts on
    the event or time. Turn to U.S. history texts for the 1960s,
   to your library's electronic databases for artir es on any
   one of the events, or search the Internet for ir formation.
   Prepare a one- or two-page fact sheet for your classmates. Cite your source(s) according to MLA guidelines
   for documentation.
5. We know that Asian (and European) students regularly
   outscore American students in math and science. We also

know that, as a group, students from more affluent school districts outscore students from less affluent districts. What are four strategies for improving American education that you would seek to implement if you were appointed "Education Czar"? What might be some political problems you would have trying to implement your four-point plan?

TOPICS FOR WRITING

1. In an essay, contrast two stories, two movies, or two TV shows you know well. Select two works that have something in common but differ in important and/or interesting ways so that you have a clear purpose in writing.
2. If you have attended two schools that differed significantly or if you have lived in two quite different places, draw on one of these experiences for a contrast essay. Organize your essay by specific points of difference that together support a thesis statement that announces your contrast purpose. (Example: California and Virginia are not just miles apart; they are worlds apart.)
3. Do you know a neighborhood, city, or area of the country that has changed significantly for better or worse? If so, develop an essay that contrasts specific differences between the place you once knew and the place as it is now. Your purpose is to demonstrate that the changes have made the place either better or worse. (Example: The _____ neighborhood of _____ is no longer the attractive, family-oriented community in which I grew up.)
4. You have had many teachers during your years of schooling. Think of ones you liked and ones you didn't like. Think about why you enjoyed some but not others. Then select two to contrast for the purpose of revealing traits that make a good teacher. Write about specific traits (e.g., knowledge of field, energy, clarity, fairness, humor), not just generalizations (e.g., she was nice).
5. How do you view today's college students—or some portion of them? What traits, characteristics, attitudes toward learning, and reasons for being in school do you see? Can

you think of an animal, fantasy creature, individual, or group from history who in your view has the traits that are more appropriate for college students? If so, then you can develop an analogy. Remember to have specific differences between students and the animal, creature, or historical figure you are using.

6. As a variation of topic 5, develop an analogy that compares rather than contrasts today's students with some animal, fantasy creature, or historical figure. Use specific points of similarity and establish a point to the comparison, a thesis about students that is supported through the fanciful comparison.

7. Most of us have had at least one experience that did not turn out as we thought it would. Sometimes, nervous about a new situation, we expect the worst only to discover that we are happy or successful participating in the actual experience. Probably more often we look forward to an upcoming event only to be disappointed. Or, we have childhood memories that are inconsistent with our re-experiencing a place or person from the past. Reflect about any experience you have had that fits the pattern of contrast between perception (expectation) and reality. (Possible experiences include a first date, a special event such as Thanksgiving or a wedding, a first experience with a new sport, a recent reunion with a childhood friend, or a return to your childhood home.)

The point of your contrast is to offer some insight into why we so often have expectations that do not match reality. Why do we remember our grandparents' old house as larger and more exciting than it appears to us today? The student essay in this chapter is an example of one student's response to this topic.

A CHECKLIST FOR COMPARISON AND CONTRAST ESSAYS

Inventing

☐ Have I selected a topic and comparison or contrast approach consistent with the instructor's guidelines for this assignment?

☐ Have I chosen among the possible topics one that fits my knowledge and experience?

☐ Have I reflected on the topic to create a tentative thesis that establishes my main idea in a clear comparison or contrast structure?

☐ Have I found, from my reflection, specific points of similarity or difference?

☐ Have I given thought to a specific order in which to present the points of similarity or difference?

Drafting

☐ Have I succeeded in completing a first draft at one sitting so that I can "see" the whole?

☐ Do I have enough—enough to meet assignment demands and enough to develop and support my thesis? If not, do I need new paragraphs or more details or reflection within paragraphs?

☐ Does the order work? If not, what needs to be moved—and where?

☐ Am I satisfied with the way I have expressed the insights to be gained? Have I been too heavy-handed with a message?

☐ Do I have adequate, effective details to illustrate each point of similarity or difference?

Revising

☐ Have I made any needed additions, deletions, or changes in order based on answering the questions about my draft?

☐ Have I revised my draft to produce coherent paragraphs, using transition and connecting words that reveal my comparison or contrast structure?

Polishing

☐ Have I eliminated wordiness and clichés?

☐ Have I avoided or removed any discriminatory language?

☐ Have I used my word processor's spell check and proofread a printed copy with great care?

☐ Do I have an appropriate and interesting title?

5

Explaining and Illustrating
Examining Media Images

"How do you know that?" "Where is your evidence?" "Can you be specific?" These questions are raised by the avid dinner companion who wants you to illustrate and support your ideas. As a writer, you need to keep in mind that the engaged reader is going to ask the same kinds of questions. For you to be an effective writer, you must answer these questions. You must provide examples.

Illustrating ideas and opinions with examples seems so obvious a way to develop and support views that you may wonder why the strategy warrants its own chapter. Even though providing examples may be the most frequently used writing technique, as with many "obvious truths," we can all benefit from being reminded of its importance.

When to Use Examples

The smart writer searches for examples as part of the process of generating ideas. Indeed, when brainstorming or in other ways inventing ideas for an essay, you may find that specifics come to mind more easily than general points. Whether you are a generalizer who needs to find illustrations for ideas or a generator of specifics who needs to reflect on what the examples illustrate, the end result will be a blend of general points and concrete examples. When should you select the use of examples as your primary strategy of development? When you are presenting information or discussing ideas that can best be understood and absorbed by readers with the aid of specifics. And that's just about any time you write.

How to Use Examples

To use examples effectively, think about what kinds of examples are needed to develop your thesis, about how many you need, and about how to introduce and discuss them effectively. First, the *kinds* of examples. You will need to find illustrations that clearly and logically support your generalizations. When Dimitri Christakis disagrees that TV makes children dumb, we expect him to give examples of educational TV shows for children and to explain how they improve children's abilities. If he mentioned only one show, or failed to provide evidence from studies of children watching educational shows, we might doubt his claim that the right TV shows can actually make kids smarter.

We also expect *enough* examples. If Vincent Bzdek mentioned only one superhero in the comics and movies, we would probably doubt his assertion that superheroes are once again popular in the movies. Occasionally, a writer will select one *extended* example rather than a number of separate examples. Jack McGarvey uses one extended example, his and his students' experience of being on TV, to show the celebrity-making power of television. To develop his example, McGarvey uses techniques of narration and description, reminding us that few pieces of writing are developed using only one strategy. Typically, though, the writer who develops a thesis primarily through illustration presents a goodly number of appropriate examples. How many make a "goodly" number will vary with each essay, but be assured that few writers include too many examples.

How many examples an essay needs depends in part on how they are introduced and discussed, and on how many facets of a topic need to be covered. Christakis does not just list several quality shows for children. He also provides results of extensive studies to support his assertion that quality TV can make youngsters smarter. Remember that if all the examples were so obvious that just a brief list would work, we would already have reached the writer's conclusions and would not need to read the article. As common to our lives as advertising, TV, movies, and song lyrics are, we still have much to learn from this chapter's writers because they are the ones who have looked closely at and listened intently to the swirl of words and images bombarding us through the media. Sometimes examples are startling enough to speak for themselves. Usually the writer's task is not only to present good illustrations but to explain how they support the essay's main ideas.

When presenting and explaining illustrations, give some thought to ordering them and to moving smoothly from one to another to create coherence. Look first for some logical basis for organizing your examples. If there is no clear reason to put one example before another, then you are probably wise to put your most important example last. Examples that add to your point can be connected by such transitions as

for instance	in addition
also	next
another example	moreover
further	finally

Occasionally, brief examples can be listed as a series in one sentence. Examples that offer contrast need contrast connectors:

by contrast	on the other hand
however	instead

Remember that a list does not make an essay. Explain *how* your examples support your thesis.

WRITING FOCUS
VARY YOUR SENTENCES

Effective writing stays focused on a controlling idea (thesis), is concrete and vivid, and shows a command of grammar, mechanics, and correct word choice. Yet readers recognize that although two essays may follow these guidelines, one essay will "read" better than another. What accounts for the difference? One answer is content; some writers are more insightful than others. Another answer is style, the selection and arrangement of words into sentences. Do not settle for the first way that you write down an idea or detail; revise and polish sentences for both variety and emphasis. Think about ways to restructure a series of short sentences into fewer sentences—even one sentence—creating variety and also greater power.

In a comparison of the life of the squirrel with her students, Liane Ellison Norman could have opened her essay this way:

> The squirrel is curious. He darts around. He looks partially at me and stays alert for enemies. So, I see only one bright eye.

Notice that each sentence begins with subject and verb, and all have about the same weight or feel. But, here is what Norman actually wrote:

> The squirrel is curious. He darts and edges, profile first, one bright black eye on me, the other alert for his enemies on the other side.

The first sentence is arresting in its brevity. Then the next few ideas have been gathered into one longer, more dramatic sentence.

Consider the following details: *It was a battered face. It was a noble face. It commanded immediate respect.* There are several ways to combine these ideas into one sentence, one more interesting and effective than the three original brief sentences. Here are two possibilities:

> It was a battered but noble face, commanding immediate respect.
> A battered but noble face, it commanded immediate respect.

Which of these two sentences is, in your view, the most effective? Why?

Here are some guidelines for varying your sentences for greater punch:

1. Combine short sentences on the same subject into one longer sentence, as shown above.
2. Use more than one way to combine ideas. Instead of joining two short sentences with "and," use a dependent clause *(Because it was a noble, though battered, face)*, or verbal phrases *(commanding immediate respect)*, or modifying words *(A battered but noble face)*.

3. Do not always begin a sentence with its subject. Instead use an introductory clause or phrase *(Squinting into the afternoon sunlight, the driver wheeled his truck into the lot.)*

4. Vary sentence length. Mix short sentences for emphasis with longer sentences as Norman illustrates above.

5. When combining and rearranging ideas, be sure to keep the most important idea in the main clause, placing less important ideas in modifying clauses, phrases, and words—as this sentence illustrates.

Getting Started:
Thinking about Advertising

Here are eight questions to help you think about advertising, one of the topics of this chapter represented by the four ads that follow. Reflect on these examples of current advertising by answering the questions for each ad.

Questions

1. What is each ad's purpose? To sell a product? An idea? An image of the company? Some combination?
2. What audience is the ad designed to reach?
3. What kind of relationship does it establish with its audience?
4. What social values does it express?
5. To what degree are those values held by the target audience? To what degree are they the values of a different social class or group?
6. Does the ad use metaphors? Puns? Rhyme? Does the company establish and repeat a logo or slogan for the product? How well known are the logo, the slogan, or both?
7. Does the ad use symbols? To what extent do the symbols help express the ad's social values? How is their association with the product appropriate?
8. Is the ad's appeal primarily direct and explicit or indirect and associative?

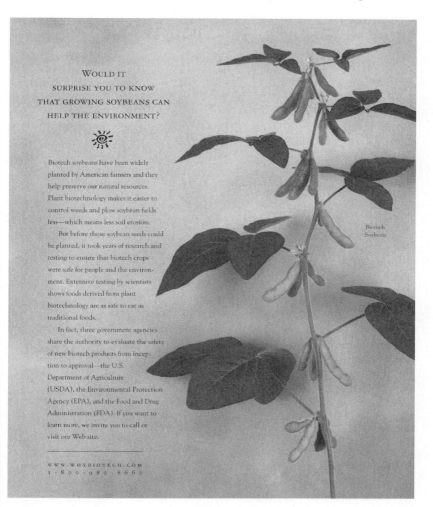

WOULD IT
SURPRISE YOU TO KNOW
THAT GROWING SOYBEANS CAN
HELP THE ENVIRONMENT?

Biotech soybeans have been widely
planted by American farmers and they
help preserve our natural resources.
Plant biotechnology makes it easier to
control weeds and plow soybean fields
less—which means less soil erosion.

But before those soybean seeds could
be planted, it took years of research and
testing to ensure that biotech crops
were safe for people and the environment. Extensive testing by scientists
shows foods derived from plant
biotechnology are as safe to eat as
traditional foods.

In fact, three government agencies
share the authority to evaluate the safety
of new biotech products from incep-
tion to approval—the U.S.
Department of Agriculture
(USDA), the Environmental Protection
Agency (EPA), and the Food and Drug
Administration (FDA). If you want to
learn more, we invite you to call or
visit our Web site.

WWW.WHYBIOTECH.COM
1-800-980-8660

Biotech
Soybean

COUNCIL FOR
BIOTECHNOLOGY
INFORMATION

good ideas are growing

To Be or Not to Be as Defined by TV

JACK McGARVEY

Jack McGarvey completed his master's degree at the University of Connecticut and taught in the Westport, Connecticut, school system for many years. He has also published many articles, short stories, and poems in the *New York Times, McCall's, Parents*, and other newspapers and magazines. The following article, a report on his experience with the power of television, appeared in 1982 in the journal *Today's Education*.

Questions to Guide Your Reading and Reflection

1. What is the source of part of the author's title? What does he gain by his reference to that source?
2. Do you view people who appear on TV talk shows as celebrities? Why or why not?

A couple of years ago, a television crew came to film my ninth grade English class at Bedford Junior High School in Westport, Connecticut. I'm still trying to understand what happened. 1

I was doing some work with my students, teaching them to analyze the language used in television commercials. After dissecting the advertising claims, most of the class became upset over what they felt were misleading—and in a few cases, untruthful—uses of language. We decided to write to the companies that presented their products inaccurately or offensively. Most of them responded with chirpy letters and cents-off coupons. Some did not respond at all. 2

I then decided to contact *Buyline*, a consumer advocate program aired on New York City's WNBC-TV at the time. The show and its host, Betty Furness, were well-known for their investigation of consumer complaints. I sent off a packet of the unanswered letters with a brief explanation of the class's work. 3

About a week later, the show's producer telephoned me. She said that she'd seen the letters and was interested in the class's 4 project. Could she and her director come to Westport to have a look?

5 I said sure and told her about a role-playing activity I was planning to do with my students. I said I was going to organize my class of 24 students into four committees—each one consisting of two representatives from the Federal Trade Commission (FTC), the agency that monitors truth in advertising; two advertising executives anxious to have their material used; and two TV executives caught somewhere in the middle—wanting to please the advertisers while not offending the FTC. Then, I would ask each committee to assume that there had been a complaint about the language used in a TV commercial, and that the committees had to resolve the complaint. "That sounds great! I'll bring a crew," she said.

6 I obtained clearance from my school district's office, and the next morning, as I was walking into the school, I met one of my students and casually let out the word: "WNBC's coming to film our class this afternoon."

7 I was totally unprepared for what happened. Word spread around school within five minutes. Students who barely knew me rushed up to squeal, "Is it true? Is it really, really true? A TV crew is coming to Bedford to film?" A girl who was not in my class pinned me into a corner near the magazine rack in the library to ask me whether she could sit in my class for the day. Another girl went to her counselor and requested an immediate change in English classes, claiming a long-standing personality conflict with her current teacher.

8 Later, things calmed down a bit, but as I took my regular turn as cafeteria supervisor, I saw students staring wide-eyed at me, then turning to whisper excitedly to their friends. I'd become a celebrity simply because I was the one responsible for bringing a TV crew to school.

9 Right after lunch, the show's producer and director came to my class to look it over and watch the role-playing activity; they planned to tape near the end of the school day. The two women were gracious and self-effacing, taking pains not to create any disturbance; but the students, of course, knew why they were there. There were no vacant stares, no hair brushes, no gum chewers, and no note scribblers. It was total concentration, and I enjoyed one of my best classes in more than 15 years of teaching.

After the class, I met with the producer and director to plan   10
the taping. They talked about some of the students they'd seen
and mentioned Susan. "She's terribly photogenic and very,
very good with words." They mentioned Steve. "He really
chaired his committee well. Real leadership there. Handsome
boy, too." They mentioned Jim, Pete, Randy, and Jenny and
their insights into advertising claims. Gradually I became
aware that we were engaged in a talent hunt; we were looking
for a strong and attractive group to be featured in the taping.

We continued the discussion, deciding on the players. We   11
also discussed the sequencing of the taping session. First, I'd do
an introduction, explaining the role-playing activity as if the class
had never heard of it. Then, I'd follow with the conclusion—summarizing remarks ending with a cheery "See you tomorrow!"—
and dismiss the class. The bit players would leave the school
and go home. We'd then rearrange the set and film the photogenic and perceptive featured players while they discussed
advertising claims as a committee. Obviously, this is not the
way I'd conduct an actual class, but it made sense. After all, I
wanted my students to look good, and I wanted to look good.

"It'll be very hard work," the producer cautioned. "I trust   12
your students understand that."

"It's already been hard work," I remarked as I thought of   13
possible jealousies and bruised feelings over our choices of
featured players.

About a half hour before school's end, the crew set up cam-   14
eras and lights in the hall near the classroom we'd be working
in, a room in an isolated part of the building. But as the crew
began filming background shots of the normal passing of
students through the hall, near chaos broke out.

Hordes of students suddenly appeared. A basketball star   15
gangled through the milling mob to do an imitation of
Nureyev,[1] topping off a pirouette by feigning a couple of jump
shots. A pretty girl walked back and forth in front of the
cameras at least a dozen times before she was snared by a home
economics teacher. Three boys did a noisy pantomime of opening jammed lockers, none of which were theirs. A faculty member, seen rarely in this part of the building, managed to work

[1]Famous ballet star—Ed

his way through the crowd, smiling broadly. And as members of my class struggled through the press of bodies, they were hailed, clutched at, patted on the back, and hugged.

16 "Knock 'em dead!" I heard a student call.

17 It took the vice-principal and five teachers 10 minutes to clear the hall.

18 We assembled the cast, arranged the furniture, erased several mild obscenities from the chalkboard, and pulled down the window shades—disappointing a clutch of spectators outside. The producers then introduced the crew and explained their work.

19 I was wired with a mike and the crew set up a boom microphone, while the girls checked each other's make-up and the boys sat squirming.

20 Finally, the taping began. It was show business, a performance, a total alteration of the reality I know as a teacher. As soon as I began the introduction, 26 pairs of eyes focused on me as if I were Billy Joel about to sing. I was instantly startled and self-conscious. When I asked a question, some of the usually quieter students leaped to respond. This so unsettled me that I forgot what I was saying and had to begin again.

21 The novelty of being on camera, however, soon passed. We had to do retakes because the soundman missed student responses from the rear of the room. The director asked me to rephrase a question and asked a student to rephrase a response. There were delays while technicians adjusted equipment.

22 We all became very much aware of being performers, and some of the students who had been most excited about making their TV debut began to grumble about the hard work. That pleased me, for a new reality began to creep in: Television is not altogether glamorous.

23 We taped for almost five hours, on more than 3,200 feet of videotape. That is almost an hour-and-a-half's worth, more than double a normal class period. And out of that mass of celluloid the producer said she'd use seven minutes on the program!

24 Two days later, five students and I went to the NBC studios at Rockefeller Center to do a taping of a final segment. The producer wanted to do a studio recreation of the role-playing game. This time, however, the game would include real executives—one from advertising, one from the NBC network,

and one from the FTC. We'd be part of a panel discussion moderated by Betty Furness. My students would challenge the TV and the advertising executives, asking them to justify some of the bothersome language used in current commercials.

This was the most arduous part of the experience. The tap- 25 ing was live, meaning that the cameras would run for no longer than eight minutes. As we ate turkey and ham during a break with Ms. Furness and the guest executives, I realized that we were with people who were totally comfortable with television. I began to worry. How could mere 14-year-olds compete in a debate with those to whom being on television is as ordinary as riding a school bus?

But my concern soon disappeared. As Ms. Furness began 26 reading her TelePrompTer, Susan leaned over and whispered, "This is fun!" And it was Susan who struck first. " 'You can see how luxurious my hair feels' is a perfect example of the silly language your ad writers use," she said with all the poise of a Barbara Walters. "It's impossible to *see* how something feels," she went on.

That pleased me, for as an English teacher, I've always empha- 27 sized the value of striving for precision in the use of language. The work we'd done with TV commercials, where suggestibility is the rule, had taken hold, I thought, as the ad executive fumbled for a response. The tension vanished, and we did well.

The show aired two weeks later, and I had it taped so the 28 class could view it together. It was a slick production, complete with music—"Hey, Big Spender"—to develop a theme for Ms. Furness' introduction. "Teens are big business these days," she said. "Does television advertising influence how they spend their money?" Then followed a shot of students in the hall— edited to show none of the wildness that actually occurred. Next, three of my students appeared in brief clips of interviews. They were asked, "Have you ever been disappointed by television advertising?" The responses were, "Yes, of course," and I was pleased with their detailed answers. Finally, the classroom appeared, and there I was, lounging against my desk, smiling calmly. I looked good—a young, unrumpled Orson Bean, with a cool blue-and-brown paisley tie. My voice was mellifluous. Gee, I thought as I saw the tape, I could have been a TV personality.

29   Now, I am probably no more vain than most people. But television does strange things to the ego. I became so absorbed in studying the image of myself that the whole point of the show passed me by. I didn't even notice that I'd made a goof analyzing a commercial until I'd seen the show three times. The students who participated were the same; watching themselves on videotape, they missed what they had said. I had an enormous struggle to get both them and me to recall the hard work and to see the obvious editing. It was as if reality had been reversed: The actual process of putting together the tape was not real, but the product was.

30   I showed the tape again last year to my ninth grade class. I carefully explained to this delightful gang of fault-finders how the taping had been done. I told them about the changed sequence, the selection of the featured players, the takes and retakes. They themselves had just been through the same role-playing activity, and I asked them to listen carefully to what was said. They nodded happily and set their flinty minds to look at things critically. But as the tape ended, they wanted to tease me about how ugly and wrinkled I looked. They wanted to say, "That's Randy! He goes to Compo Beach all the time." "Jenny's eye shadow—horrible!" "When will you get us on TV?"

31   The visual image had worked its magic once again: They had missed the point of the show altogether. And, as I dismissed them, I felt something vibrating in their glances and voices—the celebrity image at work again. I was no longer their mundane English teacher: I was a TV personality.

32   I decided to show the tape again the next day. I reviewed the hard work, the editing, the slick packaging. I passed out questions so we could focus on what had been said on the program. I turned on the recorder and turned off the picture to let them hear only the sound. They protested loudly, of course. But I was determined to force them to respond to how effectively the previous year's class had taken apart the language used in the claims of commercials. This was, after all, the point of the program. And it worked, finally.

33   As class ended, one of the students drifted up to me. "What are we going to do next?" she asked.

34   "We're going to make some comparisons between TV news shows and what's written in newspapers," I replied.

"Do they put together news shows the way they filmed your class?"   35

"It's similar and usually much quicker," I answered.   36

She smiled and shook her head. "It's getting hard to believe anything anymore."   37

In that comment lies what every TV viewer should have—a healthy measure of beautiful, glorious skepticism. But as I said, I'm still trying to understand that taping session. And I'm aware of how hard it is to practice skepticism. Every time I see the *Buyline* tape, I'm struck by how good a teacher TV made me. Am I really that warm, intelligent, creative, and good looking? Of course not. But TV made me that way. I like it, and sometimes I find myself still hoping that I am what television defined me to be.   38

I sometimes think children have superior knowledge of TV. They know, from many years of watching it, that the product in all its edited glory is the only reality. Shortly after the program aired on that February Saturday two years ago, our telephone rang. The voice belonged to my daughter's 11-year-old friend. She said, "I just saw you on TV. May I have your autograph?"   39

I was baffled. After all, this was the boisterous girl who played with my daughter just about every day and who mostly regarded me as a piece of furniture that occasionally mumbled something about lowering your voices. "Are you serious?" I croaked.   40

"May I have your autograph?" she repeated, ignoring my question. "I can come over right now." Her voice was without guile.   41

She came. And I signed while she scrutinized my face, her eyes still aglow with Chromacolor.   42

To Stephanie, television had transformed a kindly grump into something real. And there is no doubt in my mind whatsoever that in the deepest part of her soul is the fervent dream that her being, too, will someday be defined and literally affirmed by an appearance on television.   43

Lately, my ninth grade class has been growing restless. Shall I move up the TV unit and bring out the tape again? Shall I remind them what a great teacher they have? Shall I remind myself what a fine teacher I am? Shall I renew their—and my—hope?   44

45   To be or not to be as defined by TV? Does that question suggest what makes television so totally unlike any other medium?

Expanding Vocabulary

Match each word in column A with its definition in column B. When
in doubt, first find the word in the essay and look for context clues to
aid your understanding of the word's meaning. Then, if necessary, use
your dictionary to complete the matching exercise. The number in
parentheses is the number of the paragraph in which the word
appears.

Column A	Column B
dissecting (2)	smoothly flowing
advocate (3)	attractive when photographed
photogenic (10)	examined carefully
sequencing (11)	walked with long-legged awkwardness
gangled (15)	careless mistake
pirouette (15)	separating, analyzing
snared (15)	ordinary
pantomime (15)	full spin of the body on the toes or
arduous (25)	ball of the foot (in ballet)
mellifluous (28)	speak in favor of
goof (29)	act of communicating with bodily
flinty (30)	or facial expressions and gestures
mundane (31)	trapped, caught
skepticism (38)	cunning, deceit
boisterous (40)	very difficult
guile (41)	emotional, zealous
scrutinized (42)	arranging in a series
fervent (43)	hard, tough
	loud, unrestrained
	doubting, questioning attitude

Understanding Content

1. What had McGarvey's English class been studying before the TV
   crew came? What response did the class receive from their letters
   to companies?
2. What was the response of students to the news of the coming
   crew? How did McGarvey's students behave with the crew
   watching their classes?
3. How did the TV producer want to sequence the class discussion?
   On what basis did Mc Crew select students to tape? How long did

the taping take? How representative of a typical class would the taped version be?

4. How did McGarvey respond when he watched the finished tape? How did his class respond? And future classes?

Drawing Inferences about Thesis and Purpose

1. What attitude, according to McGarvey, should we hold toward what we see on TV? Why did he, and his students, have trouble maintaining that attitude?
2. What is McGarvey's thesis, the main points he wants to make about television?

Analyzing Strategies and Style

1. McGarvey develops his observations about TV through one example, one event that he recounts at length. What makes one long example an effective way to illustrate his thesis?
2. McGarvey includes a clever description of students (and teachers) showing off for the TV cameras in the school hallway. Examine this passage again (paragraphs 14 and 15). What makes this an effective description? What strategies does the author use here?

Thinking Critically

1. Are you skeptical about everything you see on television? That is, do you understand that much of what is presumably "live" has been taped and carefully edited? If you aren't skeptical, should you be?
2. Do you want to be on TV? If so, why? If not, why not?
3. Is there something wrong with a society in which a seven-minute TV segment can suddenly turn an ordinary person into a celebrity? Why are celebrities so appealing? Do we put too much emphasis on them?

Smarter Kids, Brought to You
by the Letters T and V

DIMITRI A. CHRISTAKIS

Dimitri Christakis is a pediatrician at the Children's Hospital in Seattle and a professor at the University of Washington's School of Medicine. His research has been published in over 100 articles and serves as the basis for a pediatrics textbook. With colleague Frederick Zimmerman he is the author of *The Elephant in the Living Room: Make Television Work for Your Kids* (2006). In this essay, published December 31, 2006, Christakis defends some TV programs for children.

Questions to Guide Your Reading and Reflection

1. What are some advantages of television for children?
2. What TV shows did you most enjoy as a youngster? Why were they your favorites?

1   The digital divide used to separate rich from poor; now it separates parents from their children. Whether it's infants watching the new 24-hour Baby's First TV channel, or teenagers instant messaging while they watch last night's Daily Show on their iPods, television is an enormous presence in the lives of kids today. The average American child spends three to five hours a day watching it. And they start their viewing careers much earlier than ever before: In 1961, the average child began to watch television at age 3; today it is 9 months.

2   Yet, for all the television kids are watching, much of what parents think they know about television's impact on their children is wrong. For instance, in the early 1970s, it was common knowledge that television was bad for your eyes: My own parents were convinced that my bad eyesight was the result of sitting too close to the screen, and they therefore made me stay at least six feet from it. Today, most people know that television viewing does not cause vision problems, but a host of new myths have emerged, still ripe for debunking:

3   **1. TV makes kids dumb**. Actually, high-quality TV shows such as *Sesame Street* and *Blues Clues* improve children's cognitive abilities. Study after study has shown that children 3 to 5 years old who watch *Sesame Street* for an hour a day are better able to recognize numbers, letters and shapes than those who don't. When 500 kids who had participated in some of those studies were followed up as teenagers, those who had watched educational programs as preschoolers had higher grades, were reading more books, placed more value on achievement and were more creative than those who had not.

2. TV makes kids violent. The real story is more compli-   4
cated. In 1994, researchers reviewed hundreds of studies
involving thousands of children and concluded that there was
clear evidence that watching violence on TV makes children
more aggressive. Similarly, preteens and teenagers exposed to
sexual content on television are more much more likely to
engage in the kinds of activities they see on the screen.

But a study of more than 5,000 children also found that "pro-   5
social" programs (think *Mr. Rogers' Neighborhood*) make children kinder and more tolerant. In fact the linkage between good
behavior and watching good programming is as strong as the
link between bad behavior and bad programming. The problem
is that kids are increasingly watching shows with violence and
sex instead of programming that is appropriate for their age.

3. Educational videos make infants smarter. The   6
names—such as Baby Einstein and Brainy Baby—suggest
one thing, but the data suggest otherwise. According to a
2005 report by the Kaiser Family Foundation, no program
targeting children younger than 2 has demonstrated *any*
educational benefit.

Evidence from studies my colleagues and I have done sug-   7
gests that early viewing (under age 3) may be harmful to
children's cognitive development. We found that children who
watch TV before age 3 score worse on tests of letter and number recognition upon entering school than those who do not.
And for each hour of television a child watches on average per
day before age 3, the chances that child will have attention
problems at age 7 increase by 10 percent. A 2005 University of
Pennsylvania study found that even watching *Sesame Street*
before age 3 delayed a child's ability to develop language skills.

4. Sitting around watching television—instead of playing   8
outside—makes kids overweight. In fact, being a couch potato
is not what causes obesity. Kids sit around to read, too, but no
one suggests that reading causes obesity. A 1999 Stanford University experiment found that when elementary school children
watched less television, they did lose excess weight; however,
reducing their television time did not make them more active.

What that suggests is that television-watching itself—unlike   9
other sedentary activities such as reading, block-building or
working on art projects—encourages overeating. Snacking in

front of the tube is a widespread habit (for kids as well as adults) and the barrage of junk food advertisements only heightens that temptation. About 70 percent of the ads children see on television are for food products, and virtually none of them are for healthy choices. A 2005 Harvard University study found that, on average, children eat about 170 more calories per day for each hour of television they watch, and all of those calories are derived from foods commonly advertised in television commercials.

10   **5. Television helps kids get to sleep.** The opposite is true. In a 2005 study of more than 2,000 children, my colleagues and I found that the more television children watch, the more likely they are to have irregular sleep and nap patterns. As common as it is—about three-fourths of children had television as part of their bedtime ritual, according to a national survey—allowing kids to watch television because they can't sleep is part of the problem, not the solution.

11   **6. Kids watch too much television.** Actually, the bigger problem is what they watch and how they watch it. In what some consider the halcyon days of television, families used to gather around a single centrally located set and watched high-quality, family-centered programming together.

12   Nowadays, the typical U.S. household has multiple television sets; family members (including young children) sit alone and watch programs that too often are violent and sexualized. When parents watch with their children, the value of the best television programs is enhanced—and the harm of negative programming can be curtailed.

Expanding Vocabulary

Examine the following words in their contexts in the essay and then write a brief definition or synonym for each one. Do not use a dictionary; try to guess the word's meaning from its context. The number in parentheses is the number of the paragraph in which the word appears.

debunking (2)	halcyon (11)
cognitive (3)	enhanced (12)
barrage (9)	curtailed (12)

Understanding Content

1. How much do children watch TV? When do they start watching?
2. How does watching quality TV shows for children influence them as teens?
3. What do studies reveal about the impact of videos for babies on children?
4. What do the studies suggest about TV watching and obesity in children?

Drawing Inferences about Thesis and Purpose

1. What is the author's purpose in writing?
2. What, in general, is Christakis's attitude toward children watching TV?
3. How can parents get the best of TV for their children? What are they wise to restrict in their children's TV experience?

Analyzing Strategies and Style

1. How does Christakis organize and present, visually, his essay? What makes his presentation effective?
2. Look again at the opening. What strategy does the author use to get readers' attention?

Thinking Critically

1. Does the author's partial defense of TV for children make sense to you? If so, what in his presentation convinces you? If not, why not?
2. Does it make sense to you that TV watching contributes to obesity while reading does not? Explain.
3. Is there any hope of getting families to share TV viewing again? If so, how? What advice do you have for parents based on your reflecting on Christakis's article?

We Are Our Own Worst Imuses

JONETTA ROSE BARRAS

A graduate of Trinity College, award-winning journalist J. B. Barras has been recognized as a new voice for black America. Published in newspapers and news magazines, Barras has also appeared on National Public Radio and a number of political talk shows. She is the author of three books, most recently *Bridges: Reuniting Daughters and Daddies* (2005). In the following article, published in the *Washington Post* on March 15, 2007, Barras takes on the language and culture of rap and hip-hop.

Questions to Guide Your Reading and Reflection

1. Who is Don Imus? If you do not know, see what you can learn about him from an Internet search.
2. Does the denigration of women in rap music bother you? Why or why not?

---

1   They wanted to slay Don Imus and they did. Jesse Jackson and Al Sharpton, the NAACP, the National Association of Black Journalists and their posse knocked the shock jock off his throne at CBS Radio and MSNBC. But behind the scenes in the black community where I live and work, the outcry all along has been for something else.

2   Rather than blast the talk-show host for his derogatory description of the Rutgers University women's basketball team, many African Americans I spoke to in my work as a radio commentator said all along that black folks, including and perhaps chiefly those who led the charge against Imus, should take a long look in the mirror.

3   I think they're right.

4   The sensational indignation that got Imus fired last week struck many of us as hypocritical. It cast African Americans principally as the victims of discrimination—and ignored the fact that they are the chief purveyors of the demeaning language being decried. It ignored the realities of how culture gets transmitted in contemporary society and the prominent role that African Americans play in that transfer. It failed to recognize the market forces at play. And it held blacks unaccountable for any of the damage, saddling whites with all the blame.

5   I have no tears for Imus. His style of commentary is as outdated as black-and-white TV, and he deserved to be sent packing. But here's the point: If African Americans wanted to hold Imus accountable and punish him, shouldn't they take similar actions against some in their own group?

Urban American pop culture is fast becoming a black—and   6
sometimes Hispanic—thing, and a bunch of people are getting
filthy rich from it. The dirty little secret here is that the fight
over Imus may not have been so much about his terminal foot-
in-mouth disease as about who has dominion over that culture
and who collects the cash.

"Imus didn't say anything that hasn't been included in thou-   7
sands of records," said Misty Brown, a local arts consultant.
"We have been called far worse, and by our own people."

It was black rap artists who created the image of African   8
American women as "bitches and hos." That image has been
marketed and distributed by large corporations—Warner Brothers,
Viacom, Black Entertainment Television—and purchased all
over the world by regular folks, white and black, including, no
doubt, some of the same people who called for Imus's head.

As a result, there isn't anything sacred in black culture any-   9
more, said local hip-hop artist Bomani Armah, "because it isn't
sacred among us."

Some black radio stations "allow songs to be played that   10
clearly disrespect black women," said Michael Francis, a criminal justice expert and social commentator in the District, who
cautions that not all the blame for the denigration of black
women can be placed at rap's door. The antecedents can be
found in slavery, when black women were bred, whipped and
put on the block to work for others.

But even though it was poorly executed Imus-speak,   11
"nappy-headed ho" is, in fact, a progeny of black street/thug
culture. It is a culture whose symbols, idioms and fashions
have not only seeped into the American mainstream over the
past 20 years but have been enthusiastically embraced. We see
and hear this culture every day in the 'hood, in high schools, in
the movie ticket line, in the uppercrust college dorm.

Consider that last year's Academy Award for Best Original   12
Song went to "It's Hard Out Here for a Pimp" from the movie
Hustle and Flow. That Howard University gave rapper P. Diddy
the same postgraduate achievement award that it once
bestowed upon famed African American author Zora Neale
Hurston. Or that in 2001 the NAACP gave its prestigious
Image Award to R. Kelly, a black singer accused of having sex
with underage girls.

13   We know this "thug" culture by its awful and extensive body tattoos; its denigrating language that sculpts every woman—regardless of color—into a sex object or a joke. We know it by its so-called urban fashion, which includes the butt-revealing pants, the flashy and often fake gold—around the neck, on the arms, in the mouth. And yes, by the lyrics we hear and the videos we see. Nowadays, it has also spread into comedy, said Armah, who notes a rise in politically incorrect jokes and skits.

14   African Americans "have created the atmosphere where people feel comfortable making derogatory statements," said D.C. small-business owner Edwin Chin-Shue, who managed several record stores for years. "If we want to boycott Imus, then we have to boycott Warner Brothers and Sony. We have to boycott Spike Lee and radio stations that play rap music."

15   The Imus controversy was an extension of the battle over use of the N-word. African Americans can throw around the most demeaning terminology, seeking to cash in at major record companies, production studios or publishing houses (check out the chick-lit phenom, which in many cases is just blaxploitation movies put to print). But the moment certain whites walk into that world, blacks are insulted, deeply offended. Spike Lee can use the word "jiggaboo" in his movie *School Daze*. Imus and his producer sidekick had better step back.

16   Who is caretaker of the authentic thug culture, including when and how to use the phrases "nappy head" or "bitches and hos"? That is the question.

17   The day after Imus was fired, rapper Snoop Dogg was quoted as saying that what Imus did and what rappers do "are two separate things." Rappers "have these songs coming from our minds and our souls that are relevant to what we feel," he said "I will not let them [expletive] say we in the same league as him."

18   But as American society becomes more colorized, more reflective of its multicultural roots and features, blacks may be unable to retain sole rights of proprietorship, even through bullying and demonstrations. Expressions seep into mainstream culture and become universal property.

19   "People start thinking [a phrase] is cool," said Deborah Tannen, professor of linguistics at Georgetown University. "You

use it because you have the feeling of being with it, being on the cutting edge. It's also about the youth culture" and "the allure associated with youth."

So we heard the aging Imus attempting to replicate the language of youthful African American thug culture. And we saw Bush adviser Karl Rove onstage at a recent radio correspondents' dinner, clumsily trying out the menacing gangsta pose and confrontational hand gestures as he shouted out the lame lyrics to a faux rap song. It was American street culture come to the White House. 20

And street culture's introduction into mainstream America, though incremental, is not accidental. It is orchestrated by image- and opinion-makers—black and white—and corporations champing at the bit for new markets and the cash they promise. The public aids and abets the process. It's less about being cool and more about the money. Ka-ching. 21

Each year rap/hip-hop brings more than $4 billion to the music industry. The urban apparel market racks up more than $2 billion in sales annually, according to various trade publications. 22

"In a capitalist environment, what is mainstream is what sells," said WAMU Radio talk show host Kojo Nnamdi. "The denigration of women has been a huge seller in the last 20 years. Black men do it and even black women do it." 23

And that denigration gets picked up and tossed around freely. "You should hear some of the things the young ladies I work with call themselves." said Janice Ferebee, president of Got It Goin On, which provides self-esteem and life-skills services for girls and young women in the United States, South Africa and Ghana. 24

So it's fair to ask: Why now? Why all the heat and bother? Surely it's not the first time that African Americans have heard rap-speak in mainstream America. And why won't blacks chastise their own? 25

The same machine that fed Imus has made an awful lot of black folks millionaires. So this matter of who is paraded in the public square for an old-fashioned butt-kicking must be a finely executed dance. Although Sharpton and others may claim that they have flogged rap artists, one thing is certain: They haven't flogged P. Diddy, Snoop Dogg or many of the others with the same vengeance that they did Imus. They haven't sought to strip 26 them of their sponsors and their livelihood. One reason may be that money from these trash-talkers keeps the wheels of more than a few black organizations turning. The last person who had the guts to challenge those within the race was the late C. Delores Tucker, who led the National Congress of Black Women.

27   "People have been allowed to continue living out this most amazing double standard." said Nnamdi. It's time that double standard were slain.

Expanding Vocabulary

Match each word in column A with its definition in column B. When in doubt, first find the word in the essay and look for context clues to aid your understanding of the word's meaning. Then, if necessary, use your dictionary to complete the matching exercise. The number in parentheses is the number of the paragraph in which the word appears.

Column A	*Column B*
posse (1)	providers
derogatory (2)	attack one's reputation
purveyors (4)	offspring, descendant of
demeaning (4)	unusual occurrence
decried (4)	a group called by a sheriff to help
denigration (10)	enforce law
progeny (11)	increasing in small amounts
sculpts (13)	openly condemned
phenom (15)	disparaging, belittling
allure (19)	debasing, putting down
incremental (21)	severely criticize
chastise (25)	shapes, defines
	appeal

Understanding Content

1. What is the occasion for Barras's article? What did Imus do? What was the result?
2. According to the author, African Americans should stop seeing themselves as victims; what should they admit to instead?
3. What is the source of the language and attitudes expressed by Imus?
4. Barras asks "who is the caretaker of the authentic thug culture?" How do many blacks, especially rappers, answer that question?
5. What motivates blacks to want to be in control of rap language and the culture it has spawned?

Drawing Inferences about Thesis and Purpose

1. When Barras suggests that blacks complaining about Imus should look in the mirror, what does she want readers to understand?
2. When she concludes with the assertion that is it time to get rid of the double standard, what double standard is she referring to? Who benefits from not "slaying" the double standard?
3. What is Barras's thesis?

Analyzing Strategies and Style

1. How would you characterize Barras's style? What tone or feel does her writing have?
2. The author includes quotations from quite a few people she has interviewed. What does she accomplish with this strategy?
3. Early in her article Barras writes: "I have no tears for Imus." Why does she include that statement?

Thinking Critically

1. The usual view toward name calling is that people within a group can refer to themselves in a derogatory way, but people outside that group cannot. With this concept, the complaint should be entirely against Imus. Do you agree with Barras's complaint against African Americans? Why or why not?
2. Is there any justification for the debasing language of rap and the thug culture? How do the rappers defend their lyrics? Do you agree? Why or why not?

Notes from the Hip-Hop Underground

SHELBY STEELE

With a Ph.D. from the University of Utah, Shelby Steele is a research fellow at Stanford University's Hoover Institution. He has written many essays on race, some of which have been collected into his book *The Content of Our Character* (1990). His latest book is *A Dream Deferred: The Second Betrayal of Black Freedom in America* (1998). His essay on hip-hop music was published March 30, 2001, in the *Wall Street Journal*.

Questions to Guide Your Reading and Reflection
1. What are the traits of the mythic BN?
2. Are you drawn to rap music? If so, why? If not, why not?

1   Think about it. If you were a slave, what sort of legend or myth would most warm your soul? One of the great legends in black American culture has always been that of the Bad Nigger. This figure flaunts the constraints, laws and taboos that bind a person in slavery. The BN is unbound and contemptuous, and takes his vengeance on the master's women simply to assert the broadest possible freedom. His very indifference to human feeling makes him a revolution incarnate. Nat Turner, a slave who in 1831 led an insurrection in which some 60 whites were massacred, was the BN come to life.

2   But for the most part, the BN is the imagination's compensation for the all-too-real impotence and confinement that slaves and segregated blacks actually endured. He lives out a compensatory grandiosity—a self-preening superiority combined with a trickster's cunning and a hyperbolic masculinity in which sexual potency is a vengeful and revolutionary force.

3   This cultural archetype, I believe, is at the center of rap or hip-hop culture. From "cop killer" Ice T, Tupac Shakur and, today most noticeably, Sean "Puffy" Combs and Eminem (who is white), we get versions of the BN in all his sneering and inflated masculinity.

4   Having beaten gun and bribery charges in a high-profile New York trial, Mr. Combs—who has just announced that he wishes to be known, henceforth, as "P. Diddy"—is the baddest BN for the moment. A man with both the entrepreneurial genius and the fortune (estimated to be in the hundreds of millions of dollars) to live far above the fray, he has nevertheless tried to live out the BN archetype in a series of ego feuds, thuggish assaults, and late-night escapades that ought to bore a man of his talent and wealth.

5   But Mr. Combs is caught in a contradiction. At the very least, he must posture, if not act out, BN themes, even as the actual condition of his life becomes conspicuously bourgeois. Rap culture essentially markets BN themes to American youth as an ideal form of adolescent rebellion. And this meeting of a black

cultural archetype with the universal impulse of youth to find themselves by thumbing their nose at adults is extremely profitable. But the rappers and promoters themselves are pressured toward a thug life, simply to stay credible, by the very BN themes they sell. A rap promoter without an arrest record can start to look a lot like Dick Clark.

But the Puffys of the world cannot market to an indifferent   6
youth. The important question is how the BN archetype—the slave's projection of lawless power and revenge—has become the MTV generation's metaphor for rebellion. And are conservatives right to see all this as yet more evidence of America's decline?

I think the answer to these questions begins in one fact: that   7
what many of today's youth ironically share with yesterday's slave is a need for myths and images that compensate for a sense of alienation and ineffectuality.

Of course, today's youth do not remotely live the lives of   8
slaves and know nothing of the alienation and impotence out of which slaves conjured the BN myth. Still, the injury to family life in America over the past 30 years (from high divorce and illegitimacy rates, a sweeping sexual revolution, dual-career households, etc.) may well have given us the most interpersonally alienated generation in our history.

Too many of today's youth experienced a faithlessness and   9
tenuousness even in that all-important relationship with their parents. And outside the home, institutions rarely offer the constancy, structure, high expectations, and personal values they once did. So here is another kind of alienation that also diminishes and generates a sense of helplessness, that sets up the need for compensation—for an imagined self that is bigger than life, unbound, and powerful. Here the suburban white kid, gawky and materially privileged, is oddly simpatico with the black American experience.

The success of people like Mr. Combs is built on this sense   10
of the simpatico. By some estimates, 80% of rap music is bought by white youth. And this makes for another irony. The blooming of white alienation has brought us the first generation of black entrepreneurs with wide-open access to the American mainstream. Russell Simmons, known as the "Godfather" of rap entrepreneurs, as well as Mr. Combs, Master P and

others, have launched clothing lines, restaurant chains, record labels, and production companies—possibilities seeded, in a sense, by this strong new sympathy between black and white alienation.

11   Rap's adaptation, or update, of the BN archetype began in the post-'60s black underclass. As is now well established, this was essentially a matriarchal world in which welfare-supported women became the center of households and men became satellite fathers only sporadically supporting or visiting their children by different women. The children of this world were not primed to support a music of teen romance—of "Stop in the Name of Love." The alienation was too withering. Not even the blues would do.

12   I think the appeal of the BN, on the deepest level, was his existential indifference to feeling—what might be called his immunity to feeling. The slave wanted not to feel the loves and fears that bound him to other people and thus weakened him into an accommodation with slavery. Better not to love at all if it meant such an accommodation. So the BN felt nothing for anyone and had no fear even of death. He could slap a white man around with no regard for the consequences.

13   Rappers, too, gain freedom through immunity to feeling. Women are "bitches" and "hos," objects of lust, but not of feeling. In many inner cities, where the illegitimacy rate is over 80%, where welfare has outbid the male as head of the household, where marriage is all but nonexistent, and where the decimation of drugs is everywhere—in such places, a young person of tender feelings is certain to be devastated. Everything about rap—the misogynistic lyrics, the heaving swagger, the violent sexuality, the cynical hipness—screams "I'm bad because I don't feel." Nonfeeling is freedom. And it is important to note that this has nothing to do with race. In rap, the BN nurtures indifference toward those he is most likely to love.

14   Conservatives have rightly attacked rap for its misogyny, violence and over-the-top vulgarity. But it is important to remember that this music is a fairly accurate message from a part of society where human connections are fractured and impossible, so fraught with disappointments and pain that only an assault on human feeling itself can assuage. Rap makes the conservative argument about what happens when family

life is eroded either by welfare and drugs, or by the stresses and indulgences of middle-class life.

I listened carefully to Eminem's recent Grammy performance expecting, I guess, to be disgusted. Instead I was drawn into a compelling rap about a boy who becomes a figure of terrible pathos. He is a male groupie who selfishly longs for the autograph of a rap star while he has his girlfriend tied up in the trunk of his car. Easy to be aghast at this until I remembered that Dostoyevsky's *Notes from the Underground*—the first modern novel written more than 150 years ago—was also about a pathetic antihero whose alienation from modernity made him spiteful and finally cruel toward an innocent female.   15

Both works protest what we all protest—societies that lose people to alienation. This does not excuse the vulgarity of rap. But the real problem is not as much rap's cartoonish bravado as what it compensates for.   16

Expanding Vocabulary

Match each word in column A with its definition in column B. When in doubt, first find the word in the essay and look for context clues to aid your understanding of the word's meaning. Then, if necessary, use your dictionary to complete the matching exercise. The number in parentheses is the number of the paragraph in which the word appears.

Column A	Column B
flaunts (1)	given life to
taboos (1)	ideal example or type
incarnate (1)	ease, soften
grandiosity (2)	shows contempt for
hyperbolic (2)	irregularly occurring
archetype (3)	false show of toughness
conspicuously (5)	behavior opposed by social custom
alienation (7)	overstated
simpatico (9)	noticeably, obviously
sporadically (11)	hatred of women
withering (11)	state of separation between self and
decimation (13)	the world
misogynistic (13)	pomposity
assuage (14)	large scale destruction
bravado (16)	compatible
	devastating

Understanding Content

1. What, in Steele's view, does the BN compensate for?
2. Where do we find this mythic figure today?
3. How must rappers live—or appear to live—in order to be consistent with the BN image? What makes this a contradiction?
4. Even though today's young people have no concept of a slave life, they are still drawn to hip-hop. Why?

Drawing Inferences about Thesis and Purpose

1. Steele writes that "the appeal of the BN . . . was his existential indifference to feeling." What does he mean by this statement? Why is not feeling a kind of freedom?
2. What are some of the causes, today, for feelings of alienation?
3. What is Steele's thesis?

Analyzing Strategies and Style

1. Steele writes that conservatives are correct when they complain about the language and attitudes of rap music. Why does he include this statement?
2. Examine the author's examples of rappers: What do they have in common?
3. Examine Steele's handling of rap language and his key term. How does he write concretely while showing a sensitivity to language offensive to many readers?

Thinking Critically

1. Is Steele's concept of the mythic BN, as it relates to modern hip-hop, a new idea for you? Does it make sense? Why or why not?
2. Do you agree with the author's analyses of the causes of white youth's alienation? If not, how do you account for the appeal of rap for white, suburban youth?

The Real Media Divide

MARKUS PRIOR

Markus Prior holds a Ph.D. from Stanford University and is assistant professor of politics and public affairs at Princeton University and its Woodrow Wilson School. His shared interests in communications and politics come together in his book *Post-Broadcast Democracy: How Media Choice Increases Inequality in Political Involvement and Polarizes Elections* (2007). His article on the media divide, published in the *Washington Post* on July 16, 2007, draws on the research in *Post-Broadcast Democracy*.

Questions to Guide Your Reading and Reflection

1. "The Real Media Divide" implies a contrast with what people *think* the divide is. What do you think the media divide refers to?
2. Are you a news junkie? If not, why not?

Today's news world is a political junkie's oyster. Cable TV offers CNN, Fox News, MSNBC and C-SPAN. *The Washington Post, BBC online, The Note* and many, many more news Web sites are only a click away. But that's where they remain for many Americans. Decades into the "information age," the public is as uninformed as before the rise of cable television and the Internet.

Greater access to media, ironically, has reduced the share of Americans who are politically informed. The most significant effect of more media choice is not the wider dissemination of political news but mounting inequality in political involvement. Some people follow news more closely than in the past, but many others avoid it altogether.

Now that Americans can choose among countless channels and Web sites, the role of motivation is key. Many people's reasons for watching television or surfing the Web do not include learning about politics. Today's media users seek out the extent they really like. Unfortunately for a political system that benefits from an informed citizenry, few people really like the news.

Consider the broadcast networks' desperate struggle to hold on to an evershrinking news audience. The problem is not that shallow, loud or negative coverage of politics causes viewers to tune out in disgust. It's that for many people shallow, loud entertainment offers greater satisfaction, and it always has. Now, such entertainment is available around the clock and in unprecedented variety. Television viewers have not abandoned the evening news out of frustration—they just found something more enjoyable. Even Katie Couric can't stanch that trend.

5   The flip side of the entertainment fan who doesn't have to watch the news is the news junkie who now can follow it constantly. A relatively small segment of the population—my own research indicates it's less than a fifth—specializes in news content. But such people consume so much of it that the total amount of time Americans spend watching, reading and listening to news has not declined even though many people have tuned out.

6   The new fault line of civic involvement is between news junkies and entertainment fans. Entertainment fans are abandoning news and politics not because it has become harder to be involved but because they have decided to devote their time to content that promises greater immediate gratification. As a result, they learn less about politics and are less likely to vote at a time when news junkies are becoming even more engaged. Unlike most forms of inequality, this rising divergence in political involvement is a result of voluntary consumption decisions. Making sure everybody has access to media won't fix the problem—it is exactly the cause.

7   When media users get what they want all the time, does anyone get hurt? Well, yes. The expansion of news choices has many worried about partisan bias. Such worries are overstated. Fox News's Bill O'Reilly preaches mostly to the converted; there have always been passionate conservatives, and exposure to one-sided media will hardly make them more conservative. Plus, a little O'Reilly doesn't harm anybody. The danger lies not in larger audiences for politically biased news outlets per se but in exclusive exposure to outlets all biased in the same direction. But many Fox News viewers also watch CNN and MSNBC.

8   More troubling is that entertainment fans reduce the political representation of their interests when they avoid news and cut down on their political participation. Politicians pay more attention to voters than to nonvoters, so the views of these less-involved entertainment fans may not be reflected in political outcomes as much as they were in the past.

9   Greater madia choice is both gratifying and a powerful political asset for those people who read op-eds and then move on to NPR, Instapundit and Wolf Blitzer. It is more treacherous for entertainment fans. Happy as they are with a remote control in one hand and a computer mouse in the other, they never

consciously weigh the pleasure of constant entertainment against the cost of leaving politics to news junkies and politicians. The danger is not that they are seduced by the views of Ann Coulter or Arianna Huffington but that they don't know who such people are. And not that they cast more ideologically extreme votes but that they no longer vote at all.

Expanding Vocabulary

Study the contexts in which the following words are used, or study their definitions in your dictionary, and then use each word in a separate sentence. The number in parentheses is the number of the paragraph in which the word appears.

dissemination (2)	partisan (7)
divergence (6)	ideologically (9)

Understanding Content

1. What has been the result of the big increase in cable news stations and news websites?
2. How might one think that people are divided by their media news?
3. Ironically, how are people actually divided regarding their knowledge of the news?
4. In addition to differences in time spent with the news, what also divides the news junkies from the entertainment fans?
5. As a result of the media divide, what problem worries some? What is the bigger problem?

Drawing Inferences about Thesis and Purpose

1. What is ironic about the real media divide? (Check the definition of irony in the Glossary, if necessary.)
2. What is the author's purpose in writing? Is he chiefly interested in pointing out the results of his research? Is there more to his purpose?
3. What is Prior's thesis?

Analyzing Strategies and Style

1. Prior's primary examples are two general groups: "media junkies" and "entertainment fans." But he does give some specific examples as well. Identify each news source in paragraph 1. What should you know about Fox News?
2. Identify each person mentioned in the essay. What, in general, do these people represent?

Thinking Critically

1. One result of the media divide is that fewer entertainment fans vote. Is this a problem? Should we be worried about the poor voter turnout in the U.S.? Why or why not?
2. Did you know most of the newscasters and political analysts mentioned by Prior? If not, do you think this is a problem? What can happen if people do not know the political biases of various commentators?

More Powerful Than . . . Ever: On-Screen and Off, Superheroes Are a Force to Reckon With

VINCENT P. BZDEK

News Editor for the *Washington Post,* Vincent P Bzdek also writes articles on popular culture for the paper and has had articles published in the Asian and European editions of the *Wall Street Journal* and *Wired* magazine. His degree is in English literature from Colorado College. First published February 6, 2005, his essay here is a somewhat shortened version of a richly detailed study of popular films featuring superheroes.

Questions to Guide Your Reading and Reflection

1. What is the basis for Bzdek's title—what does it refer to?
2. Do you enjoy superhero films, such as *Spider-Man*? If so, why?

1   Holy spandex, Batman.

2   Seventy years after a pair of Cleveland teenagers created the first superhero out of a primordial soup of pulp magazines, rough neighborhoods and absent dads, primary-colored crime-fighters are more popular than ever. Just ask Hollywood.

3   No fewer than 18 big-budget movies scheduled for release this year were inspired by comic books or superheroes, including, this spring and summer, *Batman Begins, Fantastic Four, Constantine, Sin City, Ultraviolet* and *Sky High.*

The boom was already well underway last year. Eight super-   4
hero movies made it to multiplexes in 2004, led by two of the
year's five biggest box-office draws, *Spider-Man 2* and *The
Incredibles*. Together, *Spider-Man* (2002) and *Spider-Man 2* have
made more than $1.6 billion in the United States, making them
the sixth and eighth most popular movies ever here.

And the hero worship doesn't seem likely to stop any time   5
soon. *Superman Returns*, under the direction of Bryan Singer (*X-
Men, X2*), is scheduled for release in 2006, the first new Superman movie in 20 years. DC Comics hopes to release films of
Wonder Woman, The Flash and *Shazam* in the next couple of
years. Its rival, Marvel Comics, has ambitious plans to bring
more of its wards to the big screen, too, including *Captain America, The Phantom, Ghost Rider*, and sequels—or additional
sequels—to *Hulk, X-Men* and *Spider-Man*.

If you look at the success of *Spider-Man* and the success of   6
The Incredibles, Hollywood is saying: "Hey, there's gold in them
thar hills," said Joe Quesada, editor in chief of Marvel Comics.
"The superhero genre is today's western."

Gerard Jones, who sits on the advisory board of the MIT   7
Comparative Media Studies program, recently published *Men
of Tomorrow*, a book that chronicles the history of superheroes,
the birth of comic books and their impact on American culture.

"No other icon comes back so strong again and again after   8
so many decades, and just keeps going," Jones says. "Adults
aren't embarrassed anymore about their interest in a genre
that used to be regarded as kid stuff," he said, adding that
superheroes are "one of the major shaping influences of pop
culture."

So why have tights-clad geek fantasies vaulted to the pinna-   9
cle of Mediapolis at this moment in history? And how to
explain their superhuman resonance and longevity in a culture
with the attention span of a newt?

For one thing, the caped crusaders have a great pedigree.   10
"The familiarity and built-in nostalgia of superheroes makes
them a relatively safe bet in an increasingly risk-averse studio
system," said David Cook, author of *A History of Narrative Film*
and director of film studies at Emory University.

"These stories are presold," Cook says. "There's a public out   11
there that is already familiar with the narrative and characters.

More and more, Hollywood tends to recycle and borrow icons from popular culture. They ran out of ideas 50 years ago."

12   Though a few superhero movies have bombed recently (*Catwoman* and *Elektra* come to mind), the two *Spider-Man* and *X-Men* films seem to have cured producers of their qualms about the genre after the Batman sequels went bust in the early '90s.

13   Another reason for the proliferation of super-films now is simply that technology is catching up to subject matter. With the evolution of computer animation, directors are finally able to realistically simulate the fantastic feats that comic artists dreamed up on pulp. . . .

14   At the same time, the super stunts have grown extraordinarily realistic and engaging in the past few years. Seeing Spider-Man swing convincingly through the real-life canyons of Manhattan certainly wows children, but it also satisfies a deep-seated desire of many adults to see how the movie version of their favorite superhero stacks up with the image that has been locked inside their heads since their comics-reading childhood.

15   That ability to cross generational lines is a large part of why superhero movies do so well when done right. Thanks to the repeat showings made possible by videos and DVD, children's movies have become one of the primary vehicles by which children and parents bond. Watching superhero movies together, the kids get to dream about being more powerful than Mom and Dad, and the parents get to laugh at the inside jokes while resampling the joys of their own childhoods.

16   Four of the five most lucrative movies of 2004 were nominally children's movies: *Spider-Man 2, The Incredibles, Shrek 2* and *Harry Potter and the Prisoner of Azkaban*. Together they made more than $1.3 billion at the box office worldwide. . . .

17   Many of the shapers of pop culture today were weaned on Marvel Comics, which enjoyed its heyday 40 years ago when Spider-Man, the X-Men, the Fantastic Four and the Incredible Hulk all came into being.

18   "You have no idea how many closet comics lovers there are," says Avi Arad, president of Marvel Studios.

19   "The thing about comics and graphic novels, they're ready-made storyboards for movies," says Cook. "They lend themselves incredibly well to filmic adaptation.". . .

Few in Hollywood turn up their noses at superhero films   20
these days. Christian Bale, not yet a major star, is this season's
Bruce Wayne in *Batman Begins*—but that movie will also feature Academy Award winner Michael Caine and Oscar nomi-
nees Morgan Freeman and Liam Neeson, as well as director
Christopher Nolan (*Memento*). Kevin Spacey has signed on to
be Lex Luthor in *Superman Returns*, and British actor Ioan
Gruffudd, the lead in A&E's *Horatio Hornblower* films, is Mr.
Fantastic in *Fantastic Four* this summer.

Well-regarded filmmakers, Quentin Tarantino, Robert   21
Rodriguez and Bryan Singer among them, have used comic
books as source material in recent work. Kevin Smith, director
of *Clerks* and *Jay and Silent Bob Strike Back*, is writing and producing the upcoming *Green Hornet*. Michael Chabon, the novelist who won a Pulitzer Prize in 2001 for *The Amazing
Adventures of Kavalier and Clay*, his fictionalized history of the
birth of the superhero, co-wrote the screenplay for last year's
Spider-Man 2. . . .

Jones thinks superhero fans have helped trigger a huge shift   22
in how popular culture is created. "This geek-nerd culture that
they were part of really has taken over as the shaping, dominant force in pop culture," he says.

These fans have erected an entire industry of consumer mass-   23
market fantasy. Comic-book characters are being converted not
just into movies but into entertainment franchises, replete with
profitable tie-ins such as video games, computer games, toys,
action figures and costumes. Related comic books and graphic
novels also get a bump when a superhero movie succeeds. . . .

Superhero Web sites such as SuperheroHype.com,   24
Efavata.com and SuperheroTimes.com keep the fan base
stoked, tracking all the latest developments in the world of
comic books and superheroes. A popular new Internet game,
City of Heroes, even allows players to create their own superheroes and do battle against each other in cyberspace.

Reality TV is next on the bandwagon. This month MTV will   25
start producing *Who Wants to be a Superhero?*, a show in which
contestants will dress, act and compete as superheroes against
other wannabe superheroes and an assortment of stock villains.
The grand prize winner's invented character will be published
in a comic book. . . .

26   But there may be something deeper afoot. During the past century, Americans often turned to superheroes as an escape in times of national jitteriness. The comic book *Superman* made its debut in 1938, as war clouds were gathering over Europe. Within five years of Action Comics No. 1, 90 percent of kids were reading superhero comic books, which enjoyed a kind of golden age during World War II.

27   "The desire for some big, bright escape that had something to do with fighting off big, bad scary things was a big part of that," Jones says.

28   Superheroes nearly disappeared from pop culture after the war, but reemerged in a new, more morally complicated way during the Vietnam War. The Marvel superheroes who made their debuts in the '60s often found they did more harm than good with their powers.

29   Spider-Man, the Hulk and Daredevil "were real people first, acting in real places, like New York and Brooklyn," and dealing with real-world problems, Quesada says. "Their alter egos became the real story."

30   And now, as we wring our hands over Iraq and terrorism, America's superheroes have arrived en masse on movie screens. . . .

31   Rainer points out that Hollywood has always been evasive about portraying what's going on in the real world—in real time—when it's grim news. Hardly any movies during Vietnam were directly about Vietnam. Instead, movies deal with the violence and anxiety of such periods in code. "This is how Hollywood talks about Iraq: with superheroes," he says.

32   Superheroes are experiencing something more than just a new round of popularity, however. They've evolved into much more complex and ambiguous beings in recent movies. They're being taken seriously by critics, directors and scholars as a unique American storytelling form.

33   "The cruel irony is that these superheroes are more complicated than many real actors in live action movies today," Rainer says. "They have more shades of feeling, and there is tremendous psychic conflict that they come out of."

34   *X-Men* was really a story about prejudice, substituting mutants as the persecuted and cast-out minority. Ang Lee, the director of *Sense and Sensibility* and *The Ice Storm*, made *Hulk*

(2003), a story about the wounds that egomaniacal parents can inflict on their children. And on one level, *The Incredibles* was a meditation on midlife crises.

In his book *Superman on the Couch*, Danny Fingeroth identi- 35 fies several different mythological archetypes in superhero movies, such as the angry young man (Wolverine of *X-Men*), the avenging orphan (Batman), the dual personality (Super- man) and the empowered Amazon (Wonder Woman).

Other countries, too, have superheroes—Turkey, in particu- 36 lar, has a love affair with low-budget superhero movies, and Japan prints millions more comic books a year than does the United States. But most foreign-born heroes are derivative of America's. It's here that they started and here that they main- tain their strongest pull.

Arad makes an analogy to jazz, which was once regarded by 37 cultural arbiters as junk music but gained acceptance and cachet over time until it achieved a reputation as one of Amer- ica's most original art forms. "Superheroes are the jazz of art history," Arad says.

Still, their metamorphosis into icons wouldn't have happened 38 if they hadn't touched some primal nerves from the get-go.

Fingeroth, Jones, Cook, and others speculate that we're 39 drawn to superheroes because they tap strongly felt emotions clustered around helplessness, identity issues, and an ancient ache to connect to something more powerful, higher and nobler. . . .

Superheroes also express our "hope (and fear) that there 40 may be more to this world than what we see," Fingeroth writes in *Superman on the Couch*. Religion taps the same yearning, in a different, more serious and ritualistic way.

Jerry Siegel created Superman when he was in his late teens, 41 a time when a person's limitations are keenly felt in contrast to his powers. Siegel may have felt the helplessness that results from that power gap more than others. In *Men of Tomorrow*, Jones reveals that just a few years before Siegel and his artist/partner Joe Shuster committed their first Superman sto- ries and sketches to paper, Siegel's father had been shot and killed in his Cleveland haberdashery. It was a crime that was never solved, and an incident Siegel never talked about pub- licly the rest of his life.

42   Instead he created a bulletproof father figure who brought the bad guys to justice over and over again. What Siegel gave us was a playful format for the expression of a very painful and universal human frustration.

43   Siegel's creation of the first superhero didn't provide him the kind of catharsis and pleasure he brought to so many others, until very late in his life. Shortly after Superman first appeared, Siegel and Shuster sold the rights to their invention for $130. For 40 years they received none of the royalties that accrued to America's most popular fictional character.

44   It was the movies that finally brought Siegel a measure of vindication. In 1975, when he heard that Warner Bros. was paying $3 million for the rights to film *Superman* and he wasn't getting a penny, Siegel began a full-out public campaign for better compensation, reviving efforts to settle a lawsuit that had languished for a decade.

45   The press soon picked up the story, which touched a nerve in a public fed up with corporate scandals and Watergate. The pressure built until Warner Bros. and DC Comics decided it was best to clear the decks of the Siegel lawsuit before the movie opened.

46   On Dec. 19, 1975, Siegel and Shuster received a settlement of more than $20,000 a year for life. More important, they were promised credit as the creators of Superman on all printed matter, TV and movies in perpetuity. When *Superman Returns* comes out next year, at some point the screen will announce: "The character of Superman was created by Jerry Siegel and Joe Shuster."

Expanding Vocabulary

Match each word in column A with its definition in column B. When in doubt, first find the word in the essay and look for context clues to aid your understanding of the word's meaning. Then, if necessary, use your dictionary to complete the matching exercise. The number in parentheses is the number of the paragraph in which the word appears.

Column A	*Column B*
icon (8)	continuance, powerful influence
genre (8)	anxieties, doubts
pinnacle (9)	businesses
resonance (9)	altogether
pedigree (10)	those judging, deciding

nostalgia (10)
qualms (12)
proliferation (13)
franchises (23)
en masse (30)
evasive (31)
egomaniacal (34)
arbiters (37)
cachet (37)
catharsis (43)

illustrative history
mark of distinction
image or representation
excessively focused on the self
purging of painful memories
type or category, often applied to
    literary types
intentionally vague
bittersweet longing for the past
highest point
extensive increase

Understanding Content

1. What is Bzdek's subject?
2. What is the source of most film superheroes?
3. How successful have the superhero movies been?
4. What reasons does the author give for these films' current popularity? Be able to state each reason in your own words.
5. Explain the concept of the "primal nerves" that superheroes touch in us.

Drawing Inferences about Thesis and Purpose

1. What is Bzdek's primary purpose in writing? What additional purpose does he have? (See paragraph 9.)
2. Write a thesis statement for the essay that includes both purposes.

Analyzing Strategies and Style

1. A good use of examples, we've said, means having "enough" and making them relevant to the support of the thesis. Does the author succeed in providing enough appropriate examples to develop and support his ideas? What is one good lesson you can learn from Bzdek?
2. Bzdek also presents the views of various people in the film or comic business. How does this strategy add to his essay?
3. Find three examples of clever or amusing word choice in the essay and explain why you have made your choice.

Thinking Critically

1. Many cultures of the past have stories about heroes. Why do you think humans feel a need to create such tales? Has Bzdek given you some increased insight into the causes? Explain.

2. There are many interesting studies of "the hero," the traits, experiences, and goals necessary to get the label. See what you can find in your library's book or periodicals collection or on the Internet to help you define the hero. How well does your definition fit the superheroes of comics and film mentioned by Bzdek?
3. Suppose someone said to you that these films are silly children's fluff. How would you respond to that comment?

A Date to Remember

LISA MUNDY

Lisa Mundy holds a master's degree in English literature from the University of Virginia and is a staff writer and columnist for the *Washington Post*. The following column, appearing in the paper's Sunday magazine on July 14, 2002, offers a thoughtful analysis of our times.

Questions to Guide Your Reading and Reflection

1. There are many dates to remember. After reading the essay's title, what date did you expect to read about? Were you correct in your expectation?
2. What do you remember about 9/11?

Photo: Brian Noyes

There's a Web site now that shows you how to fold the new   1
$20 bill to create a strange little origami construction that
depicts, on one side, a scene that looks uncannily like the World
Trade Center on fire and, on the other, one that resembles the
Pentagon with flames coming out of the center. The site, www.
allbrevard.net, makes much of what it calls the "amazing $20
bill 9/11 coincidence," and goes on to explore any number of
insane conspiracy theories, such as whether the U.S. government planned the attacks, whether it means anything that you
can also fold the $50 bill to depict a *plume of smoke*, etc. Pre-
dictably, responders to the site alternately glom onto these
nutty ideas or excoriate the site for using them to sell its own
Web-hosting service. Me, I was struck by something else; the
way "9/11" has entered our consciousness to the point when
even on a site clearly meant to appeal to the stupidest among
us, it needs no explanation. The numbers are there. Nine,
Eleven. We know instantly what they signify.

Up to now, there was no event in American history that we   2
designated digitally, if you will, by lining numerals up in a row.
Many people continue to say "September 11" it's true, and
somehow using the word, like that, seems more formal, possibly more sad. But many others use the short form, without
intending any disrespect. There are any number of Web sites
and relief funds for the "victims of 9/11"; and just the other
day Sen. Charles Schumer of New York used the short version
in a Senate hearing, pointing out that "before 9/11, the FBI's
computers were less sophisticated than the one I bought for my
son for $1,400."

Up to now, the signal events of our history were known,   3
more often than not, by place names. Pearl Harbor is the analogy everybody thought of when the attacks happened; the
worst disaster the nation had known will be forever associated
with a lyrically named spot in Hawaii, the very name of which
conjures up images of horrified Americans hearing the news by
radio, sailors tapping vainly on their ship's hull for days, it is
said, before they died. It's synecdoche, the part standing for the
whole, and it's how we have always remembered our major
military events. Bunker Hill, Valley Forge, Gettysburg, Little
Big Horn: Great and terrible moments have traditionally been
evoked by the places where they happened, here and, often,

around the world. Historically, battles are known by names like Hastings, Gallipoli, the Somme; treaties by names like Yalta; trials by names like Nuremberg; assassinations by names like Dallas, a word that connotes not only the shooting of a president but the end of a national innocence. Why did we not adopt, similarly, a place name for the national innocence that ended last fall? Was it because it happened in planes, in the air, everywhere and nowhere?

4   I think that's part of it. This was an assault with a strangely un-regional quality; despite the intensity with which the attacks were felt in New York and Washington, they were also experienced by those watching, live, on television. All of America was the target. The attack happened on a single day, a singular day, a day that shocked us not only with the attacks themselves but with the sudden recognition that the forces that caused them had been gathering, unknown to most of us, for a long time. In the same way, those relatively few historical events that are remembered by their dates—July 4th, Cinco de Mayo, Juneteenth—are days when something that had been coming for a long time happened; the social order had been changing, but now the change burst into the open. Nine-eleven is the dark opposite of those celebratory occasions. It's the dark opposite of D-Day, too, another event we remember as just that, a day, its name evocative of the operational codes of World War II and the military determination of an era.

5   In the same way, the phrase "9/11" evokes something about our own era. We would never refer to Independence Day as 7/4; that would seem anachronistic. But 9/11 fits. We are all digital thinkers now, accustomed to looking at our calendars, our watches, and seeing numerals. Granted, there is some especially odd thing about these numerals; it *is* weird that 911 is what people punched on their cell phones, often in vain, to seek help that day. There's significance in numbers, menace in numbers. It's a ridiculous stretch when one *allbrevard.net* link points out that 9 + 11 = 20 ($20, get it?), but serious counterterrorism people have actually studied these numbers to see if there really is a pattern, a portent. Numbers involve ancient superstitions and modern habits. So do terrorists. Nine-eleven was a disaster born of an old evil, an old hatred, but one that could have happened only in the communication age, when

terrorists can hook up using satellite phones and e-mail accounts and synchronized Casio watches. Funny how 9/11 exactly expresses all that: the menace, the placelessness, the precision of time. Like the event itself, our use of numbers to describe what happened signifies that something about us, and the way we think, has changed, possibly forever.

Expanding Vocabulary

Examine the following words in their contexts in the essay and then write a brief definition or synonym for each one. Do not use a dictionary. Try to guess the word's meaning from its context. The number in parentheses is the number of the paragraph in which the word appears.

origami (1)	evocative (4)
glom (1)	anachronistic (5)
excoriate (1)	portent (5)
synecdoche (3)	

Understanding Content

1. How have we traditionally referred to important moments in our history?
2. What is characteristic of the few events remembered by their dates?
3. What is different about our use of "9/11"?
4. In the author's view, how does the use of "9/11" fit our times?

Drawing Inferences about Thesis and Purpose

1. Mundy asserts that 9/11 is an event that could have happened only in our communications age. Why is that?
2. What is the author's purpose in writing? What does she want us to understand about our times?

Analyzing Strategies and Style

1. What does the photograph depicting the image on the website contribute to the essay?
2. In her opening paragraph, Mundy rather strongly ridicules the website and comments of those who responded to it. What does she accomplish by that?
3. What do her place-name examples have in common? (Look at the details she gives about them.) How does her discussion of these events contribute to the tone of her essay?

4. Identify all examples of places in paragraph 3. Identify the events noted by dates in paragraph 4.

Thinking Critically

1. Mundy asserts that "numbers involve ancient superstitions and modern habits." What numbers are connected to superstitions? If you don't have much knowledge of numbers with special meanings, you may want to do some research on this interesting topic.
2. Do you think that 9/11 has changed "the way we think," "possibly forever"? Why or why not?
3. Is it troubling, in any way, to consider that a digital "shorthand" represents our times?

STUDENT ESSAY—USING EXAMPLES

RAP'S REFUSAL OF INJUSTICE
Michael King

The caustic manner in which rap music questions its surroundings provides most critics with a dilemma: does one focus on the negative or the positive qualities of the genre? Rap's frequent revelry in misogyny, homophobia, and violence blunts its virtues, and its preoccupation with the rejection of contemporary paradigms rather than a synthesis of new and old ideas has hindered progress in dialogues about race. Still, for all of its bravado, hip-hop's move away from the overly didactic writing of the civil rights era and into a period of angry rejection is the inevitable reaction to continued inequality. The

Introduction recognizes negative attitudes toward rap.

rage found in rap music is a reaction to continued injustice and a means of empowerment. It is, therefore, politically significant.

Opening paragraph moves to a thesis statement.

Unfortunately, the dynamic nature of rap music makes defining its political importance a challenge. While today's better rap groups continue to reflect the rage associated with inequality, one risks generalizing by placing every group into one category. However, three groups stand out for their use of rage as a political tool. Although their expression of rage differed, Public Enemy, N.W.A., and Scarface have become archetypal rather than stereotypical, representing the best rap has to offer.

Transitional paragraph introduces the three examples.

Formed somewhere between the Black Nationalist movement of the seventies and New York's economic collapse in the eighties, Public Enemy's sonic and political rage moved hip-hop from a benign oddity to a force that uprooted the cultural norms of the time. Labeled by many critics as hateful, Public Enemy's refusal to accept the superficial truce between the haves and have-nots represented not only a move away from white America but moderate black America as well. In Public Enemy's world, middle

First example: Public Enemy

class values, the de facto norms of American culture, were tantamount to racism. Their support of former Black Panther and political exile Assata Shakur on "Rebel Without a Pause" and their vilification of both Elvis and John Wayne in the group's best known song, "Fight the Power," successfully redefined the cultural heroes of the time, giving both black and white youth a new, more culturally diverse value system. Similarly, their song, "Black Steel in the Hour of Chaos," dealing with the imprisonment and eventual escape of a black war objector, jettisoned the values rooted in America's white hierarchy, while the group's support of Minister Farrakhan in "Bring the Noise" implicitly rejected the goal of integration of the more moderate civil rights leaders.

Three songs by Public Enemy analyzed.

While Public Enemy searched for ideological empowerment, N.W.A.'s first album, *Straight Out of Compton*, took a more visceral but nonetheless important stand against injustice. At first glance, the group's brand of reaction seemed to be little more than violent hedonism, a juvenile reaction to a complex problem, but the group's behavior represented an important shift in approach. N.W.A.

Second example: NWA

First album and two songs analyzed

removed the shackles of propriety and rooted its raps in both the language and reality of ghettos across the country. Even the title of their album suggested a geographical context, and in doing so, N.W.A. identified with the residents of Compton. Seemingly unredeemable songs like "Gangsta Gangsta" found solace in its populist approach to empowerment. No longer were communities like Compton places for their residents to be embarrassed about; instead "Gangsta Gangsta" insisted that Compton, long ignored by politicians and citizens alike, must redefine their goals and produce their own—albeit equally corrupt—brand of success. In confronting police brutality in their most controversial song, "_ _ _ _ Tha Police," the group further defied cultural norms by outlining the tension between minorities and police. Justice, the song cried, was not found behind a badge, and with each chorus sung, "_ _ _ _ Tha Police" warned of the impending 1992 L.A. riots.

Perhaps the most worrisome rapper of the nineties, Houston's Scarface became the most easily made case for censorship. His vivid tales of murder and violence were not without redemption. His

Third example introduced.

exploration of psychological desperation revealed a source for the rage first articulated by N.W.A., and through shocking detail exposed the humanity of violence. "Diary of a Madman," his first solo effort, presented listeners with a character so void of opportunity that he descends into madness. Confessional in nature, the song served as both an apologetic exploration of insanity and a critique of the opportunities presented to the poor. Similarly, "I Seen a Man Die" expanded the theme developed in "Diary of a Madman," producing a more sophisticated analysis of desperation. Unlike previous gangsta rap songs that removed the ugliness of violence, "I Seen a Man Die" forced listeners to confront the victim, making it impossible to romanticize the act, and refusing the larger paradigm of remorseless murderers. Ultimately, Scarface's success lay in his ability to show not only the consequences of violence but also the consequences of inequality.

Two songs analyzed.

With seventeen years since the release of both Public Enemy's *It Takes a Nation of Millions to Hold Us Back* and N.W.A.'s *Straight Out of Compton*, and thirteen years since the release of Scarface's first solo effort, rap music's relevance

Conclusion reminds readers of the three examples of rap artists and restates the essay's thesis.

continues to rest in its ability to
reflect the cultural disconnects found in
race, economics, age, and ideology.
Whether one finds rap's presentation
depraved or acceptable, the insights provided in the music are essential to
understanding the community that
embraces the music.

MAKING CONNECTIONS

---

1. An ongoing topic of debate is violence in the media, whether in song lyrics or the movies. Because children and teenagers are big listeners and watchers, they are growing up exposed to a considerable amount of violence. Of course, fairy tales also contain much violence, but some experts believe that their violence is healthy for children. Are there different kinds or levels of violence? Should distinctions be made, and some kinds of violence banned or available to adults only? Consider the examples the writers in this chapter use and those you know, and then try to define the kinds of violence that may be tolerated and the kinds that should be controlled in some way. To aid your reflection, find some statistics on violence in the media. Explore essays in electronic databases in your library or do an online search.
2. If violence in lyrics and on television should be controlled, who should do the controlling? Is the task one for parents, for education through the schools and TV, for voluntary control by the media, for federal guidelines and restrictions? Decide on the approaches you would take if you were "media czar."
3. McGarvey, Barras, Steele, and Prior are stating or implying the power of the media. The media create images that sanction the dress, language, and behavior presented in those images. And children are not the only ones influenced by those images, as McGarvey's experience demonstrates.

How should children be instructed to understand the media, especially television, movies, and advertising, so that they can distinguish between image and reality? Consider the suggestions stated or implied in this chapter and reflect on other possibilities as well.

4. Marcus Prior reminds us that the news—in print and on TV—can be quite biased. How can we know who is accurate and reliable? Think about strategies readers can use to guide their reading of both print and websites, and of their listening to TV news.

5. Studies show that TV programs are filled with stereotypes. What about advertising? Conduct an online search to see what you can learn about stereotyping in print or TV ads, or in television shows. Search with keywords such as "advertising and stereotyping." One useful site to visit is: *http://www.media-awareness.ca.*

TOPICS FOR WRITING

1. What makes your favorite type of television program so good, or what makes your least favorite type of program so bad? Do you most enjoy (or least enjoy) watching news, sports, sitcoms, soaps, a movie channel? Select your most (or least) favorite type and then support a thesis with specific examples from particular shows.

2. The columnist George Will has described the names of some foods as "printed noise." (Think of the names of ice cream flavors, for example.) Are there other words or pictures that should be labeled verbal or visual litter—words or pictures that are silly, inaccurate, overstated, childish? Think about product commercials; political advertising; repeated coverage of particular issues in the media; repeated "lectures" from teachers, parents, friends that you now simply tune out.

3. Examine current political campaigns to see whether any use negative advertising that distorts the issues and misleads voters. For evidence, listen to radio and TV ads for specific examples with which to develop your essay. Your

thesis will be that the _____ campaign uses misleading negative tactics, or the _____ campaign uses only fair and accurate campaign tactics.

4. Shelby Steele is concerned about violence in song lyrics and in the lives of rap musicians. Are you? Examine examples of lyrics and/or TV images (e.g., MTV videos), decide on your point of view, and then support it.

5. Do you watch "live" TV shows—game shows, talk shows, competitions, survivor shows? If so, reflect on what these shows have in common and what attracts viewers to them. Develop and support a thesis about "live" TV.

6. When a product's name is clever, that name becomes an ongoing advertisement for the product. Many product names are highly connotative or suggestive, such as Lestoil cleaner. Think about the names used for one type of product, such as cleaning materials, perfumes, diet foods, or cigarettes. (You may want to explore your favorite grocery store or shopping mall for ideas.) In an essay, explain the effects of the various product names, grouping the names by their different effects (their purpose or the desired impact on buyers), and illustrate those effects with specific examples. You probably need at least ten specific items (e.g., White Shoulders) in the product category (e.g., perfumes).

7. Writing fables or parables to make a point about human character traits or about morality can be fun. Try writing one to make some point about advertising or about what motivates humans to buy particular products. Think, for example, about the many different car models—what types of people are drawn to each model—or the array of sports equipment or kinds of drinks. When planning your story, follow these guidelines: (a) keep your story short, no more than two or three pages; (b) make it a story—not an essay—with characters, dialogue, and a sequence of events; (c) remember that characters do not have to be human; (d) fill your story with specific details; (e) avoid any direct statement of your story's point; (f) consider using humor as a way to imply your point.

A CHECKLIST FOR ESSAYS USING EXAMPLES

Inventing

☐ Have I selected a topic consistent with the instructor's guidelines for this assignment?

☐ Have I chosen among the possible topics one that fits my knowledge and experience?

☐ Have I reflected on the topic to write a tentative thesis that invites the use of examples for support?

☐ Have I generated a good list of possible examples to use?

☐ Have I given thought to a meaningful order in which to introduce each example?

Drafting

☐ Have I succeeded in completing a first draft at one sitting so that I can "see" the whole?

☐ Do I have enough—enough to meet assignment demands and enough to develop and support my thesis? If not, do I need new paragraphs or more examples or reflection within paragraphs?

☐ Have I explained *how* the examples support my thesis?

☐ Does the order work? If not, what needs to be moved—and where?

☐ Am I satisfied with the way I have expressed the insights to be gained? Have I been too heavy-handed with a message?

Revising

☐ Have I made any needed additions, deletions, or changes in order based on answering the questions about my draft?

☐ Have I revised my draft to produce coherent paragraphs, using transition and connecting words that reveal my use of several examples?

Polishing

☐ Have I eliminated wordiness and clichés?

☐ Have I avoided or removed any discriminatory language?

☐ Have I used my word processor's spell check and proofread a printed copy with great care?

☐ Do I have an appropriate and interesting title?

6

Using Process Analysis
How We Work and Play

How does it work? How do we do it? How did it happen? These questions are answered when you provide a process analysis. You live with process analysis every day. The directions to the library that you give to a visitor, the mechanic's explanation of how your car engine is supposed to be working, your history text's account of the planning and execution of the D-Day invasion of Normandy, the biology instructor's explanation of the steps to follow in dissecting a frog: All of these directions, accounts, and instructions are examples of process analysis.

When to Use Process Analysis

The label "process analysis" tells us about this kind of writing. It is, first, *process* because we are talking about an activity or procedure that takes us from one situation to another, that results in some change, some goal reached. You follow the instructions on the recipe card to produce the desired carrot cake, or on the box to put together the new bookcase. You listen to the instructor's guidelines carefully so that you will end with a properly dissected frog. Process is also a type of *analysis* because the good writer of process breaks down the activity into a clear series of steps or stages. Getting the steps in a process right—absolutely right!—is essential. You have come to value the person who gives clear directions, the instructor whose guidelines help you through the stages that shaped an important period in history. You value those who write process analyses well because you have probably experienced more than one occasion of frustration over directions that were unclear, incomplete, or just plain wrong. When you have a topic that can most logically be developed as steps or stages in a process, then you will want to be one of those writers who presents the steps or stages clearly and completely for your readers.

How to Use Process Analysis

To write a clear, effective process analysis you need to keep several points in mind. First, when you are assigned a process analysis—or, more accurately, topics that can best be developed by using process analysis—you are not writing a *list* of instructions. You are writing an essay. This means that you must begin the way you begin any essay—with decisions about audience and purpose. You would not give the same directions for using a camera to a fifth-grade class that you would give to an advanced photography class at an adult education center. Similarly, when planning a process essay, you must assess your readers' knowledge of the subject as a basis for deciding how much background information and explanation are appropriate. These are really two separate decisions. One answers the question: Where do I start? The other answers the question: How detailed is my discussion of each step or stage in the process? Many "how-to" books are not really written for beginners, as you may have discovered. Instead, the author assumes more background than the beginner has.

When the process is complex, the writing challenge lies in giving sufficient explanation of each step so that readers are not too confused with step one to comprehend step two. Unless you are given an assignment that calls for a particular audience, think of directing your essays to a general adult audience made up of people like your classmates. Few of them are likely to be as knowledgeable as you are about a topic you select for your process analysis. When planning the essay, take time to include the background and explanations needed by readers who probably don't have your knowledge and expertise.

The good essay is not only directed to a clearly defined audience; it is also unified around a clear thesis. In those instructions with the bookcase pieces, the implied thesis is: If you follow these directions you will put the bookcase together correctly. In a process essay, the thesis extends beyond the completing of the process. You must ask yourself why a reader should be interested in learning about the process topic you have selected. Ernest Hemingway wants to keep inexperienced campers from having so miserable a time that they will swear never to camp again. John Aigner explains a process for preparing for a job interview so that readers will be able to do well in their interviews and get the job.

Finally, the good essay is the interesting essay. The *HTML for Dummies* manual doesn't have to be interesting; it just has to be clear so that the computer user can complete the desired documents. But the essay, whatever its purpose or organizational strategy, needs to engage its reader, to make an audience for itself through clear explanations and interesting details. Be sure to guide your reader through the time sequence that is your basic organizational strategy. Search for transitions that are more lively than "the first step," "the second step," and so on. Here are some transition words that often appear in process essays:

after	following	second	before
later	next	then	finally
last	now	when	

In addition, when you present each step or stage, provide vivid details and concrete examples. Hemingway does not tell us in general terms to fry in the frying pan and boil in the kettle. He prepares trout and pancakes and macaroni, and an apple pie. The reader, mouth watering, is ready to start packing. Make your analysis right, make it clear, but, above all, make it interesting.

WRITING FOCUS
PUNCTUATING PROPERLY

When you punctuate sentences properly, you show readers how the parts connect and what groups of words go together. Incorrect punctuation can confuse readers—and sometimes create unintended humor. There are many rules, but only a handful cover most situations. Here they are.

1. Use commas to separate items in a series.
  Winston Churchill spoke of blood, sweat, toil, and tears.

It was Mario's idea, Ruth's organization, and Brian's technical skill that produced the winning project.

2. **Use commas to separate adjectives modifying the same noun.**

The frisky, black, floppy-eared spaniel trotted next to her youthful, happy owner.

3. **Use a comma to set off lengthy introductory phrases and clauses.**

Struggling to get his sentences punctuated properly, the student carefully reviewed the rules.

Although the deli's sandwiches are just okay, its pizza is really good.

Avoid using commas to set off short introductory elements.

No: Yesterday, a little, old lady bought a new, red Miata.

4. **Use commas to set off parenthetical material, or interrupters.**

Chuck, who is lazy, will lose his job.

Do not set off restrictive material:

Workers who are lazy will lose their jobs.

5. **Use a comma with a coordinating conjunction (and, or, but, for, nor, yet, so) to separate two independent clauses. (Independent clauses can stand alone as complete sentences.)**

Some say Woods is the greatest golfer ever, but others argue that the honor still goes to Nicklaus.

6. **Use a semicolon (NOT a comma) to separate two independent clauses not joined with a coordinating conjunction.**

Some say Woods is the greatest golfer ever; others argue that the honor still goes to Nicklaus.

7. **DO NOT use a comma between compound words or phrases.**

The boat sailed out of the cove⊙and into the bay.

The football team trotted onto the field⊙ and prepared for the opening kickoff.

8. **Use a comma to prevent misreading.**

Inside, the church was dimly lit.

While the dog ate, the cat hid under the sofa.

Getting Started: Reflections on Your Favorite Game

If you were going to teach some element of your favorite game or sport to a beginner, how would you break down the element into steps to be taught in sequence? For example, if you were to teach the tennis serve, you might go through the following steps: the stance, the toss, the backswing, contact with the ball, and the follow-through. List steps in the process of teaching some movement, play, or strategy in your favorite game. Try this process analysis in your journal or prepare it for class discussion.

Putting Your Job Interview into Rehearsal

JOHN P. AIGNER

A graduate of City College of New York, John Aigner is the founder and president of Network Résumés, a New York City career services firm. Aigner has taught courses for career counselors in addition to running his company, which helps job seekers with the process of finding desired positions. His article on preparing for a job interview was originally published in the *New York Times* on August 16, 1983.

Questions to Guide Your Reading and Reflection

1. What are the three broad steps in preparation for a job interview?
2. Have you rehearsed before interviews or class presentations?

No actor would be so foolish as to walk onto a stage in front   1
of a first-night audience without weeks of rehearsal. Yet every day thousands of job seekers at all stages of their careers walk into interviews without even a minimum of preparation. Hours of effort and expense invested in an effective résumé that successfully obtained the interview are thrown away through lack of preparation.

2   There are three key areas in which preparation can pay big dividends:

- Creating and rehearsing a personal script.
- Developing a "power vocabulary."
- Researching information about the job, company and industry.

3   Creation of a script and a power vocabulary are essentially one-time projects that will likely remain useful with only minor variations throughout a job search. General industry-oriented information also has an extended utility during a search. The gathering of information about the company or opportunity will need to be repeated for each occasion.

4   Persons who might be uncertain about the basic shoulds and shouldn'ts preliminary to successful interviewing—proper dress, on-time arrival, appropriate greeting—might try reading *Sweaty Palms*, by Anthony Medley, or *How to Win in a Job Interview*, by Jason Robertson.

Preparing the Script

5   Devising a strategy for handling difficult questions will enable you to answer them calmly and with confidence. A particularly successful approach is to make a list of the most feared questions (some excellent examples may be found in *How to Turn an Interview Into a Job*, by Jeffrey G. Allen, or *Outinterviewing the Interviewer*, by Steven Merman and John McLaughlin), and prepare a written answer to each. Then record your answers on a cassette, listen to yourself and practice, practice, practice.

6   Be aware that most interviewers cover the same ground, and the same basic questions will appear in most interviews. This makes it relatively simple to prepare your answers. Following are some difficult questions that job-seekers may encounter, with suggestions for answering them:

- "Why did you leave your last job?" or "Why do you want to leave your present job?" Remember to be positive, not defensive. Acceptable answers are: greater opportunity, changing conditions, seeking greater responsibility. The best answers are both honest and brief.
- "Why should we hire you?" You may say that from your research you have learned that the interviewer's company is a leader in your field and you believe that your skills and its needs are well matched.

- "What are your strengths and weaknesses?" For many interviewees this question is the most intimidating. This is where preparation and a positive approach are most rewarding. One of the best ways to deal with a weakness is to refer to it as "an area in which I am working to strengthen my skills." Some career advisers suggest responding with, "Well, I don't really have any major weaknesses, but . . ." This is not a satisfactory answer, and would annoy me if I were the interviewer.

One general rule is never to answer a serious or really diffi- 7
cult question off the top of your head. Ask for an opportunity to think the question over, and promise to get back to the interviewer the next day. This approach has the added benefit of giving you a follow-up, second opportunity to sell yourself.

Have a friend or relative ask you the questions as many 8
times as necessary for you to feel comfortable with the answers. Three to six hours spent practicing in this way will result in greatly improved confidence during interviews. If you think of additional questions later or if an interviewer throws you a curve, you can update your recorded answers.

The interviewer controls the flow of an interview, but the 9
interviewee controls the content. If you know what you want to say, you will be more likely to say it, and you will have provided yourself with a powerful tool to maintain control of even a difficult interview.

The Power Vocabulary

A survey conducted among personnel executives by the 10
Bureau of National Affairs concluded that the interview was the single most important factor in landing a job and that most applicants were rejected because they didn't promote themselves well during the interview. They frequently preface their description of an experience with, "Well, I only . . ." or "That wasn't a major part of my job." By such a deprecating phrase, they devalue their experience.

This lack of confidence about self-promotion is particularly 11
true of women, an American Management Association study has concluded. Men, it seems, have had more practice at competition and are less reticent when it comes to advertising their accomplishments.

You should consider the interviewer to be in the same cate- 12
gory as the tax auditor. He or she is not your friend, and you

are under no obligation to volunteer any information that won't help you. In short, telling the truth and telling everything are not the same thing. If you performed well at a project, such as setting up a computer installation or devising a new method of taking inventory, it is not necessary to volunteer, for example, that the project lasted only a short while. If asked directly, of course answer honestly.

13   The words you select to describe yourself during the interview will have a powerful effect on the outcome. These words can be planned in advance. In the same way that you planned a script for the interview, you can also plan a vocabulary of "power" words that will create an accumulation of positive impressions about you and your accomplishments.

14   Consider this example: "I reduced costs" versus "I trimmed costs." The word "reduce" conjures up a fat person who is trying to lose weight. The word "trim" brings to mind someone who is fit and healthy.

15   Or: "While at company X, I . . ." versus "I am proud of the fact that while at company X, I . . ." The latter approach is much stronger and more positive.

16   Use only positive words, ones that create strong mental images, adjectives such as accurate, dynamic, proficient, reliable, thorough, and verbs such as expedite, generate, improve, motivate, persuade, solve. These descriptors will add spice if you pepper your interview with them.

17   You can learn to develop a winning interview style by selecting ten winning words each week and writing them on index cards. Practice using them in sentences about yourself, using one word per sentence. Select words with which you feel comfortable and work them into phrases within your script. You'll quickly discover that these words affect your self-image and the image that others have of you.

18   Avoid complaints of any kind. Do not criticize your previous company, supervisor or position. A complaint is always negative, and that is not the impression you wish to create.

Gathering Information

19   Valuable information about an industry, and about particular companies within it, can be acquired through a library source

such as Standard & Poor's, or annual reports, or through the trade press. This is an excellent way to learn the jargon of an industry. These special-interest professional and business publications have mushroomed like cable channels, and are frequently overlooked by job seekers because most are not available on newsstands and are not sold to the general public. There are thousands of these publications—privately circulated newsletters, weekly newspapers, slick monthlies, annual directories and everything in between. They contain a wealth of insider information—for example, industrywide trends and concerns, corporate plans, new-product announcements, trade jargon.

A sample copy or even a free subscription is generally available for the asking. To track down the trade press in your industry, check the *Standard Periodical Directory, Gebbe Press All-in-One Directory, The Encyclopedia of Business Information Sources, Ayers Guide to Periodicals* or *Standard Rate and Data*. For articles on particular business subjects, check the *Business Periodicals Index*. 20

Being current on industry concerns in general and company problems in particular can go a long way toward making an interview successful. 21

Expanding Vocabulary

Examine the following words in their contexts in the essay and then write a brief definition or synonym of each one. Do not use a dictionary; try to guess each word's meaning from its context. The number in parentheses is the number of the paragraph in which the word appears.

preliminary (4)	accumulation (13)
intimidating (6)	descriptors (16)
deprecating (10)	jargon (19)
devalue (10)	mushroomed (19)
reticent (11)	

Understanding Content

1. List the specific steps within the first step: preparing the script. Why is it possible to prepare basically one script?
2. List the specific steps for developing a power vocabulary.

3. Why does it help to think of the interviewer as similar to a tax auditor?
4. What is the procedure for gathering information? What are the advantages beyond preparation for a specific interview?

Drawing Inferences about Thesis and Purpose

1. What is Aigner's thesis—what is the point of his process analysis?
2. When advising people on how to sell themselves, one invites the charge of encouraging misrepresentation, of "packaging" the interviewee. How does Aigner seek to avoid this charge? How does he try to balance polishing one's interview skills with a fair presentation of one's qualifications?

Analyzing Strategies and Style

1. What analogy does Aigner use throughout his article? Where does he introduce the comparison? Where does he refer to it again? Is this an effective analogy? Why or why not?
2. Aigner's introduction runs to several paragraphs, but his conclusion is only one paragraph containing one sentence. Does it seem too abrupt to you? Can you make the case that it is an effective ending?
3. Examine Aigner's metaphors in paragraphs 1, 8, and 16. How are they effective? What do they contribute to the article?

Thinking Critically

1. Will you now prepare for an interview in any of the ways Aigner suggests? If so, do you think the process helped you in the interview? If not, would you follow Aigner's steps the next time? Why or why not?
2. Is there one step in Aigner's process that would be especially important in your career field? If so, how would it make you a better interviewee in your career field?
3. Aigner emphasizes the similarity of most job interviews. Had you thought about this point before? Does the idea seem sensible? How can understanding this characteristic of interviews help to make the interview process a little easier?
4. Aigner gives the most space to developing a power vocabulary. Is there some good advice here that extends beyond the interview process? How important are positive attitudes about ourselves?

Improving Your Body Language Skills

SUZETTE H. ELGIN

A professor emeritus in linguistics from San Diego State University, Suzette Elgin is the author of several books on language use, including *Try to Feel It My Way* (1996) and *How to Disagree Without Being Disagreeable* (1997). She has also written several science fiction novels. "Improving Your Body Language Skills" is a section from Elgin's book *Genderspeak* (1997). Here Elgin offers guidelines for finding the most respected way of speaking American English and for understanding the messages in body language.

Questions to Guide Your Reading and Reflection

1. What are the characteristics of the ideal adult voice for American speakers of English?
2. When you speak, what do others "hear" in your voice?

Body language problems between men and women who are speakers of American Mainstream English [AME] today begin at the most basic of nonverbal levels: with the *pitch* of the voice. The admired voice for the AME culture is the adult male voice; the deeper and richer it is, and the less nasal it is, the more it is admired. Women tend to pitch their voices higher than men do, and this is a strike against them in almost every language interaction. Not because there is anything inherently wrong with high-pitched voices, but because AME speakers associate them with children. A high-pitched voice that's also nasal is heard as the voice of a *whiny* child. People know, of course, that they're hearing an adult woman (or, for the occasional man with a high-pitched voice, an adult male). But at a level below conscious awareness they tend to perceive the voice as the voice of a child. This perception, however much it is in conflict with reality, affects their response to and their behavior toward the speaker.

The contrast in voice pitch isn't really a *physiological* matter; the difference between adult male and female vocal tracts is too minor to account for it in the majority of people. In many other cultures, male voices are higher than those of AME-speaking men, although the physical characteristics of the males are the same. When American adults speak to infants, they pitch their voices lower as they talk to boys, and the infants respond in the same way. Females learn, literally in the bassinet and playpen, that they are expected to make higher-pitched sounds than males are.

3   In addition to the difference in baseline pitch, AME-speaking women's voices have more of the quality called *dynamism:* They use more varied pitch levels, they move from one pitch to another more frequently, and they are more likely than men's voices are to move from one pitch to another that's quite a bit higher or lower. In other situations the term "dynamic" is a compliment, while "monotonous," its opposite, is a negative label. But not in language; not in the AME culture. The less monotonous a woman's voice is, the more likely it is that her speech will be described by others as "emotional" or "melo-dramatic." Monotony in the male voice, however, is ordinarily perceived as evidence of strength and stability. (For a detailed discussion of these differences, see McConnell-Ginet 1983.)

4   Certainly male/female body language differences go beyond the voice. There are positions and gestures and facial expressions that are more typical of one gender than of the other. But the effect one gender achieves by learning to use such items of body language from the other gender is rarely positive. A woman who hooks her thumbs into her belt, spreads her feet wide, and juts out her chin usually looks foolish, as does a man who carefully crosses his legs at the ankles. There are a few stereotypically feminine items that reinforce the "childish" perception which a woman can be careful *not* to use, such as giggling behind her hand or batting her eyelashes. But the most useful thing any woman—or man—can do to get rid of the perceptually filtered "I'm listening to a child" effect is to make the voice lower, and less nasal, and more resonant, so that it will be perceived as an *adult* voice.

5   This is something that anyone not handicapped by a physi-cal disability that interferes with voice quality can do. One way to do it is to put yourself in the hands of a competent voice *coach.* If you have the time and money to do that, and you live where such experts are available, that's an excellent idea. On

the other hand, it's also something you can do by yourself, using an ancient technique that in the *Gentle Art* system is called *simultaneous modeling.* . . .

Let me make one thing clear, however, before we go on. I'm not suggesting that anyone, of either gender, "should" try to change the quality of their voice. As is true for many linguistic questions, this is not a moral issue but an issue of cultural fashion. Low voices are not "better" than high voices. In the same way that some people insist on their right to wear jeans in an office where everyone else dresses more formally, people have every right to take the position that the voice they have is the voice they prefer to have. I approve of that, one hundred percent. However, because that decision can have grave consequences, people need to be aware that the consequences exist and that the choice is theirs to make. 6

It's unacceptable for someone to be unaware that the primary reason for his or her communication problems is a high-pitched voice, and to assume that the problems are caused by the lack of a "powerful vocabulary," or a thin enough body, or a sufficiently expensive blazer, or some such thing. It's also unacceptable for those who do realize what the problem is to believe they're helpless to do anything about it. Except in cases requiring medical attention, *anyone*, working alone, can change his or her voice to make it closer to what our culture perceives as the ideal and adult voice. When a medical condition complicates the issue, the potential for improvement may be less, but even limited change toward the ideal can bring about significant positive effects. 7

The facts about body language and its critical importance to communication can be frightening. We don't study body language in school, and few of us are given formal training in the subject. We read everywhere that "a more powerful vocabulary" is our ticket to communication success, and that seems easy— just buy a book or a software program and learn some new words. Improving our body language skills seems mysterious and difficult by contrast. But there's no need to be intimidated; it's simpler than you think. 8

Your internal grammar, the same one that you use to put the right endings on your words and arrange your words in the proper order in your sentences, contains all the rules for body 9 language in your culture. You just haven't had convenient *access* to that information that would let you use it consciously and strategically. The sections that follow will help you establish that access.

Developing Your Observational Skills

10   The first step in developing observational skills for nonverbal communication is simply learning to PAY ATTENTION to the speaker's body and voice. Men in the AME culture tend not to do this, and to be unaware that it matters; when they do pay attention they usually follow a rule that tells them to pay attention only to the speaker's face. Women do somewhat better, not because they have any built-in biological advantage, but because it is universally true that those having less power pay more attention to the body language of those having more power. (In the most primitive situations, this means being alert to the movements of the powerful person so that you will be able to get out of the way before the powerful person grabs or hits you.)

11   This gender difference is well known. In 1975 a footnote in the *Virginia Law Review* suggested that perhaps women should be excluded from jury duty, because their skill at observing and interpreting nonverbal communication might make them excessively vulnerable to body language effects, interfering with the defendant's right to an independent and unbiased jury. ("Notes: Judges' Nonverbal Behavior in Jury Trials: A Threat to Judicial Impartiality," *Virginia Law Review*, 1975, 61:1266–1298. For a review of research and an account of experiments proving that the body language of trial judges has a significant impact on jury decisions, see Blanck et al. 1985.)

12   Sometimes this language skill is an advantage for women; sometimes it's not. Like any other skill, it depends on how it is used. Nobody likes the idea that another person is able to read his or her mind. The woman who expresses in words what a man's body language tells her—with claims such as "I can tell by the look on your face that you don't want to go to St. Louis" or "Don't try to tell me you want to go to St. Louis; the way you keep wiggling your index fingers gives you away every time"—is almost sure to provoke hostility. Such remarks are

equally counterproductive coming from men who have well-developed body language reading skills.

The only way to learn to pay attention to body language is 13 to *practice*. You have to work at it consciously until you become so skilled that you do it automatically, just as you would work at your tennis or your golf or a favorite handicraft. If you're not accustomed to body language observation, you'll find it extremely difficult at first. You'll keep *forgetting* to do it.

You've probably had the experience of "coming to" as you 14 take the last highway exit on your drive home and realizing that you have no memory of your previous ten minutes on the road. In the same way, you'll start out carefully observing someone's body language and then suddenly realize that it's been five minutes since you were consciously aware of anything but the words, and perhaps the facial expression, of the speaker. If you continue to work at it, however, you'll get past this stage. As a first practice partner, I strongly recommend your television set. Unlike living persons, the TV set doesn't get tired, doesn't wonder why you're staring at it, is always available at your convenience, and—best of all—never gets its feelings hurt.

Establishing Baseline Values—and Spotting Deviations from Them—in Body Language

Body language baselines are profiles of people's speech 15 when they're relaxed, as in casual conversations with close friends. Baselines include such information as the typical pitch of the voice, rate of speed for speech, frequency of eyeblink, body posture, number of hand gestures, etc., for the individual you're interacting with, during *relaxed communication*. This information is important because a *deviation* from the baseline—a move away from these typical values—is a signal to be alert. It indicates some sort of emotional involvement, positive or negative; it indicates that something is happening; sometimes it indicates an attempt to deceive or mislead you.

You will have read books or listened to tapes telling you that 16 when you see a person cross his arms or scratch her nose it *means* a particular thing. You'll read that crossed arms signal defensiveness and disagreement with what you're saying; you'll hear that scratching the nose signals anxiety. Sometimes that's true, of course; but much of the time it means the person you're observing is cold or has a nose that itches. When such items *are* reliable, they hold for a restricted population in specific circumstances—usually for the middle class or upper class dominant white male in a business situation. Learning to establish baseline values for the other person and spotting deviations from that baseline is a great deal more reliable, and will be useful to you in every communication situation, including interactions with people from outside your own culture.

17   For example, one of the most reliable clues to anxiety, a lack of sincere commitment to what's being said, and a possible intention to deceive is a change to a higher voice pitch. But you won't know there's been a change unless you have first learned what pitch the speaker uses in normal everyday conversation. The same thing is true for other deviations from baseline values. Here are two simple and practical ways to get the necessary information:

- Make a phone call to the individual in advance of your meeting and discuss something entirely neutral, like how to get to the meeting site.
- When you're with the other person, don't begin by talking about anything important. Instead, spend five minutes—or as long as it takes—making small talk on neutral subjects.

18   Now we can move on to improving your body language *performance* skills, as opposed to observation alone.

Simultaneous Modeling

19   When students learn t'ai chi, they learn not by watching the teacher and then trying out the posture or movement by themselves but by watching and then moving *with* the teacher. This technique has been successful for thousands of years. If you've studied a foreign language, you're familiar with the traditional procedure: Listen to a sequence of the foreign language, and then, during the pause provided, repeat what you've just heard. At the University of California San Diego, instead of repeating the foreign language sequence *after* the recorded model, students listen to it several times to become familiar with the content and then speak simultaneously *with* the model. This technique (developed at UCSD by linguist

Leonard Newmark) consistently produces results far superior to the traditional method. And there are many cultures in which people learn to do things (weaving, for example) by first watching someone who already knows how and then sitting down beside that person and working along with her or him.

These are all examples of *simultaneous modeling*. They take *advantage* of the way human brains work instead of fighting against it. When you change your behavior to make it like someone else's you have to make many small adjustments all over your body, all at once. You can't do that very well *consciously*. But your brain can do it competently and success-fully, if you just stay out of its way. You can use this informa-tion and your brain's built-in skills to improve the quality of your voice, by adapting Newmark's foreign language teaching method.

Changing voice quality requires an array of small but cru-cial adjustments. You have to change the tension of the muscles of your tongue and throat and chest, you have to move the parts of your vocal tract in ways that you're not used to, and so on. When you listen to a foreign language sequence and try to repeat it afterward, you not only have to make all those adjust-ments but you have to *remember* the sequence. The final result is that you change your speech to match the sequence you *remember* instead of the one you actually heard. When you speak *with* the model voice instead of repeating on your own, this doesn't happen. Your brain takes over and does all the adjustments, matching your voice to the model.

Working with the Tape Recorder

You need a tape recorder (an inexpensive one will do), a few blank tapes, and a tape about thirty minutes long by someone of your own gender whose voice sounds the way you'd like to sound. For men, I recommend television anchorman Peter Jen-nings, or one of the male announcers on National Public Radio's regular news programs ("Morning Edition" or "All Things Considered," for example). For women I recommend a tape of Diane Sawyer or one of the female NPR newscasters. If you prefer someone else, either a public figure or someone in your own circle, that's fine. Just be sure the voice you choose as your model is one that you and others perceive as strong,

20

21

22

resonant, pleasant, compelling, and—above all—the voice of a *mature adult*. Then follow the steps below, at your own convenience, at your own speed, and in privacy.

23   1. Make a twenty- to thirty-minute baseline tape of your own speech, write down the date on which it was made, and keep it for comparison with tapes you make later on. Don't read aloud, and don't say something memorized—just talk. Talk about your childhood, or why you have trouble communicating with people of the opposite sex, or anything else you can talk about easily and naturally.

24   2. Listen to the tape you've chosen as a model, all the way through, to get a general idea of its content. Don't write it down, and don't try to memorize it—doing either of those things just gets in the way and keeps you from succeeding.

25   3. Choose a sentence of average length to work with, from any point on the tape. Listen to it a couple of times, to become familiar with it. Then repeat it, SPEAKING ALONG WITH THE TAPE, SIMULTANE-OUSLY. Rewind the tape and do it again, as many times as you feel are necessary—ten times is not in any way unusual. Your goal is to be able to speak smoothly and easily with the model. Don't *struggle*. Trust your brain and let it carry out its functions without interference.

26   4. When you're bored with the sentence you chose, pick another sentence and repeat Step #3. You should also move on whenever you realize that you know a sentence so well that you've stopped needing the model voice; you aren't interested in learning to *recite* the tape. Continue in this way until you've finished the tape or achieved your goal, whichever happens first. (And go on to another model tape if you find that you need one.)

27   5. After about ten hours of practice (and after every additional five or six hours), make a new baseline tape of your own speech. Listen to it, and compare it with the earlier ones. When you're satisfied with the change you hear, STOP. The point of this technique is to improve your *own* voice. You don't want people to think you're doing Peter Jennings or Diane Sawyer imitations when you talk; if you go on too long, that's exactly what will happen.

28   How long this will take will depend on the amount of time you have for practice, how tired you are, whether you are a person who learns well by listening, and other individual factors. Try to make each practice session at least fifteen minutes long;

thirty minutes is even better. Try to practice every other day, roughly. If all you can manage is ten minutes once a week, put in those ten minutes—just be prepared for it to take you much longer to achieve results on that basis. Remember: It doesn't make any difference how long it takes. You're not paying by the hour when you use this technique, and there won't be a final exam. Relax and let it take as long as it takes. Some of my clients have noticed substantial improvement in six weeks; others have needed six months or more for the same results.

The fact that you can't just take a Voice Quality Pill and change   29
instantly is actually a good thing. The people you interact with regularly (and especially the person or persons you live with) need to be able to get used to the change in your voice gradually. You don't want your partner to leave in the morning, accustomed to the voice you've always had, and come home that night to someone who sounds like an entirely different person. A pleasant adult voice is a powerful tool for improving your relationships, but it shouldn't come as a *shock* to those around you.

Note: You can also use this procedure to learn to speak other   30
varieties of English—other dialects or other registers—at will. If you feel that your native accent sometimes holds you back in the American Mainstream English environment, simultaneous modeling is a good way to learn a variety of English that's more helpful. Moving back and forth among varieties—called *codeswitching*—is a valuable skill.

Working with the Television Set

A voice coach (or an "image" coach) may be beyond the   31
financial limits for many of us. It's fortunate that we have our television sets available to use as free coaches. In exactly the same way that you can improve your voice quality by speaking along with a tape recorded model, you can improve the rest of your body language by *moving* simultaneously with a model on videotape. Ideally, you will also have a VCR, so that you can work with a single tape over a period of time. If you have a video camera (or can rent one), to let you make a baseline video of your body language, that's also a plus. But if those items aren't available to you, choose as a model someone of your own gender that you can see on television several times a week, and practice moving simultaneously with that person at

those times. As with voice quality, stop *before* you find yourself doing impersonations of your model.

32   I don't recommend that women try to learn "male body language" by working with a videotape of a male speaker, or that men work with a videotape of a woman to learn "female body language." (The fact that the latter alternative is wildly unlikely outside the entertainment field is consistent with the power relationships in our society.) Cross-gender modeling is a bad idea, full of hidden hazards and boobytraps, and it almost always backfires. If you're gifted with the sort of superb acting ability that would let you do this *well*, like Dustin Hoffman playing the heroine in the movie *Tootsie*, you're not someone who needs improved body language anyway. You will be far more successful with the body language of a strong and competent adult of your own gender.

33   If you believe you have a long way to go in acquiring satisfactory body language skills, if you feel self-conscious trying to acquire them, if your opportunities to practice them are few and far between, by all means rely on the TV set. You can move on to practice with live partners when you feel more at ease.

Expanding Vocabulary

Study the definitions of any of the following words that are unfamiliar to you. Then use each of the words in a separate sentence. The number in parentheses is the number of the paragraph in which the word appears.

perceptually (4)	vulnerable (11)
resonant (4)	boobytraps (32)
intimidated (8)	

Understanding Content

1. What are the characteristics of a "whiny child's" voice?
2. How hard is it to improve body language skills?
3. What is the first step to improving body language skills? What is a good way to practice?
4. What are body language baseline profiles? Why are they useful to establish?
5. How do you establish baseline profiles?
6. What is meant by "simultaneous modeling"? Why does it work well?

7. What can you change using simultaneous modeling?
8. Summarize the process of using a tape recorder to change your voice quality.
9. Summarize the process of working with a TV to improve your body language. What should be your standard to work with?

Drawing Inferences about Thesis and Purpose

1. What is Elgin's position on changing one's voice quality? Should the typical male voice be set as a standard for everyone?
2. What is Elgin's purpose in writing?
3. What is her thesis?

Analyzing Strategies and Style

1. What tone of voice do you "hear" in this essay? Do you respond to the author as a sympathetic teacher? Support your response.
2. Elgin uses italics and even all caps for some words. Why? What do they contribute?

Thinking Critically

1. Have you thought about the idea that the typical male voice is considered standard and that many women are perceived as talking like children? Does the idea make sense to you? Why or why not?
2. Why is it important to develop sensitivity to body-language messages?
3. Do you agree that women tend to be better at this sensitivity than men? Does Elgin's explanation for this tendency make sense? Why or why not?
4. Are you going to tape yourself and examine your voice quality and body language? Why or why not?

How to Get Unstuck Now!

GAIL SALTZ

Dr. Saltz is a psychoanalyst with a private practice; she is also on the faculty of the New York Presbyterian Hospital, is a health contributor to several TV shows, and writes a weekly column on MSNBC.com. Her first book, *Becoming Real: Defeating the*

Stories We Tell Ourselves That Hold Us Back, was published in 2004. *Changing You: A Guide to Body Changes and Sexuality* (2007), a book for parents and children, was written with Lynn Avril Cravath. The following article appeared in *Parade* magazine on March 20, 2005.

Questions to Guide Your Reading and Reflection

1. What kinds of people make up the two groups of procrastinators?
2. Do you ever procrastinate? If so, would you like to get "unstuck"?

1   David looks miserable as he tells me that, once again, he has to pay a late penalty for failing to turn in his taxes on time. He feels angry and guilty that this delay will now cost him the money he was saving for the family vacation. His family and friends have been calling him lazy for years. It seems to him that the harder he tries to "get it right," the worse his procrastinating gets. "It's ruining my relationships and holding me back at work," he says. "Why am I doing this?"

2   Maria, on the other hand, had always gotten things done on time—until she was up for a promotion. Suddenly, this very conscientious woman was late with her assignments. She knew that she was screwing up her chances for advancement yet was baffled as to why she kept doing it.

Who Procrastinates?

3   David is one of the 20 percent of Americans considered "chronic procrastinators." Maria, like the majority of us, is an occasional procrastinator whose repeated delays take place in a particular realm.

4   Almost everyone procrastinates some of the time. The results can range from annoyance to misery—for both the person doing it and those affected by it. Research has shown that procrastinators tend to feel extremely stressed, resulting in more insomnia, colds and stomachaches than nonprocrastinators suffer. In one survey of 300 college students who confessed to being procrastinators, nearly half said they would rather donate blood than write an assigned paper; almost a third said they would rather visit the dentist; and

more than one in five said they would rather pick up trash on campus.

Both men and women suffer from anxiety as a result of pro- 5
crastination. Interestingly, women suffer from guilt as well—
nearly twice as often as men.

Why We Procrastinate

Too often procrastinators receive the advice from profes- 6
sionals or others to just "quit it." Would that it were really that
simple! The idea that procrastinators are simply lazy is a myth,
and their behavior rarely is changed by just deciding to stop.
Laziness might respond to giving yourself a good kick in the
pants. Procrastination doesn't.

Unlike laziness, procrastination is caused by fears—the result 7
of emotional stories that each of us carries around inside us.
Understanding the reasons why you procrastinate ultimately can
change your behavior and your life. To do that, think about what
it means to you to get things done and about the stuff you're
putting off. See which of the following stories resonates with you:

"I'm so afraid of failing that I would rather not try than to 8
try but fail." Fear of failure probably is the most common story.
If that's you, you may be a perfectionist who feels that doing a
"just OK" task is mortifying. These types also believe that they
need to please others in order to be accepted. In the extreme,
they may believe that they are only lovable and worthwhile if
their performance is outstanding.

"I'm afraid to be successful because people will envy me or 9
see me as a threat, and then I'll lose them." Fear of success can
lead to procrastination as well. You may imagine that if you
succeed, you'll then be expected to be wildly successful all the
time, or that you'll become a workaholic, or even that on some
level you'll feel you are not deserving of success. All are common reasons for procrastination.

"I need to be defiant, or they will rule me and win." This too 10
is a common story. If it's yours, you may believe that all of life
is a battle for control. Perhaps you grew up in a home with an
authoritarian parent who was extremely controlling. Sometimes people with this story respond to the whole world as if it
were that parent and seek to passive-aggressively control that
world by procrastinating.

11   "This task holds no interest for me unless it is so last-minute as to be perilous and thrilling." People who say this to themselves generally are chronic procrastinators who, unlike the others, do not appear anxious. They are the thrill-seeking, risk-taking drama lovers. If you are such a procrastinator, you may feel that the daily grind is boring, and boredom is terrifying. Waiting until the last moment lets thrill-seeking procrastinators shake things up by creating their own crisis.

Understanding Your Own Story

12   Figuring out what your fears are is an important first step. So is taking notice of which situations tend to trigger your procrastinating. Is it work, your love life, friends, your body or money? The specific arena of life in which you procrastinate is a clue as to where you feel most conflicted and afraid. That's likely to be the arena that is most important to you at this time.

13   David, the chronically late tax-filer, came to understand that he was afraid of failing. He imagined messing up his taxes, failing at his job and even disappointing his loved ones. So he avoided doing many things in order to spare himself the chance of failure. Eventually, he came to see that he had damaged them all by procrastinating. This understanding helped him to change his behaviors.

14   Maria tapped into her knowledge that her success threatened her competitive husband. Once she understood that, she was able to catch herself delaying her work and to forge ahead. She also was able to discuss the issue with her husband, who ultimately became more supportive.

Break the Pattern

15   These steps can help you (or someone you know) break the pattern of procrastination:

1. **Articulate what you get out of procrastinating.** (Examples: "I avoid risking failure"; "I can't stand to not have fun.") This is what keeps you locked in.
2. **Consider the problems your procrastination creates vs. what you think you get out of it.** (Example: "I like being a victim, but that means I never get ahead in life.")

3. **Start small.** Do the least-noxious task to get yourself rolling. Remind yourself along the way—or enlist someone else to remind you—that the actual cost of not doing it is greater than the imagined fear of getting it done.
4. **Help a procrastinator.** Living or working with a procrastinator can be exasperating. It's easier to be objective about someone else's state of mind than your own. Plus, you aren't being bogged down by anxiety or fear. But rather than blame the procrastinator in your life—which merely perpetuates the cycle of anxiety and delay—describe the story you see him or her acting out. Offer to help break the cycle.

Tackle It Now

- **Prioritize tasks.** If everything seems like a priority, you'll feel overwhelmed and get none of it done. And if nothing seems important, nothing will get done. Create a "to do" list, ranking tasks in order of priority. Marking a specific number of hours to work and to play on your calendar also helps. 16
- **Question your beliefs.** Do you tell yourself that you work better under pressure? Prove it. Do one task at the last minute and one ahead. Test other myths, such as "I don't have the ability" and "It has to be done perfectly."
- **Control your impulsiveness.** Most procrastinators jump from one task to the next and never finish anything. Make yourself complete one task before moving on to another.
- **Old habits die hard.** Don't expect it to change overnight. If you change one thing a week, you are making progress, and that progress will show you that more change is possible.

Expanding Vocabulary

Match each word in column A with its definition in column B. When in doubt, first find the word in the essay and look for context clues to aid your understanding of the word's meaning. Then, if necessary, use your dictionary to complete the matching exercise. The number in parentheses is the number of the paragraph in which the word appears.

Column A	*Column B*
procrastinating (1)	area, part of one's life
conscientious (2)	echoes, makes sense
realm (3)	annoying, frustrating

resonates (7)	steadily push ahead
mortifying (8)	unpleasant, poisonous
perilous (11)	putting off doing something
forge (14)	humiliating
articulate (16)	principled, thorough
noxious (18)	express in words
exasperating (19)	dangerous

Understanding Content

1. What are some consequences of procrastinating?
2. How does procrastination differ from laziness?
3. Explain each of the four "stories" that account for the behavior of most procrastinators.
4. What is the first—and most critical—step toward change? Explain the next four steps in your own words.

Drawing Inferences about Thesis and Purpose

1. Saltz opens with some interesting information about procrastination. What, though, is her primary purpose in writing? What does she want to accomplish?
2. Write a thesis for the essay that indicates that process analysis will be used as a structure for the essay.

Analyzing Strategies and Style

1. What formatting strategies aid the presentation of information? How do they help?
2. The author begins by introducing David and Maria. What does she accomplish with her opening strategy?

Thinking Critically

1. Are you a procrastinator? If so, have you found your "story"? Do you think recognizing the reasons for procrastinating will help a procrastinator change? Why or why not?
2. Saltz writes that many college students said they would rather donate blood or go to the dentist than write a paper. Does this describe your attitude toward writing? Or the attitude of students you know? How can you take Saltz's process steps and apply them specifically to paper assignments? Explain.
3. How important is it to understand the causes of our behavior? Explain.

The Five Stages of Crisis Management

JACK WELCH

The CEO of General Electric from 1981 to 2001, Jack Welch trimmed the bureaucracy at GE, created more informality, fired the weakest managers and rewarded the best, and increased the value of the company manifold during his tenure at the top. In 1999 *Fortune* magazine named him "Manager of the Century." He is the author of three books and co-author, with his wife Suzy Welch, of his latest book *Winning* (2005). His essay in response to Hurricane Katrina appeared in the *Wall Street Journal* on September 14, 2005.

Questions to Guide Your Reading and Reflection

1. Before reading, think about Welch's title. What do you think some of the stages might be?
2. How well do you handle difficult situations in your life?

Our last day in Nantucket this summer, we bumped into a   1
crusty old islander we know, a sea-hand who has seen his share of hurricanes. We asked him about the storm bearing down on New Orleans. "Probably just another overhyped Weather Channel event," he mused. We saw him again the next day, a few hours after the storm's landfall, and he repeated his take, this time with relief. We agreed—the pictures on TV weren't that bad.

Then, of course, the levees broke and all hell broke loose   2
with them.

In the terrible days since then, there has been a hurricane of   3
debate about what went wrong in New Orleans and who is to blame. Mother Nature, perhaps for the first time in the case of a bona fide natural disaster, has been given a pass. Instead, the shouting has been about crisis-management—or the lack thereof. Everyone from President Bush to the police chief in a small parish on the outskirts of the city has been accused of making shockingly bad mistakes and misjudgments. The Katrina crisis, you would think, is unlike any before it.

4   Unfortunately, that's not completely true.

5   Yes, there has never been a natural disaster of Katrina's magnitude in our history. An entire city has been devastated, hundreds of lives lost, and hundreds of thousands of people displaced. In terms of impact, only an extended catastrophe like the Great Depression can compare in scope.

6   And yet, Hurricane Katrina is practically a case study of the five stages people seem to have to go through during severe crisis. Over the past 40 years, I've seen these stages unfold in companies large and small, of every type, in every part of the world, and I went through them myself at my own company more than a few times.

7   New Orleans, of course, is not a company, but like any city, it is an organization. And there can be no denying that New Orleans' crisis is tragic in a way that company crises are not. But contrary to the sound and fury out there right now, the Katrina crisis follows a well-worn pattern.

8   The first stage of that pattern is *denial*. The problem isn't that bad, the thinking usually goes, it can't be, because bad things don't happen here, to us. The second is *containment*. This is the stage where people, including perfectly capable leaders, try to make the problem disappear by giving it to someone else to solve. The third stage is *shame-mongering*, in which all parties with a stake in the problem enter into a frantic dance of self-defense, assigning blame and claiming credit. Fourth comes *blood on the floor*. In just about every crisis, a high profile person pays with his job, and sometimes he takes a crowd with him. In the fifth and final stage, *the crisis gets fixed* and, despite prophecies of permanent doom, life goes on, usually for the better.

9   We are a way off from the fifth stage in New Orleans, but the first four played out like an old movie.

Denial

10   In the days and even hours before the hurricane struck, officials at every level of the government demonstrated a lack of urgency about the storm that seems crazy now. No one operated out of malice—that can be said for certain. But the facts reveal the kinds of paralysis so often brought on by panic and its ironically common side-effect, inertia. The federal government received hourly updates on the storm, but the head of FEMA,

the ill-fated Michael Brown, waited 24 hours, by the most generous estimations, before ordering personnel into the area. The state's governor, in her early communications with the president, mainly asked for financial aid for the city's clean-up efforts. On the local level, the mayor let a critical 12 hours elapse before ordering an evacuation of the city.

Denial in the face of disaster is human. It is the main and   11 immediate emotion people feel at the receiving end of any really bad news. That doesn't excuse what happened in New Orleans. In fact, one of the marks of good leadership is the ability to dispense with denial quickly and face into hard stuff with eyes open and fists raised. With particularly bad crises facing them, good leaders also define reality, set direction and inspire people to move forward. Just think of Giuliani after 9/11 or Churchill during World War II. Denial doesn't exactly come to mind—a forthright, calm, fierce boldness does.

All that was in short supply during the disaster in New   12 Orleans. But it might be argued that denial in and about New Orleans started long ago. New Orleans was a city with more than 20% living below the poverty line, a homicide rate almost 10 times higher than New York, and an intractable tradition of political corruption.

Why did it take a hurricane to reveal these unacceptable   13 conditions?

New Orleans was also well aware that its levee system was   14 inadequate for a major storm and that the economic plight of its citizenry, with their lack of cars and cash, rendered evacuation plans meaningless.

Why did it take a hurricane to prove those points?   15

In both cases, the only answer is denial, that predictable first   16 phase of crisis, which in Katrina's case, happened before, during, and after the actual storm.

Containment

For this second predictable phase in crisis, Katrina was no   17 exception. In companies, containment usually plays out with leaders trying to keep the "matter" quiet—a total waste of energy, as all problems, and especially messy ones, eventually get out and explode. In Katrina's case, containment came in a related form, buck-passing—pushing responsibility for the disaster from one part of government to another in hopes of making it go away. The city and state screamed for federal help, the feds said they couldn't send in the troops (literally) until the state asked for them, the state said it wouldn't approve the federal relief plan, and round and round went the baton.

18   No layer is a good layer. Bureaucracy, with its pettiness and formalities, slows action and initiative in any situation, business or otherwise. In a crisis like Katrina, it can be deadly. The terrible part is that Katrina might have avoided some of its bureaucratic bumbling if FEMA had not been buried in the Department of Homeland Security. As an independent entity for decades prior, FEMA fared better. But inside Homeland Security, FEMA was a layer down, twisted in and hobbled by government hierarchy. And to make matters worse, its head, Michael Brown, appears to have been an inexperienced political operative—making his appointment an example of bureaucratic inefficiency at its worst.

Shame-Mongering

19   This is a period in which all stakeholders fight to get their side of the story told, with themselves as the heroes at the center. Katrina's shame-mongering had blasted into overdrive by Tuesday, about 48 hours after landfall. I would wager that never before has a storm become so politicized. Very quickly, Katrina wasn't a hurricane—it was a test of George Bush's leadership, it was a reflection of race and poverty in America, it was a metaphor for Iraq. The Democrats used the event to define George Bush for their own purposes; the Republicans— after a delay and with markedly less gusto—used it to define them back. The key word here is delay. Because in any crisis, effective leaders get their message out strongly, clearly—and early. George Bush and his team in Washington didn't do that, and they are paying for it.

Blood on the Floor

20   From the moment it became obvious that Katrina was a crisis-management disaster, you knew someone's head was going to roll. That's what usually happens in the fourth stage of crises. People need to feel that someone has paid, and paid dearly, for

what went wrong. Michael Brown was the obvious choice—a guy who had few hard credentials in his bag of defenses. And if Katrina is like most crises, his blood won't be the last spilled. In a few weeks, more personnel changes in FEMA and Homeland Security are sure to come, and politicians in New Orleans and Louisiana will be both made and ruined by what they did during the storm.

Eventually, all crises go away, and New Orleans' will too. 21 The waters will recede; people will return and rebuild. In a year, the media will report that progress toward normalcy has been made. In three years, the best levees ever constructed will be completed with great fanfare; the Superdome or its replacement will have been outfitted to keep thousands of people housed and fed for a month. In five years, the before-and-after photos of New Orleans will boggle the mind.

History shows us that crises almost always seem to give way 22 to something better. Maybe that's because crises reveal how and where the system is broken in ways that make denial no longer feasible. They have a way of forcing real solutions to happen.

Hurricane Katrina has the potential to do that in New 23 Orleans—to compel leaders in government and business to find ways to break the city's cycle of poverty and corruption. The opportunities are huge because the losses were. There is a blank slate for change to begin, and it most likely will. Just watch the entrepreneurs rush in with ideas and energy, revitalizing old and creating new businesses with the help of the money politicians will be outbidding one another to throw at the problem. Just watch the residents of New Orleans flock to the jobs that are created with a new spirit of optimism. Crises like Katrina have a way of galvanizing people toward a better future. That's the fifth and final part of the pattern—the best part.

Now, you may be wondering that if most every crisis fol- 24 lows a pattern, why can't we manage them better, or even prevent them?

In business, we very often do. Over time, organizations may 25 go through several crises, but very rarely do they go through the same type twice. The reason? Companies typically go to extremes after a crisis. They throw up fortresses of rules, controls and procedures to fix what went wrong in the first place. In that way, they build a kind of immunity to the sickness that felled them. It is very unlikely, for instance, that Johnson & Johnson will ever have another product-tampering disaster like Tylenol.

26   Immunity to crises comes from learning. Crises teach us where the system is broken and how to repair it so it won't break again. Ultimately, learning is why disasters, in business and in nature, have the potential to make the organizations that survive them so much stronger in the long run. And learning will reveal the crisis management of Katrina for what it was— an age-old pattern meant to be broken.

Expanding Vocabulary

Examine the following words in their contexts in the essay and then write a brief definition or synonym for each one. Do not use a dictionary. Try to guess the word's meaning from its context. The number in parentheses is the number of the paragraph in which the word appears.

bona fide (3)	hierarchy (18)
ironically (10)	galvanizing (23)
inertia (10)	immunity (25)
intractable (12)	

Understanding Content

1. What are the five stages of response to a crisis?
2. How do leaders get past the denial stage?
3. What were other marks of denial in New Orleans before Katrina came?
4. What did the containment stage reveal about FEMA and Homeland Security?
5. What did the shame-mongering stage keep Bush from doing?
6. What are Welch's predictions for the outcome of the Katrina disaster?

Drawing Inferences about Thesis and Purpose

1. What seems to be the author's attitude toward bureaucracy?
2. Welch suggests that business and government bureaucracies are much the same. Does his analysis of crisis management after Katrina support this view?
3. What is Welch's thesis?

Analyzing Strategies and Style

1. What is the essay's tone? How does Welch's tone contribute to his essay?
2. How does Welch begin his essay? What makes the opening paragraphs an effective introduction?

Thinking Critically

1. Examine the author's predictions for New Orleans. Has he been on target? If not, what predictions have not been fulfilled? What, if any, predictions have become reality?
2. Should FEMA be a part of Homeland Security or a separate agency? Be prepared to defend your views.
3. Can Welch's five stages be applied to individuals facing difficult situations? If so, how? If not, why not?

Restoring Recess

CAROL KRUCOFF

A journalist, Carol Krucoff is a freelance writer on health and exercise topics, a syndicated health columnist, and the author of *Healing Moves* (2000). Krucoff runs and holds a black belt in karate. In "Restoring Recess," which appeared in the *Washington Post*'s Health section on January 12, 1999, Krucoff encourages readers to treat daily exercise not as work but as play.

Questions to Guide Your Reading and Reflection

1. How do adults who exercise regularly feel about it?
2. How do you feel about regular exercise?

So here we are, just a few weeks into the new year, and if 1 you're like most Americans you're already struggling to keep your resolution to shape up. Despite good intentions, the sad fact is that half of all adults who start a new exercise program drop out within six months.

Adopting a new habit isn't easy. As Sir Isaac Newton 2 pointed out, a body at rest will tend to remain at rest. Even the promise of better health and improved appearance won't get most people to exercise regularly.

3   But there is one motivator that can pry even the most con-firmed "potato" off the couch. Freud called it the pleasure prin-ciple: People do things that feel good and avoid things that feel bad. Most American adults get little or no exercise and more than half are overweight because many of them consider exer-cise to be hard, painful work—a distasteful chore they must force themselves to endure.

4   Yet as children we didn't feel this way about moving our bodies. Most kids see physical pursuits, like skipping and running, as exciting play to be enjoyed.

5   So this year, meet your fitness goals by turning exercise into child's play. Scratch the resolution to work out. Instead, vow to play actively for 30 minutes most days. Think of it as recess, and try to recapture the feeling you had as a child of being released onto the playground to swing, play ball or do whatever your little heart—and body—desired. Don't worry about flattening your abs or losing weight. Just enjoy the sensations of moving your body, breathing deeply and experiencing the moment.

6   This is your personalized playtime, so pick any form of movement that you like—a solitary walk, shooting hoops with a friend, a dance class, gardening, ping-pong, cycling. The options are vast, and nearly anything that gets you moving is fine, since even light-to-moderate exercise can yield significant health benefits.

7   The point is to stop thinking of your workout as one more demanding task you must cram into your busy day and start viewing it as a welcome recess that frees you from the con-fines of your chair. Most regular exercisers will tell you that this is the reason they remain active. Yes, they exercise to lose weight, build strong bones and all those other healthy rea-sons. But scratch deeper and most will admit that a central reason they're out there day after day is that it's fun—their exercise satisfies body and soul, and is a cherished highlight of their lives.

8   If you think this attitude adjustment is merely a mind game, you're right. Getting in shape is, after all, a matter of mind over body. But it's also a healthy way of approaching fitness, to enjoy the journey as much as reaching the destination. Goals

can be helpful motivators to shape up. But once you drop a clothing size, then what?

So instead of being caught up in reaching a certain scale   9
weight, view taking care of your physical self—which can play a key role in boosting your emotional self—as an opportunity for active play. This may be difficult in our culture, which considers play a frivolous time-waster. Yet "the ability to play is one of the principal criteria of mental health," wrote anthropologist Ashley Montague in his book, *Growing Young*.

Just as kids need the release of recess to get the "wiggles"   10
out of the bodies, adults also need relief from the stiffness caused by sitting and the chance to oxygenate sluggish brains.

Next time a problem has you stumped, take it out on a walk   11
in the fresh air—and bring along a pencil and paper. Solutions will appear on the move that eluded you at your desk.

To make your play breaks happen, schedule them into your   12
life. Lack of time is the main reason people say they don't exercise, and it's true that most of us lead very busy lives. But it's also true that we find time for things that are important to us. It's a matter of making choices.

You may need to get up a half hour earlier—and go to bed a   13
half hour earlier—to make your play break happen. You might have to turn off the TV, cut short a phone call or eat lunch at your desk to squeeze in recess. But if it's fun, it won't be a terrible sacrifice—it'll be a willing trade-off. Besides, as a wise person once said, "If you don't make time to exercise, you'll have to take time to be sick."

To keep your break fun, remember to: 14

1. Start slowly and progress gradually. If you've been inactive, begin with as little as five minutes of your chosen activity. Add on five more minutes each week with the goal of playing actively for 30 minutes on most days.
2. Avoid negative talk about yourself. Instead of obsessing about your thunder thighs, have an attitude of gratitude about your body and all that it does for you.
3. Choose a positive exercise environment. Just as fresh air and music may enhance your recess, mirrors may detract from your experience if you're self-critical. If so, play outdoors or in a mirror-free room.
4. Consider a few sessions with a personal trainer if you need help getting started. For a referral, call the American Council on Exercise's consumer hot line at 1-800-529-8227.

5. Vary your activity. If you like doing the same thing, day after day, great. But it's fine to move in different ways on different days, depending on your mood, the weather and other factors you find relevant.
6. Focus on behaviors, not on outcomes. If you consistently exercise and eat right, results will come.
7. Avoid rushing back to routine. Take a few minutes to breathe deeply and bring the refreshing spirit of playfulness back to your grown-up world.

Expanding Vocabulary

Study the definitions of any of the following words that are unfamiliar to you. Then use each of the words in a separate sentence. The number in parentheses is the number of the paragraph in which the word appears.

pry (3)   oxygenate (10)
confines (7)   sluggish (10)
frivolous (9)   eluded (11)

Understanding Content

1. How many adults drop out of an exercise program within six months?
2. How many Americans are overweight?
3. How did most of us feel about movement and play when we were children?
4. How much exercise and what kinds of exercise does the author recommend?
5. What steps should we take to get back to "recess"?

Drawing Inferences about Thesis and Purpose

1. What are the advantages of exercise suggested throughout Krucoff's essay?
2. What is Krucoff's thesis?

Analyzing Strategies and Style

1. How does the author use New Year's resolutions as both an opening strategy and a way develop her essay?
2. Krucoff writes with brief paragraphs and ends with a list. What is the effect of these strategies? How does her style connect to audience and purpose?

Thinking Critically

1. Do you make New Year's resolutions to exercise more? If so, do you keep them? If not, why not?
2. Do you exercise regularly? If not, why not? How would you defend your inactivity to Krucoff?
3. Do you agree that we choose to do what is important to us? Do you think that most of us could find thirty minutes most days for exercise if we really wanted to? Explain your response.
4. Has Krucoff convinced you to treat exercise as play and to start playing more? Why or why not?

Camping Out

ERNEST HEMINGWAY

One of the most popular of twentieth-century fiction writers, Ernest Hemingway (1899–1961) is best known for his short stories and novels, especially *A Farewell to Arms, The Sun Also Rises*, and *The Old Man and the Sea*. Hemingway, winner of the Nobel Prize for Literature, began his writing career as a journalist and returned to journalism from time to time, most notably as a correspondent during the Spanish Civil War and World War II. His guidelines for a successful camping trip, first published in the *Toronto Star Weekly* in 1920, continue to provide good advice for today's campers.

Questions to Guide Your Reading and Reflection

1. What is Hemingway's purpose in writing about camping? What does he want to accomplish?
2. From your camping experience, what is one piece of advice you would give to other campers?

Thousands of people will go into the bush this summer to   1
cut the high cost of living. A man who gets his two weeks' salary while he is on vacation should be able to put those two weeks in fishing and camping and be able to save one week's salary clear. He ought to be able to sleep comfortably every night, to eat well every day and to return to the city rested and in good condition.

2   But if he goes into the woods with a frying pan, an ignorance of black flies and mosquitoes, and a great and abiding lack of knowledge about cookery, the chances are that his return will be very different. He will come back with enough mosquito bites to make the back of his neck look like a relief map of the Caucasus. His digestion will be wrecked after a valiant battle to assimilate half-cooked or charred grub. And he won't have had a decent night's sleep while he has been gone.

3   He will solemnly raise his right hand and inform you that he has joined the grand army of never-agains. The call of the wild may be all right, but it's a dog's life. He's heard the call of the tame with both ears. Waiter, bring him an order of milk toast.

4   In the first place he overlooked the insects. Black flies, no-see-ums, deer flies, gnats and mosquitoes were instituted by the devil to force people to live in cities where he could get at them better. If it weren't for them everybody would live in the bush and he would be out of work. It was a rather success-ful invention.

5   But there are lots of dopes that will counteract the pests. The simplest perhaps is oil of citronella. Two bits' worth of this pur-chased at any pharmacist's will be enough to last for two weeks in the worst fly- and mosquito-ridden country.

6   Rub a little on the back of your neck, your forehead and your wrists before you start fishing, and the blacks and skeeters will shun you. The odor of citronella is not offensive to people. It smells like gun oil. But the bugs do hate it.

7   Oil of pennyroyal and eucalyptol are also much hated by mosquitoes, and with citronella they form the basis for many proprietary preparations. But it is cheaper and better to buy the straight citronella. Put a little on the mosquito netting that covers the front of your pup tent or canoe tent at night, and you won't be bothered.

8   To be really rested and get any benefit out of a vacation a man must get a good night's sleep every night. The first requi-site for this is to have plenty of cover. It is twice as cold as you expect it will be in the bush four nights out of five, and a good plan is to take just double the bedding that you think you will need. An old quilt that you can wrap up in is as warm as two blankets.

Nearly all outdoor writers rhapsodize over the browse bed. 9
It is all right for the man who knows how to make one and has
plenty of time. But in a succession of one-night camps on a
canoe trip all you need is level ground for your tent floor and
you will sleep all right if you have plenty of covers under you.
Take twice as much cover as you think that you will need, and
then put two-thirds of it under you. You will sleep warm and
get your rest.

When it is clear weather you don't need to pitch your tent if 10
you are only stopping for the night. Drive four stakes at the
head of your made-up bed and drape your mosquito bar over
that, then you can sleep like a log and laugh at the mosquitoes.

Outside of insects and bum sleeping, the rock that wrecks 11
most camping trips is cooking. The average tyro's idea of cooking is to fry everything and fry it good and plenty. Now, a frying pan is a most necessary thing to any trip, but you also need
the old stew kettle and the folding reflector baker.

A pan of fried trout can't be bettered and they don't cost any 12
more than ever. But there is a good and bad way of frying them.

The beginner puts his trout and his bacon in and, over a 13
brightly burning fire, the bacon curls up and dries into a dry
tasteless cinder, and the trout is burned outside while it is still
raw inside. He eats them and it is all right if he is only out for
the day and going home to a good meal at night. But if he is
going to face more trout and bacon the next morning and other
equally well-cooked dishes for the remainder of two weeks, he
is on the pathway to nervous dyspepsia.

The proper way is to cook over coals. Have several cans of 14
Crisco or Cotosuet or one of the vegetable shortenings along
that are as good as lard and excellent for all kinds of shorten-
ing. Put the bacon in and when it is about half cooked lay the
trout in the hot grease, dipping them in cornmeal first. Then
put the bacon on top of the trout and it will baste them as it
slowly cooks.

The coffee can be boiling at the same time and in a smaller 15
skillet pancakes being made that are satisfying the other
campers while they are waiting for the trout.

With the prepared pancake flours you take a cupful of pan- 16
cake flour and add a cup of water. Mix the water and flour and
as soon as the lumps are out it is ready for cooking. Have the

skillet hot and keep it well greased. Drop the batter in and as soon as it is done on one side loosen it in the skillet and flip it over. Apple butter, syrup or cinnamon and sugar go well with the cakes.

17   While the crowd have taken the edge from their appetites with flapjacks, the trout have been cooked and they and the bacon are ready to serve. The trout are crisp outside and firm and pink inside and the bacon is well done—but not too done. If there is anything better than that combination the writer has yet to taste it in a lifetime devoted largely and studiously to eating.

18   The stew kettle will cook you dried apricots when they have resumed their predried plumpness after a night of soaking, it will serve to concoct a mulligan in, and it will cook macaroni. When you are not using it, it should be boiling water for the dishes.

19   In the baker, mere man comes into his own, for he can make a pie that to his bush appetite will have it all over the product that mother used to make, like a tent. Men have always believed that there was something mysterious and difficult about making a pie. Here is a great secret. There is nothing to it. We've been kidded for years. Any man of average office intelligence can make at least as good a pie as his wife.

20   All there is to a pie is a cup and a half of flour, one-half tea-spoonful of salt, one-half cup of lard and cold water. That will make piecrust that will bring tears of joy into your camping partner's eyes.

21   Mix the salt with the flour, work the lard into the flour, make it up into a good workmanlike dough with cold water. Spread some flour on the back of a box or something flat, and pat the dough around a while. Then roll it out with whatever kind of round bottle you prefer. Put a little more lard on the surface of the sheet of dough and then slosh a little flour on and roll it up and then roll it out again with the bottle.

22   Cut out a piece of the rolled-out dough big enough to line a pie tin. I like the kind with holes in the bottom. Then put in your dried apples that have soaked all night and been sweet-ened, or your apricots, or your blueberries, and then take another sheet of the dough and drape it gracefully over the top, soldering it down at the edges with your fingers. Cut a couple of slits in the top dough sheet and prick it a few times with a fork in an artistic manner.

Put it in the baker with a good slow fire for forty-five min- 23
utes and then take it out, and if your pals are Frenchmen they
will kiss you. The penalty for knowing how to cook is that the
others will make you do all the cooking.

It is all right to talk about roughing it in the woods. But the 24
real woodsman is the man who can be really comfortable in the
bush.

Expanding Vocabulary

Examine the following words in their contexts in the essay and then
write a definition for each one. Do not use a dictionary. Try to guess
the word's meaning from its context. The number in parentheses is the
number of the paragraph in which the word appears.

relief map (2)	requisite (8)
Caucasus (2)	rhapsodize (9)
valiant (2)	browse bed (9)
assimilate (2)	tyro (11)
grub (2)	dyspepsia (13)
dopes (5)	concoct (18)
skeeters (6)	mulligan (18)
proprietary (7)	

Understanding Content

1. Explain the processes for coping with each of the first two problems Hemingway addresses.
2. Hemingway devotes most of his article to the third problem. Why?
3. How does he organize his guidelines for cooking?
4. When explaining pie-making, what misconception does Hemingway
   clear up?

Drawing Inferences about Thesis and Purpose

1. Hemingway's title announces the broad subject of camping but
   not his specific subject. State his subject by completing the phrase:
   "how to _____."
2. State a thesis for the essay.

Analyzing Strategies and Style

1. Hemingway has written a lively and entertaining essay, not a list
   of impersonal instructions. How did he make his process essay
   interesting? Discuss specific passages that you think are effective.

2. When Hemingway writes, in paragraph 4, "It was a rather successful invention," what writing technique is he using? What tone do we hear in the line?

3. Who is Hemingway's anticipated audience? Who does he think are potential campers among the newspaper's readers? What passages reveal his assumption?

4. Camping out has changed since the 1920s. Writers on this topic today would not assume a male audience, and they would be careful not to write in a sexist manner. How would this essay have to be edited to eliminate sexist writing? What specific changes would you make?

5. The essay's conclusion is brief—only two sentences. Why is it effective in spite of its brevity? How does it connect to the essay's thesis?

Thinking Critically

1. What reasons for camping does Hemingway suggest? Are these still the reasons most people camp out today?

2. Are the problems Hemingway addresses—bugs, uncomfortable sleeping, bad food—still the basic problems to be solved to enjoy a camping trip? What modern equipment can help campers with these problems?

3. Many people today go "camping" in well-equipped RVs. Is this really camping? What would Hemingway say? What do you say? Why?

Learning to Love

TIFFANY SHARPLES

Tiffany Sharples is a feature writer for *Time* magazine. Her article on the stages of practicing the art of love appeared in *Time* on January 18, 2008.

Questions to Guide Your Reading and Reflection

1. When do we first start learning to flirt?

2. Have you learned how to be in a loving relationship? Or, do you think you still have some practicing to do?

There's a very thin line between being thrilled and being ter- 1
rified, and Candice Feiring saw both emotions on her son's
face. The sixth-grader had just gotten off the phone with a girl
in his class who called to ask if he'd like to go to the movies—
just the two of them. It sounded a whole lot like a date to him.
"Don't I have something to do tomorrow?" he asked his
mother. A psychologist and an editor of *The Development of
Romantic Relationships in Adolescence*, Feiring was uniquely prepared to field that question and give her son the answer that,
for now, he needed. "I think you're too young to go out
one-on-one," she said. His face broke into a relieved grin.

A year later, even a month later, Feiring's adolescent son 2
might have reacted very differently to being told he was not
ready to date. That moment-to-moment mutability of his interest in—never mind his readiness for—courtship is only one
tiny part of the exhilarating, exhausting, confounding path all
humans travel as they make their halting way into the world
of love. From the moment we're born—when the world is
mostly sensation, and nothing much matters beyond a full
belly, a warm embrace and a clean diaper—until we finally
emerge into adulthood and understand the rich mix of tactile,
sexual and emotional experiences that come with loving
another adult, we are in a constant state of learning and
rehearsing. Along with language, romance may be one of the
hardest skills we'll ever be called on to acquire. But while we're
more or less fluent in speech by the time we're 5, romance takes
a lot longer. Most Western romance research involves Western
cultures, where things may move at a very different pace from
that of, say, the Far East or the Muslim world. While not all of
the studies yield universal truths, they all suggest that people
are wired to pick up their love skills in very specific stages.

Infancy and Babyhood

Babies may not have much to do right after they're born, but 3
the stakes are vitally high that they do it right. One of the first
skills newborns must learn is how to woo the adults in their
world. "For a baby, literally you're going to be dead without
love, so getting people around you to love you is a really good
strategy," says Alison Gopnik, a cognitive psychologist at the
University of California, Berkeley.

4   Babies do this much the way adults do: by flirting. Within a couple of months, infants may move and coo, bob and blink in concert with anyone who's paying attention to them. Smiling is a critical and cleverly timed part of this phase. Babies usually manage a first smile by the time they're 6 weeks old, which, coincidentally or not, is about the time the novelty of a newborn has worn off and sleep-deprived parents are craving some peace. A smile can be a powerful way to win them back.

5   Even before we know how to turn on the charm, touch and chemistry are bonding us firmly to our parents—and bonding them to us. Oxytocin—a hormone sometimes called the cuddle chemical—surges in new mothers and, to a lesser extent, in new fathers, making their baby instantly irresistible to them. One thing grownups particularly can't resist doing is picking a baby up, and that too is a key to survival. "Babies need physical contact with human hands to grow and thrive," says Lisa Diamond, a psychologist at the University of Utah. Years of data have shown that premature babies who are regularly touched fare much better than those who aren't.

6   As babies seduce and adults respond, a sophisticated dynamic develops. Mothers learn to synch their behavior with their newborn's, so that they offer a smile when their baby smiles, food when their baby's hungry. That's a pleasingly reciprocal deal, and while adults are already aware that when you give pleasure and comfort, you get it in return, it's news for the baby. "Babies are building up ideas about how close relationships work," says Gopnik.

Toddlerhood and Preschool

7   When kids reach 2, mom and dad aren't paying quite the same attention they used to. You feed yourself, you play on your own, you get held less often. That's not to say you need your parents less—and you're not shy about letting them know it. Children from ages 2 to 5 have yet to develop what's known as a theory of mind—the understanding that other people have hidden thoughts that are different from yours and that you can conceal your thoughts too. Without that knowledge, kids conceal nothing. "They love you," says Gopnik, "and they really, really express it."

At the same time, kids are learning something about sensual   8
pleasures. They explore their bodies more, discovering that
certain areas yield more electrifying feelings than others. This
simultaneous emotional development and physical experience
can lead to surprising behavior. "Three- and 4-year-olds are
very sexual beings," says Gopnik, "and a lot of that is directed
at their parents." Some of this can get generalized to other
adults too, as when a small child develops a crush on a teacher
or seems to flirt with an aunt or uncle. While a number of
things are at work when this happens, the most important is
playacting and the valuable rehearsal for later life it provides.
"Kids are trying to play out a set of roles and be more like
adults," says psychologist Andrew Collins of the University of
Minnesota's Institute of Child Development.

The same kind of training behavior can show up with play-   9
mates and friends, often accompanied by unexpectedly powerful feelings. Social psychologist Elaine Hatfield of the
University of Hawaii is best known for co-creating the Passionate Love Scale, a questionnaire with which she can gauge
feelings of romantic connectedness in adults. She has modified
the test to elicit similar information from children. In early
work, she studied 114 boys and 122 girls, some as young as 4,
presenting them with statements like "I am always thinking
about ____" or "I would rather be with ____ than anybody
else." The kids filled in the name of someone they loved, and
Hatfield asked them to rate the intensity of feelings with stacks
of checkers: the higher the stack, the more they felt. In some
instances, the kids became overwhelmed with emotion, as in
the case of a 5-year-old girl who wept at the thought of a boy
she would never see again. "Little kids fall in love too," Hatfield
says plainly.

School Age and Puberty

As with so much else in childhood, things get more compli-   10
cated once kids reach the social incubator of elementary school.
Nowhere near sexually mature, they nonetheless become sexually active—in their own fashion. The opposite-sex teasing
and chasing that are rife on playgrounds may give teachers
headaches, but they teach boys and girls a lot. The games, after
all, are about pursuit and emotional arousal, two critical

elements of sex. "There are a lot of erotic forms of play," says Barrie Thorne, a sociologist at the University of California, Berkeley, and the author of *Gender Play: Boys and Girls in School.* "It can be titillating, and it may involve sexual meaning, but it comes and goes."

11   More enduring—for a while at least—is the gender segregation that begins at this age. Boys and girls who once played in mixed groups at school begin to drift apart into single-sex camps, drawing social boundaries that will stay in place for years. In her 1986 study that is still cited today, Thorne looked at 802 elementary-school students from California and Massachusetts to determine just what goes on behind these gender fortifications and why they're established in the first place.

12   To no one's surprise, both groups spend a lot of time talking and thinking about the opposite sex, but they do it in very different ways. Boys experiment more with sexually explicit vocabulary and, later, sexual fantasies. Girls focus more heavily—but hardly exclusively—on romantic fantasies. The two-gender world they'll eventually re-enter will be a lot more complex than that, but for now the boys are simply practicing being boys—albeit in a very rudimentary way—and the girls are practicing being girls. "Among the boys, for example, there's a lot of bragging talk," says Thorne. "You're supposed to be powerful and not vulnerable."

13   When puberty hits, the wall between the worlds begins to crumble—a bit. Surging hormones make the opposite sex irresistible, but the rapprochement happens collectively, with single-gender groups beginning to merge into co-ed social circles within which individual boys and girls can flirt and experiment. Generally, kids who pair off with a love interest and begin dating will hold onto a return ticket to the mixed-gender group. Jennifer Connolly, a psychologist at York University in Toronto, studied 174 high school students in grades nine to 11 and found that when things go awry with couples, the kids are quickly absorbed back into the co-ed circle, with the old single-sex group increasingly eclipsed. "Once the progression has started," Connolly says, "we don't see kids retreating back into only same-gender interaction."

14   Almost all of these early relationships are, not surprisingly, short-lived—and a good thing too. If the purpose is to pick a

mate for life, you're hardly likely to find a suitable one on your very first go. What's more, even if you did get lucky, you'd almost certainly not have the emotional wherewithal to keep the relationship going. Adults often lament the love they had and lost in high school and wonder what would have happened if they had met just a few years later. But the only way to acquire the skills to conduct a lifetime relationship is to practice on ones you may destroy in the process. "Kids don't really have a sense of working to preserve a relationship," Connolly says. "Adolescence is a time for experimentation."

Sexual experimentation is a big part of that—and it's a part 15 that's especially fraught. Pregnancy and sexually transmitted diseases are just two of the things that make sex perilous. There are also emotional conflicts kids bring into their early experiences with intimacy. Psychologists have long warned that children who grow up in a hostile home or one in which warmth is withheld are likelier to start having sex earlier and engage in it more frequently. In a study that will be published in March, Trish Williams, a neuropsychology fellow at Alberta Children's Hospital, studied a group of 1,959 kids ages 11 to 13 and did find a striking correlation between a volatile home and earlier sexual behavior. A few of the children had had intercourse at as young an age as 12, and while the number of sexually active kids wasn't high—just 2% of the total—the cause was clear. "Hostile parenting is highly associated with problem behavior," says Williams.

Even kids without such emotional scarring can be pretty 16 undiscriminating in their sexual choices. Two studies conducted by sociologist Wendy Manning in 2005 and 2006 showed that while 75% of kids have their first sexual experience with a partner they're dating—a figure that may bring at least some comfort to worried parents—more than 60% will eventually have sex with someone with whom they're not in any kind of meaningful dating relationship. Hooking up—very informal sex between two people with no intent of pursuing a deeper relationship—takes this casualness even further. A 2004 study Manning worked on showed that the overwhelming majority of hookups involve alcohol use—an impairer of sexual judgment if ever there was one—and according to the work of other researchers, more than half the times kids hook up, they do not use a condom. Manning's studies suggest that hooking up prevents kids from practicing the interpersonal skills they'll need in a permanent relationship and may lead to lowered expectations of what those relationships should be like—and a greater willingness to settle for less.

17   For all these perils, the fact is, most people manage to shake off even such high-stakes behavior and find a satisfying life partner, and that says something about the resilience of humans as romantic creatures. In the U.S., by the time we're 18, about 80% of us have had at least one meaningful romantic relationship. As adults, up to 75% of us marry. Certainly, nature doesn't make things easy. From babyhood on, it equips us with the tools we'll need for the hardest social role we'll ever play— the role of romantic—and then chooses the moment when we're drunk on the hormones of adolescence and least confi-dent in ourselves to push us on stage to perform. That we go on at all is a mark of our courage. That we learn the part so well is a mark of how much is at stake.

Expanding Vocabulary

Study the definitions of each of the following words in your dictio-nary. Then select five words and use each one in a separate sentence. The number in parentheses is the number of the paragraph in which the word appears.

mutability (2)	eclipsed (13)
synch (6)	fraught (15)
reciprocal (6)	perilous (15)
elicit (9)	volatile (15)
rapprochement (13)	resilience (17)
awry (13)	

Understanding Content

1. What is Sharples's subject?
2. What are the stages of learning we go through?
3. What are babies learning?
4. What are toddlers learning? How strong are their feelings?
5. What is happening during the play of younger school-aged boys and girls?
6. How do teens group and regroup? How successful is their prac-tice at relationships?

Drawing Inferences about Thesis and Purpose

1. What is Sharples's primary purpose in writing?
2. What attitudes about human development emerge as she explores her topic?
3. What is the author's thesis?

Analyzing Strategies and Style

1. Sharples's opening paragraph is an extended example. How is it effective in suggesting one of her key points?
2. How is the essay organized? How is that organization made clear?
3. From what type of sources do most of the details come? What is effective about this strategy?

Thinking Critically

1. Are you surprised by the idea that we practice for romantic relationships from infancy? Does this make sense to you? If not, why not?
2. What are the dangers of "hooking up"? Can one argue that the greatest peril may be psychological? Explain.
3. What are some ways that parents can help their children learn how to love? If you were counseling parents, what advice would you give?

MAKING CONNECTIONS

---

1. John Aigner emphasizes the importance of being prepared. Preparation is a major key to success. Does this make sense to you? If you agree, think how you would convince unprepared students of the value of preparation. If you disagree, think how you would challenge these writers.
2. John Aigner encourages interviewees to develop a power vocabulary and learn to speak only positively about themselves. Suzette Elgin gives directions for changing one's speech to be more effective. Are these writers providing useful self-help guidelines for success? Or, are they encouraging us to misrepresent ourselves to get ahead? Or, are they implying that society fails to accept diverse styles? Be prepared to debate these issues.

3. Suzette Elgin and Gail saltz encourage readers to know themselves. How important is it to know yourself as a basis for success in your career? Reflect on this question as a preparation for class discussion or a possible essay topic.

4. How are we expected to behave in the workplace today? Look for guides in your library's book collection or search online for advice on office behavior.

5. Take an informal survey of those with whom you work or those you know at school to analyze their conversational styles. Are most direct or indirect in their speech? Are there other observations about conversational styles that are useful to note?

6. Select a company (e.g., Nike) or a sports organization (e.g., the United States Tennis Association) you are interested in and visit their Website. Analyze the Website, looking at color and graphics and the information. Does it provide useful information? Is it organized clearly? Is it engaging visually? Be prepared to discuss your Website analysis with classmates.

7. E-mailing is an important function in today's workplace. Do an online search of e-mail etiquette (netiquette) to see what you can learn about the appropriate way to use, write, and send e-mails. Consider: Should you follow these guidelines when e-mailing your professors?

TOPICS FOR WRITING

---

1. In an essay examine some process of change that has taken place in your life. Consider physical, emotional, intellectual, or occupational changes. Although you will use chronological order, make certain that you focus on specific *stages* or *steps* that led to the change so that you write a process analysis, not a narrative. Possible topics include: how you grew (or shrank) to the size you are now, how you developed your skill in some sport or hobby, how you changed your taste in music, how you decided on a career. Analyze the change into at least three separate stages. Explain and illustrate each stage. Reflect on *your* reason for writing about the change in your life. Then state your

thesis in your first paragraph and restate it, enlarging on it, in your concluding paragraph.

2. Select a change in human society that has occurred in stages over time and that has had a significant effect on the way we live. Your thesis is the significance of the development— significance for good or ill. Develop that thesis by analyzing the process of change, the stages in development. Be sure to analyze the change into several distinct stages of development. Possible topics include technological changes (e.g., the generations of computers), changes in the classroom or school buildings, changes in recreation, and changes in dress.

3. Do you have advice to give someone preparing for a job interview, advice that is different from or in addition to the advice given by John Aigner in "Putting Your Job Interview into Rehearsal"? If so, organize your advice into a series of specific steps and write your guide to the successful interview. Your thesis, stated or implied, is that following these steps will improve one's chances of obtaining the desired position.

4. Have you taken the same type of vacation (camping, renting a beach house, sightseeing by car, traveling abroad) several times? If so, you may have learned the hard way what to do and what not to do to have a successful vacation. In an essay, pass your knowledge along to readers. Organize your essay into a process—a series of steps or directions—but also approach your analysis by explaining both the wrong way and the right way to complete each step. Ernest Hemingway's "Camping Out" is your model for this topic.

5. Many people have misconceptions about processes or tasks they are unfamiliar with, particularly if those activities are a part of a different culture. Do you understand how to do something that others might have misconceptions about? If so, prepare a process analysis that will explain the activity and thereby clear up the reader's misconceptions. In your opening paragraph you might refer to the typical misconceptions that people have and then move on to explain how the task or activity is actually done. If your activity is part of a particular culture (how to

cook with a wok, how to prepare pita bread, how to serve a Japanese dinner, how to wrap a sari), enrich your process analysis with appropriate details about that culture.

6. Some social situations can be difficult to handle successfully. If you have had success in one of them (such as asking someone for a date, meeting a close friend's or a fiancé's family, attending a large family reunion, attending the office Christmas party), then explain how to handle the situation with ease and charm. Select either a chronological ordering of steps or a list of specific instructions, including dos and don'ts. Humorous examples can be used with this topic to produce lively writing.

7. Prepare a detailed, knowledgeable explanation of a particular activity or task from your work or play for interested nonspecialists. You are the expert carefully explaining the process of, for example, bunting down the third-base line, booting up the computer, tuning an engine, building a deck, sewing a dress, or whatever you know well. Be sure to give encouragement as you give directions.

A CHECKLIST FOR PROCESS ESSAYS

Inventing

☐ Have I selected a topic consistent with the instructor's guidelines for this assignment?

☐ Have I chosen among the possible topics one that fits my knowledge and experience?

☐ Have I reflected on the topic to write a tentative thesis that invites the use of process analysis for support?

☐ Have I organized my thinking into clear steps or stages?

☐ Have I considered my audience as a guide to where and when to start the process or how much information to include about each step?

☐ Do I have the correct order for the process?

Drafting

☐ Have I succeeded in completing a first draft at one sitting so that I can "see" the whole?

☐ Do I have enough—enough to meet assignment demands and enough to develop and support my thesis? If not, do I need new paragraphs or more examples or reflection within paragraphs?

☐ Do the steps in the process connect to and support my thesis?

☐ Does the order work? If not, what needs to be moved—and where? Have I left out any steps?

☐ Am I satisfied with the way I have expressed the insights to be gained? Have I been too heavy-handed with a message?

Revising

☐ Have I made any needed additions, deletions, or changes in order based on answering the questions about my draft?

☐ Have I revised my draft to produce coherent paragraphs, using transition and connecting words that reveal the steps or stages in the process?

Polishing

☐ Have I eliminated wordiness and clichés?

☐ Have I avoided and removed any discriminatory language?

☐ Have I used my word processor's spell check and proofread a printed copy with great care?

☐ Do I have an appropriate and interesting title?

7

Using Division and Classification
Understanding Human Connections

You have probably discovered by now that your college library organizes its book collection not by the Dewey decimal system but by the Library of Congress *classification* system. And you are probably taking courses offered by several different departments. Those departments, English for example, may be further *classified* by colleges—the college of arts of sciences. If you needed to find an apartment near campus or a part-time job, you may have looked in the newspaper's *classified* section. We *divide* or separate individual items and then group or *classify* them into logical categories because order is more convenient than disorder and because the process helps us make sense of a complex world. Just think how frustrated you would be if you had to search through a random listing of want ads rather than being able to look under several headings for specific jobs, or if you had to search up and down shelves of books because they were not grouped by any system.

When to Use Division and Classification

Division and classification are not similar but distinct strategies, as are comparison and contrast. Rather, division and classification work together; they are part of the same thinking process that brings order to a mass of items, data, ideas, forms of behavior, groups of people, or whatever else someone chooses to organize. Division is another term for analysis, the breaking down of something into its parts. Division, or analysis, provides the plan or pattern of grouping. To devise a classification system for books, books have to be divided by type: books on history, or art, or botany. Then large categories need to be subdivided: U.S. history, British history, Russian history. Then each individual book can be given a number that is its very own but also shows into what categories it has been classified, twentieth-century U.S. history, for example. The categories have been developed after thoughtful analysis; each book can be placed in one of the established categories.

A thinking process that has served us so well, solving organizational problems from the biologist's classification of the animal kingdom to the phone company's classification of businesses in the Yellow Pages must surely be a useful strategy for writers. And indeed it is. If you have written essays using examples and have sought to group examples to support different parts of your topic, you have already started working with the process of division and classification. The difference between the essays in Chapter 5 ("Explaining and Illustrating") and those in this chapter lies in the rigor of the classification system. To use classification effectively, you need a logical, consistent principle of division, and your classification needs to be complete. So, when thinking about possible topics for an essay and when thinking about purpose in writing, ask yourself: Am I interested in giving some specific examples to develop an idea, or am I interested in analyzing a topic, dividing it logically into its parts?

How to Use Division and Classification

Thinking and Organizing

Suppose that you are asked to write about some element of campus life. Reflecting on the fun you have had getting acquainted with classmates over meals in nearby restaurants, you decide to write about the various restaurants available to college students. How many and how varied are the restaurants within walking distance of the campus? To be thorough, you may not want to trust your memory; better to walk around, making a complete list of the area restaurants. Next, analyze your list to see the possible categories into which the restaurants can be grouped. You may see more than one way to classify them, perhaps by type of food (French, Chinese, Italian) and by cost (cheap, moderate, expensive). You need to avoid overlapping categories and to classify examples according to the division you select. The following chart illustrates the general principle:

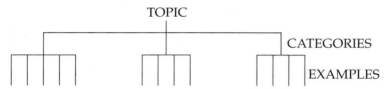

Thesis

The divisions and classifications you create must also support a thesis. What do you want to explain to your readers? This is the key question to answer in deciding on a classification pattern. If you decide to stress the variety of food available to students, for example, then you will want to classify your examples of restaurants by food type, not by cost.

In your essay on restaurants, division and classification provide an effective strategy for developing your thesis. Sometimes, though, a writer's thesis *is* the classification pattern. Put another way, what the writer has learned is that the subject can best be grasped by understanding the author's classification of that subject. Ralph Whitehead, writing about American class structure, asserts that the old categories are no longer accurate and that his new categories give us more insight into American society.

Much of what is important in your division and classification essay lies in your analysis, in the logical and perhaps new way you ask readers to examine your topic. This means that you may need to explain your categories to readers, to explain how and why you have divided your subject in your particular way and to show, if necessary, why the categories do not overlap. In "The Science and Secrets of Personal Space," Curt Suplee defines the required distances for each category or zone—intimate, personal, social, and public— but then explains how various cultures modify their space requirements. Remember, too, that you need to illustrate each of your divisions. In the essay on restaurants, the student needs to name and describe sample restaurants in each of the categories.

WRITING FOCUS
WORDS TO LIVE WITHOUT!

Student writers have been known to assure instructors that they would revise more energetically if they only knew what to look for to change or toss out. Here are several categories of words, with some examples of each, that you can watch for in your drafts and get in the habit of cutting or changing. Indeed, you can improve your writing overnight if you will commit to live without these types of words.

Unnecessary Qualifiers
How often have you written:

> *In my opinion, it seems to me* that gun laws . . .
> *I believe that possibly* we should have a . . .
> *What I got out of the poem is just* that the poet . . .

Whether the goal is padding or genuine concern about "being wrong," the writing suffers. Delete these kinds of words and phrases in all of your writing.

Vague, General Language
Some words that are hard to live without in casual speech do not belong in writing. These include such words as: *very, thing, good, bad, nice, aspect, factor.* In your writing you have the opportunity to substitute more powerful, concrete words for these overworked and now powerless words.

Loaded Words
Avoid language that puts down someone based on gender, age, race, ethnicity, or disability. Educated writers today make every effort to write in ways that do not

offend, at least when that is not the point of the writing. Here are some examples and the edits you can make: *firemen* (firefighters), *man* (human), *poetess* (poet for both genders). Also avoid all racial or ethnic slur words and be careful about political name calling as well (e.g., *radical, right wing, communist, reactionary*).

Getting Started: Classifying Recent Reading or Viewing

Make a list of all the works (books, magazines, newspapers, texts, etc.) you have read in the past three months. Study your list, thinking of several classifying principles you could use to organize your reading. Consider: Which pattern seems the most logical and complete? Could several patterns work, depending on your purpose in classifying? Alternately, complete the same exercise for all the movies or all the television shows you have seen in the past three months.

The Roles of Manners

JUDITH MARTIN

Judith Martin is "Miss Manners." After graduating from Wellesley College, Martin began her career as a reporter for the *Washington Post*. She is best known now for her syndicated column, "Miss Manners." She has published ten books, including *Miss Manners' Guide to Rearing Perfect Children* (1984), *Common Courtesy* (1985), and *Miss Manners: A Citizen's Guide to Civility*. In the following, a slightly shortened version of an article that appeared in the Spring 1996 issue of *The Responsive Community*, Martin analyzes the several roles of manners.

Questions to Guide Your Reading and Reflection

1. When you do not follow expected codes in society, how are you perceived? What do you appear to be doing?
2. What is your reaction to those who do not follow expected codes of behavior?

Ritual serves one of three major functions of manners.   1
Oddly enough, the greatest scoffers at the traditions of American
etiquette, who scorn the rituals of their own society as stupid
and stultifying, voice respect for the custom and folklore of
Native Americans, less industrialized peoples, and other societies they find more "authentic" than their own.

Americans who disdain etiquette in everyday life often go   2
into an etiquette tailspin in connection with marriage.
Although the premise on which the 20th-century American
wedding forms were based—that a young girl is given by the
father whose protection she leaves to a husband who will perform the same function—has changed, the forms retain their
emotional value. If it happens that the bride has been supporting the bridegroom for years in their own household, she may
well ask their own toddler age son to "give her away" just to
preserve the ritual.

Ritual provides a reassuring sense of social belonging far   3
more satisfying than behavior improvised under emotionally complicated circumstances. Rituals of mourning other
than funerals have been nearly abandoned, but at a great
emotional cost. Not only are the bereaved unprotected from
normal social demands by customs of seclusion and
symbols of vulnerability, but they are encouraged to act as
if nothing had happened—only to be deemed heartless if
they actually succeed.

A second function of manners is the symbolic one. It is the   4
symbolic function that confuses and upsets people who claim
that etiquette is "simply a matter of common sense" when actually the symbols cannot be deduced from first principles, but
must be learned in each society, and, within that society, for
different times, places, ages, and social classes.

Because symbols are arbitrary, it can happen that opposite   5
forms of behavior may symbolize the same idea, as when a man
takes off his hat to show respect in a church, but puts on his hat
to show respect in a synagogue. But once these rules are learned,
they provide people with a tremendous fund of nonverbal
knowledge about one another, helping them to deal appropriately with a wide range of social situations and relationships.
Forms of greeting, dressing, eating, and restraining bodily functions can all be read as symbols of degrees of friendliness or

hostility, respect or contempt, solidarity with the community or alienation from it. It is safe to assume that a person who advances on you with an outstretched hand is symbolizing an intent to treat you better than one who spits on the ground at the sight of you.

6   The law, the military, diplomacy, the church, and athletics have particularly strict codes of etiquette, compliance with which is taken to symbolize adherence to the particular values that these professions require: fairness, obedience, respect, piety, or valor. And following the conventions of the society is taken as a measure of respect for it—which is why people who are facing juries are advised by their own lawyers to dress and behave with the utmost convention.

7   It does not matter how arbitrary any of the violated rules may be—ignoring them is interpreted as defiance of, or indifference to, or antagonism toward, the interests of the person or community whose standard is being ignored. The person who wears blue jeans to a formal wedding, or a three-piece suit at a beach party, may protest all he likes that his choice had only to do with a clothing preference, but it is hard to imagine anyone so naive as to believe that the people whose standards he is violating will not interpret the choice as disdain. In New York, a 15-year-old was shot on the street in a gang fight started over his refusal to return another teenager's high five sign of greeting. "Dissin'," the current term for showing disrespect, is cited as a leading provocation for modern murder.

8   The third function of etiquette is the regulative function, which is less troublesome to the literal-minded, because those rules can be understood functionally. Between them, etiquette and law divide the task of regulating social conduct in the interest of community harmony, with the law addressing grave conflicts, such as those threatening life or property, and administering serious punishments, while etiquette seeks to forestall such conflicts, relying on voluntary compliance with its restraints.

9   This is why etiquette restricts freedom of self-expression more than the law does (and why etiquette rejects encounter group theories of achieving harmony through total communication). It is within my legal right to tell you that you are ugly,

or that your baby is, but this is likely to lead to ugly—which is to say dangerous—behavior, which it will require the law to address, no longer as a mere insult, but as a more serious charge of slander, libel, or mental cruelty.

But the danger of attempting to expand the dominion of the   10 law to take over the function of etiquette—to deal with such violations as students calling one another nasty names, or protesters doing provocative things with flags—is that it may compromise our constitutional rights. For all its strictness, a generally understood community standard of etiquette is more flexible than the law and, because it depends on voluntary compliance, less threatening.

Jurisprudence itself cannot function without etiquette. In   11 enforcing standards of dress, rules about when to sit and when to stand, restricting offensive language and requiring people to speak only in proper turn, courtroom etiquette overrides many of the very rights it may protect. So does the etiquette of legislatures, such as that specified in *Robert's Rules of Order*. This is necessary because the more orderly is the form of a social structure, the more conflict it can support. Etiquette requires participants in adversarial proceedings to present their opposing views in a restrained manner, to provide a disciplined and respectful ambience in which to settle conflicts peacefully.

Responding to Changing Times

That we cannot live peacefully in communities without   12 etiquette, using only the law to prevent or resolve conflicts in everyday life, has become increasingly obvious to the public. And so there has been, in the last few years, a "return to etiquette," a movement for which I am not totally blameless. It has been hampered by the idea that etiquette need not involve self-restriction. Those who must decry rudeness in others are full of schemes to punish those transgressors by treating them even more rudely in return. But the well-meaning are also sometimes stymied, because they understand "etiquette" to consist of the social rules that were in effect approximately a generation ago, when women rarely held significant jobs, and answering machines and Call Waiting had not yet been invented. As the same social conditions do not apply, they assume that there can be no etiquette system, or that each individual may make up his or her own rules.

13   One often hears that etiquette is "only a matter of being considerate of others," and that is certainly a good basis for good behavior. Obviously, however, it does not guide one in the realms of symbolic or ritual etiquette. And if each individual improvises, the variety of resulting actions would be open to misinterpretations and conflicts, which a mutually intelligible code of behavior seeks to prevent.

14   Yet many of the surface etiquette issues of today were addressed under the codes of earlier times, which need only be adapted for the present. . . . [A] system of precedence must exist, although it need not be "ladies first." One must regulate the access of others to one's attention—if not with a butler announcing the conventional fiction that "Madam is not at home," then by a machine that says, "If you leave a message after the beep. . . . " But dropping one unfinished conversation to begin another has always been rude, and that applies to Call Waiting. Usually, changes happen gradually, as, for example, most people have come to accept the unmarried couple socially, or to issue their wedding invitations in time for guests to take advantage of bargain travel prices.

15   There is, of course, ideologically motivated civil disobedience of etiquette, just as there is of law. But people who mean to change the behavior of the community for its own supposed benefit by such acts must be prepared to accept the punitive consequences of their defiance. They would be well advised to disobey only the rule that offends them, carefully adhering to other conventions, if they do not wish to have their protests perceived as a general contempt for other people. Thanks to her symbolic meaning, the well-dressed, soft-spoken grandmother is a more effective agitator than the unkempt, obscenity-spouting youth.

16   Ignorance of etiquette rules is not an easily accepted excuse, except on behalf of small children or strangers to the community. An incapacity to comply is acceptable, but only if convincingly explained. To refuse to shake someone's hand will be interpreted as an insult, unless an explanation, such as that one has crippling arthritis, is provided.

Such excuses as "Oh, I never write letters" or "I just wasn't   17
in the mood" or "I'm not comfortable with that" are classified
as insolence and disallowed. Etiquette cannot be universally
abandoned in the name of individual freedom, honesty,
creativity, or comfort, without social consequences.

In 1978, when I began chronicling and guiding the legiti-   18
mate changes in etiquette, and applying the rules in specific
cases, where there may be extenuating circumstances or
conflicting rules—as a judge does in considering a case—
it was difficult to get people to agree that etiquette was
needed. Now it is only difficult to get people to comply
with its rules.

Expanding Vocabulary

Match each word in column A with its definition in column B. When
in doubt, first find the word in the essay and look for context clues
to aid your understanding of the word's meaning. Then, if necessary, use your dictionary to complete the matching exercise. The
number in parentheses is the number of the paragraph in which the
word appears.

Column A	Column B
scoffers (1)	inflicting punishment
stultifying (1)	thwarted
tailspin (2)	left desolate, especially by death
bereaved (3)	unity of sympathies or interests
arbitrary (5)	within a group
solidarity (5)	state of estrangement, feeling of
alienation (5)	separation from others
adherence (6)	sudden deep decline or slump
naive (7)	simple, lacking worldliness
provocative (10)	act of inciting anger or stirring action
adversarial (11)	special atmosphere of a particular place
ambiance (11)	those expressing scorn
decry (12)	openly condemn
stymied (12)	antagonistic, behaving as an opponent
punitive (15)	determined by chance or whim
extenuating (18)	devotion to or commitment to
	providing partial excuses
	limiting or stifling

Understanding Content

1. What is often illogical about marriage rituals today? Why do we continue with these rituals anyway?
2. Why is it incorrect to insist that manners are simply common sense?
3. When you follow the codes of etiquette, diplomacy, or athletics, what does your behavior symbolize?
4. What is the relationship between the law and etiquette? What may happen if we try to get the law to take over the role of etiquette?
5. If you want to change particular etiquette, what should you do to be most successful?
6. Why is ignorance not usually accepted as an excuse for being unmannerly?

Drawing Inferences about Thesis and Purpose

1. What is Martin's purpose in writing? Does she have more than one? Try to write a thesis that makes her purpose clear.
2. Does Martin think that people today are more—or less—likely to follow codes of etiquette? How do you know?
3. What is the author's attitude toward Call Waiting? How do you know?

Analyzing Strategies and Style

1. Think about the ordering of the three roles of manners. What does the author gain by her choice of order?
2. Why does the author put *authentic* in quotation marks in paragraph 1? What do they signify to the reader?

Thinking Critically

1. Have you thought before about the ritual and symbolic roles of manners? If not, does Martin's explanation make sense to you?
2. Why are rituals helpful? Think of ways that the rituals of etiquette can aid us—and think of specific examples to illustrate your points.
3. Do you agree that etiquette can be a better choice than laws in controlling some kinds of behavior and that we should not turn to the law as a way to make people behave? Look specifically at Martin's examples and see whether you agree or disagree with her. Explain your position.
4. Many have argued that there has been a loss of manners in our time. What do you suggest that we do about the loss?

Hot Boxes for Ex-Smokers

FRANKLIN E. ZIMRING

Franklin Zimring completed his law degree at the University of Chicago in 1967 and taught there until 1985 before moving to Berkeley's School of Law and its Center for Studies in Criminal Justice. Zimring has published extensively, both articles and books, usually on such legal issues as capital punishment, youth crime, the criminal justice system, and violence in society. One important book is *American Youth Violence* (1998). The following article, appearing in *Newsweek* on April 20, 1987, departs from legal issues to draw on the writer's experience as an ex-smoker.

Questions to Guide Your Reading and Reflection

1. Into which of his "boxes" does the author fit?
2. How would you describe the author's tone?

Americans can be divided into three groups—smokers, nonsmokers, and that expanding pack of us who have quit. Those who have never smoked don't know what they're missing, but former smokers, ex-smokers, reformed smokers can never forget. We are veterans of a personal war, linked by that watershed experience of ceasing to smoke and by the temptation to have just one more cigarette. For almost all of us ex-smokers, smoking continues to play an important part in our lives. And now that it is being restricted in restaurants around the country and will be banned in almost all indoor public places in New York state starting next month, it is vital that everyone understand the different emotional states cessation of smoking can cause. I have observed four of them; and in the interest of science I have classified them as those of the zealot, the evangelist, the elect, and the serene. Each day, each category gains new recruits.

Not all antitobacco zealots are former smokers, but a substantial number of fire-and-brimstone opponents do come from the ranks of the reformed. Zealots believe that those who continue to smoke are degenerates who deserve scorn, not pity, and the penalties that will deter offensive behavior in public as well. Relations between these people and those who continue to smoke are strained.

3   One explanation for the zealot's fervor in seeking to outlaw tobacco consumption is his own tenuous hold on abstaining from smoking. But I think part of the emotional force arises from sheer envy as he watches and identifies with each lung-filling puff. By making smoking in public a crime, the zealot seeks reassurance that he will not revert to bad habits; give him strong social penalties and he won't become a recidivist.

4   No systematic survey has been done yet, but anecdotal evidence suggests that a disproportionate number of doctors who have quit smoking can be found among the fanatics. Just as the most enthusiastic revolutionary tends to make the most enthusiastic counterrevolutionary, many of today's vitriolic zealots include those who had been deeply committed to tobacco habits.

5   By contrast, the antismoking evangelist does not condemn smokers. Unlike the zealot, he regards smoking as an easily curable condition, as a social disease, and not a sin. The evangelist spends an enormous amount of time seeking and preaching to the unconverted. He argues that kicking the habit is not *that* difficult. After all, *he* did it; moreover, as he describes it, the benefits of quitting are beyond measure and the disadvantages are nil.

6   The hallmark of the evangelist is his insistence that he never misses tobacco. Though he is less hostile to smokers than the zealot, he is resented more. Friends and loved ones who have been the targets of his preachments frequently greet the resumption of smoking by the evangelist as an occasion for unmitigated glee.

7   Among former smokers, the distinctions between the evangelist and the elect are much the same as the differences between proselytizing and nonproselytizing religious sects. While the evangelists preach the ease and desirability of abstinence, the elect do not attempt to convert their friends. They think that virtue is its own reward and subscribe to the Puritan theory of predestination.[1] Since they have proved themselves capable of abstaining from tobacco, they are therefore different

---

[1]Puritans believed that those of the elect, those saved, have been chosen by God.—Ed.

from friends and relatives who continue to smoke. They feel superior, secure that their salvation was foreordained. These ex-smokers rarely give personal testimony on their conversion. They rarely speak about their tobacco habits, while evangelists talk about little else. Of course, active smokers find such bluenosed[2] behavior far less offensive than that of the evangelist or the zealot, yet they resent the elect simply because they are smug. Their air of self-satisfaction rarely escapes the notice of those lighting up. For active smokers, life with a member of the ex-smoking elect is less stormy than with a zealot or evangelist, but it is subtly oppressive nonetheless.

I have labeled my final category of former smokers the   8 serene. This classification is meant to encourage those who find the other psychic styles of ex-smokers disagreeable. Serenity is quieter than zealotry and evangelism, and those who qualify are not as self-righteous as the elect. The serene ex-smoker accepts himself and also accepts those around him who continue to smoke. This kind of serenity does not come easily, nor does it seem to be an immediate option for those who have stopped. Rather it is a goal, an end stage in a process of development during which some former smokers progress through one or more of the less-than-positive psychological points en route. For former smokers, serenity is thus a positive possibility that exists at the end of the rainbow. But all former smokers cannot reach that promised land.

What is it that permits some former smokers to become   9 serene? I think the key is self-acceptance and gratitude. The fully mature former smoker knows he has the soul of an addict and is grateful for the knowledge. He may sit up front in an airplane, but he knows he belongs in the smoking section in back. He doesn't regret that he quit smoking, nor any of his previous adventures with tobacco. As a former smoker, he is grateful for the experience and memory of craving a cigarette.

Serenity comes from accepting the lessons of one's life. And   10 ex-smokers who have reached this point in their worldview have much to be grateful for. They have learned about the potential and limits of change. In becoming the right kind of former smoker, they developed a healthy sense of self. This

---

[2]Puritanical.—Ed.

former smoker, for one, believes that it is better to crave (one hopes only occasionally) and not to smoke than never to have craved at all. And by accepting that fact, the reformed smoker does not need to excoriate, envy, or dissociate himself from those who continue to smoke.

Expanding Vocabulary

Match each word in column A with its definition in column B. When in doubt, first find the word in the essay and look for context clues to aid your understanding of the word's meaning. Then, if necessary, use your dictionary to complete the matching exercise. The number in parentheses is the number of the paragraph in which the word appears.

Column A	Column B
watershed (1)	flimsy, uncertain
cessation (1)	deliberate self-restraint
zealot (1)	based on casual accounts rather than strong evidence
degenerates (2)	
tenuous (3)	one fanatically devoted to a cause
recidivist (3)	seeking to convert others from one belief to another
anecdotal (4)	
vitriolic (4)	self-satisfied
proselytizing (7)	turning point
sects (7)	scathing, caustic, sarcastic
abstinence (7)	mental, behavioral
foreordained (7)	declines in quality
smug (7)	denounce strongly
psychic (8)	ceasing, halt
excoriate (10)	narrowly defined religious groups
	predestined
	one who lapses into previous behavior

Understanding Content

1. How does the zealot feel about smokers? What motivates the zealot? What group of ex-smokers can often be found among the zealots?
2. What is the evangelist's attitude toward quitting? How do smokers feel about the evangelist?
3. How do the elect differ from evangelists? What attitude of the elect bothers smokers?

4. How do the serene differ from the other ex-smokers? How should ex-smokers view this category? What is the psychological state of the serene ex-smoker?

Drawing Inferences about Thesis and Purpose

1. What is the author's purpose in writng?
2. What is Zimring's thesis in his classification of ex-smokers?

Analyzing Strategies and Style

1. Zimring draws one word (*recidivist*) from his field, the law, but many of his words come from what other field or subject area? What does he gain from using so many words from this field?
2. Zimring announces early in his essay that he is an ex-smoker. Why is it important for him to tell this to readers?

Thinking Critically

1. Are you an ex-smoker? If so, do you see yourself in one of Zimring's categories? Are there other categories that he should add?
2. Are you a smoker? If so, do you recognize Zimring's classification of ex-smokers? Which type bothers you the most? (Why are you still smoking?)
3. Is it always best to serenely accept what others do—their habits, their speech, their lifestyles? Or is there a role for zealots or evangelists? Support your position.

The Science and Secrets of Personal Space

CURT SUPLEE

Curt Suplee is a science writer and editor for the *Washington Post*. He has written *Everyday Science Explained* (1996) and *Physics in the 20th Century* (1999). His analysis of personal and public spaces appeared in the *Post*'s Horizon section on June 9, 1999.

Questions to Guide Your Reading and Reflection

1. How can the police use knowledge of personal space to aid their work?
2. What is your comfort level for personal space?

1   It's a free country, right? Well, not exactly. Every day, all day long, the specific position of your body and the state of your mind are under the control of a powerful and authoritative force of which you are almost entirely unaware.

2   It's the system of personal space. Every culture has its own, and some are so drastically different that they can cause friction—or at least extreme unease—when groups such as Arabs and northern Europeans get together.

3   Individual idiosyncracies and social context can modify the rules slightly, as we shall see. But within a culture, the code usually is firmly imprinted by age 12 and remains surprisingly constant from town to town and region to region.

4   For the average American, according to anthropologist Edward T. Hall, there are four distinctive spacial zones, each with a well-understood spectrum of appropriate behavior.

5   The nearest Hall calls the "intimate" zone, which extends outward from the skin about 18 inches. This is the range within which lovers touch and parents communicate with infants. At that distance, it is difficult to focus on another person's face, which appears larger than your entire field of vision. That is one reason why people often kiss with their eyes closed.

6   Within this zone, the sense of smell is important; and body heat is felt immediately. For example, sexual arousal customarily floods the abdomen with blood. Many people say they can sense the condition of a partner, even during cocktail conversation or formal ballroom dancing, by feeling the radiated heat.

7   The next, or "personal," zone, extends from 18 inches to about 4 feet. Within this range, you discuss private or serious matters and confer with literally "close" friends. Touch is easy throughout the nearest part of this space, up to about 30 inches. Alternatively, you can keep someone "at arm's length."

8   (Although you may be unaware of the rules of personal space, your language is not. Many of our familiar phrases reflect our cultural code and what happens when somebody is too close for comfort.)

9   Within the personal zone, you can focus sharply on another person's face and read very subtle details of expression. But you'll probably move your eyes a lot to focus on various parts of the other person's face. Watch somebody else talking at this distance, and you'll see his or her gaze flick rapidly from one spot to another.

You'll also notice that personal groups larger than two or   10
three are very rare, because it becomes difficult to maintain
appropriate spacing with more people.

Casual acquaintances or people who just want to tell you   11
something relatively unimportant had better stay well outside
the 30-inch inner personal zone. If they don't, they'll make you
very uncomfortable, and you may find yourself inadvertently
backing up until you're trapped against a wall.

One reason that economy-class air travel frequently is so   12
ghastly is that the strangers who are your seatmates are way
inside the close personal zone. Worse yet, side-by-side seating
is widely felt to be the most intimate arrangement. Men will
not voluntarily choose it unless the alternative is sitting too far
apart to talk.

In one study, American, English, Dutch, Swedish and   13
Pakistani subjects all ranked the side-by-side position as psychologically closest, followed by corner seating, face-to-face,
and various diagonal arrangements.

The "social-consultive" zone, in which most day-to-day   14
work and ordinary conversation occurs, starts at 4 feet and
goes to about 10 feet. In American culture, eight feet is the point
at which you pretty much have to acknowledge another person's presence. Beyond that, you can ignore someone without
giving obvious offense.

Usually, there are no smell or heat sensations at 4 to 10   15
feet, and much nonverbal information is conveyed by large-
scale body language. The whole body is visible as a unit at
about seven feet, although you can only focus on part
because the clearest vision occurs in a cone of about 15
degrees from the eyeball.

Finally, there is an all-purpose "public" zone that begins at   16
about 10 feet and extends to 25 feet. Thirty feet is the customary
nearest distance for addresses by public officials or celebrities.

Studies have shown that people are more likely to interact   17
with somebody who looks weird if that person stays well outside the personal zone. In one experiment, a researcher dressed
as a punk rocker pretended to be looking for help from people
sitting at tables in a shopping mall food court.

"Although only one in 15 people consented to help the   18
punker when she sat right next to them, 40 percent agreed to

help when she sat at a medium distance," the researchers found. But "80 percent of the people agreed to help her when she took the seat farthest away."

Over the Line

19   When someone does something that violates the tacit rules of the zone system, we are perplexed, annoyed or both. For example, if a person wanted a date with you and asked you out from 10 feet away—two feet beyond the farthest range of business conversation—you'd certainly think twice about agreeing, even if you were initially inclined to go.

20   On the other hand, a Latin American or French person, from a culture with a much closer personal interaction distance, could seem to be too "forward" or "coming on too strong" if he or she made the request from two feet away.

21   Sometimes, the resulting discomfort is intentional. Psychologist Robert Sommer notes in his book *Personal Space* that police interrogators are taught to intrude well inside the personal zone when questioning suspects.

22   Similarly, we often decide that someone is wearing "too much" perfume or cologne if the scent extends past the distance of personal space. So if you can smell a woman's perfume 8 feet away, you may find it irritating—not just because of the odor itself but because she is making what should be an intimate olfactory statement in public space. . . .

Size Does Matter

23   Variations abound. In much of India, there are only two zones: intimate and public. Some Mediterranean cultures have personal zones that begin much closer than those typical of Americans or northern Europeans. That's why Americans sometimes feel crowded or stressed in France or Italy.

24   And, of course, some cultures simply build things differently. Japanese rooms seem too small by Western standards, and the furniture tends to be placed in the center rather than along the walls. What we don't know is that the traditional Japanese room configuration can be changed by moving the lightweight walls.

25   Thus, what we perceive as a permanent space is merely a temporary arrangement from another perspective. Conversely,

our fondness for big spaces with furniture at the edges can make Western rooms look barren to the Japanese eye.

In 1967, Hong Kong's housing authority was constructing 26 apartments with 35 square feet per occupant. That's 5-by-7, about the size of a modern work "cubicle." When a westerner asked why the design was so stingy, a construction supervisor replied, "With 60 square feet per person, the tenants would sublet."

Birth and Turf

But each culture's rules arise from the same fundamental 27 biological impetus, which extends throughout the animal kingdom—the tendency to mark and defend one's own territory or to avoid intruding on someone else's.

Think about that next time you sit down in a cafeteria or 28 library. If you find an empty table that can seat six or eight, you're probably going to sit at one of the corner chairs—an "avoidance" position, according to psychologists—and you'll most likely face the door because some ancestral instinct says you might have to flee.

Dogs mark their territory by urinating at the boundaries. 29 Happily, human civilization has not evolved this trait. But we're constantly doing the equivalent.

Everyone has been vaguely irritated by the person in a 30 movie theater who spreads coats and bags across six seats and then goes off for popcorn. Nonetheless, we'll bypass any space that faintly appears to be "marked" by an absentee squatter. One study showed that, even in a busy and crowded library, a simple stack of magazines in front of a chair kept that seat open for more than an hour.

Analogously, you may find that when you enter someone's 31 home, you carefully avoid sitting in what seems to be the father's "personal" chair. Or you may notice how some passengers in the Metro system claim two spaces—an "aggressive" position—by putting a briefcase next to them or taking the outermost of the two side-by-side seats. . . .

Eyes Right

Space can be invaded by vision as well as another's presence, 32 and visual territories also differ from culture to culture. Unlike, say, the French, whose "frank" stares can be intimidating to outsiders, Americans rarely look directly at each other for very long, even during intense conversation.

33   In the animal kingdom, an averted gaze often indicates a passive stance. But in America, it is merely polite. We consider it an invasion of personal space to "stare" at someone, even briefly, and sensitivity varies by distance.

34   Thus, when the door closes on a crowded elevator, you'll usually notice two behaviors. First, the occupants automatically adjust their positions to create the same amount of space between each. Then most people either look down at their feet or up at the floor indicator rather than at one another.

35   In fact, one experiment showed that people will sit closer to a picture of a person with the eyes closed than to an otherwise identical image with the eyes open.

36   The English, on the other hand, regard it as rude not to look directly at the other person during conversation. To do otherwise makes it appear that you're not paying attention.

37   But in order to hold the head still and the gaze steady while listening to someone, one has to be far enough away so the eyes aren't constantly shifting around the other person's face. Thus the English tend to stand near the outer limits of American personal space, making them seem aloof, reserved or literally "stand-offish."

Expanding Vocabulary

Examine the following words in their contexts in the essay and then write a brief definition or synonym of each one. Do not use a dictionary. Try to guess each word's meaning from the context. The number in parentheses is the number of the paragraph in which the word appears.

idiosyncracies (3)	interrogators (21)
spectrum (4)	olfactory (22)
inadvertently (11)	impetus (27)
tacit (19)	analogously (31)

Understanding Content

1. What are the characteristics of the intimate zone?
2. What are the dimensions and uses of the personal zone?
3. What terms have evolved from the dynamics of the personal zone?

4. How do most people view sitting next to strangers?
5. What are the dimensions and characteristics of the third zone? At what distance do we usually have to acknowledge another person?
6. What are the dimensions of the public zone?
7. What are some of the ways we "mark" our personal space?
8. How do American and British and French patterns differ regarding looking directly at someone?

Drawing Inferences about Thesis and Purpose

1. Why are we irritated by people who spread their belongings over several chairs?
2. What is Suplee's purpose in writing? State his thesis.

Analyzing Strategies and Style

1. What are the sources of the author's information? How does he provide this information for readers?
2. Describe the strategies Suplee uses to introduce each of his four space zones.
3. What *type* of information does the author provide for each of the zones?

Thinking Critically

1. Are you familiar with this information about personal space? If not, does Suplee's analysis make sense to you? Think about your own experiences on elevators and in movie theaters.
2. What information about zones is most helpful for our personal relationships? Explain your response.
3. What information is most helpful for our dealings with people we don't know? Explain your response.

The Ways We Lie

─────────

STEPHANIE ERICSSON

A screenwriter and advertising copywriter, Stephanie Ericsson is the author of *Companion Through the Darkness: Inner Dialogues on Grief* (1992) and *Companion into the Dawn: Inner Dialogues on Loving* (1994). After losing her husband while pregnant with

their child, Ericsson kept a journal which has served as the basis
for her writing and for her frequent speaking engagements on
the subject of loss. The following analysis of the various types
of lies we tell was published originally in the Nov./Dec. 1992
issue of the *Utne Reader.*

Questions to Guide Your Reading and Reflection

1. What is the definition of the term *lie*?
2. Do you define all false impressions as lies?

---

1   The bank called today and I told them my deposit was in the
mail, even though I hadn't written a check yet. It'd been a
rough day. The baby I'm pregnant with decided to do aerobics
on my lungs for two hours, our three-year-old daughter
painted the living-room couch with lipstick, the IRS put me on
hold for an hour, and I was late to a business meeting because
I was tired.

2   I told my client that the traffic had been bad. When my partner came home, his haggard face told me his day hadn't gone
any better than mine, so when he asked, "How was your day?"
I said, "Oh, fine," knowing that one more straw might break
his back. A friend called and wanted to take me to lunch. I said
I was busy. Four lies in the course of a day, none of which I felt
the least bit guilty about.

3   We lie. We all do. We exaggerate, we minimize, we avoid
confrontation, we spare people's feelings, we conveniently forget, we keep secrets, we justify lying to the big-guy institutions.
Like most people, I indulge in small falsehoods and still think
of myself as an honest person. Sure I lie, but it doesn't hurt anything. Or does it?

4   I once tried going a whole week without telling a lie, and it
was paralyzing. I discovered that telling the truth all the time
is nearly impossible. It means living with some serious consequences: The bank charges me $60 in overdraft fees, my part-
ner keels over when I tell him about my travails, my client fires
me for telling her I didn't feel like being on time, and my friend
takes it personally when I say I'm not hungry. There must be
some merit to lying.

5   But if I justify lying, what makes me any different from
slick politicians or the corporate robbers who raided the S&L

industry? Saying it's okay to lie one way and not another is hedging. I cannot seem to escape the voice deep inside me that tells me: When someone lies, someone loses.

What far-reaching consequences will I, or others, pay as a result of my lie? Will someone's trust be destroyed? Will someone else pay penance because I ducked out? We must consider the *meaning of our actions*. Deception, lies, capital crimes, and misdemeanors all carry meanings. *Webster's* definition of *lie* is specific:

1. a false statement or action especially made with the intent to deceive;
2. anything that gives or is meant to give a false impression.

A definition like this implies that there are many, many ways to tell a lie. Here are just a few.

The White Lie

A man who won't lie to a woman has very little consideration for her feelings.

—Bergen Evans

The white lie assumes that the truth will cause more damage than a simple, harmless untruth. Telling a friend he looks great when he looks like hell can be based on a decision that the friend needs a compliment more than a frank opinion. But, in effect, it is the liar deciding what is best for the lied to. Ultimately, it is a vote of no confidence. It is an act of subtle arrogance for anyone to decide what is best for someone else.

Yet not all circumstances are quite so cut and dried. Take, for instance, the sergeant in Vietnam who knew one of his men was killed in action but listed him as missing so that the man's family would receive indefinite compensation instead of the lump-sum pittance the military gives widows and children. His intent was honorable. Yet for twenty years this family kept their hopes alive, unable to move on to a new life.

Facades

Et tu, Brute?

—Caesar

10   We all put up facades to one degree or another. When I put on a suit to go to see a client, I feel as though I am putting on another face, obeying the expectation that serious businesspeople wear suits rather than sweatpants. But I'm a writer. Normally, I get up, get the kid off to school, and sit at my computer in my pajamas until four in the afternoon. When I answer the phone, the caller thinks I'm wearing a suit (though the UPS man knows better).

11   But facades can be destructive because they are used to seduce others into an illusion. For instance, I recently realized that a former friend was a liar. He presented himself with all the right looks and the right words and offered lots of new consciousness theories, fabulous books to read, and fascinating insights. Then I did some business with him, and the time came for him to pay me. He turned out to be all talk and no walk. I heard a plethora of reasonable excuses, including in-depth descriptions of the big break around the corner. In six months of work, I saw less than a hundred bucks. When I confronted him, he raised both eyebrows and tried to convince me that I'd heard him wrong, that he'd made no commitment to me. A simple investigation into his past revealed a crowded graveyard of disenchanted former friends.

Ignoring the Plain Facts
Well, you must understand that Father Porter is only human . . .
—A Massachusetts Priest

12   In the sixties, the Catholic Church in Massachusetts began hearing complaints that Father James Porter was sexually molesting children. Rather than relieving him of his duties, the ecclesiastical authorities simply moved him from one parish to another between 1960 and 1967, actually providing him with a fresh supply of unsuspecting families and innocent children to abuse. After treatment in 1967 for pedophilia, he went back to work, this time in Minnesota. The new diocese was aware of Father Porter's obsession with children, but they needed priests and recklessly believed treatment had cured him. More children were abused until he was relieved of his duties a year

later. By his own admission, Porter may have abused as many as a hundred children.

Ignoring the facts may not in and of itself be a form of lying, 13 but consider the context of this situation. If a lie is *a false action done with the intention to deceive*, then the Catholic Church's conscious covering for Porter created irreparable consequences. The church became a co-perpetrator with Porter.

Deflecting

When you have no basis for an argument, abuse the plaintiff.
—Cicero

I've discovered that I can keep anyone from seeing the true 14 me by being selectively blatant. I set a precedent of being upfront about intimate issues, but I never bring up the things I truly want to hide; I just let people assume I'm revealing everything. It's an effective way of hiding.

Any good liar knows that the way to perpetuate an untruth 15 is to deflect attention from it. When Clarence Thomas exploded with accusations that the Senate hearings were a "high-tech lynching," he simply switched the focus from a highly charged subject to a radioactive subject. Rather than defending himself, he took the offensive and accused the country of racism. It was a brilliant maneuver. Racism is now politically incorrect in official circles—unlike sexual harassment, which still rewards those who can get away with it.

Some of the most skillful deflectors are passive-aggressive 16 people who, when accused of inappropriate behavior, refuse to respond to the accusations. This you-don't-exist stance infuriates the accuser, who, understandably, screams something obscene out of frustration. The trap is sprung and the act of deflection successful, because now the passive-aggressive person can indignantly say, "Who can talk to someone as unreasonable as you?" The real issue is forgotten and the sins of the original victim become the focus. Feeling guilty of name-calling, the victim is fully tamed and crawls into a hole, ashamed. I have watched this fighting technique work thousands of times in disputes between men and women, and what I've learned is that the real culprit is not necessarily the one who swears the loudest.

Omission

The cruelest lies are often told in silence.
—R. L. Stevenson

17   Omission involves telling most of the truth minus one or two key facts whose absence changes the story completely. You break a pair of glasses that are guaranteed under normal use and get a new pair, without mentioning that the first pair broke during a rowdy game of basketball. Who hasn't tried something like that? But what about omission of information that could make a difference in how a person lives his or her life?

18   For instance, one day I found out that rabbinical legends tell of another woman in the Garden of Eden before Eve. I was stunned. The omission of the Sumerian goddess Lilith from Genesis—as well as her demonization by ancient misogynists as an embodiment of female evil—felt like spiritual robbery. I felt like I'd just found out my mother was really my stepmother. To take seriously the tradition that Adam was created out of the same mud as his equal counterpart, Lilith, redefines all of Judeo-Christian history.

19   Some renegade Catholic feminists introduced me to a view of Lilith that had been suppressed during the many centuries when this strong goddess was seen only as a spirit of evil. Lilith was a proud goddess who defied Adam's need to control her, attempted negotiations, and when this failed, said adios and left the Garden of Eden.

20   This omission of Lilith from the Bible was a patriarchal strategy to keep women weak. Omitting the strong-woman archetype of Lilith from Western religions and starting the story with Eve the Rib has helped keep Christian and Jewish women believing they were the lesser sex for thousands of years.

Stereotypes and Clichés

Where opinion does not exist, the status quo becomes stereotyped and all originality is discouraged.
—Bertrand Russell

21   Stereotype and cliché serve a purpose as a form of shorthand. Our need for vast amounts of information in nanoseconds has made the stereotype vital to modern communication.

Unfortunately, it often shuts down original thinking, giving those hungry for truth a candy bar of misinformation instead of a balanced meal. The stereotype explains a situation with just enough truth to seem unquestionable.

All the *isms*—racism, sexism, ageism, et al.—are founded on 22 and fueled by the stereotype and the cliché, which are lies of exaggeration, omission, and ignorance. They are always dangerous. They take a single tree and make it a landscape. They destroy curiosity. They close minds and separate people. The single mother on welfare is assumed to be cheating. Any black male could tell you how much of his identity is obliterated daily by stereotypes. Fat people, ugly people, beautiful people, old people, large-breasted women, short men, the mentally ill, and the homeless all could tell you how much more they are like us than we want to think. I once admitted to a group of people that I had a mouth like a truck driver. Much to my surprise, a man stood up and said, "I'm a truck driver, and I never cuss." Needless to say, I was humbled.

Groupthink

Who is more foolish, the child afraid of the dark, or the man afraid of the light.

—Maurice Freehill

Irving Janis, in *Victims of GroupThink*, defines this sort of lie 23 as a psychological phenomenon within decision-making groups in which loyalty to the group has become more important than any other value, with the result that dissent and the appraisal of alternatives are suppressed. If you've ever worked on a committee or in a corporation, you've encountered groupthink. It requires a combination of other forms of lying—ignoring facts, selective memory, omission, and denial, to name a few.

The textbook example of groupthink came on December 7, 24 1941. From as early as the fall of 1941, the warnings came in, one after another, that Japan was preparing for a massive military operation. The Navy command in Hawaii assumed Pearl Harbor was invulnerable—the Japanese weren't stupid enough to attack the United States' most important base. On the other hand, racist stereotypes said the Japanese weren't smart enough to invent a torpedo effective in less than 60 feet of water (the fleet was docked in 30 feet); after all, U.S. technology hadn't been able to do it.

25   On Friday, December 5, normal weekend leave was granted to all the commanders at Pearl Harbor, even though the Japanese consulate in Hawaii was busy burning papers. Within the tight, good-ole-boy cohesiveness of the U.S. command in Hawaii, the myth of invulnerability stayed well entrenched. No one in the group considered the alternatives. The rest is history.

Out-and-Out Lies

The only form of lying that is beyond reproach is lying for its own sake.
—Oscar Wilde

26   Of all the ways to lie, I like this one the best, probably because I get tired of trying to figure out the real meanings behind things. At least I can trust the bald-faced lie. I once asked my five-year-old nephew, "Who broke the fence?" (I had seen him do it.) He answered, "The murderers." Who could argue?

27   At least when this sort of lie is told it can be easily confronted. As the person who is lied to, I know where I stand. The bald-faced lie doesn't toy with my perceptions—it argues with them. It doesn't try to refashion reality, it tries to refute it. *Read my* lips . . . No sleight of hand. No guessing. If this were the only form of lying, there would be no such thing as floating anxiety or the adult-children of alcoholics movement.

Dismissal

Pay no attention to that man behind the curtain! I am the Great Oz!
—The Wizard of Oz

28   Dismissal is perhaps the slipperiest of all lies. Dismissing feelings, perceptions, or even the raw facts of a situation ranks as a kind of lie that can do as much damage to a person as any other kind of lie.

29   The roots of many mental disorders can be traced back to the dismissal of reality. Imagine that a person is told from the time she is a tot that her perceptions are inaccurate. *"Mommy. I'm scared."* "No you're not, darling." *"I don't like that man next door,*

he makes me feel icky." "Johnny, that's a terrible thing to say, of course you like him. You go over there right now and be nice to him."

I've often mused over the idea that madness is actually a sane reaction to an insane world. Psychologist R.D. Laing supports this hypothesis in *Sanity, Madness & The Family*, an account of his investigations into the families of schizophrenics. The common thread that ran through all of the families he studied was a deliberate, staunch dismissal of the patient's perceptions from a very early age. Each of the patients started out with an accurate grasp of reality, which, through meticulous and methodical dismissal, was demolished until the only reality the patient could trust was catatonia.

Dismissal runs the gamut. Mild dismissal can be quite handy for forgiving the foibles of others in our day-to-day lives. Toddlers who have just learned to manipulate their parents' attention sometimes are dismissed out of necessity. Absolute attention from the parents would require so much energy that no one would get to eat dinner. But we must be careful and attentive about how far we take our "necessary" dismissals. Dismissal is a dangerous tool, because it's nothing less than a lie.

Delusion

We lie loudest when we lie to ourselves.
　　　　—Eric Hoffer

I could write the book on this one. Delusion, a cousin of dismissal, is the tendency to see excuses as facts. It's a powerful lying tool because it filters out information that contradicts what we want to believe. Alcoholics who believe that the problems in their lives are legitimate reasons for drinking rather than results of the drinking offer the classic example of deluded thinking. Delusion uses the mind's ability to see things in myriad ways to support what it wants to be the truth.

But delusion is also a survival mechanism we all use. If we were to fully contemplate the consequences of our stockpiles of nuclear weapons or global warming, we could hardly function on a day-to-day level. We don't want to incorporate that much reality into our lives because to do so would be paralyzing.

34   Delusion acts as an adhesive to keep the status quo intact. It shamelessly employs dismissal, omission, and amnesia, among other sorts of lies. Its most cunning defense is that it cannot see itself.

> *The liar's punishment . . . is that he cannot believe anyone else.*
> —George Bernard Shaw

35   These are only a few of the ways we lie. Or are lied to. As I said earlier, it's not easy to entirely eliminate lies from our lives. No matter how pious we may try to be, we will still embellish, hedge, and omit to lubricate the daily machinery of living. But there is a world of difference between telling functional lies and living a lie. Martin Buber once said, "The lie is the spirit committing treason against itself." Our acceptance of lies becomes a cultural cancer that eventually shrouds and reorders reality until moral garbage becomes as invisible to us as water is to a fish.

36   How much do we tolerate before we become sick and tired of being sick and tired? When will we stand up and declare our right to trust? When do we stop accepting that the real truth is in the fine print? Whose lips do we read this year when we vote for president? When will we stop being so reticent about making judgments? When do we stop turning over our personal power and responsibility to liars?

37   Maybe if I don't tell the bank the check's in the mail I'll be less tolerant of the lies told to me every day. A country song I once heard said it all for me: "You've got to stand for something or you'll fall for anything."

Expanding Vocabulary

Match each word in column A with its definition in column B. When in doubt, first find the word in the essay and look for context clues to aid your understanding of the word's meaning. Then, if necessary, use your dictionary to complete the matching exercise. The number in parentheses is the number of the paragraph in which the word appears.

Column A	*Column B*
travails (4)	careful and precise
hedging (5)	love of children that is abusive

penance (6)	cause to turn aside, to blunt the force of
facades (10)	impossible to repair
plethora (11)	those who hate women
pedophilia (12)	prolong the existence of
irreparable (13)	many
blatant (14)	struggles
perpetuate (15)	strong, solid
deflect (15)	abnormal condition often marked
misogynists (18)	by withdrawal
obliterated (22)	something that conceals
staunch (29)	deceptive appearances
meticulous (29)	completely wiped out
catatonia (29)	atonement for one's sins
foibles (30)	super-abundance
myriad (31)	offensively obvious
shrouds (34)	minor weaknesses of character
	making an ambiguous statement

Understanding Content

1. What is the fundamental problem with the white lie?
2. What is destructive about facades?
3. How can ignoring obvious facts be a form of lying?
4. How does the lie by deflecting work? What makes it effective?
5. How do we lie by omission?
6. What lying strategies underlie the stereotype? Groupthink?
7. What happened on December 7, 1941?
8. Why is dismissal dangerous?
9. What is useful about delusion? What is dangerous about it?
10. Who may suffer the most from our lying? Why?

Drawing Inferences about Thesis and Purpose

1. Ericsson begins paragraph 6 with three questions. How are we supposed to answer these questions?
2. What is Ericsson's purpose in writing?
3. Write a thesis that reveals the author's use of a classification strategy.

Analyzing Strategies and Style

1. The author begins by recounting four lies she told in one day. What does she gain by this opening?

2. In paragraph 21 Ericsson uses a metaphor to make her point. Explain the metaphor.
3. The author introduces each category of lying with a quotation. How do these quotations contribute to the essay?

Thinking Critically

1. Ericsson suggests that lying is self-destructive. Does this idea make sense to you? Why or why not?
2. Which types of lies seem to have the greatest potential for damaging others? Explain your choice.
3. Which quotation, for you, offers the greatest insight? Why?

Class Acts: America's Changing Middle Class

RALPH WHITEHEAD JR.

Beginning his career as a journalist in Chicago, Ralph White-head became a professor of journalism at the University of Massachusetts in 1973. He is the author of many articles on social structures and public opinion and has been a consultant to political and labor groups and to the U.S. Department of Labor. His study of the changing social/economic hierarchy in American society was first published in the Jan./Feb. 1990 issue of the *Utne Reader*.

Questions to Guide Your Reading and Reflection

1. What does Whitehead mean by his use of "collar," as in "bright collar" and "new collar"? What does "collar" stand for?
2. Into what social class would you place yourself? On what basis?

1   As we enter the 1990s, American society exhibits a vastly different social and economic makeup from the one that we grew accustomed to in the thirty years that followed World War II. The gap between the top and bottom is far greater now, of course, but the economic position of people in the middle is

changing, too. This new social ladder is seen most vividly in the lives of our younger generations, the baby boom and the later baby bust. Because the new ladder is so much steeper than the old one, it's creating an alarming new degree of polarization in American life.

As it held sway for roughly the first three decades after 2 World War II, the old social ladder was shaped largely by the continuing expansion of the middle class. For the first time, many people could afford to buy a house, a car (or two), a washer and dryer, an outdoor grill, adequate health coverage, maybe a motor boat, and possibly college for the kids. And for the first time, a growing number of blacks and Hispanics could enter the middle class.

Within this expanding middle class, there were a couple of 3 fairly well-defined ways of life: white-collar life and blue-collar life. White-collar life was typified by TV characters like Ward and June Cleaver and later Mike and Carol Brady. Blue-collar life was typified by characters like Ralph and Alice Kramden and later Archie and Edith Bunker.

At the top of the old social ladder stood a small number of 4 rich people. A larger but declining number of poor people stood at the bottom, and the rest of the ladder was taken up by the middle-class. The old social ladder looked roughly like this:

THE RICH

THE EXPANDING MIDDLE CLASS:
White collar
Blue collar

THE POOR

The new social ladder is markedly different. Within the baby 5 boom and baby bust generations, the middle class is no longer expanding. Therefore the new social ladder is shaped by—and at the same time is helping to shape—a new polarization between the haves and the have-nots. The social ladder of the 1990s looks roughly like this:

UPSCALE AMERICA:
The Rich
The Overclass

THE DIVERGING MIDDLE CLASS:
Bright collar
New collar
Blue collar
DOWNSCALE AMERICA:
The Poor
The Underclass

The rich are still on top, of course. But the new generation of rich people is typified by Donald Trump, the billionaire developer of luxury buildings for the newly rich, rather than by someone like his father, Fred Trump, a developer who made millions building modestly priced postwar homes and apartments for the expanding middle class—the kinds of homes in which the Kramdens and Bunkers lived.

6   The poor are still with us, of course, but they're no longer at the bottom. It's not because they've risen to the middle class but rather because some of them have fallen into the underclass. Because definitions of the underclass vary, so do estimates of its size. However, it does include at least two million people who lead lives that aren't typified in America's popular culture. To belong to the underclass is to be without a face and without a voice.

7   Just as an underclass has emerged, so has an overclass, which occupies the rung just below the rich. Located chiefly in a dozen metropolises and heavily concentrated in lucrative management and professional jobs, the overclass is roughly the same size as the underclass. Its significance lies not in its numbers, however, but in its immense power throughout American society. The overclass holds the highest level positions in the fields of entertainment, media, marketing, advertising, real estate, finance, and politics. It's pursued for its consumption dollars and cajoled for its investment dollars. It is crudely typified by the media stereotype of the yuppie.

8   What clearly stood out on the old social ladder that shaped American society during the fifties and sixties was the dominant presence of an expanding middle class. What is noticeable about the new social ladder is the unmistakable emergence of distinct upper and lower rungs, and the vast social, economic, and psychological distance between them. Together, the rich

and the overclass form Upscale America. Together, the underclass and the poor form Downscale America.

The expanding middle class, with its white and blue collars,   9
has given way in the baby boom and baby bust generations to
a diverging middle class. It consists largely of three kinds of
workers:

- **Bright collars**. Within the ranks of managerial and professional   10
  workers a new category of job has emerged. The white-collar
  worker is receding and the bright-collar worker is advancing. The
  bright collars are the 20 million knowledge workers born since 1945:
  lawyers and teachers, architects and social workers, accountants
  and budget analysts, engineers and consultants, rising executives
  and midlevel administrators. They earn their living by taking intellectual initiatives. They face the luxury and the necessity of making
  their own decisions on the job and in their personal lives.

  Bright-collar people lack the touchstones that guided white-   11
  collar workers like Ward Cleaver in the 1950s and 1960s. The white
  collars believed in institutions; bright collars are skeptical of them.
  The corporate chain of command, a strong force in white-collar life
  then, is far weaker for bright collars today. They place a premium
  on individuality, on standing out rather than fitting in. Although
  the older white collars knew the rules and played by them, bright
  collars can't be sure what the rules are and must think up their
  own. The white collars were organization men and women (mostly
  men); bright collars are entrepreneurs interested in building
  careers for themselves outside big corporations.

  Three quarters of the managers and professionals of the 1950s   12
  were men. Today half are women. Seven percent are black or Hispanic or Asian. Bright collars make up a third of the baby boom
  work force. They're typified by figures like *L.A. Law's* attorneys.
- **Blue collars**. Within the manufacturing workplace, blue-collar   13
  work endures, but on a much smaller scale. Thirty years ago
  almost 40 percent of the adult work force did blue-collar work.
  Today, after the relative decline of American heavy industry, it's
  done by less than 25 percent of baby boom workers. During the
  fifties and sixties, blue-collar wages rose steadily, thus helping fuel
  the expansion of the middle class. In the past 15 years these wages
  have been relatively flat. Young blue collars often must live near
  the economic margins.

  The blue-collar world is still a man's world. Roughly three   14
  quarters of today's younger blue collars are men—the same percentage as in the 1950s. Twelve percent are black, Hispanic, or
  Asian. Within a growing number of innovative manufacturing

workplaces, new models of blue-collar work have begun to emerge, but they haven't yet advanced enough to trigger a new category of American worker. In the popular culture the new generation of blue collars finds a voice in Bruce Springsteen, but it still hasn't found a face.

15 • New collars. These people aren't managers and professionals, and they don't do physical labor. Their jobs fall between those two worlds. They're secretaries, clerks, telephone operators, key-punch operators, inside salespeople, police officers. They often avoid the grime and regimentation of blue-collar work. Two thirds of the new collars are women. More than 15 percent are black, Hispanic, or Asian. The new collars make up at least 35 percent of the baby boom work force.

16   Federal Express truck drivers are typical new-collar workers. They design pickup and delivery routes, explain the company's services and fees, provide mailing supplies, and handle relatively sophisticated information technology in their trucks. They aren't traditional truck drivers so much as sales clerks in offices on wheels.

17   The rise of the new social ladder has helped to drive a number of changes in American life, but one of them, already evident, should be underscored: the dramatic shift of power within both the middle class and the society as a whole.

18   As members of the expanding middle class of the postwar years, blue collars once held considerable leverage. In the electorate, for every vote cast by the white collars in 1960, the blue collars cast two. In the workplace, they acted through powerful unions. In the marketplace, they were valued as consumers. As a result, blue collars dealt with white collars as equals. In the fifties and sixties, whatever class lines still divided the two groups seemed to be dissolving.

19   Within the diverging middle class today, the balance of power is much different. In the electorate, for every vote cast by younger blue collars in 1988, bright collars cast two. In the workplace, younger blue-collar workers are losing union power, while bright collars exert the power of their knowledge and privilege of their status. In the marketplace, blue-collar consumers are written off as too downscale, while the bright-collar consumer is courted as an aspiring member of the overclass. Deep divisions have sprung up between bright collars and blue collars. They look a lot like class lines.

The rise of an overclass throws the decline of blue-collar 20
life into sharper relief, and vice versa. Upscale yuppie haunts
spring up: the health club, the gourmet takeout shop, the
pricy boutique, the atrium building. Downscale blue-collar
haunts wither: the union hall, the lodge, the beauty parlor,
the mill. The guys with red suspenders began showing up in
the beer commercials right about the time the loggers and
guys with air hammers began to disappear. The overclass's
stock portfolios began to get fat just as blue-collar families
were losing their pensions and health insurance. Condo
prices were climbing in Atlanta just as bungalow prices
fell in Buffalo. It seems that there's a battle here, a zero-
sum game, whereby the rise of one comes at the expense of
the other.

The contrast between the rich and the underclass is sharper 21
than ever. If you look at the new social ladder in New York, you
see Donald Trump in his penthouse and the homeless people
in the subways.

This situation intensifies the shift of power in society as a 22
whole. With the middle class divided, the center cannot hold.
The dominant forces in society become Upscale America and
Downscale America—or, more precisely, Upscale America
versus Downscale America. Upscale America uses its power
to secure privileges such as proposed cuts in the capital gains
tax. Downscale America strikes back blindly through rising
rates of crime. Through the old social ladder, the
expanding middle class acted as the nation's glue. With the
new social ladder, the diverging middle class is merely caught
in the crossfire.

Expanding Vocabulary

Study the definitions for any of the following words that you do not
know. Then select five words and use each one in a separate sentence.
The number in parentheses is the number of the paragraph in which
the word appears.

polarization (1)	innovative (10)
lucrative (7)	sophisticated (16)
cajoled (7)	leverage (18)
yuppie (7)	zero-sum (20)
entrepreneurs (11)	

Understanding Content

1. In the social ladder that existed for thirty years after World War II, what was happening to the middle class?
2. What were the four categories on the older social ladder?
3. What two important changes are taking place in the middle class?
4. What are the characteristics of the underclass?
5. Who makes up the new overclass?
6. What are the characteristics of the three new categories of workers in the new middle class?
7. How has power changed in the new bright collar and blue collar classes?

Drawing Inferences about Thesis and Purpose

1. What is Whitehead's purpose in writing? Does he have more than one? State his thesis.
2. What does Whitehead mean when he writes of a "zero-sum game" played between upscale and downscale America (paragraph 20)?
3. What implications for America do we find in the final paragraph?

Analyzing Strategies and Style

1. What does the author gain by the visual presentation of both the former and the current class categories?
2. Whitehead uses several TV characters as examples. How are they effective? What do they imply about his expected audience?
3. The author uses contrast within his classification structure. Find several nicely balanced contrast sentences and consider why they are effective.

Thinking Critically

1. Does Whitehead's classification of contemporary American class structure seem on target? Why or why not?
2. Many Americans like to believe that we are a "classless" society; everybody is the same. Whitehead doesn't do anything to address, or counter, this attitude. What might this tell us about his expected audience?
3. Do you agree with Whitehead that the diverging middle class and the conflict between upscale and downscale America pose serious social problems for the United States? Why or why not?

Psst! Human Capital

DAVID BROOKS

A syndicated columnist and author of several books, David Brooks writes regularly for the *New York Times*, examining both political and cultural issues. Brooks, a recognized conservative, also appears on National Public Radio and the *Jim Lehrer Report* on PBS. His study of human capital was published November 13, 2005.

Questions to Guide Your Reading and Reflection

1. What does "human capital" mean? What do you expect this essay to be about?
2. What would you list as your human capital?

Help! I'm turning into the "plastics" guy from *The Graduate*. I'm   1
pulling people aside at parties and whispering that if they want to understand the future, it's just two words: "Human Capital."

If we want to keep up with the Chinese and the Indians,   2
we've got to develop our Human Capital. If we want to remain a just, fluid society: Human Capital. If we want to head off underclass riots: Human Capital.

As people drift away from me at these parties by pretending   3
to recognize long-lost friends across the room, I'm convinced that they don't really understand what human capital is.

Most people think of human capital the way economists and   4
policy makers do—as the skills and knowledge people need to get jobs and thrive in a modern economy. When President [George W.] Bush proposed his big education reform, he insisted on tests to measure skills and knowledge. When commissions issue reports, they call for longer school years, revamped curriculums and more funds so teachers can transmit skills and knowledge.

But skills and knowledge—the stuff you can measure with   5
tests—is only the most superficial component of human capital. U.S. education reforms have generally failed because they try to improve the skills of students without addressing the underlying components of human capital.

6   These underlying components are hard to measure and uncomfortable to talk about, but they are the foundation of everything that follows.

7   There's cultural capital: the habits, assumptions, emotional dispositions and linguistic capacities we unconsciously pick up from families, neighbors and ethnic groups—usually by age 3. In a classic study, James S. Coleman found that what happens in the family shapes a child's educational achievement more than what happens in school. In more recent research, James Heckman and Pedro Carneiro found that "most of the gaps in college attendance and delay are determined by early family factors."

8   There's social capital: the knowledge of how to behave in groups and within institutions. This can mean, for example, knowing what to do if your community college loses your transcript. Or it can mean knowing the basic rules of politeness. The University of North Carolina now offers seminars to poorer students so they'll know how to behave in restaurants.

9   There's moral capital: the ability to be trustworthy. Students who drop out of high school, but take the G.E.D. exam, tend to be smarter than high school dropouts. But their lifetime wages tend to be no higher than they are for those with no high school diplomas. That's because many people who pass the G.E.D. are less organized and less dependable than their less educated peers—as employers soon discover. Brains and skills don't matter if you don't show up on time.

10   There's cognitive capital. This can mean pure, inherited brainpower. But important cognitive skills are not measured by IQ tests and are not fixed. Some people know how to evaluate themselves and their abilities, while others with higher IQ's are clueless. Some low-IQ people can sense what others are feeling, while brainier peers cannot. Such skills can be improved over a lifetime.

11   Then there's aspirational capital: the fire-in-the-belly ambition to achieve. In his book *The Millionaire Mind*, Thomas J. Stanley reports that the average millionaire had a B-minus collegiate G.P.A.—not very good. But millionaires often had this experience: People told them they were too stupid to achieve something, so they set out to prove the naysayers wrong.

12   Over the past quarter-century, researchers have done a lot of work trying to understand the different parts of human

capital. Their work has been almost completely ignored by policy makers, who continue to treat human capital as just skills and knowledge. The result? A series of expensive policy failures.

We now spend more per capita on education than just about   13
any other country on earth, and the results are mediocre. No Child Left Behind treats students as skill-acquiring cogs in an economic wheel, and the results have been disappointing. We pour money into Title I and Head Start, but the long-term gains are insignificant.

These programs are not designed for the way people really   14
are. The only things that work are local, human-to-human immersions that transform the students down to their very beings. Extraordinary schools, which create intense cultures of achievement, work. Extraordinary teachers, who inspire students to transform their lives, work. The programs that work touch all the components of human capital.

There's a great future in Human Capital, buddy. Enough said.   15

Expanding Vocabulary

Examine the following words in their contexts in the essay. Then write a brief definition or synonym for each one. Do not use a dictionary; try to guess the word's meaning from its context. The number in parentheses is the number of the paragraph in which the word appears.

dispositions (7)	aspirational (11)
linguistic (7)	per capita (13)
cognitive (10)	immersions (14)

Understanding Content

1. How do most people define human capital, according to Brooks?
2. How do these misconceptions affect education in this country?
3. Explain, in your own words, each of the five types of human capital.

Drawing Inferences about Thesis and Purpose

1. Brooks asserts that components of human capital are "uncomfortable to talk about." Of the five types, which ones most typically make people "uncomfortable"? Why?
2. What is most important to Brooks, explaining types of human capital—or something else?
3. Write a thesis statement for this essay.

Analyzing Strategies and Style

1. Brooks begins and ends by presenting himself as a character in the movie *The Graduate*. What does he gain by this "frame" strategy? What is the risk of such strategies?
2. How does the author introduce each category of human capital? What makes this a useful technique?

Thinking Critically

1. Do you agree that schools put too much emphasis on knowledge and skills? If so, what would you add/change to develop Brooks's human capital traits?
2. Are there some types of human capital that schools cannot readily develop? Explain.
3. Do you agree with Brooks that these five components are vitally important? Why or why not? Do you think some are more important than others? If so, why?

The Dog Ate My Disk and Other Tales of Woe

CAROLYN FOSTER SEGAL

With a Ph.D. in English from Lehigh University, Carolyn Foster Segal teaches English at Cedar Crest College in Pennsylvania. She is the author of poetry and fiction as well as essays and likes to assert that all writing "begins with observation." The following essay, popularly received by many faculty, was published on August 11, 2000, in the *Chronicle of Higher Education*.

Questions to Guide Your Reading and Reflection

1. If you were to list students' favorite excuses, what would be on your list?
2. Do you often turn work in late and try to get by with excuses? If so, why don't you just do the work on time?

1   Taped to the door of my office is a cartoon that features a cat explaining to his feline teacher, "The dog ate my homework." It is intended as a gently humorous reminder to my students

that I will not accept excuses for late work, and it, like the lengthy warning on my syllabus, has had absolutely no effect. With a show of energy and creativity that would be admirable if applied to the (missing) assignments in question, my students persist, week after week, semester after semester, year after year, in offering excuses about why their work is not ready. Those reasons fall into several broad categories: the family, the best friend, the evils of dorm life, the evils of technology, and the totally bizarre.

The Family

The death of the grandfather/grandmother is, of course, the   2
grandmother of all excuses. What heartless teacher would dare to question a student's grief or veracity? What heartless student would lie, wishing death on a revered family member, just to avoid a deadline? Creative students may win extra extensions (and days off) with a little careful planning and fuller plot development, as in the sequence of "My grandfather/grandmother is sick"; "Now my grandfather/grandmother is in the hospital"; and finally, "We could all see it coming—my grandfather/grandmother is dead."

Another favorite excuse is "the family emergency," which   3
(always) goes like this: "There was an emergency at home, and I had to help my family." It's a lovely sentiment, one that conjures up images of Louisa May Alcott's[1] little women rushing off with baskets of food and copies of *Pilgrim's Progress*,[2] but I do not understand why anyone would turn to my most irresponsible students in times of trouble.

The Best Friend

This heartwarming concern for others extends beyond the   4
family to friends, as in, "My best friend was up all night and I had to (a) stay up with her in the dorm, (b) drive her to the hospital, or (c) drive to her college because (1) her boyfriend broke up with her, (2) she was throwing up blood [no one catches a cold anymore; everyone throws up blood], or (3) her grandfather/grandmother died."

[1]Nineteenth-century author of the novel *Little Women*—Ed.
[2]Eighteenth-century book by John Bunyan—Ed.

5   At one private university where I worked as an adjunct, I heard an interesting spin that incorporated the motifs of both best friend and dead relative: "My best friend's mother killed herself." One has to admire the cleverness here: A mysterious woman in the prime of her life has allegedly committed suicide, and no professor can prove otherwise! And I admit I was moved, until finally I had to point out to my students that it was amazing how the simple act of my assigning a topic for a paper seemed to drive large numbers of otherwise happy and healthy middle-aged women to their deaths. I was careful to make that point during an off week, during which no deaths were reported.

The Evils of Dorm Life

6   These stories are usually fairly predictable; almost always feature the evil roommate or hallmate, with my student in the role of the innocent victim; and can be summed up as follows: My roommate, who is a horrible person, likes to party, and I, who am a good person, cannot concentrate on my work when he or she is partying. Variations include stories about the two people next door who were running around and crying loudly last night because (a) one of them had boyfriend/girlfriend problems; (b) one of them was throwing up blood; or (c) someone, somewhere, died. A friend of mine in graduate school had a student who claimed that his roommate attacked him with a hammer. That, in fact, was a true story; it came out in court when the bad roommate was tried for killing his grandfather.

The Evils of Technology

7   The computer age has revolutionized the student story, inspiring almost as many new excuses as it has Internet businesses. Here are just a few electronically enhanced explanations:

- The computer wouldn't let me save my work.
- The printer wouldn't print.
- The printer wouldn't print this disk.
- The printer wouldn't give me time to proofread.
- The printer made a black line run through all my words, and I know you can't read this, but do you still want it, or wait, here, take my disk. File name? I don't know what you mean.
- I swear I attached it.

- It's my roommate's computer, and she usually helps me, but she had to go to the hospital because she was throwing up blood.
- I did write to the newsgroup, but all my messages came back to me.
- I just found out that all my other newsgroup messages came up under a diferent name. I just want you to know that its really me who wrote all those messages, you can tel which ones our mine because I didnt use the spelcheck! But it was yours truely:) Anyway, just in case you missed those messages or dont belief its my writting. I'll repeat what I sad: I thought the last movie we watched in clas was borring.

The Totally Bizarre

I call the first story "The Pennsylvania Chain Saw Episode."   8
A commuter student called to explain why she had missed my morning class. She had gotten up early so that she would be wide awake for class. Having a bit of extra time, she walked outside to see her neighbor, who was cutting some wood. She called out to him, and he waved back to her with the saw. Wouldn't you know it, the safety catch wasn't on or was broken, and the blade flew right out of the saw and across his lawn and over her fence and across her yard and severed a tendon in her right hand. So she was calling me from the hospital, where she was waiting for surgery. Luckily, she reassured me, she had remembered to bring her paper and a stamped envelope (in a plastic bag, to avoid bloodstains) along with her in the ambulance, and a nurse was mailing everything to me even as we spoke.

That wasn't her first absence. In fact, this student had   9
missed most of the class meetings, and I had already recommended that she withdraw from the course. Now I suggested again that it might be best if she dropped the class. I didn't harp on the absences (what if even some of this story were true?). I did mention that she would need time to recuperate and that making up so much missed work might be difficult. "Oh, no," she said, "I can't drop this course. I had been planning to go on to medical school and become a surgeon, but since I won't be able to operate because of my accident, I'll have to major in English, and this course is more important than ever to me." She did come to the next class, wearing—as evidence of her recent trauma—a bedraggled Ace bandage on her left hand.

10   You may be thinking that nothing could top that excuse, but in fact I have one more story, provided by the same student, who sent me a letter to explain why her final assignment would be late. While recuperating from her surgery, she had begun corresponding on the Internet with a man who lived in Germany. After a one-week, whirlwind Web romance, they had agreed to meet in Rome, to rendezvous (her phrase) at the papal Easter Mass. Regrettably, the time of her flight made it impossible for her to attend class, but she trusted that I—just this once—would accept late work if the pope wrote a note.

Expanding Vocabulary

Study definitions of each of the following words and then use each one in a separate sentence. The number in parentheses is the number of the paragraph in which the word appears.

bizarre (1)	enhanced (7)
veracity (2)	recuperate (9)
conjures (3)	trauma (9)
motifs (5)	

Understanding Content

1. What are the five types of excuses?
2. How do students try to stretch the dead grandparent excuse?
3. What do the technology excuses have in common?

Drawing Inferences about Thesis and Purpose

1. From her choice of heading, what does the author suggest about her last category of excuses? How do you suppose she reacts to students whose excuses are categorized in this section?
2. What is Segal's thesis? Where does she state it?

Analyzing Strategies and Style

1. What does Segal use that visually reinforces her classification strategy? How do the bullets under "The Evils of Technology" reinforce her point that the Internet has inspired a host of new excuses?
2. Consider Segal's ending. How would you characterize it? What makes it effective?
3. The author's original audience was composed of instructors. Do her style and tone seem appropriate for that audience? What readers might not be so amused by her approach to her subject?

Thinking Critically

1. Why do people make excuses when they have already been informed that excuses will not change outcomes? Reflect on this element of human behavior and be prepared to debate the topic in class.
2. Do you think that Segal is unsympathetic to her students? If so, why? What would Segal's response be to this question?
3. Look again at the examples of excuses the author provides. Which, if any, would you believe to be true? Which, if any, would you accept? Why?

STUDENT ESSAY—DIVISION AND CLASSIFICATION

BUYING TIME
Garrett Berger

Chances are you own at least one wristwatch. Watches allow us immediate access to the correct time. They are indispensable items in our modern world, where, as the saying goes, time is money. Today the primary function of a wristwatch does not necessarily guide its design; like clothes, houses, and cars, watches have become fashion statements and a way to flaunt one's wealth.

Introduction connects to reader.

To learn how watches are being sold, I surveyed all of the full-page ads from the November issues of four magazines. The first two, GQ and Vogue, are well-known fashion magazines. The Robb Report is a rather new magazine that caters to the overclass. Forbes is of course a well-known

Student explains his methodology of collecting ads. Paragraph concludes with his thesis.

financial magazine. I was rather surprised at the number of advertisements I found. After surveying 86 ads, marketing 59 brands, I have concluded that today watches are being sold through five main strategies: DESIGN/BRAND appeal, CRAFTS-MANSHIP, ASSOCIATION, FASHION appeal, and EMOTIONAL appeal.

In most DESIGN/BRAND appeal ads, only a picture and the brand name are used. A subset of this category uses the same basic strategy with a slogan or phrases to emphasize something about the brand or product. A Mont Blanc ad shows a watch profile with a contorted metal link band, asking the question, "Is that you?" The reputation of the name and the appeal of the design sell the watch. Rolex, perhaps the best-known name in high-end watches, advertises, in <u>Vogue</u>, its "Oyster Perpetual Lady-Date Pearlmaster." A close-up of the watch face showcases the white, mother-of-pearl dial, sapphire bezel, and diamond-set band. A smaller, more complete picture crouches underneath, showing the watch on its side. The model name is displayed along a gray band that runs near the bottom. The Rolex crest anchors the bottom of the

Discussion of first category.

page. Forty-five ads marketing 29 brands use the DESIGN/BRAND strategy. A large picture of the product centered on a solid background is the norm.

CRAFTSMANSHIP, the second strategy, focuses on the maker, the horologer, and the technical sides of form and function. Brand heritage and a unique, hand-crafted design are major selling points. All of these ads are targeted at men, appearing in every magazine except Vogue. Collector pieces and limited editions were commonly sold using this strategy. The focus is on accuracy and technical excellence. Pictures of the inner works and cutaways, technical information, and explanations of movements and features are popular. Quality and exclusivity are all-important.

Discussion of second category.

A Cronoswiss ad from The Robb Report is a good example. The top third pictures a horologer, identified as "Gerard Lange, master watchmaker and founder of Cronoswiss in Munich," directly below. The middle third of the ad shows a watch, white-faced with a black leather band. The logo and slogan appear next to the watch. The bottom third contains copy beginning with the words: "My watches are a hundred years behind the times." The rest explains what that statement means.

Detailed examples to illustrate second category.

Mr. Lange apparently believes that technical perfection in horology has already been attained. He also offers his book, <u>The Fascination of Mechanics</u>, free of charge along with the "sole distributor for North America" at the bottom. A "Daniel Roth" ad from the same magazine displays the name across the top of a white page; towards the top, left-hand corner a gold buckle and black band lead your eye to the center, where a gold watch with a transparent face displays its inner works exquisitely. Above and to the right, copy explains the exclusive and unique design accomplished by inverting the movement, allowing it to be viewed from above.

The third strategy is to sell the watch by establishing an ASSOCIATION with an object, experience, or person, implying that its value and quality are beyond question. In the six ads I found using this approach, watches are associated with violins, pilots, astronauts, hot air balloons, and a hero of the free world. This is similar to the first strategy, but relies on a reputation other than that of the maker. The watch is presented as being desirable for the connections created in the ad.

Discussion of third category.

Parmigiani ran an ad in <u>The Robb Report</u> featuring a gold watch with a black face and band illuminated by some unseen source. A blue-tinted violin rises in the background; the rest of the page is black. The brief copy reads: "For those who think a Stradivarius is only a violin. The Parmigiani Toric Chronograph is only a wristwatch." "The Moon Watch" proclaims an Omega ad from <u>GO</u>. Inset on a white background is a picture of an astronaut on the moon saluting the American flag. The silver watch with a black face lies across the lower part of the page. The caption reads: "Speedmaster Professional. The first and only watch worn on the moon." Omega's logo appears at the bottom.

The fourth strategy is to present the watch simply as a FASHION statement. In this line of attack, the ads appeal to our need to be current, accepted, to fit in and be like everyone else, or to make a statement, setting us apart from others as hip and cool. The product is presented as a necessary part of our wardrobes. The watch is fashionable and will send the "right" message. Design and style are the foremost concerns; "the look" sells the watch.

Discussion of fourth category.

Techno Marine has an ad in GO which shows a large close-up of a watch running down the entire length of the left side of the page. Two alternate color schemes are pictured on the right, separating small bits of copy. At the bottom on the right are the name and logo. The first words at the top read: "Keeping time—you keep your closet up to the minute, why not your wrist? The latest addition to your watch wardrobe should be the AlphaSport." Longines uses a similar strategy in Vogue. Its ad is divided in half lengthwise. On the left is a black-and-white picture of Audrey Hepburn. The right side is white with the Longines' logo at the top and two ladies' watches in the center. Near the bottom is the phrase, "Elegance is an Attitude." Retailers appear at the bottom. The same ad ran in GO, but with a man's watch and a picture of Humphrey Bogart. A kind of association is made, but quality and value aren't the overriding concerns. The point is to have an elegant attitude like these fashionable stars did, one that these watches can provide and enhance.

The fifth and final strategy is that of EMOTIONAL appeal. The ads using this approach strive to influence our

Discussion of fifth category.

emotional responses and allege to influence the emotions of others towards us. Their power and appeal are exerted through the feelings they evoke in us. Nine out of ten ads rely on a picture as the main device to trigger an emotional link between the product and the viewer. Copy is scant; words are used mainly to guide the viewer to the advertiser's desired conclusions.

A Frederique Constant ad pictures a man, wearing a watch, mulling over a chess game. Above his head are the words "Inner Passion." The man's gaze is odd; he is looking at something on the right side of the page, but a large picture of a watch superimposed over the picture hides whatever it is that he is looking at. So we are led to the watch. The bottom third is white and contains the maker's logo and the slogan "Live your Passion." An ad in GO shows a man holding a woman. He leans against a rock; she reclines in his arms. Their eyes are closed, and both have peaceful, smiling expressions. He is wearing a Tommy Hilfiger watch. The ad spans two pages; a close-up of the watch is presented on the right half of the second page. The only words are the ones in the logo. This is perhaps one of those pictures that are worth a thousand words. The message is he got the girl because he's got the watch.

Even more than selling a particular watch, all of these ads focus on building the brand's image. I found many of the ads extremely effective at conveying their messages. Many of the better-known brands favor the comparatively simple DESIGN/BRAND appeal strategy, to reach a broader audience. Lesser-known, high-end makers contribute many of the more specialized strategies. We all count and mark the passing hours and minutes. And society places great importance on time, valuing punctuality. But these ads strive to convince us that having "the right time" means so much more than "the time."

Strong conclusion; the effect of watch ads.

MAKING CONNECTIONS

1. The writers in this chapter have examined many ways in which humans connect to one another. Sometimes the connections are good ones (using manners, serene ex-smokers); sometimes the connections are less than ideal (intruding on someone's space, not accepting someone's excuse). What can you learn from these writers about human needs in relationships? What do we need to feel good? What missing needs lead to conflicts in human relationships?

2. Review the questions about advertising at the beginning of Chapter 5. Then think about what human needs are

appealed to in the advertising of various products. How, for example, are perfumes (or cars) sold to us? To what specific needs do perfume (or car) ads appeal? You may want to do some reading on this subject, beginning with Maslow's hierarchy of needs—which you can read about online.

3. Which writer in this chapter offers the greatest insight into human connections? To answer this question, you will need to define *greatest*. The term could mean most profound, or most useful to readers, or most original or startling. You may want to classify the writers into these three categories—or others of your own—before deciding whom to select as having the greatest insight. Your initial analysis then becomes the basis for the defense of your choice.

4. Think about the concepts of social and moral capital discussed by David Books. How do the essays by Judith Martin, Curt Suplee, and Carolyn Segal relate to these two types of human capital? What conclusions can you draw about the nature and significance of both social and moral capital?

5. Often conflicts in human relationships result from people with different personalities not understanding each other's ways of seeing the world or making decisions. Some of these conflicts can be avoided if we know ourselves better and can recognize specific traits in others we interact with. One strategy is to take the Myers/Briggs personality test to know yourself better and to understand elements of personality. At some colleges, students can arrange to take this test and have a counselor "score" it and discuss the results with the student. You can learn more about Myers/Briggs online and see if you are interested in following through on this approach to learning about yourself. A good site to explore is: *www.teamtechnology.co.uk/ad.html.*

TOPICS FOR WRITING

---

1. Look over your Getting Started exercise—your classification of recent reading, movies, or television shows. Do you think your reading (or viewing) habits are fairly typical of someone in your situation? Or are your reading (or viewing)

habits unusual, reflecting, perhaps, a hobby or special interest? If you see some point—a thesis—that your classification of reading (or viewing) can support, then you have an essay topic.

2. Reflect on the parents, teachers, or coaches you have known. Can they be divided into categories based on their ways of using discipline? Select one group (parents, teachers, or coaches), and then classify that group according to their strategies for disciplining. (You might want to give each type or category a label, as Zimring labels ex-smokers.)

3. Along the same lines as in topic 2, reflect on a particular group of people you know well—teachers, students, dates, workers in a particular field, athletes, and so on. Select one group and classify it according to the different types within that group. Try to make your classification complete. You are saying to your reader that these are the types of dates—or teachers—that one could conceivably know. Make your divisions clear by labeling each type, and then define and illustrate each type. One possible thesis could be your view of the best and worst types in the group you are writing about.

4. Watch (and perhaps tape so that you can review) at least six evenings of the ABC, NBC, or CBS evening news. Analyze the news programs according to the types of news stories and determine the amount of time given to each type of story, to commercials, and to "what's coming" segments. What have you learned? How much serious news do we get in a half hour? How much time (in minutes or seconds) is devoted to each type of story? Report the results of your study in an essay. Introduce your topic in paragraph 1, explain how you conducted your analysis in paragraph 2, and then report on the results of your study. Illustrate your categories with specific examples from the programs you watched. (For example, if one type of story that appears regularly is what can be called "national news," then what news stories from the shows you watched fit into that category? You might explain and illustrate the category with several stories about the president or Congress.)

5. What are some of the "games" that people play in their relationships with one another? That is, what strategies are used by people to get along or get ahead? In what

situations are they likely to use particular games? If you have been a careful observer of human behavior or if you have watched people behaving in one particular situation, you potentially have an essay on this topic. Take one of two approaches. (1) Write on the games people play, classifying game playing as fully as you can. Explain and illustrate each game with examples. Remember that you can use hypothetical (made-up) examples as well as those drawn from your experience. (2) Write on the ways that people behave in a particular situation you know well. That is, how can people be classified by their behavior in the classroom, at the doctor's (or dentist's) office, in the library, at the beach, while driving, or at the movies. This second approach can be serious or humorous.

6. Think of one job category you know well (such as small business, farming, the medical profession, teaching, or banking). Then, within that one category, think of all the various workers and classify them according to Whitehead's new class divisions. Your point will be to show that not everyone in a job category is in the same class, although you may discover that not all categories are represented. For example, would anyone in teaching be placed in the underclass?

A CHECKLIST FOR DIVISION AND CLASSIFICATION ESSAYS

Inventing

☐ Have I selected a topic consistent with the instructor's guidelines for this assignment?

☐ Have I chosen among the possible topics one that fits my knowledge and experience?

☐ Have I reflected on the topic to write a tentative thesis that establishes the use of division and classification?

☐ Have I thought through the categories I need to best organize my subject matter?

☐ Is my classification plan complete, providing a category for all elements of the subject?

☐ Have I thought about the most effective order for my categories?

Drafting

☐ Have I succeeded in completing a first draft at one sitting so that I can "see" the whole?

☐ Do I have enough—enough to meet assignment demands and enough to develop and support my thesis? If not, do I need new paragraphs or more examples or details or more reflection within some paragraphs?

☐ Have I clearly explained the differences among my categories and justified my classification strategy? If not, do I need to rethink my classification system?

☐ Do I have good examples and details to illustrate each category?

☐ Does the order work? If not, what needs to be moved—and where?

☐ Am I satisfied with the way I have expressed the insights to be gained? Have I been too heavy-handed with a message?

Revising

☐ Have I made any needed additions, deletions, or changes in order based on answering the questions about my draft?

☐ Have I revised my draft to produce coherent paragraphs, using transition and connecting words that reveal my classification system?

Polishing

☐ Have I eliminated wordiness and clichés?

☐ Have I avoided or removed any discriminatory language?

☐ Have I used my word processor's spell check and proofread a printed copy with great care?

☐ Do I have an appropriate and interesting title?

8

Using Definition
Explaining Ideas and Values

"Define your terms!" someone shouts in the middle of a heated debate. Although yelling may not be the best strategy, the advice is sound. Quite frequently the basis for a disagreement turns out to be a key word used differently by those whose discussion can now best be defined as an argument. We cannot let words mean whatever we want them to and still communicate, but, as you know from your study of vocabulary, many words have more than one dictionary definition (*denotation*). If we add to those meanings a word's *connotation* (associations and emotional suggestions), it is no wonder that we disagree over a word's meaning. To some, civil disobedience is illegal behavior; to others it is an example of patriotism. When we don't disagree over a word's generally understood meaning, we can still disagree over its connotation.

When to Use Definition

When do you need to define terms to avoid confusion? First, define words that most readers are not likely to know. If you need to use a technical term in an essay directed to nonspecialists, then you should provide a brief definition. Textbooks are, as you know, filled with definitions as the authors guide students through the vocabulary of a new subject. Second, define any word that you are using in a special way or in one of its special meanings. If you were to write: "We need to teach discrimination at an early age," you probably should add: "By discrimination I do not mean prejudice; I mean discernment, the ability to see differences." (*Sesame Street* has been teaching children this good kind of discrimination for years.)

A third occasion for using definition occurs when a writer chooses to develop a detailed explanation of the meaning of a complex, abstract, frequently debated, or emotion-laden term. Words such as *freedom, happiness, wisdom,* and *honesty* need to be reexamined, debated, and clarified in discussions that go beyond a dictionary's brief entry. We use the term *extended definition* to refer to the essay that has, as its primary purpose, the examination of a word's meaning. Sometimes the writer's purpose is to clarify our thinking: what does it mean to be *happy*? Sometimes a writer wants to reclaim a word from its current negative (or positive) connotations. This is what Robert Miller does when he argues that *discrimination* can have—and should be used with—a positive connotation.

How to Develop an Extended Definition

Extended definition describes a writing purpose. It does not suggest a particular organizational strategy. To develop an extended definition, you need to use some of the writing strategies that you have already been practicing. Suppose three Martians landed in your backyard, saw your Burmese cat, and asked, "What is that?" They are curious to know more than just the name of your pet. You could begin to answer their question with a dictionary-styled definition: a cat is a domesticated mammal (placing the object in a class) with retractable claws (distinguishing it from other members of the class—such as dogs). Your Martian friends, possibly interested in taking some cats home, want more information, so you continue with *descriptive details*: soft fur, usually long tails, padded feet, agile climbers (onto furniture, trees, and rooftops), rumbling sounds when contented. Developing your definition further, you can *contrast* cats with dogs: cats are more independent, can be trained to a box, will clean themselves. You can continue by providing *examples*: there are Siamese cats, Persian cats, tabby cats, and so on.

"This is all very interesting," the Martians respond, "but what do cats do, what are cats for?" You answer by explaining *use* or *function*: cats are pets, friends and companions, fun to play with and cuddle. Some people have even worshipped cats as gods, you add, providing *history*. A variation of providing history is to explain *word origin* or *etymology*. Often we get clues about a word's meaning by studying its origin and the changes in meaning over time. This information can be found in dictionaries that specialize in etymology, the *Oxford English Dictionary (OED)*, for example. (Your library will have the *OED*, probably both in a print format and online.)

The previous two paragraphs list and illustrate a number of strategies for developing an extended definition:

descriptive details	comparison/contrast
examples	use or function
etymology	

To write a definition essay, you need to select those strategies that best suit your word and your particular purpose in defining that word. Remembering that effective writing is concrete writing, you want to include plenty of details and examples. Also give thought to the most effective organization of specifics so that the result is a unified essay, not a vocabulary exercise. Keep in mind that one of the most important strategies is contrast, for your purpose in defining is to discriminate, to explain subtle differences among words. (For example, what is the difference between wisdom and knowledge? Can one be wise without having knowledge? Or, how do self-esteem and self-respect differ? Is one better than the other?) Keep in mind that one kind of comparison, the metaphor, is especially useful because metaphors help make the abstract concrete. The Getting Started exercise below shows you how one writer used metaphors to define the concept *democracy*.

WRITING FOCUS
USING METAPHORS, AVOIDING CLICHÉS

Just as there are colorless words—vague, general words such as *nice* and *thing*—so there are colorless expressions. These are metaphors that once had freshness but now are dulled by overuse. "In the twinkling of an eye" we become "starry-eyed" and are on "pins and needles" awaiting our true love's call. Or, in today's "fast-paced world" we have trouble avoiding "the rat race." To these expressions, called clichés, readers stop listening because they have heard them too many times before. So, when you are about to write that your friend was "as hungry as a bear," stop, ask yourself if this is *your* expression of an idea or a pat phrase you've pulled out of the air, and then erase all tuneless clichés.

Fresh metaphors, on the other hand, both delight readers and give them insight into a writer's thoughts and feelings. Here are some metaphors you will find in this chapter's essays.

Andrew Vachss writes that a "veil of secrecy and protection then descends."

John Ciardi writes that the concept of happiness "will not sit still for easy definition."

David Fischer writes that the words *freedom* and *liberty* have an "old tension between them" that "persists like a coiled spring in our culture."

Find your own clever metaphors when you can. When you can't, write simply and directly, avoiding the pat phrases that so easily come to mind.

Getting Started: Reflections on E. B. White's Ideas of Democracy

E. B. White, essayist and author of children's books, once defined democracy largely through a series of metaphors. Three of his metaphors are

1. Democracy is "the line that forms on the right"
2. Democracy is "the hole in the stuffed shirt through which the sawdust slowly trickles"
3. Democracy is "the score at the beginning of the ninth"

First, analyze each metaphor. For each one, explain what the concrete situation is to which democracy is being compared. Ask yourself, how is that situation democratic? That is, what is White saying about democracy through the comparison? Then select the metaphor you like best and expand the idea that it suggests into a paragraph of your own on democracy. Try to include at least one metaphor of your own in your paragraph.

Is Everybody Happy?

JOHN CIARDI

A graduate of Tufts and the University of Michigan, John Ciardi (1916–1986) was a lecturer, critic, and, primarily, a poet. Ciardi published collections of poetry, including some delightful poems for children. His major critical study is *On Poetry and the Poetic Process* (1971). Ciardi was also for many years poetry editor of *Saturday Review*. In the following essay, from *Saturday Review* (May 14, 1964), Ciardi defines happiness as never perfectly attainable and requiring effort.

Questions to Guide Your Reading and Reflection
1. What seems to be the American concept of happiness?
2. How would you define happiness?

The right to pursue happiness is issued to Americans with their birth certificates, but no one seems quite sure which way it ran. It may be we are issued a hunting license but offered no game. Jonathan Swift[1] seemed to think so when he attacked the idea of happiness as "the possession of being well-deceived," the felicity of being "a fool among knaves." For Swift saw society as Vanity Fair, the land of false goals.

It is, of course, un-American to think in terms of fools and knaves. We do, however, seem to be dedicated to the idea of buying our way to happiness. We shall all have made it to Heaven when we possess enough.

And at the same time the forces of American commercialism are hugely dedicated to making us deliberately unhappy. Advertising is one of our major industries, and advertising exists not to satisfy desires but to create them—and to create them faster than any man's budget can satisfy them. For that matter, our whole economy is based on a dedicated insatiability. We are taught that to possess is to be happy, and then we are made to want. We are even told it is our duty to want. It was only a few years ago, to cite a single example, that car dealers

[1]Irish-born English clergyman and satiric writer, 1667–1745.—Ed.

across the country were flying banners that read "You Auto Buy Now." They were calling upon Americans, as an act approaching patriotism, to buy at once, with money they did not have, automobiles they did not really need, and which they would be required to grow tired of by the time next year's models were released.

4   Or look at any of the women's magazines. There, as Bernard DeVoto[2] once pointed out, advertising begins as poetry in the front pages and ends as pharmacopoeia and therapy in the back pages. The poetry of the front matter is the dream of perfect beauty. This is the baby skin that must be hers. These, the flawless teeth. This, the perfumed breath she must exhale. This, the sixteen-year-old figure she must display at forty, at fifty, at sixty, and forever.

5   Once past the vaguely uplifting fiction and feature articles, the reader finds the other face of the dream in the back matter. This is the harness into which Mother must strap herself in order to display that perfect figure. These, the chin straps she must sleep in. This is the salve that restores all, this is her laxative, these are the tablets that melt away fat, these are the hormones of perpetual youth, these are the stockings that hide varicose veins.

6   Obviously no half-sane person can be completely persuaded either by such poetry or by such pharmacopoeia and orthopedics. Yet someone is obviously trying to buy the dream as offered and spending billions every year in the attempt. Clearly the happiness-market is not running out of customers, but what is it trying to buy?

7   The idea "happiness," to be sure, will not sit still for easy definition: the best one can do is try to set some extremes to the idea and then work in toward the middle. To think of happiness as acquisitive and competitive will do to set the materialistic extreme. To think of it as the idea one senses in, say, a holy man of India will do to set the spiritual extreme. That holy man's idea of happiness is in needing nothing from outside himself. In wanting nothing, he lacks nothing. He sits immobile, rapt in contemplation, free even of his own body. Or nearly free of it. If devout admirers bring him food he eats it; if not, he

[2]American novelist and critic, 1897–1955.—Ed.

starves indifferently. Why be concerned? What is physical is an illusion to him. Contemplation is his joy and he achieves it through a fantastically demanding discipline, the accomplishment of which is itself a joy within him.

Is he a happy man? Perhaps his happiness is only another sort of illusion. But who can take it from him? And who will dare say it is more illusory than happiness on the installment plan?

But, perhaps because I am Western, I doubt such catatonic happiness, as I doubt the dreams of the happiness-market. What is certain is that his way of happiness would be torture to almost any Western man. Yet these extremes will still serve to frame the area within which all of us must find some sort of balance. Thoreau[3]—a creature of both Eastern and Western thought—had his own firm sense of that balance. His aim was to save on the low levels in order to spend on the high.

Possession for its own sake or in competition with the rest of the neighborhood would have been Thoreau's idea of the low levels. The active discipline of heightening one's perception of what is enduring in nature would have been his idea of the high. What he saved from the low was time and effort he could spend on the high. Thoreau certainly disapproved of starvation, but he would put into feeding himself only as much effort as would keep him functioning for more important efforts.

Effort is the gist of it. There is no happiness except as we take on life-engaging difficulties. Short of the impossible, as Yeats[4] put it, the satisfactions we get from a lifetime depend on how high we choose our difficulties. Robert Frost[5] was thinking in something like the same terms when he spoke of "The pleasure of taking pains." The mortal flaw in the advertised version of happiness is in the fact that it purports to be effortless.

We demand difficulty even in our games. We demand it because without difficulty there can be no game. A game is a way of making something hard for the fun of it. The rules of the game are an arbitrary imposition of difficulty. When the spoilsport ruins the fun, he always does so by refusing to play by the rules. It is easier to win at chess if you are free, at your

8

9

10

11

12

[3]American author and naturalist, 1817–62.—Ed.
[4]Irish essayist, dramatist, and poet, 1865–1939.—Ed.
[5]American poet, 1874–1963.—Ed.

pleasure, to change the wholly arbitrary rules, but the fun is in winning within the rules. No difficulty, no fun.

13   The buyers and sellers at the happiness-market seem too often to have lost their sense of pleasure of difficulty. Heaven knows what they are playing, but it seems a dull game. And the Indian holy man seems dull to us, I suppose, because he seems to be refusing to play anything at all. The Western weakness may be in the illusion that happiness can be bought. Perhaps the Eastern weakness is in the idea that there is such a thing as perfect (and therefore static) happiness.

14   Happiness is never more than partial. There are no pure states of mankind. Whatever else happiness may be, it is neither in having nor in being, but in becoming. What the Founding Fathers declared for us as an inherent right, we should do well to remember, was not happiness but the *pursuit* of happiness. What they might have underlined, could they have foreseen the happiness-market, is the cardinal fact that happiness is in the pursuit itself, in the meaningful pursuit of what is life-engaging and life-revealing, which is to say, in the idea of *becoming*. A nation is not measured by what it possesses or wants to possess, but by what it wants to become.

15   By all means let the happiness-market sell us minor satisfactions and even minor follies so long as we keep them in scale and buy them out of spiritual change. I am no customer for either puritanism or asceticism. But drop any real spiritual capital at those bazaars, and what you come home to will be your own poorhouse.

Expanding Vocabulary

Match each word in column A with its definition in column B. When in doubt, first find the word in the essay and look for context clues to aid your understanding of the word's meaning. Then, if necessary, use your dictionary to complete the matching exercise. The number in parentheses is the number of the paragraph in which the word appears.

Column A	*Column B*
insatiability (3)	ointment that soothes or heals
pharmacopoeia (4)	beliefs of Puritans who regarded
therapy (4)	pleasure as sinful
salve (5)	medical specialty dealing with injuries
varicose (5)	to the skeleton

orthopedics (6)
acquisitive (7)
catatonic (9)
purports (11)
inherent (14)
puritanism (15)
asceticism (15)

in a stupor, with rigid body
stock of drugs
professes to be
treatment of illness
intrinsic, essential characteristic
belief in life of austerity
eager to possess, grasping
abnormally swollen or knotted
state of not being satisfied

Understanding Content

1. How would Jonathan Swift have described people who thought they were happy?
2. Why does Ciardi reject both extremes of happiness?
3. How do the extremes help to define happiness? What must we find to begin to achieve happiness?
4. What else is essential to happiness? What role does this ingredient play in our games? Why is the advertised version of happiness flawed? Why is the Eastern version flawed?
5. Ciardi says that "happiness is never more than partial." What is another characteristic of happiness?

Drawing Inferences about Thesis and Purpose

1. What are the ingredients for happiness that Ciardi presents? State, in your own words, the key elements of his definition.
2. Examine Ciardi's discussion of American advertising in paragraphs 3 through 5. What is his attitude toward advertising? How do you know?

Analyzing Strategies and Style

1. In developing his definition, Ciardi refers to five writers. What do these references tell you about the author? What do they suggest about Ciardi's anticipated audience?
2. Ciardi begins and ends his essay with metaphors. Explain the metaphor in his first two sentences and the metaphor in his last two sentences. What points about happiness does each metaphor suggest?
3. List all the strategies that Ciardi uses to develop his definition, giving an example of each one.

Thinking Critically

1. Ciardi thinks that happiness is a difficult term to define. Do you agree? Would you agree that it is the sort of concept that we think we understand until we are pressed to define it?
2. Ciardi asserts that "there is no happiness except as we take on life-engaging difficulties." Do you agree? Why or why not?
3. Ciardi does not think that happiness can be found in "getting the most toys," to use a modern expression. What is the relationship between money and happiness? Can some money help? Does having money make happiness more difficult to obtain? Be prepared to explain and defend your views.

Discrimination Is a Virtue

ROBERT KEITH MILLER

Holding a Ph.D. from Columbia University, Robert Keith Miller is a professor of English at St. Thomas University. He has published scholarly articles and books on such writers as Mark Twain, Oscar Wilde, and Willa Cather and has written for popular magazines and newspapers as well. In the following essay, which appeared in *Newsweek*'s "My Turn" column in 1980, Miller seeks to rescue the word *discrimination* from its misuse in our time.

Questions to Guide Your Reading and Reflection

1. What does *discrimination* mean, as Miller defines it?
2. How do most Americans use this word today?

1   When I was a child, my grandmother used to tell me a story about a king who had three daughters and decided to test their love. He asked each of them "How much do you love me?" The first replied that she loved him as much as all the diamonds and pearls in the world. The second said that she loved him more than life itself. The third replied "I love you as fresh meat loves salt."

2   This answer enraged the king; he was convinced that his youngest daughter was making fun of him. So he banished her from his realm and left all of his property to her elder sisters.

As the story unfolded it became clear, even to a 6-year-old, 3
that the king had made a terrible mistake. The two older girls
were hypocrites, and as soon as they had profited from their
father's generosity, they began to treat him very badly. A wiser
man would have realized that the youngest daughter was the
truest. Without attempting to flatter, she had said, in effect,
"We go together naturally; we are a perfect team."

Years later, when I came to read Shakespeare, I realized that 4
my grandmother's story was loosely based upon the story of
King Lear, who put his daughters to a similar test and did not
know how to judge the results. Attempting to save the king
from the consequences of his foolishness, a loyal friend pleads,
"Come sir, arise, away! I'll teach you differences." Unfortunately, the lesson comes too late. Because Lear could not tell the
difference between true love and false, he loses his kingdom
and eventually his life.

We have a word in English which means "the ability to 5
tell differences." That word is *discrimination*. But within the
last twenty years, this word has been so frequently misused
that an entire generation has grown up believing that "discrimination" means "racism." People are always proclaim-
ing that "discrimination" is something that should be done
away with. Should that ever happen, it would prove to be
our undoing.

Discrimination means discernment; it means the ability to 6
perceive the truth, to use good judgment and to profit accordingly. The *Oxford English Dictionary* traces this understanding
of the word back to 1648 and demonstrates that, for the next
300 years, "discrimination" was a virtue, not a vice. Thus,
when a character in a nineteenth-century novel makes a happy
marriage, Dickens has another character remark, "It does credit
to your discrimination that you should have found such a very
excellent young woman."

Of course, "the ability to tell differences" assumes that 7
differences exist, and this is unsettling for a culture obsessed
with the notion of equality. The contemporary belief that discrimination is a vice stems from the compound "discriminate
against." What we need to remember, however, is that some
things deserve to be judged harshly: we should not leave our
kingdoms to the selfish and the wicked.

8   Discrimination is wrong only when someone or something is discriminated against because of prejudice. But to use the word in this sense, as so many people do, is to destroy its true meaning. If you discriminate against something because of general preconceptions rather than particular insights, then you are not discriminating—bias has clouded the clarity of vision which discrimination demands.

9   One of the great ironies of American life is that we manage to discriminate in the practical decisions of daily life, but usually fail to discriminate when we make public policies. Most people are very discriminating when it comes to buying a car, for example, because they realize that cars have differences. Similarly, an increasing number of people have learned to discriminate in what they eat. Some foods are better than others—and indiscriminate eating can undermine one's health.

10   Yet in public affairs, good judgment is depressingly rare. In many areas which involve the common good, we see a failure to tell differences.

11   Consider, for example, some of the thinking behind modern education. On the one hand, there is a refreshing realization that there are differences among children, and some children—be they gifted or handicapped—require special education. On the other hand, we are politically unable to accept the consequences of this perception. The trend in recent years has been to group together students of radically different ability. We call this process "mainstreaming," and it strikes me as a characteristically American response to the discovery of differences: we try to pretend that differences do not matter.

12   Similarly, we try to pretend that there is little difference between the sane and the insane. A fashionable line of argument has it that "everybody is a little mad" and that few mental patients deserve long-term hospitalization. As a consequence of such reasoning, thousands of seriously ill men and women have been evicted from their hospital beds and returned to what is euphemistically called "the community"—which often means being left to sleep on city streets, where confused and helpless people now live out of paper bags as the direct result of our refusal to discriminate.

13   Or to choose a final example from a different area: how many recent elections reflect thoughtful consideration of the

genuine differences among candidates? Benumbed by television commercials that market aspiring officeholders as if they were a new brand of tooth paste or hair spray, too many Americans vote with only a fuzzy understanding of the issues in question. Like Lear, we seem too eager to leave the responsibility of government to others and too ready to trust those who tell us whatever we want to hear.

So as we look around us, we should recognize that "discrimination" is a virtue which we desperately need. We must try to avoid making unfair and arbitrary distinctions, but we must not go to the other extreme and pretend that there are no distinctions to be made. The ability to make intelligent judgments is essential both for the success of one's personal life and for the functioning of society as a whole. Let us be open-minded by all means, but not so open-minded that our brains fall out.   14

Expanding Vocabulary

Examine the following words in their contexts in the essay and then write a brief definition or synonym for each one. Do not use a dictionary. Try to guess the word's meanings from its context. The number in parentheses is the number of the paragraph in which the word appears

banished (2)	undermine (9)
realm (2)	evicted (12)
hypocrites (3)	euphemistically (12)
discernment (6)	benumbed (13)
preconceptions (8)	

Understanding Content

1. Currently, how is the word *discrimination* being used? How does the current use of the word change its connotation? (See the Glossary, if necessary, for the definition of *connotation*.)
2. When is discrimination wrong? When it is wrong, what should it be called? What has actually happened to one's ability to discriminate?
3. Under what circumstances do people usually discriminate? In what area of life do we often fail to discriminate?

Drawing Inferences about Thesis and Purpose

1. What is Miller's purpose in defining *discrimination*? What point does he want to make about the word?
2. State Miller's thesis.

Analyzing Strategies and Style

1. What opening strategy does Miller use? How does it lead into his subject?
2. What are Miller's examples of public policy failures in discrimination? Are they effective examples, showing a range of public policy problems?
3. Examine Miller's closing paragraph. Is it effective in its balanced language? What makes the final sentence clever?

Thinking Critically

1. Is the definition of *discrimination* that Miller wants to highlight familiar to you, or do you know the word only as it means to show prejudice? Do you see how the two meanings could develop in the same word?
2. Do you agree with Miller that we are "benumbed by television commercials" and "vote with only a fuzzy understanding of the issues"? Have you voted with a good knowledge of the candidates and the issues? (Have you voted? If not, why not?)
3. Is the American focus on equality keeping us from learning to discern differences? Explain.
4. Should differences in ability be ignored in education in favor of "mainstreaming"? Why or why not?

The Difference Between "Sick" and "Evil"

ANDREW VACHSS

A lawyer whose only clients are children, Andrew Vachss is also the author of more than a dozen novels. More information about Mr. Vachss, and more articles written by him, can be found at www.vachss.com. In response to the news coverage of Roman Catholic priests accused of child abuse, Vachss has written the following essay, which appeared in *Parade* magazine July 14, 2002.

Questions to Guide Your Reading and Reflection

1. What is the context in which the author raises the question of the difference between sick and evil?
2. What should the Roman Catholic Church do about pedophile priests?

The shock waves caused by the recent exposures of so-called   1
"pedophile priests" have reverberated throughout America.
But beneath our anger and revulsion, a fundamental question
pulsates: Are those who abuse positions of trust to prey upon
children—a category certainly not limited to those in religious
orders—sick . . . or are they evil?

We need the answer to that fundamental question. Because,   2
without the truth, we cannot act. And until we act, nothing
will change.

My job is protecting children. It has taken me from big cities   3
to rural outposts, from ghettos to penthouses and from court-
rooms to genocidal battlefields. But whatever the venue, the
truth remains constant: Some humans intentionally hurt children. They commit unspeakable acts—for their pleasure, their
profit, or both.

Many people who hear of my cases against humans who   4
rape, torture and package children for sale or rent immediately
respond with, "That's sick!" Crimes against children seem so
grotesquely abnormal that the most obvious explanation is that
the perpetrator must be mentally ill—helpless in the grip of a
force beyond his or her control.

But that very natural reaction has, inadvertently, created   5
a special category of "blameless predator." That confusion of
"sick" with "sickening" is the single greatest barrier to our
primary biological and ethical mandate: the protection of
our children.

The difference between sick and evil cannot be dismissed   6
with facile eye-of-the-beholder rhetoric. There are specific criteria we can employ to give us the answers in every case,
every time.

Some of those answers are self-evident and beyond dispute: 7
A mother who puts her baby in the oven because she hears
voices commanding her to bake the devil out of the child's
spirit is sick; and a mother who sells or rents her baby to child
pornographers is evil. But most cases of child sexual abuse—
especially those whose "nonviolent" perpetrators come from
within the child's circle of trust—seem, on their surface, to be
far more complex.

That complexity is an illusion. The truth is as simple as it is   8
terrifying:

Sickness is a condition.   9

10   Evil is a behavior.

11   Evil is always a matter of choice. Evil is not thought; it is conduct. And that conduct is always volitional.

12   And just as evil is always a choice, sickness is always the absence of choice. Sickness happens. Evil is inflicted.

13   Until we perceive the difference clearly, we will continue to give aid and comfort to our most pernicious enemies. We, as a society, decide whether something is sick or evil. Either decision confers an obligation upon us. Sickness should be treated. Evil must be fought.

14   If a person has desires or fantasies about sexually exploiting children, that individual may be sick. (Indeed, if such desires are disturbing, as opposed to gratifying to the individual, there may even be a "cure.") But if the individual chooses to act upon those feelings, that conduct is evil. People are not what they think; they are what they do.

15   Our society distrusts the term "evil." It has an almost biblical ring to it—something we believe in (or not) but never actually understand. We prefer scientific-sounding terms, such as "sociopath." But sociopathy is not a mental condition; it is a specific cluster of behaviors. The diagnosis is only made from actual criminal conduct.

16   No reputable psychiatrist claims to be able to cure a sociopath—or, for that matter, a predatory pedophile. Even the most optimistic professionals do not aim to change such a person's thoughts and feelings. What they hope is that the predator can learn self-control, leading to a change in behavior.

17   Such hopes ignore the inescapable fact that the overwhelming majority of those who prey upon children don't want to change their behavior—they want only to minimize the consequences of being caught at it.

18   In the animal kingdom, there is a food chain—predators and prey. But among humans, there is no such natural order. Among our species, predators select themselves for that role.

19   Psychology has given us many insights of great value. But it also has clouded our vision with euphemisms. To say a person suffers from the "disease" of pedophilia is to absolve the predator of responsibility for his behavior.

20   Imagine if an attorney, defending someone accused of committing a dozen holdups, told the jury his poor client was

suffering from "armed-robberia." That jury would decide that the only crazy person in the courtroom was the lawyer.

When a perpetrator claims to be sick, the *timing* of that claim 21
is critical to discovering the truth. Predatory pedophiles carefully insinuate themselves into positions of trust. They select
their prey and approach cautiously. Gradually, sometimes over
a period of years, they gain greater control over their victims.
Eventually, they leave dozens of permanently damaged
children in their wake.

But only when they are caught do predatory pedophiles 22
declare themselves to be sick. And the higher the victim count,
the sicker (and therefore less responsible) they claim to be.

In too many cases, a veil of secrecy and protection then 23
descends. The predator's own organization appoints itself
judge and jury. The perpetrator is deemed sick and sent off for
in-house "treatment." The truth is never made public. And
when some secret tribunal decides that a cure has been
achieved, the perpetrator's rights and privileges are restored,
and he or she is given a new assignment.

In fact, such privileged predators actually are assisted. They 24
enter new communities with the blessing of their own organization, their history and propensities kept secret. As a direct
result, unsuspecting parents entrust their children to them.
Inevitably, the predator eventually resumes his or her conduct
and preys upon children again. And when that conduct comes
to light, the claim of "sickness" re-emerges as well.

Too often, our society contorts itself to excuse such preda- 25
tors. We are so eager to call those who sexually abuse children
"sick," so quick to understand their demons. Why? Because
sickness not only offers the possibility of finding a cure but also
assures us that the predator didn't really mean it. After all, it is
human nature to try to understand inhuman conduct.

Conversely, the concept of evil terrifies us. The idea that some 26
humans *choose* to prey upon our children is frightening, and
their demonstrated skill at camouflage only heightens this fear.

For some, the question, "Does evil exist?" is philosophical. 27
But for those who have confronted or been victimized by predatory pedophiles, there is no question at all. We are what we do.

Just as conduct is a choice, so is our present helplessness. We 28
may be powerless to change the arrogance of those who believe

they alone should have the authority to decide whether predatory pedophiles are "sick" or when they are "cured." But, as with the perpetrators themselves, we do have the power to change their behavior.

29   In every state, laws designate certain professions that regularly come into contact with children—such as teachers, doctors, social workers and day-care employees—as "mandated reporters." Such personnel are required to report reasonable suspicion of child abuse when it comes to their attention. Failure to do so is a crime.

30   Until now, we have exempted religious organizations from mandated-reporter laws. Recent events have proved the catastrophic consequences of this exemption. We must demand— now—that our legislators close this pathway to evil.

31   A predatory pedophile who is recycled into an unsuspecting community enters it cloaked with a protection no other sex offender enjoys. If members of religious orders were mandated reporters, we would not have to rely on their good-faith belief that a predator is cured. We could make our own informed decisions on this most vital issue.

32   Modifying the law in this way would not interfere with priest-penitent privileges: When child victims or their parents disclose abuse, they are not confessing, they are crying for help. Neither confidentiality nor religious freedom would in any way be compromised by mandatory reporting.

33   Changing the laws so that religious orders join the ranks of mandated reporters is the right thing to do. And the time is right now.

Expanding Vocabulary

Match each word in column A with its definition in column B. When in doubt, first find the word in the essay and look for context clues to aid your understanding of the word's meaning. Then, if necessary, use your dictionary to complete the matching exercise. The number in parentheses is the number of the paragraph in which the word appears.

Column A	*Column B*
pedophile (1)	vibrates
reverberated (1)	one who is guilty of, responsible for
revulsion (1)	site, place

pulsates (1)
genocidal (3)
venue (3)
grotesquely (4)
perpetrator (4)
mandate (5)
facile (6)
volitional (11)
inflicted (12)
pernicious (13)
sociopath (15)
euphemisms (19)
insinuate (21)
tribunal (23)
propensities (24)
contorts (25)
camouflage (26)
designate (29)
exempted (30)

psychopath with aggressive,
    antisocial behavior
conscious choice
destructive, cruel, evil
select, specify
echoed repeatedly, resounded
inoffensive terms used for offensive
    ones
imposed on
cleverly place
hiding
command
natural inclinations
binds and twists out of shape
one who has a preference for children
freed from obligation
distortedly, bizarrely
simple, easy
disgust, loathing
court or committee giving a legal decision
engaged in planned killing of a particular
    group

Understanding Content

1. Is Vachss writing only about pedophile priests? How do you know?
2. What, according to the author, is our primary mandate? In what sense is it our primary biological mandate?
3. What is the difference between *sick* and *evil?*
4. What should be our response to sickness? To evil?
5. Why do we have problems with the word *evil?*
6. How have some child abusers avoided punishment?
7. What does Vachss want to see changed? How does he think this will improve the situation—that is, help protect more children?

Drawing Inferences about Thesis and Purpose

1. What is Vachss's thesis? You may need to use more than one sentence to give a definition of evil and to connect that to the author's call for action.
2. Vachss says that psychology "has clouded our vision with euphemisms." Explain his meaning.

Analyzing Strategies and Style

1. How would you describe the author's tone? You may need to use more than one word, for example, "outrageously silly" or "deeply caring."
2. Generally, Vachss's paragraphs are short, but paragraphs 8 through 12 are especially brief. Why? What does he gain by short sentences and paragraphs in this part of his essay?

Thinking Critically

1. Do you agree with Vachss's definitions of *sick* and *evil?* Why or why not?
2. Do you agree that today we have trouble with the term *evil?* Why or why not?
3. Should religious organizations be covered under the mandated-reporter law? Why or why not?
4. Is our society doing an adequate job of caring for and protecting our children? Explain your views.

Freedom's Not Just Another Word

DAVID HACKETT FISCHER

Holding a Ph.D. from Johns Hopkins, Dr. Fischer is a professor of history at Brandeis University and the author of many articles and books on American history, including *Bound Away: Virginia and the Westward Movement* (2000) and *Liberty and Freedom: A Visual History of America's Founding Ideas* (2004). His *New York Times* essay on the terms *liberty* and *freedom* appeared on February 7, 2005.

Questions to Guide Your Reading and Reflection

1. What is the relationship of these terms' meanings and history and culture?
2. Do you see a distinction between the terms *liberty* and *freedom?*

1   In Baghdad's Fardus Square, where Iraqi civilians and American marines so famously pulled down the statue of Saddam Hussein in the spring of 2003, Iraqi artists have raised

a new sculpture on the same pedestal. It is a monument to liberty and freedom, and unlike any other in the world.

In Europe and America, the favorite symbols of liberty and freedom are individual figures like Marianne or the Statue of Liberty. This Iraqi statue is a family group: mother, father and child so close together that they become one being. Above them are a crescent moon and sun, emblems of Islamic faith and Sumerian culture. One of its creators remarked that both civilizations "have called for love, peace and freedom."

The Baghdad monument was the work of a group of Iraqi artists called Najeen, or the Survivors. After the Persian Gulf war in 1991, they worked underground to keep alive the spirit of liberty and freedom. Their monument has a message about that. "Freedom is not a gift from people with tanks," Basim Hassad, a Najeen member, told a BBC reporter. "What we see in our country could be the first signs of freedom. What remains is a history that we will make together with the Najeen group at its heart."

Foreigners who opposed the Iraqi war were not impressed. "On top of the marble column where Saddam's statue stood, someone put up the most hideous monstrosity I've ever seen," one wrote contemptuously," A green statue with a face that's not recognizable as anything human. It's supposed to be some kind of 'goddess of liberty,' but it looks like nothing in any of the worlds."

The writer missed the meaning of the monument, which in fact has much to teach us about liberty and freedom. These ideas are growing and changing rapidly today, and their long history is more dynamic and diverse than our thoughts about it. There is no one true definition of liberty and freedom in the world, though many people to the left and right believe that they have found it. And, yet, there is one great historical process in which liberty and freedom have developed, often in unexpected ways.

The words themselves have a surprising history. The oldest known word with such a meaning comes to us from ancient Iraq. The Sumerian "ama-ar-gi," found on tablets in the ruins of the city-state of Lagash, which flourished four millenniums ago, derived from the verb "ama-gi," which literally meant "going home to mother." It described the condition of emancipated servants who returned to their own free families—an interesting link to the monument in Baghdad. (In contemporary America, the ancient characters for "ama-ar-gi" have become the logos of some libertarian organizations, as well as tattoos among members of politically conservative motorcycle gangs, who may not know that the inscriptions on their biceps mean heading home to mom.)

7   Equally surprising are the origins of our English words liberty and, especially, freedom. They have very different roots. The Latin *libertas* and Greek *eleutheria* both indicated a condition of independence, unlike a slave. (In science, *eleutherodactylic* means separate fingers or toes.) Freedom, however, comes from the same root as friend, an Indo-European word that meant "dear" or "beloved." It meant a connection to other free people by bonds of kinship or affection, also unlike a slave. Liberty and freedom both meant "unlike a slave." But liberty meant privileges of independence; freedom referred to rights of belonging.

8   We English-speakers are possibly unique in having both "liberty" and "freedom" in our ordinary speech. The two words have blurred together in modern usage, but the old tension between them persists like a coiled spring in our culture. It has inspired an astonishing fertility of thought. Americans have invented many ideas of liberty and freedom. Some are close to independence, others to rights of belonging. Most are highly creative combinations. For most people they are not academic abstractions or political ideologies, but inherited ideas that we hold as what Tocqueville called "habits of the heart." They tend to be entire visions of a free society, and we see them in our mind's eye through symbols and emblems, much as Najeen envisions symbols in Iraq.

9   I have counted more than 500 such literal symbols of liberty and freedom in America alone. In the American Revolution they included New England's Liberty Tree with its collective sense of town-born rights, Philadelphia's great Quaker Bell ringing for all humanity, Virginia's hierarchical Liberty Goddess, South Carolina's Liberty Crescent, and the rattlesnake of individual independence, with its motto, "Don't Tread on Me." Other emblems were invented by German immigrants, African slaves, trans-Atlantic

artisans and Loyalist elites. All were different combinations of liberty and freedom.

The Civil War, of course, was a conflict between visions of 10 liberty, freedom, union and rights of belonging on one side; and ideas of states' rights, separation and liberty to keep a slave on the other. Many competing images of liberty and freedom appeared in the Progressive Era, and again in the 1930's when President Franklin D. Roosevelt's "broader definition of liberty" and "greater freedom, greater security" were fiercely opposed by the conservative Liberty League. It happened again in the 1950's and 60's, with the Rev. Dr. Martin Luther King Jr.'s dream of freedom as rights of belonging, and Barry Goldwater's impassioned idea of liberty as independence from intrusive government. But perhaps the most fertile period of invention was the late 20th century. Through 16 generations, American ideas of liberty and freedom have grown larger, deeper, more diverse and yet more inclusive in these collisions of contested visions.

One can observe this growth not only in America as a whole, 11 but also in the thought of individual Americans. An example, of course, is George W. Bush. His speeches before 2001 centered on a particular idea of personal liberty, private property, individual responsibility and minimal government. By his second inaugural last month, that vision had grown larger. It preserved the idea of individual liberty, but also quoted Franklin Roosevelt's "broader definition of liberty" and "greater freedom from want and fear." It embraced Dr. King's "freedom now," and adopted the universal Quaker vision of "liberty throughout all the land," even enlarging it to "liberty throughout all the world."

How these words will be defined by acts in Mr. Bush's 12 second term remains to be seen. His first administration was very careless of civil liberties for others, and little interested in civil rights; he spoke often of the rights of the unborn but enacted fiscal policies that betrayed the rights of generations to come. One hopes that the larger spirit of the second inaugural address will appear in political acts to come.

I found it most striking that Mr. Bush also explicitly 13 recognized that liberty and freedom take different forms throughout the world, where "others find their own voice, attain their own freedom, and make their own way." His phrasing would seem to recognize that this is a global process that is broader than the American experience of liberty and freedom, and yet preserves the same dynamics.

14   In India, for example, leaders of the Congress Party have combined Western ideas with Hindu and Buddhist beliefs to create old-new visions of liberty and freedom that are unique to that republic. In Beijing, the students who constructed the Goddess of Tiananmen Square in 1989 created a new symbol that combined American liberty and freedom, Russian socialism and Chinese culture, a radical new vision of a free world. The people of Eastern Europe have invented their own visions from traditions like Poland's collective memory of its "golden freedom" during the 17th century. The same thing is happening in Ukraine and the Balkans, Latin America and Africa, Southeast Asia and the Pacific.

15   Most of all it is happening in Islam today. We find it in the Baghdad monument that links liberty and freedom to the faith of Islam and the history of Mesopotamia. We see it in the ink-stained fingers of millions of Iraqis, held upright in a new symbol of courage against tyranny, pride in an ancient past, and hope for the future of a free world.

16   The catch, of course, is that people become more truly free only when the central ideas are respected: liberty as the rights of individual independence, freedom in the rights of collective belonging. Many on the right and left continue to call for one idea without the other, but the strongest ground is in the center, where they come together.

17   People across the globe will continue to create new combinations of liberty and freedom, with an inexhaustible fertility of invention. These visions are profoundly different from one another, but they are all part of one great historical process that is more open and free than any one idea of liberty or freedom has ever been, or even wished to be.

Expanding Vocabulary

Study the definitions for any of the following words that you do not know. Then select four of the words and use each one in a separate sentence. The number in parentheses is the number of the paragraph in which the word appears.

crescent (2)   ideologies (8)
Sumerian (2)   hierarchical (9)
contemptuously (4)   intrusive (10)
emancipated (6)

Understanding Content

1. What is the oldest source of a word for *liberty* or *freedom*? What does the word mean?
2. What do the origins of the English words *liberty* and *freedom* have in common? How do their original definitions differ?
3. What has been the relationship of the two words in America's history?
4. How should Americans see their meanings of the words in relationship to other cultures?
5. When did Iraqis hold up ink-stained fingers as a new symbol of hope for freedom?

Drawing Inferences about Thesis and Purpose

1. Fischer writes that the words *freedom* and *liberty* exist in a "tension" "like a coiled spring." What does he suggest with this metaphor?
2. How does Fischer want the terms to connect? Write a thesis for his essay.

Analyzing Strategies and Style

1. Fischer's rather lengthy introduction discusses a new statue in Baghdad's Fardus Square. What does the statue mean to Iraqis? How does the opening connect to Fischer's topic?
2. List all the strategies the author uses to develop his definition.

Thinking Critically

1. Fischer refers to a number of symbols of liberty. Why do we have so many symbols for this term?
2. The author connects the meanings of *liberty* and *freedom* to history and to culture. Why is it important to recognize that there is not one, unchanging definition of these terms?
3. How do the differing definitions of these terms in American culture help us to understand conflicts between Republicans and Democrats?

The Greatness Gap

CHARLES KRAUTHAMMER

A graduate of Harvard Medical School and board certified in psychiatry, Charles Krauthammer is a syndicated columnist and a regular on the political talk show *Inside Washington*. He has won a Pulitzer Prize for political commentary. Showing his versatility, Krauthammer examines sports greats in the following column, originally published in *Time* magazine on July 1, 2002.

Questions to Guide Your Reading and Reflection

1. What does Krauthammer mean by the "greatness gap"?
2. Who would you list as among the world's greatest athletes?

1   There is excellence, and there is greatness—cosmic, transcendent, Einsteinian. We know it when we see it, we think. But how to measure it? Among Tiger Woods' varied contributions to contemporary American life is that he shows us how.

2   As just demonstrated yet again at the U.S. Open, Woods is the greatest golfer who ever lived. How do we know? You could try Method 1: Compare him directly with the former greatest golfer, Jack Nicklaus. For example, take their total scores in their first 22 major championships (of which Nicklaus won seven, Woods eight). Nicklaus was 40 strokes over par; Tiger was 81 under—an astonishing 121 strokes better.

3   But that is not the right way to compare. You cannot compare greatness directly across the ages. There are so many intervening variables: changes in technology, training, terrain, equipment, often rules and customs.

4   How then do we determine who is greatest? Method 2: The Gap. Situate each among his contemporaries. Who towers? Who is, like the U.S. today, a hyperpower with no second in sight?

5   The mark of true transcendence is running alone. Nicklaus was great, but he ran with peers: Palmer, Player, Watson. Tiger has none. Of the past 11 majors, Woods has won seven. That means whenever and wherever the greatest players in the world gather, Woods wins twice and the third trophy is distributed among the next, oh, 150.

In 2000–01, Woods won four majors in a row. The *Washington*   6
Post's Thomas Boswell found that if you take these four and
add the 2001 Players Championship (considered the next most
important tournament), Tiger shot a cumulative 1,357 strokes—
55 strokes better than the next guy.

To find true greatness, you must apply the "next guy" test.   7
Then the clouds part and the deities appear. In 1921 Babe Ruth
hit 59 home runs. The next four hit 24, 24, 23, and 23. Ruth alone
hit more home runs than half the teams in the major leagues.

In the 1981–82 season, Wayne Gretzky scored 212 points.   8
The next two guys scored 147 and 139. Not for nothing had he
been known as the Great One—since age 9.

Gaps like these are rare as the gods that produce them. By   9
1968, no one had ever long-jumped more than 27 ft. $4\frac{3}{4}$ in. In the
Mexico City Olympics that year, Bob Beamon jumped 29 ft. $2\frac{1}{2}$ in.
—this in a sport in which records are broken by increments of
a few inches, sometimes fractions. (Yes, the air is thin in Mexico City, but it was a legal jump and the record stood for an
astonishing 23 years.)

In physics, a quantum leap means jumping to a higher level   10
without ever stopping—indeed, without even traveling through—
anywhere in between. In our ordinary understanding of things,
that is impossible. In sports, it defines greatness.

Not only did Michael Jordan play a game of basketball so   11
beautiful that it defied physics, but he racked up numbers that
put him in a league of his own. Jordan has averaged 31 points
a game, a huge gap over the (future) Hall of Famers he played
against (e.g., Karl Malone, 25.7; Charles Barkley, 22.1).

The most striking visual representation of the Gap is the   12
photograph of Secretariat crossing the finish line at the
Belmont Stakes, 31(!) lengths ahead of the next horse. You can
barely see the others—the fastest horses in the world, mind
you—in the distance.

In 1971, Bobby Fischer played World Championship elimi-   13
nation rounds against the best players on the planet. These
were open-ended matches that finished only when one player
had won six games. Such matches could take months, because
great chess masters are so evenly matched that 80% of tournament games end in draws. Victories come at rare intervals;
six wins can take forever. Not this time. Fischer conducted a

campaign unrivaled since Scipio Africanus leveled Carthage. He beat two challengers six games in a row, which combined with wins before and after, produced a streak of 20 straight victories against the very best—something never seen before and likely never to be seen again.

14   That's a Gap. To enter the pantheon—any pantheon—you've got to be so far above and beyond your contemporaries that it is said of you, as Jack Nicklaus once said of Tiger Woods, "He's playing a game I'm not familiar with."

15   The biologist and philosopher Lewis Thomas was asked what record of human achievements he would launch into space to be discovered one day by some transgalactic civilization. A continual broadcast of Bach would do, Thomas suggested, though "that would be boasting."

16   Why not make it a music video? A Bach fugue over Tiger hitting those miraculous irons from the deep rough onto the greens at Bethpage Black. Nah. The aliens will think we did it all with computer graphics.

Expanding Vocabulary

1. Krauthammer refers to two important people: Einsteinian (1) and Scipio Africanus (13). Learn about each person, if necessary, and then use each one in a separate sentence.
2. Study the definitions of each of the following words that are unfamiliar to you. Then use each of the words in a separate sentence. The number in parentheses is the number of the paragraph in which the word appears.

variables (3)	defied (11)
Situate (4)	pantheon (14)
increments (9)	transgalactic (15)

Understanding Content

1. What is Method 1 for judging Tiger Woods's greatness? Why is it not a good method?
2. How is Method 2 applied?
3. Who are Krauthammer's greats, using Method 2?

Drawing Inferences about Thesis and Purpose

1. What is the author's primary purpose in writing? To argue for Woods's greatness? Something else?
2. What is the author's thesis?

Analyzing Strategies and Style

1. What does Krauthammer gain by first considering Method 1?
2. When the author concludes that aliens would not believe a music video of Woods hitting irons to a Bach fugue, what is his point? What writing strategy is he using? What makes this an effective conclusion?

Thinking Critically

1. Do you agree that the gap is the best way to define greatness in sports? Why or why not? If you disagree, explain what other elements you would include to measure greatness.
2. Sports greats are often looked up to as role models. Which sports great do you think is the "greatest" in terms of what that person does (or has done) away from his or her sport? Be prepared to explain your criteria—your method—for determining the greatest as a role model.

Glamour, That Certain Something

ROBIN GIVHAN

Robin Givhan is a graduate of Princeton and holds a master's degree in journalism from the University of Michigan. She is fashion editor for the *Washington Post* and has won a Pulitzer Prize (2006) for criticism, the first time the prize has been awarded to a fashion writer. Givhan's coverage of the world of fashion frequently becomes a study of culture, as we see in the following column, published February 17, 2008, shortly before the 2008 Academy Awards show.

Questions to Guide Your Reading and Reflection

1. What is the difference between glamour and good looks?
2. What famous people do you consider glamorous?

Glamour isn't a cultural necessity, but its usefulness can't be denied.   1

It makes us feel good about ourselves by making us believe   2
that life can sparkle. Glamorous people make difficult tasks
seems effortless. They appear to cruise through life shaking off

defeat with a wry comment. No matter how hard they work for what they have, the exertion never seems to show. Yet the cool confidence they project doesn't ever drift into lassitude.

3   Hollywood attracts people of glamour—as well as the misguided souls who confuse it with mere good looks—because that is where it is richly rewarded. And the Academy Awards are the epicenter of it all. We'll watch the Oscars next Sunday to delight in the stars who glide down the red carpet like graceful swans or who swagger onto the stage looking dashing.

4   Of course, we'll watch for other reasons, too. There's always the possibility of a supremely absurd fashion moment or an acceptance speech during which the winner becomes righteously indignant—Michael Moore-style—or practically hyperventilates like Halle Berry. While Moore, a nominee, is not glamorous, he is compelling for the sheer possibility of an impolitic eruption. Berry isn't glamorous either, mostly because nothing ever looks effortless with her. (She has even expressed anguish over her beauty.) Mostly, though, we will watch in search of "old Hollywood" glamour. But really, is there any other kind?

5   Among the actors who consistently manage to evoke memories of Cary Grant or Grace Kelly are George Clooney and Cate Blanchett. There's something about the way they present themselves that speaks to discretion, sex appeal and glossy perfection. As an audience, we think we know these actors but we really don't. We know their image, the carefully crafted personality they display to the public. If they have been to rehab, they went quietly and without a crowd of paparazzi.

6   Their lives appear to be an endless stream of lovely adventures, minor mishaps that turn into cocktail party banter, charming romances and just enough gravitas to keep them from floating away on a cloud of frivolity.

7   These actors take pretty pictures because they seem supremely comfortable with themselves. It's not simply their beauty we're seeing; it's also an unapologetic pleasure in being who they are.

8   Oscar nominee Tilda Swinton has the kind of striking, handsome looks of Anjelica Huston or Lauren Bacall. But Swinton doesn't register as glamorous as much as cool. She looks a bit androgynous and favors the eccentric Dutch design team of

Viktor & Rolf, which once populated an entire runway show with Swinton doppelgangers. Coolness suggests that the person knows something or understands something that average folks haven't yet figured out. Cool people are a step ahead. Glamour is firmly situated in the now.

There's nothing particularly intimate about glamour, which 9 is why it plays so well on the big screen and why film actors who embody it can sometimes be disappointing in real life. Glamour isn't like charisma, which is typically described as the ability to make others feel important or special.

Neither quality has much to do with a person's inner life. 10 Glamour is no measure of soulfulness or integrity. It isn't about truth, but perception. *Redbook* traffics in truth. *Vogue* promotes glamour.

Although Hollywood is the natural habitat for the glitterati, 11 they exist everywhere: politics, government, sports, business. Tiger Woods brought glamour to golf with his easy confidence and his ability to make the professional game look as simple as putt-putt. Donald Trump aspires to glamour with his flashy properties and their gold-drenched decor. But his efforts are apparent, his yearning obvious. The designer Tom Ford is glamorous. The man never rumples.

In the political world, Barack Obama has glamour. Bill Clinton 12 has charisma. And Hillary Clinton has an admirable work ethic. Bill Clinton could convince voters that he felt their pain. Hillary Clinton reminds them detail by detail of how she would alleviate it. Glamour has a way of temporarily making you forget about the pain and just think the world is a beautiful place of endless possibilities.

Ronald Reagan evoked glamour. His white-tie inaugural balls 13 and morning-coat swearing-in were purposefully organized to bring a twinkle back to the American psyche. George W. Bush has charisma, a.k.a. the likability factor, although it does not appear to be helping his approval rating now. Still, he remains a back-slapper and bestower of nicknames.

Charisma is personal. Glamour taps into a universal fairy 14 tale. It's unconcerned with the nitty-gritty. Instead, it celebrates the surface gloss. And sometimes, a little shimmer can be hard to resist.

Expanding Vocabulary

Match each word in column A with its definition in column B. When in doubt, first find the word in the essay and look for context clues to aid your understanding of the word's meaning. Then, if necessary, use your dictionary to complete the matching exercise. The number in parentheses is the number of the paragraph in which the word appears.

Column A	Column B
wry (2)	unwise
lassitude (2)	playful conversation
epicenter (3)	seriousness
impolitic (4)	listlessness
paparazzi (5)	having both male and female characteristics
banter (6)	clone-like figures
gravitas (6)	those who sparkle
androgynous (8)	dryly humorous
doppelgangers (8)	spirit or soul
habitat (11)	celebrity photographers
glitterati (11)	the center of the storm, center of action
psyche (13)	environment

Understanding Content

1. How does glamour make us feel?
2. Where do we usually find glamour? Why?
3. Who today best capture Hollywood's glamour of the past?
4. What traits do the glamorous have?
5. Explain the differences among glamour, charisma, and cool.

Drawing Inferences about Thesis and Purpose

1. Do we ever really know the glamorous, cool, and charismatic celebrities? Explain.
2. What is Givhan's thesis?

Analyzing Strategies and Style

1. Examine the opening three sentences in paragraph 12. What makes them effective?
2. List all definition strategies Givhan uses and include an example of each.

Thinking Critically

1. Givhan asserts that glamour is in the present but "cool people are a step ahead." Does this contrast make sense to you? Explain.
2. Many young people aspire to be cool. How would you advise these people? What should one do, how should one behave, to be cool? Is "cool" a trait that we can "put on" if we wish? Why or why not?

Curiosity

ALASTAIR REID

A Scotsman who prefers to live in Spain, Alastair Reid is a poet, translator, essayist, writer of children's books, and lecturer. Holding a master's degree from Scotland's St. Andrews University, Reid has lectured at schools in England, Spain, and the United States. He has had several books of poems published, has translated much of the poetry of Latin American poet Pablo Neruda, and has been a staff writer for *The New Yorker*. "Curiosity" appeared first in *The New Yorker* and was then included in the collection *Weathering* (1959).

Curiosity

may have killed the cat. More likely,
the cat was just unlucky, or else curious
to see what death was like, having no cause
to go on licking paws, or fathering
litter on litter of kittens, predictably.   5

Nevertheless, to be curious
is dangerous enough. To distrust
what is always said, what seems,
to ask odd questions, interfere in dreams,
smell rats, leave home, have hunches,   10
does not endear cats to those doggy circles
where well-smelt baskets, suitable wives, good lunches
are the order of things, and where prevails
much wagging of incurious heads and tails.

15 Face it. Curiosity
will not cause us to die—
only lack of it will.
Never to want to see
the other side of the hill
20 or that improbable country
where living is an idyll
(although a probable hell)
would kill us all.
Only the curious
25 have if they live a tale
worth telling at all.
Dogs say cats love too much, are irresponsible,
are dangerous, marry too many wives,
desert their children, chill all dinner tables
30 with tales of their nine lives.

Well, they are lucky. Let them be
nine-lived and contradictory,
curious enough to change, prepared to pay
the cat-price, which is to die
35 and die again and again,
each time with no less pain.
A cat-minority of one
is all that can be counted on
to tell the truth; and what cats have to tell
40 on each return from hell
is this: that dying is what the living do,
that dying is what the loving do,
and that dead dogs are those who never know
that dying is what, to live, each has to do.

Understanding Content and Strategies

1. What is more likely than curiosity to have killed the cat?
2. Why is being curious "dangerous enough"?
3. What kind of people belong to "doggy circles"?
4. What do dogs say about cats? What traits do they ascribe to them? Are we to agree with the dogs' view of cats? How do you know?
5. What are the characteristics of the curious life? Given the rather negative-sounding elements of this life, why should we be like the curious cat rather than the incurious dog?

6. Notice that the title runs into the first line. How does Reid's use of punctuation (to stop us) or no punctuation (to keep us reading) parallel what he is observing about curiosity or the lack of it?
7. What is the term for poems that have the pattern—or lack of pattern—that you find in "Curiosity"?

Drawing Inferences about Theme

1. When the poet writes that "dying is what, to live, each has to do," what does he mean? The statement seems contradictory. What is the term for this strategy for gaining emphasis? For the statement to make sense, how do you have to take the word *dying?*
2. State the poem's meaning or theme. What does Reid want us to understand about the role of curiosity in life?

Thinking Critically

1. Do you find the use of cats and dogs an effective one? For the most part, do the personalities of cats and dogs seem to fit the distinction Reid wants to make?
2. Is curiosity an important trait? Why or why not? What are its virtues? What are its dangers?
3. Are most children more like cats or dogs? If they are like cats, then why are some adults so incurious? If they are like dogs, what are some ways they can be encouraged to develop curiosity?

STUDENT ESSAY—DEFINITION

PARAGON OR PARASITE?
Laura Mullins

Do you recognize this creature? He is low maintenance and often unnoticeable, a favorite companion of many. Requiring no special attention, he grows from the soil of pride and rejection, feeding reg-ularly on a diet of ignorance and inse-curity, scavenging for hurt feelings and defensiveness, gobbling up dainty morsels

Attention-getting introduction

of lust and scandal. Like a cult leader
clothed in a gay veneer, disguising himself as blameless, he wields power.
Bewitching unsuspecting but devoted
groupies, distracting them from honest
self-examination, deceiving them into
believing illusions of grandeur or, on
the other extreme, unredeemable worth-
lessness, he breeds jealousy, hate, and
fear; thus, he thrives. He is Gossip.

Clever extended metaphor

Subject introduced

   One of my dearest friends is a gossip.
She is an educated, honorable, compassionate, loving woman whose character and
judgment I deeply admire and respect.
After sacrificially raising six children,
she went on to study medicine and become
a doctor who graciously volunteers her
expertise. How, you may be wondering,
could a gossip deserve such praise? Then
you do not understand the word. My friend
is my daughter's godmother; she is my
gossip, or *god-sib*, meaning sister-
in-god. Derived from Middle English words
god, meaning spiritual, and *sip/sib/syp*,
meaning kinsman, this term was used to
refer to a familiar acquaintance, close
family friend, or intimate relation,
according to the *Oxford English Dictionary*. As a male, he would have joined in
fellowship and celebration with the

Etymology of gossip and early meanings

father of the newly born; if a female, she would have been a trusted friend, a birth-attendant or midwife to the mother of the baby. The term grew to include references to the type of easy, unrestrained conversation shared by these folks.

As is often the case with words, the term's meaning has certainly evolved, maybe eroded from its original idea. Is it harmless, idle chat, innocuous sharing of others' personal news, or back-biting, rumor-spreading, and manipulation? Is it a beneficial activity worthy of pursuit, or a deplorable danger to be avoided?

Current meanings

In her article "Evolution, Alienation, and Gossip" (for the Social Issues Research Centre in Oxford, England), Kate Fox writes that "gossip is not a trivial pastime; it is essential to human social, psychological, and even physical well-being." Many echo her view that gossip is a worthy activity, claiming that engaging in gossip produces endorphins, reduces stress, and aids in building intimate relationships. Gossip, seen at worst as a harmless outlet, is encouraged in the workplace. Since much of its content is not inherently critical or malicious, it is viewed as a positive activity. However, this view does nothing to encourage those

Good use of sources to develop definition

speaking or listening to evaluate or examine motive or purpose; instead, it seems
to reflect the "anything goes" thinking
so prevalent today.

Conversely, writer and high school
English and geography teacher Lennox V.
Farrell of Toronto, Canada, in his essay
titled "Gossip: An Urban Form of Sor-
cery," presents gossip as a kind of
"witchcraft . . . based on using unsub-
stantiated accusations by those who make
them, and on uncritically accepting these
by those enticed into listening." Farrell
uses gossip in its more widely understood
definition, encompassing the breaking of
confidences, inappropriate sharing of
indiscretions, destructive tale-bearing,
and malicious slander.

What, then, is gossip? We no longer use
the term to refer to our children's god-
parents. Its current definition usually
comes with derogatory implications.
Imagine a backyard garden: you see a
variety of greenery, recognizing at a
glance that you are looking at different
kinds of plants. Taking a closer look,
you will find the gossip vine; inconspic-
uously blending in, it doesn't appear
threatening, but ultimately it destroys.
If left in the garden it will choke and

*Good use of
metaphor to
depict gossip as
negative*

then suck out life from its host. Zoom in on the garden scene and follow the creeping vine up trees and along a fence where two neighbors visit. You can overhear one woman saying to the other, "I know I should be the last to tell you, but your husband is being unfaithful to me." (Caption from a cartoon by Alan De la Nougerede!)

The current popular movement to legitimize gossip seems an excuse to condone the human tendency to puff-up oneself. Compared in legal terms, gossip is to conversation as hearsay is to eyewitness testimony; it's not credible. Various religious doctrines abhor the idea and practice of gossip. An old Turkish proverb says, "He who gossips to you will gossip of you." From the Babylonian Talmud, which calls gossip the three-pronged tongue, destroying the one talking, the one listening, and the one being spoken of, to the Upanishads, to the Bible, we can conclude that no good fruit is born from gossip. Let's tend our gardens and check our motives when we have the urge to gossip. Surely we can find more noble pursuits than the self-aggrandisement we have come to know as gossip.

Conclusion states view that gossip is to be avoided—the writer's thesis.

MAKING CONNECTIONS

1. John Ciardi says that happiness is difficult to define—and to obtain. Is happiness possible without the ability to discriminate, as Robert Miller defines the term? How would each author answer this question? How would you answer the question?

2. Is happiness possible without curiosity? How would John Ciardi and Alastair Reid each answer the question? How would you answer the question?

3. John Ciardi stresses that true happiness takes effort. Andrew Vachss suggests that we shy away from distinguishing between sick and evil because it is a difficult philosophical problem. Are we getting tired? Or lazy? As a society? Individually? Examine the essays and then prepare your answer to these questions.

4. If happiness is not something we can "find" outside ourselves, what about "cool" or "glamour"? Can we become cool by deciding to be so? Can we just decide to be glamorous? How would Robin Givhan answer these questions? How would you answer them?

5. Robert Miller deplores our feeling that we can no longer use the word *discrimination* in its important meaning of discerning differences. Andrew Vachss is bothered by our unwillingness to call specific actions *evil,* to use such a strong word. Have we become hemmed in by political correctness or the attitudes of the social sciences such that we are unwilling to use precise language? Has this become an age of indirection and "softness" in language use? If so, is this a good or a bad situation? Think about how the authors would answer these questions, and think about how you would answer them.

6. Select one of the words defined in this chapter to study in the *Oxford English Dictionary,* either in its print or online version. Prepare a one to two page discussion of the word based on your study in the *OED.*

TOPICS FOR WRITING

1. In this chapter you can find definitions of *friendship, happiness,* even *curiosity.* If you have disagreed at least in part with one of the definitions presented in the chapter, write your own definition of that term. Include in your essay at least one reference to the writer with whom you disagree, discussing his or her views and contrasting them with your own. Make your purpose your own definition, but use the ideas with which you disagree as one way to develop your definition.

2. In an essay develop a definition of one of the terms below. Use at least three of the specific strategies for developing a definition discussed in the chapter's introduction. Try to make one of those strategies the metaphor, including several in your essay. And use contrast as one of your strategies, contrasting the word you select with its contrasting term in parentheses.

   patriotism (chauvinism)   wisdom (knowledge)
   courtesy (manners)   ghetto (neighborhood)
   leader (elected official)   hero (star)
   community (subdivision)   gossip (conversation)

3. In "Curiosity," Alastair Reid plays paradoxically with the terms *living* and *dying.* In an essay, define either *work* or *play,* developing your definition in part by reflecting on the word's relationship with its apparent opposite. In what situations, under what conditions, can play become work? Or, in what situations, under what conditions, can work be play? We use these terms frequently to suggest opposite activities. In your definition of one of these words, show that there are some contexts in which its "opposite" is not really opposite.

4. Define a term that is currently used to label people with particular traits and values. Possibilities include: *nerd, yuppie, freak, jock, redneck, bimbo, wimp.* Reflect, before selecting

this topic, on why you want to explain the meaning of the word you have chosen. One purpose might be to explain the term to someone from a different culture. Another purpose might be to defend people who are labeled negatively by one of these terms; that is, your goal is to show why the term should not have a negative connotation.

5. Select a word that you believe is currently misused. The word can be misused because it has taken on a negative (or positive) connotation that it did not once have, or because it has changed meaning and has lost something in the change. A few suggestions include *awful, fabulous, exceptional* (in education), *awesome, propaganda.*

6. If you are familiar with a culture other than American culture, define either *liberty* or *freedom* as the term is used in that culture.

7. *Doublespeak* is a term used to describe, negatively, language used in some government and business writing. Do an online search to learn the characteristics of doublespeak. Then check out some government Websites and/or company Webpages to see what examples you can find. Your essay will be a study of the extent and kinds of doublespeak found on government or company Websites.

A CHECKLIST FOR DEFINITION ESSAYS

Inventing

☐ Have I selected a topic consistent with the instructor's guidelines for this assignment?

☐ Have I chosen among the possible topics one that fits my knowledge and experience?

☐ Have I reflected on my topic to understand why I want to define my chosen term?

☐ Have I reflected on my topic to write a tentative thesis that establishes my purpose of definition?

☐ Have I considered all the possible strategies I can use to develop an extended definition: word origin, history of usage, descriptive details, examples, comparison and contrast, function or use, metaphors?

- [ ] Have I selected several strategies that are best suited to defining my term and fulfilling my purpose in defining?
- [ ] Have I generated specifics from the strategies I selected?
- [ ] Have I thought about the most effective order for the specifics?

Drafting

- [ ] Have I succeeded in completing a first draft at one sitting so that I can "see" the whole?
- [ ] Do I have enough—enough to meet assignment demands and enough to develop and support my thesis—my definition?
- [ ] Do I have good specifics to make my definition clear and concrete? If not, do I need to use other strategies or do I need more specifics within strategies I have used? (For example, do I need to add an explanation of word origin or do I need more examples?)
- [ ] Does the order work? If not, what needs to be moved—and where?

Revising

- [ ] Have I made any needed additions, deletions, or changes in order based on answering the questions about my draft?
- [ ] Have I revised my draft to produce coherent paragraphs, using transitions and connecting words that reveal my classification system?

Polishing

- [ ] Have I eliminated wordiness and clichés?
- [ ] Have I avoided or removed any discriminatory language?
- [ ] Have I used my word processor's spell check and proofread a printed copy with great care?
- [ ] Do I have an appropriate and interesting title?

9

Using Causal Analysis
Examining Family and Community Conflicts

You may know the old—and very bad—joke that asks why the chicken crossed the road. When we give up and ask for the answer, the jokester, laughing merrily at trapping us in such silliness, says: "to get to the other side." The joke isn't in the answer but on us because we expect a more profound explanation of cause. Human beings characteristically ask why things happen. The four-year-old who asks her mother why there are stars in the sky may grow up to be the astrophysicist who continues, in a more sophisticated manner, to probe the same question.

When to Use Causal Analysis

We want to know what produced past events (why did the Roman Empire collapse?), what is causing current situations (why is there an increased fear of violence in our society?), and what will happen if we act in a particular way (will inflation be avoided if the Federal Reserve lowers interest rates?). Whether the questions are about the past, the present, or the future, we are seeking a causal explanation. We usually make a distinction between a study of *causes* (what produced A) and a study of *effects* (what has happened or will happen as a result of B), but actually the distinction is more one of wording than of approach or way of thinking. If, for example, we think that inflation can be avoided (effect) by raising interest rates (cause), we are saying that low interest rates can cause inflation. So, when we want to know why, we need to explore cause, whether we approach the "connection" from the causal end or the effects end.

How to Use Causal Analysis

In the study of causes and effects, we need to stress the key word *analysis*. In Chapter 6, you learned that process analysis answers the question *how* something is done or was accomplished by determining the steps, in proper time sequence, to complete the activity. When we examine cause, we also need to analyze the situation, both present and past, to make certain that we recognize all contributing elements and that we sort out the more important from the less important. Fortunately, there are some terms for distinguishing among different kinds of causes that can help us examine cause in a thoughtful and thorough way.

Thinking about Cause

First, events do not occur in a vacuum. There are *conditions* that surround an event, making the finding of only one cause unlikely. Suppose you have decided to become a veterinarian, and you want to understand why you have made that career choice. The conditions of your family life and upbringing probably affected your decision. You grew up with a dog you loved and cared for; your parents tolerated all the frogs and wounded birds you brought home and taught you to value living things. Second, there are more specific *influences* that contribute to an event. Perhaps the family vet let you help when your dog needed shots or bandaging and by example influenced your career plans.

In addition to conditions and influences, there are the more *immediate causes* that shape an event, leading up to the *precipitating cause*, the triggering event. In your choice to become a veterinarian, these events may include your good grades in and enjoyment of high school chemistry and biology, a recognition that you like working with your hands and that you want to be your own boss, and two summers of working at an animal hospital. In short, going off to college and having to declare a major did not cause you to choose veterinary medicine. The search for cause is a search for deeper, more fundamental answers than the college's requirement that you state a major field of study.

In our need, as humans, to have explanations for what happens, we can sometimes fool ourselves into thinking that we understand events, and we can be comforted by "finding" simple explanations for complex situations. But the desire to settle for simplistic explanations or for explanations for which there is no clear evidence of a causal connection must be resisted, both in thinking about life and in writing about cause. Two all-too-common ways of generating illogical causal explanations are to mistake a *time relationship* for a causal one and a *correlation* between two events for a causal relationship. For example, you went out to dinner last night and awoke with an upset stomach this morning. Can you conclude that something you ate last night caused the stomach upset? Certainly not without further evidence. Perhaps you already had a stomach virus before you went to dinner. To understand the difference between a correlation and a cause, consider the relationship between IQ scores and college grades. Students who have high IQ scores generally get good grades in college, but scores on an IQ test do not *cause* the good grades. (Whatever skills or knowledge produce high IQ scores are certainly one cause, though, of good grades. On the other hand, IQ tests do not measure motivation or good study habits.)

Evidence and Thesis

Writing a causal analysis challenges both thinking and writing skills. Remember that readers will evaluate your logic and evidence. After all, your purpose in writing is to show readers that your analysis of cause is sound and therefore useful to them. So, resist simplistic thinking and consider the kinds of evidence needed to illustrate and support your analysis. In addition to drawing on your own experience, you may need, depending on your topic, to obtain some evidence from reading. You will discover, for example, that many writers in this chapter include statistical evidence drawn from their reading. If you plan to emphasize one cause of a situation because you believe others have overlooked that cause or have failed to understand its importance, be certain that readers understand this limited and focused purpose.

Organization

Several organizational strategies are appropriate, depending on your topic and purpose. If you are examining a series of causes, beginning with background conditions and early influences, then your basic plan will be time sequence. Use appropriate terms for types of causes you discuss and transitional words to guide your reader through the sequence of events. If you want to examine an overlooked cause, you could begin by briefly discussing the causes that are usually stressed and then go on to introduce and explain the cause you want to emphasize. If your goal is to demonstrate that the same cause has operated in several different circumstances, then you need to show how that cause is the single common denominator in each circumstance. Whatever your overall strategy, remember to illustrate your points and to explain how your examples serve as evidence in support of your thesis.

WRITING FOCUS
REFERENCES TO AUTHORS, WORKS, AND THE WORDS OF OTHERS

Readers expect writers to follow the standard conventions for referring to authors and titles of works and for indicating when words belong to someone other than the writer. For you to be an effective writer, you need to follow these conventions both in the academic community and the workplace.

References to People
- In the first reference give the person's full name: *Amitai Etzioni, Linda J. Waite*. In all other references to that person, use the last name (surname): *Etzioni, Waite*.
- Do not use Mr., Mrs., or Ms. Special titles such as President, Chief Justice, or Doctor may be used in the first reference with the person's full name.
- Never refer to an author by his or her first name. Write *Waite*, not *Linda*.

References to Titles

- Always write titles as titles. This involves proper capitalizing of words in the title and then using either quotation marks or italics, depending on the work.
- Capitalizing: The first and last words are capitalized. The first word of a subtitle is capitalized. All other words are capitalized except:

    Articles (*a, an, the*)

    Coordinating conjunctions (*and, or, but, for, nor, yet, so*)

    Prepositions of five or fewer letters. Longer prepositions are capitalized.

- Titles requiring quotation marks: All works published within other works, including essays ("Cos and Effect"), short stories, poems ("Dream Deferred"), chapter titles, lectures.
- Titles requiring italics: Works that are separate publications, including newspapers (*New York Times*), magazines (*Newsweek*), novels (*The Old Man and the Sea*), textbooks (*Patterns of Reflection*), films (*The Wizard of Oz*).

Quotations

- Put *all* words taken from a source within quotation marks. Never change any of the words within the quotation marks.
- Do not leave out any words in the quoted passage unless you use ellipses (three spaced dots: . . .). If you have to add words to make the passage clear, place them in square brackets ([]), not parentheses.
- Always provide the source of the quoted passage, preferably *before* the quoted passage.
- When working a quoted passage into your sentence, place commas and periods within the final quotation mark—even when you quote only one word: Etzioni asserts that one reason for our loss of a sense of duty is too much "me-ism."
- Place semicolons and colons outside the end quotation mark. Do not quote punctuation at the end of

a quoted passage; use only the punctuation you need for your sentence.

- Use single quotation marks (the apostrophe key on your keyboard) to identify quoted material within quoted material: Barnett and Rivers point out that "'family-friendly' corporate policies reduce burnout." *Note: There is no comma before the beginning of the quoted passage; it is smoothly worked into the sentence.*

- When a quoted passage runs to more than three lines of type, use a block style: indent quoted lines ten spaces from the left margin; go to the right margin; continue to double space throughout the block quotation; do not use quotation marks—the indenting indicates a direct quotation.

- Remember your reader! Keep direct quoting to a minimum; keep quoted passages brief. You probably would not use a block quotation in a short essay, although you might use one in a research essay.

Getting Started: Reflections on Why You Are in College

Why are you in college? List the main reasons for your decision to attend college. Then reflect on some of the sources of those reasons. What people (parents, teachers, friends) and what experiences helped shape your decision? What, in other words, were the conditions and influences, as well as the more immediate causes, that led to your decision? Write in your journal on these questions or prepare responses for class discussion.

When Parents Are Toxic to Children

KEITH ABLOW

Keith Ablow, a graduate of the Johns Hopkins University Medical School, is a writer and psychiatrist who practices in the Boston area. He has published several nonfiction books, including *With Mercy* (1996) and *Compulsion* (2006), and several novels. In the following article, which appeared in the *Washington Post*'s Health section in May 1996, Ablow examines the effects of bad parenting and argues for change.

Questions to Guide Your Reading and Reflection

1. Reflect on Ablow's title. What is the key word in his title? What point is he making?
2. What would you list as the worst ways parents abuse children?

---

1   I sat with a 15-year-old girl in the interview room where I meet psychiatric inpatients for the first time, watching her as she gazed through her long black hair at her forearm. She gingerly traced the superficial cuts she had made with a razor the night before when she had flirted with suicide.

2   Her chart indicated that since the age of 11 she had suffered repeated bouts of severe depression that antidepressant medication didn't touch. At times she was intermittently paranoid, believing that someone was out to steal her mind or even to take her life.

3   "I'm not going back there," she finally said, looking up at me. "I'll kill myself, if they make me live with my parents."

4   "What happens there?" I asked.

5   "Constant fighting. Screaming. Swearing. Hitting. It's been like that my whole life."

6   "Do they hit you?" I asked.

7   "They used to. A lot. They don't anymore. They hit my brothers, though. And they keep telling me I'm ugly . . . and stupid. Worthless." She looked at her arm. "I don't care where I get sent. I'll go anywhere but home."

8   I was certain she would return home. Social service agencies had been involved in her case for years. No doubt there would be another family meeting during her hospitalization, perhaps more frequent home visits by a social worker afterward. But the mental health system's prejudice in favor of keeping families intact, as well as a perennial shortage of acceptable foster parents, would likely keep my young patient with her own parents and in peril.

I have repeatedly treated teenagers like this girl whose 9
biological parents have inflicted irreparable psychological
harm on their children. Some are the victims of sexual abuse,
others of pervasive neglect. They end up in my office with
symptoms that include panic attacks, severe depression and
psychosis. Many are addicted to drugs before they even begin
high school. Some see suicide as a reasonable way to end their
pain. I prescribe them a variety of antidepressant, anti-anxiety
and sometimes antipsychotic medications, hoping that their
symptoms of mental illness are temporary, but worried that the
damage they have suffered may be permanent. Worst of all I
know that these are preventable illnesses.

Nor does the damage end with them. These teenage patients 10
are tomorrow's parents. And experience has repeatedly
demonstrated that many of them are likely to reenact the same
destructive scenarios with their own children. Most people
who harbor rage from their childhood don't expect it to surface
after they become parents. Many fail to see the traumas they
survived as sources of great risk for a new generation.

If we are to make a serious attempt to prevent some forms 11
of serious mental illness, parenting must no longer be seen as
an inalienable right, but as a privilege that can—and will—be
revoked for abuse or neglect. Society must be much less tolerant of harm to children and also must be willing to devote con-
siderably more resources to providing alternative living
situations for children and adolescents who are in danger.

Only in the most egregious cases of physical violence or 12
emotional neglect have I seen the state terminate parental
rights. It seems that damage to children must reach the level of
near catastrophe to justify cleaving a parent-child relationship
that has been anything but loving.

Parents need to get a new message. If you do a lousy job 13
parenting, you lose your job. In cases involving child custody,
blood ties must be given less weight not only by the mental health
system, but by the government and the court system. At the federal, state and local levels, keeping children with their parents can
no longer be considered more important than keeping them safe.

Another young woman I treated had been repeatedly beaten 14
by her older brothers for years. As a girl she had been raped by

her mother's boyfriend. Her moods had become erratic, and her temper unpredictable. She had turned to marijuana for relief and had been expelled from school for fighting. Yet she continued to live at home, with the blessing of the state Department of Social Services.

15   "She's got to get off these damn drugs," her mother complained in my office. "That [stuff] has got her all screwed . . ."

16   "I'm not gonna listen to you," the girl interrupted. She turned to me. "This is the woman who let me get beat on for about 10 years and let her boyfriend sneak into my bedroom, without her saying two words. How am I supposed to live as a normal human being with a mother like her?"

17   Privately I agreed with her. I felt hopeless about the situation myself. I could see that this girl was trapped in a family that was eroding her emotional resiliency, leaving her increasingly vulnerable to severe psychiatric illness. And society had no plan to rescue her from this situation. In fact, it tacitly endorsed it.

18   One of the difficulties of working as a therapist with adolescents is that they often clearly perceive the psychological dangers confronting them, but are powerless to deal with them. It's no wonder then that such experiences lay the groundwork for panic attacks, post-traumatic stress disorder, depression and paranoia that seem to come "out of the blue" later in life. The coping mechanisms of some of the teenagers I treat have short-circuited already. These patients "dissociate": They unpredictably enter altered states of consciousness in which they lose touch with reality.

19   One 17-year-old whom I treated for depression asked me plainly: "If you were me, what would you do to make sure your parents didn't get you even sicker during the next year? I mean, if I can get to 18, I can leave home, maybe join the Army or something, and they won't be able to do anything about it."

20   I told him that he needed to be less confrontational in the face of his parents' unreasonable demands for strict obedience, if only to conserve his emotional energy, not to mention avoid his father's belt. "Prisoners of war don't get in beefs every day with their captors," I told him. "They lay low until they can escape."

21   Like most of the abusive parents I have met, this young man's father, for example, made it clear to me that he too had

faced traumas as a young person, including horrific beatings. He tried to do his best for his son despite severe depression and alcoholism that limited his ability to function. Doing his best, however, was not nearly good enough.

This is why a social policy that would raise expectations for   22 healthy parenting and more frequently and quickly impose the loss of parental rights should include a vigorous attempt to educate parents on how to avoid harming their children. The loss of parental rights is a tragedy we should attempt to avoid.

Another key requirement is to recruit good foster families.   23 Too often such families have not proven to be much better for kids than the homes they have left; sometimes they are even worse. It makes no sense to take the admittedly drastic step of removing children from bad biological parents only to place them with bad foster parents.

One 19-year-old woman I met recently had spent a decade   24 living in a foster family. She had been beaten and neglected for the years prior to her placement and, even with obviously concerned and empathic foster parents, had required years of psychotherapy to cope with her traumatic past.

With the support of a new family, however, she had   25 achieved in school, shunned drugs and made close and lasting friendships. She hoped to save money to attend college. While she considered leaving her biological parents as one of the major stresses in her life, she made it clear that she would have been much worse staying with them. "I'm one of the lucky ones," she said. "I got out."

The tragedy is that too few children do.   26

Expanding Vocabulary

Match each word in column A with its definition in column B. When in doubt, first find the word in the essay and look for context clues to aid your understanding of the word's meaning. Then, if necessary, use your dictionary to complete the matching exercise. The number in parentheses is the number of the paragraph in which the word appears.

Column A	*Column B*
bouts (2)	dividing, separating
paranoid (2)	impossible to repair or fix
perennial (8)	quietly, implied rather than stated

irreparable (9)
psychosis (9)
scenarios (10)
traumas (10)
inalienable (11)
egregious (12)
cleaving (12)
eroding (17)
resiliency (17)
tacitly (17)

outlines of possible future events
serious emotional shocks that may
   result in lasting damage
notably offensive
contests, matches
destroying, eating away at
one with a disorder characterized by
   delusions of persecution or grandeur
ability to recover from serious problems
lasting through many years
what cannot be transferred to another
mental disorder marked by
   disconnection with reality
   and social dysfunction

Understanding Content

1. For what two reasons are abused children kept with the parents who are abusing them?
2. What problems do the abused teenagers experience; what are the effects of their situation? How does Ablow treat them?
3. How do abused adolescents view their situation?

Drawing Inferences about Thesis and Purpose

1. What is Ablow's thesis? What change in policy does he want to see? Where does he state his thesis?
2. What specific actions are needed to improve the health of abused children?

Analyzing Strategies and Style

1. The author provides several examples of abused teenagers; how do the examples help to advance his argument? Ablow begins and ends with extended examples that include dialogue. What makes these effective ways to begin and end?
2. What, in your view, is the most telling example, detail, or argument in the essay? Why?

Thinking Critically

1. Have you known any abused teens? If so, have you seen any good solutions to their problems, such as foster care or therapy? Do you know adolescents who need help? If so, what can you do?
2. Should bad parents lose their children? Why or why not?

3. Would you favor more resources to help abused children? Why or why not?
4. How can we improve education for prospective parents so that they will be prepared for good parenting? What suggestions do you have?

Social Science Finds: "Marriage Matters"

LINDA J. WAITE

A former senior sociologist at the Rand Corporation, Linda Waite is a professor at the University of Chicago. She has several books including *The Ties That Bind: Perspectives on Marriage and Cohabitation* (2000) and *Aging, Health, and Public Policy: Demographic and Economic Perspectives* (2004). In this article, published in *The Responsive Community* in 1996, Waite examines various studies of marriage to determine the effects that marriage has on those who are married.

Questions to Guide Your Reading and Reflection

1. What groups of people are the healthiest and live the longest?
2. Do the benefits of marriage extend to cohabitation?

As we are all too aware, the last few decades have witnessed   1
a decline in the popularity of marriage. This trend has not escaped the notice of politicians and pundits. But when critics point to the high social costs and taxpayer burden imposed by disintegrating "family values," they overlook the fact that individuals do not simply make the decisions that lead to unwed parenthood, marriage, or divorce on the basis of what is good for society. Individuals weigh the costs and benefits of each of these choices to themselves—and sometimes their children. But how much is truly known about these costs and benefits, either by the individuals making the choices or demographers like myself who study them? Put differently, what are the implications, for individuals, of the current increases in

nonmarriage? If we think of marriage as an insurance policy—which it is, in some respects—does it matter if more people are uninsured, or are insured with a term rather than a whole-life policy? I shall argue that it does matter, because marriage typically provides important and substantial benefits, benefits not enjoyed by those who live alone or cohabit.

2   A quick look at marriage patterns today compared to, say, 1950 shows the extent of recent changes. Figures from the Census Bureau show that in 1950, at the height of the baby boom, about a third of white men and women were not married. Some were waiting to marry for the first time, some were divorced or widowed and not remarried. But virtually everyone married at least once at some point in their lives, generally in their early twenties.

3   In 1950 the proportion of black men and women not married was approximately equal to the proportion unmarried among whites, but since that time the marriage behavior of blacks and whites has diverged dramatically. By 1993, 61 percent of black women and 58 percent of black men were not married, compared to 38 percent of white men and 41 percent of white women. So, in contrast to 1950 when only a little over one black adult in three was not married, now a majority of black adults are unmarried. Insofar as marriage "matters," black men and women are much less likely than whites to share in the benefits, and much less likely today than they were a generation ago.

4   The decline in marriage is directly connected to the rise in cohabitation—living with someone in a sexual relationship without being married. Although Americans are less likely to be married today than they were several decades ago, if we count both marriage and cohabitation, they are about as likely to be "coupled." If cohabitation provides the same benefits to individuals as marriage does, then we do not need to be concerned about this shift. But we may be replacing a valuable social institution with one that demands and offers less.

5   Perhaps the most disturbing change in marriage appears in its relationship to parenthood. Today a third of all births occur to women who are not married, with huge but shrinking differences between blacks and whites in this behavior. One in five births to white mothers and two-thirds of births to black mothers currently take place outside marriage. Although about

a quarter of the white unmarried mothers are living with someone when they give birth, so that their children are born into two-parent—if unmarried—families, very few black children born to unmarried mothers live with fathers too.

I believe that these changes in marriage behavior are a cause   6
for concern, because in a number of important ways married men and women do better than those who are unmarried. And I believe that the evidence suggests that they do better because they are married.

Marriage and Health

The case for marriage is quite strong. Consider the issues of   7
longevity and health. With economist Lee Lillard, I used a large national survey to follow men and women over a 20-year period. We watched them get married, get divorced, and remarry. We observed the death of spouses and of the individuals themselves. And we compared deaths of married men and women to those who were not married. We found that once we took other factors into account, married men and women faced lower risks of dying at any point than those who have never married or whose previous marriage has ended. Widowed women were much better off than divorced women or those who had never married, although they were still disadvantaged when compared with married women. But all men who were not currently married faced significantly higher risks of dying than married men, regardless of their marital history. Other scholars have found disadvantages in death rates for unmarried adults in a number of countries besides the United States.

How does marriage lengthen life? First, marriage appears to   8
reduce risky and unhealthy behaviors. For example, according to University of Texas sociologist Debra Umberson, married men show much lower rates of problem drinking than unmarried men. Umberson also found that both married men and women are less likely to take risks that could lead to injury than are the unmarried. Second, as we will see below, marriage increases material well-being—income, assets, and wealth. These can be used to purchase better medical care, better diet, and safer surroundings, which lengthen life. This material improvement seems to be especially important for women.

9   Third, marriage provides individuals—especially men—
with someone who monitors their health and health-related
behaviors and who encourages them to drink and smoke less,
to eat a healthier diet, to get enough sleep and to generally take
care of their health. In addition, husbands and wives offer each
other moral support that helps in dealing with stressful situations. Married men especially seem to be motivated to avoid
risky behaviors and to take care of their health by the sense of
meaning that marriage gives to their lives and the sense of
obligation to others that it brings.

More Wealth, Better Wages—For Most

10   Married individuals also seem to fare better when it comes
to wealth. One comprehensive measure of financial well-
being—household wealth—includes pension and Social Security wealth, real and financial assets, and the value of the
primary residence. According to economist James Smith, in
1992 married men and women ages 51–60 had median wealth
of about $66,000 per spouse, compared to $42,000 for the widowed, $35,000 for those who had never married, $34,000
among those who were divorced, and only $7,600 for those
who were separated. Although married couples have higher
incomes than others, this fact accounts for only about a quarter
of their greater wealth.

11   How does marriage increase wealth? Married couples can
share many household goods and services, such as a TV and
heat, so the cost to each individual is lower than if each one
purchased and used the same items individually. So the married spend less than the same individuals would for the same
style of life if they lived separately. Second, married people
produce more than the same individuals would if single. Each
spouse can develop some skills and neglect others, because
each can count on the other to take responsibility for some of
the household work. The resulting specialization increases effi-
ciency. We see below that this specialization leads to higher
wages for men. Married couples also seem to save more at the
same level of income than do single people.

12   The impact of marriage is again beneficial—although in this
case not for all involved—when one looks at labor market outcomes. According to recent research by economist Kermit

Daniel, both black and white men receive a wage premium if they are married: 4.5 percent for black men and 6.3 percent for white men. Black women receive a marriage premium of almost 3 percent. White women, however, pay a marriage penalty, in hourly wages, of over 4 percent. In addition, men appear to receive some of the benefit of marriage if they cohabit, but women do not.

Why should marriage increase men's wages? Some researchers 13 think that marriage makes men more productive at work, leading to higher wages. Wives may assist husbands directly with their work, offer advice or support, or take over household tasks, freeing husbands' time and energy for work. Also, as I mentioned earlier, being married reduces drinking, substance abuse, and other unhealthy behaviors that may affect men's job performance. Finally, marriage increases men's incentives to perform well at work, in order to meet obligations to family members.

For women, Daniel finds that marriage and presence of 14 children together seem to affect wages, and the effects depend on the woman's race. Childless black women earn substantially more money if they are married but the "marriage premium" drops with each child they have. Among white women only the childless receive a marriage premium. Once white women become mothers, marriage decreases their earnings compared to remaining single (with children), with very large negative effects of marriage on women's earnings for those with two children or more. White married women often choose to reduce hours of work when they have children. They also make less per hour than either unmarried mothers or childless wives.

Up to this point, all the consequences of marriage for the 15 individuals involved have been unambiguously positive— better health, longer life, more wealth, and higher earnings. But the effects of marriage and children on white women's wages are mixed, at best. Marriage and cohabitation increase women's time spent on housework; married motherhood reduces their time in the labor force and lowers their wages. Although the family as a whole might be better off with this allocation of women's time, women generally share their husbands' market earnings only when they are married. Financial well-being declines dramatically for women and their children after divorce and widowhood; women whose marriages have ended are often quite disadvantaged financially by their investment in their husbands and children rather than in their own earning power. Recent changes in divorce law—the rise in no-fault divorce and the move away from alimony—seem to have exacerbated this situation, even while increases in women's education and work experience have moderated it.

Improved Intimacy

16   Another benefit of married life is an improved sex life. Married men and women report very active sex lives—as do those who are cohabiting. But the married appear to be more satisfied with sex than others. More married men say that they find sex with their wives to be extremely physically pleasurable than do cohabiting men or single men say the same about sex with their partners. The high levels of married men's physical satisfaction with their sex lives contradicts the popular view that sexual novelty or variety improves sex for men. Physical satisfaction with sex is about the same for married women, cohabiting women, and single women with sex partners.

17   In addition to reporting more active and more physically fulfilling sex lives than the unmarried, married men and women say that they are more emotionally satisfied with their sex lives than do those who are single or cohabiting. Although cohabitants report levels of sexual activity as high as the married, both cohabiting men and women report lower levels of emotional satisfaction with their sex lives. And those who are sexually active but single report the lowest emotional satisfaction with it.

18   How does marriage improve one's sex life? Marriage and cohabitation provide individuals with a readily available sexual partner with whom they have an established, ongoing sexual relationship. This reduces the costs—in some sense—of any particular sexual contact, and leads to higher levels of sexual activity. Since married couples expect to carry on their sex lives for many years, and since the vast majority of married couples are monogamous, husbands and wives have strong incentives to learn what pleases their partner in bed and to become good at it. But I would argue that more than "skills" are at issue here. The long-term contract implicit in marriage—which is not implicit in cohabitation—facilitates emotional investment in the relationship, which should affect both frequency of and

satisfaction with sex. So the wife or husband who knows what the spouse wants is also highly motivated to provide it, both because sexual satisfaction in one's partner brings similar rewards to oneself and because the emotional commitment to the partner makes satisfying him or her important in itself.

To this point we have focused on the consequences of marriage for adults—the men and women who choose to marry (and stay married) or not. But such choices have consequences for the children born to these adults. Sociologists Sara McLanahan and Gary Sandefur compare children raised in intact, two-parent families with those raised in one-parent families, which could result either from disruption of a marriage or from unmarried childbearing. They find that approximately twice as many children raised in one-parent families than children from two-parent families drop out of high school without finishing. Children raised in one-parent families are also more likely to have a birth themselves while teenagers, and to be "idle"—both out of school and out of the labor force—as young adults. 19

Not surprisingly, children living outside an intact marriage are also more likely to be poor. McLanahan and Sandefur calculated poverty rates for children in two-parent families—including stepfamilies—and for single-parent families. They found very high rates of poverty for single-parent families, especially among blacks. Donald Hernandez, chief of marriage and family statistics at the Census Bureau, claims that the rise in mother-only families since 1959 is an important cause of increases in poverty among children. 20

Clearly poverty, in and of itself, is a bad outcome for children. In addition, however, McLanahan and Sandefur estimate that the lower incomes of single-parent families account for only half of the negative impact for children in these families. The other half comes from children's access—or lack of access—to the time and attention of two adults in two-parent families. Children in one-parent families spend less time with their fathers (this is not surprising given that they do not live with them), but they also spend less time with their mothers than children in two-parent families. Single-parent families and stepfamilies also move much more frequently than two-parent families, disrupting children's social and academic environments. Finally, children who spend part of their childhood in a single-parent family report 21 substantially lower quality relationships with their parents as adults and have less frequent contact with them, according to demographer Diane Lye.

Correlation Versus Causality

22   The obvious question, when one looks at all these "benefits" of marriage, is whether marriage is responsible for these differences. If all, or almost all, of the benefits of marriage arise because those who enjoy better health, live longer lives, or earn higher wages anyway are more likely to marry, then marriage is not "causing" any changes in these outcomes. In such a case, we as a society and we as individuals could remain neutral about each person's decision to marry or not, to divorce or remain married. But scholars from many fields who have examined the issues have come to the opposite conclusion. Daniel found that only half of the higher wages that married men enjoy could be explained by selectivity; he thus concluded that the other half is causal. In the area of mental health, social psychologist Catherine Ross—summarizing her own research and that of other social scientists—wrote, "The positive effect of marriage on well-being is strong and consistent, and the selection of the psychologically healthy into marriage or the psychologically unhealthy out of marriage cannot explain the effect." Thus marriage itself can be assumed to have independent positive effects on its participants.

23   So, we must ask, what is it about marriage that causes these benefits? I think that four factors are key. First, the institution of marriage involves a long-term contract—"'til death do us part." This contract allows the partners to make choices that carry immediate costs but eventually bring benefits. The time horizon implied by marriage makes it sensible—a rational choice is at work here—for individuals to develop some skills and to neglect others because they count on their spouse to fill in where they are weak. The institution of marriage helps individuals honor this long-term contract by providing social support for the couple as a couple and by imposing social and economic costs on those who dissolve their union.

24   Second, marriage assumes a sharing of economic and social resources and what we can think of as co-insurance. Spouses act as a sort of small insurance pool against life's uncertainties,

reducing their need to protect themselves—by themselves—from unexpected events.

Third, married couples benefit—as do cohabiting couples—from economies of scale.   25

Fourth, marriage connects people to other individuals, to their social groups (such as in-laws), and to other social institutions (such as churches and synagogues) which are themselves a source of benefits. These connections provide individuals with a sense of obligation to others, which gives life meaning beyond oneself.   26

Cohabitation has some but not all of the characteristics of marriage and so carries some but not all of the benefits. Cohabitation does not generally imply a lifetime commitment to stay together; a significant number of cohabiting couples disagree on the future of their relationship. Frances Goldscheider and Gail Kaufman believe that the shift to cohabitation from marriage signals "declining commitment within unions, of men and women to each other and to their relationship as an enduring unit, in exchange for more freedom, primarily for men." Perhaps, as a result, many view cohabitation as an especially poor bargain for women.   27

The uncertainty that accompanies cohabitation makes both investment in the relationship and specialization with this partner much riskier than in marriage and so reduces them. Cohabitants are much less likely than married couples to pool financial resources and more likely to assume that each partner is responsible for supporting himself or herself financially. And whereas marriage connects individuals to other important social institutions, cohabitation seems to distance them from these institutions.   28

Of course, all these observations concern only the average benefits of marriage. Clearly, some marriages produce substantially higher benefits for those involved. Some marriages produce no benefits and even cause harm to the men, women, and children involved. That fact needs to be recognized.   29

Reversing the Trend

Having stated this qualification, we must still ask, if the average marriage produces all of these benefits for individuals, why has it declined? Although this issue remains   30 a subject of much research and speculation, a number of factors have been mentioned as contributing. For one, because of increases in women's employment, there is less specialization by spouses now than in the past; this reduces the benefits of marriage. Clearly, employed wives have less time and energy to focus on their husbands, and are less financially and emotionally dependent on marriage than wives who work only in the home. In addition, high divorce rates decrease people's certainty about the long-run stability of their marriage, and this may reduce their willingness to invest in it, which in turn increases the chance they divorce—a sort of self-fulfilling prophecy. Also, changes in divorce laws have shifted much of the financial burden for the breakup of the marriage to women, making investment within the marriage (such as supporting a husband in medical school) a riskier proposition for them.

31   Men, in turn, may find marriage and parenthood a less attractive option when they know that divorce is common, because they may face the loss of contact with their children if their marriage dissolves. Further, women's increased earnings and young men's declining financial well-being may have made women less dependent on men's financial support and made young men less able to provide it. Finally, public policies that support single mothers and changing attitudes toward sex outside of marriage, toward unmarried childbearing, and toward divorce have all been implicated in the decline in marriage. This brief list does not exhaust the possibilities, but merely mentions some of them.

32   So how can this trend be reversed? First, as evidence accumulates and is communicated to individuals, some people will change their behavior as a result. Some will do so simply because of their new understanding of the costs and benefits, to them, of the choices involved. In addition, we have seen that attitudes frequently change toward behaviors that have been shown to have negative consequences. The attitude change then raises the social cost of the newly stigmatized behavior.

33   In addition, though, we as a society can pull some policy levers to encourage or discourage behaviors. Public policies that include asset tests (Medicaid is a good example) act to exclude the married, as do AFDC programs and most states. The "marriage penalty" in the tax code is another example. These and other policies reinforce or undermine the institution of marriage.

If, as I have argued, marriage produces individuals who drink less, smoke less, abuse substances less, live longer, earn more, are wealthier, and have children who do better, we need to give more thought and effort to supporting this valuable social institution.

Expanding Vocabulary

After studying definitions of the following words, select five and use each one in a separate sentence. The number in parentheses is the number of the paragraph in which the word appears.

pundits (1)	exacerbated (15)
demographers (1)	monogamous (18)
cohabit (1)	implicit (18)
diverged (3)	disruption (19)
unambiguously (15)	stigmatized (32)

Understanding Content

1. Waite argues that most people weigh the advantages and disadvantages of marriage based on what?
2. Although marriage has declined, what has taken its place?
3. What percentage of births occur to women who are not married? What percentage of white mothers are living with someone? What percentage of black mothers are living with someone?
4. Which arrangement type has the greatest income? Which type has the least?
5. In what ways can marriage increase wealth? Who, when married, loses in hourly wages?
6. What may be causes for increased productivity for married men?
7. Which living arrangement reports having the most physical and emotional satisfaction from sex?
8. What situations increase poverty for children?
9. What are some effects of single-parent families on children?
10. Does Waite conclude that marriage itself is a cause of the improved lives of most married people? In general, who benefits the least from marriage?

Drawing Inferences about Thesis and Purpose

1. Why, if marriage has benefits, are fewer people getting married and more getting divorced?
2. What does Waite think should be done to change the movement away from marriage?

Analyzing Strategies and Style

1. This is a longish essay. What does Waite do to help readers follow her discussion?
2. What kind of evidence, primarily, does the author provide? How is this consistent with your expectations, based on your knowledge of the author?

Thinking Critically

1. Which statistic most surprises you? Why?
2. Do you think that the evidence Waite provides should encourage people to choose marriage over divorce, cohabitation, or the single life? If so, why? If not, why not?
3. What can be done to increase marriage benefits for women, the ones who have least benefited by marriage?

Working at McDonald's

AMITAI ETZIONI

An internationally renowned sociologist, Amitai Etzioni is University Professor at the George Washington University and founder of the Communitarian Network. He is the author of many books, including *Empire to Community: A New Approach to International Relations* (2004). In a whirlwind of articles, television appearances, and speeches, Etzioni focused on the general message of encouraging a greater sense of community, with less emphasis on the self. Seemingly no social issue is insignificant, as his analysis of the effects of after-school jobs in the following essay makes clear.

Questions to Guide Your Reading and Reflection

1. What are the advantages of teens working? What are the disadvantages?
2. Do you work? Do you think that it interferes with your learning?

1   McDonald's is bad for your kids. I do not mean the flat patties and the white-flour buns; I refer to the jobs teenagers undertake, mass-producing these choice items.

As many as two-thirds of America's high school juniors and   2
seniors now hold down part-time paying jobs, according to
studies. Many of these are in fast-food chains, of which
McDonald's is the pioneer, trend-setter and symbol.

At first, such jobs may seem right out of the Founding Fathers'   3
education manual for how to bring up self-reliant, work-ethic-
driven, productive youngsters. But in fact, these jobs undermine
school attendance and involvement, impart few skills that will be
useful in later life, and simultaneously skew the values of teenagers—especially their ideas about the worth of a dollar.

It has been a longstanding American tradition that young-   4
sters ought to get paying jobs. In folklore, few pursuits are
more deeply revered than the newspaper route and the sidewalk lemonade stand. Here the youngsters are to learn how
sweet are the fruits of labor and self-discipline (papers are
delivered early in the morning, rain or shine), and the ways of
trade (if you price your lemonade too high or too low. . .).

Roy Rogers, Baskin Robbins, Kentucky Fried Chicken, *et al.*   5
may at first seem nothing but a vast extension of the lemonade
stand. They provide very large numbers of teen jobs, provide
regular employment, pay quite well compared to many other
teen jobs and, in the modern equivalent of toiling over a hot
stove, test one's stamina.

Closer examination, however, finds the McDonald's kind of   6
job highly uneducational in several ways. Far from providing
opportunities for entrepreneurship (the lemonade stand) or
self-discipline, self-supervision and self-scheduling (the paper
route), most teen jobs these days are highly structured—what
social scientists call "highly routinized."

True, you still have to have the gumption to get yourself over   7
to the hamburger stand, but once you don the prescribed uniform, your task is spelled out in minute detail. The franchise pre-
scribes the shape of the coffee cups; the weight, size, shape and
color of the patties; and the texture of the napkins (if any). Fresh
coffee is to be made every eight minutes. And so on. There is no
room for initiative, creativity, or even elementary rearrange-
ments. These are breeding grounds for robots working for
yesterday's assembly lines, not tomorrow's high-tech posts.

There are very few studies on the matter. One of the few is   8
a 1984 study by Ivan Charper and Bryan Shore Fraser. The

study relies mainly on what teen-agers write in response to the questionnaires rather than actual observations of fast-food jobs. The authors argue that the employees develop many skills such has how to operate a food-preparation machine and a cash register. However, little attention is paid to how long it takes to acquire such a skill, or what its significance is.

9   What does it matter if you spend 20 minutes to learn to use a cash register, and then—"operate" it? What "skill" have you acquired? It is a long way from learning to work with a lathe or carpenter tools in the olden days or to program computers in the modern age.

10   A study by A. V. Harrell and P. W. Wirtz found that, among those students who worked at least 25 hours per week while in school, their unemployment rate four years later was half of that of seniors who did not work. This is an impressive statistic. It must be seen, though, together with the finding that many who begin as part-time employees in fast-food chains drop out of high school and are gobbled up in the world of low-skill jobs.

11   Some say that while these jobs are rather unsuited for college-bound, white, middle-class youngsters, they are "ideal" for lower-class, "non-academic," minority youngsters. Indeed, minorities are "over-represented" in these jobs (21 percent of fast-food employees). While it is true that these places provide income, work and even some training to such youngsters, they also tend to perpetuate their disadvantaged status. They provide no career ladders, few marketable skills, and undermine school attendance and involvement.

12   The hours are often long. Among those 14 to 17, a third of fast-food employees (including some school dropouts) labor more than 30 hours per week, according to the Charper-Fraser study. Only 20 percent work 15 hours or less. The rest: between 15 and 30 hours.

13   Often the stores close late, and after closing one must clean up and tally up. In affluent Montgomery County, Md., where child labor would not seem to be a widespread economic necessity, 24 percent of the seniors at one high school in 1986 worked as much as five to seven days a week; 27 percent, three to five. There is just no way such amounts of work will not interfere with school work, especially homework. In an informal survey published in the most recent yearbook of the high

school, 58 percent of seniors acknowledge that their jobs interfere with their school work.

The Charper-Fraser study sees merit in learning teamwork   14
and working under supervision. The authors have a point here.
However, it must be noted that such learning is not automatically educational or wholesome. For example, much of the
supervision in fast-food places leans toward teaching one the
wrong kinds of compliance: blind obedience, or shared alienation with the "boss."

Supervision is often both tight and woefully inappropriate.   15
Today, fast-food chains and other such places of work (record
shops, bowling alleys) keep costs down by having teens super-
vise teens with often no adult on the premises.

There is no father or mother figure with which to identify, to   16
emulate, to provide a role model and guidance. The work-
culture varies from one place to another: Sometimes it is a
tightly run shop (must keep the cash registers ringing); sometimes a rather loose pot party interrupted by customers. However, only rarely is there a master to learn from, or much worth
learning. Indeed, far from being places where solid adult work
values are being transmitted, these are places where all too
often delinquent teen values dominate. Typically, when my son
Oren was dishing out ice cream for Baskin Robbins in upper
Manhattan, his fellow teen-workers considered him a sucker for
not helping himself to the till. Most youngsters felt they were
entitled to $50 severance "pay" on their last day on the job.

The pay, oddly, is the part of the teen work-world that is   17
most difficult to evaluate. The lemonade stand or paper route
money was for your allowance. In the old days, apprentices
learning a trade from a master contributed most, if not all, of
their income to their parents' household. Today, the teen pay
may be low by adult standards, but it is often, especially in the
middle class, spent largely or wholly by the teens. That is, the
youngsters live free at home ("after all, they are high school
kids") and are left with very substantial sums of money.

Where this money goes is not quite clear. Some use it to   18
support themselves, especially among the poor. More middle-
class kids set some money aside to help pay for college, or save
it for a major purchase—often a car. But large amounts seem to
flow to pay for an early introduction into the most trite aspects of

American consumerism: flimsy punk clothes, trinkets and whatever else is the last fast-moving teen craze.

19   One may say that this is only fair and square; they are being good American consumers and spend their money on what turns them on. At least, a cynic might add, these funds do not go into illicit drugs and booze. On the other hand, an educator might bemoan that these young, yet unformed individuals, so early in life driven to buy objects of no intrinsic educational, cultural or social merit, learn so quickly the dubious merit of keeping up with the Joneses in ever-changing fads, promoted by mass merchandising.

20   Many teens find the instant reward of money, and the youth status symbols it buys, much more alluring than credits in calculus courses, European history or foreign languages. No wonder quite a few would rather skip school—and certainly homework—and instead work longer at a Burger King. Thus, most teen work these days is not providing early lessons in the work ethic; it fosters escape from school and responsibilities, quick gratification and a short cut to the consumeristic aspects of adult life.

21   Thus, parents should look at teen employment not as automatically educational. It is an activity—like sports—that can be turned into an educational opportunity. But it can also easily be abused. Youngsters must learn to balance the quest for income with the needs to keep growing and pursue other endeavors that do not pay off instantly—above all education.

22   Go back to school.

Expanding Vocabulary

Match each word in column A with its definition in column B. When in doubt, first find the word in the essay and look for context clues to aid your understanding of the word's meaning. Then, if necessary, use your dictionary to complete the matching exercise. The number in parentheses is the number of the paragraph in which the word appears.

Column A	Column B
skew (3)	inherent, central to
entrepreneurship (6)	machine on which wood or metal is
gumption (7)	worked
lathe (9)	look up to, seek to be like
perpetuate (11)	feeling of separation from others

alienation (14)	lament, feel bad about
emulate (16)	drawer for money at a business
till (16)	experience of operating a business
severance (16)	one who does not think highly of others
cynic (19)	appealing, enticing
bemoan (19)	prolong the existence of
intrinsic (19)	questionable
dubious (19)	distort
alluring (20)	pay given to an employee who leaves a job
	boldness, initiative

Understanding Content

1. What has been the view of part-time jobs for youngsters? What can they gain from paper routes, for example?
2. How many high schoolers now have part-time jobs? How many hours do some of them work?
3. What do some people think teens gain from working at fast food restaurants? How does Etzioni respond to them?
4. What, in Etzioni's view, are the negative effects of these kinds of jobs?

Drawing Inferences about Thesis and Purpose

1. After providing statistics on hours of work, Etzioni asserts that those work hours must impact on school work. Does this seem like a sound conclusion? Explain.
2. What is Etzioni's thesis?

Analyzing Strategies and Style

1. Who is Etzioni's audience? How do you know?
2. Etzioni declares that McDonald's is the symbol of the places where many teens work. What makes it a good symbol of the kinds of jobs the author objects to?
3. Examine the author's conclusion; is it effective? Why or why not?

Thinking Critically

1. Etzioni offers a strong challenge to conventional views of kids working. Has he been successful? If you disagree with him, how would you respond?
2. Why do middle-class parents let their teens work long hours? What might be some of the reasons for their agreeing to the part-time jobs?

The Don't Blame Me Generation

PATRICIA DALTON

A clinical psychologist with a practice in Washington, DC, Patricia Dalton writes essays that occasionally appear in the *Washington Post*'s Outlook section. She has written about the consequences of the feminist revolution for women and the long work hours and lack of sleep found among women today. In this essay, published March 5, 2006, Dalton examines the effects of bad parenting on today's young generation.

Questions to Guide Your Reading and Reflection

1. What attitudes toward oneself are encouraged today by our culture?
2. How often do you and your friends blame your teachers when you get a bad grade?

1   I once got a call from a couple whose son, a student at an elite college, had run up a huge credit card debt. His parents realized they had a problem and called to make an appointment for therapy. I told them that I wanted to see them along with their son. But when the parents showed up, they told me that their son had refused to come. "Tell me," I said halfway through our discussion. "If you had insisted, would your child be here?" The mother answered quickly, "Well, yes." The dad paused, then said, "That's a very good question."

2   The incident reminded me of the Warren Zevon song:
Send lawyers, guns, and money
Dad, get me out of this.

3   Except in real life, it wasn't funny. These parents weren't requiring their son to take responsibility for his actions. And he didn't respect them enough to shoulder it. The young man was in charge, not the parents.

4   The tendency to shirk the burden of responsibility permeates our family rooms and our boardrooms. I saw it in Vice President Cheney's belated response to the shooting incident last month. And it has characterized former Enron chairman

Kenneth Lay's public statements since his company's debacle: "Of anything and everything that I could imagine might happen to me in my lifetime," Lay said in Houston in December, "the one thing I would have never even remotely speculated about was that someday I would become entangled in our country's criminal justice system."

Whether or not he is found guilty, Lay sounds like the spokesman for our culture of victimhood. It is a culture that reflects a studiously nonjudgmental attitude toward one's own behavior, while ignoring its effects on others. And it is based on a belief system like this: I am more important than most people; I am good; therefore, I am incapable of doing bad things.   5

The upshot?   6

Excuses, excuses, excuses . . .   7

Evasive attitudes are learned, refined and reinforced in the home. And they ultimately lead people to become so divorced from the impact of their actions that they freely take advantage of others.   8

My clients have included parents who shrug when they realize that their son or daughter has been stealing. One even said, "I have bigger fish to fry," referring to his true priority— which was his child's all-important transcript for college applications. And I remember hearing about local parents who were outraged when a group of high school seniors were expelled for cheating on their SATs with the result that their prized college acceptances were rescinded.   9

Parents who want to raise mature young people who will contribute to society must not only have values that infuse their own lives but must also be willing to enforce them in their children's lives. Young people need to be taught, before reaching adulthood, that taking a powerful position involves a weight of responsibility to others.   10

What is striking today is the number of parents who seem to be uncomfortable with the role of teaching their children. They let the culture do it and hope for the best. Some even side with their children against authorities.   11

Take one disturbing example I heard from a friend who teaches middle school. A girl was caught drawing in her notebook during class. When the teacher asked her to stop, she   12 looked up and kept going. The teacher then confiscated the notebook. After class, the teacher tossed the girl her notebook. She reported to the school office that her teacher threw the notebook at her, intending to hurt her. A report (mandated in cases of alleged abuse) was written up; child protective services was called in to investigate. Only after fellow students refused to go along with the girl's story was the case dismissed. All along, the parents supported their daughter and her farfetched version of events.

13   A generation ago, this kind of behavior would have been almost inconceivable. Parents' tougher approach taught us lessons critical for later life—like that lying doesn't pay and that you have to respect your boss even if you don't like him or her. Today's adults who coddle young people fail to see that they are handicapping them.

14   It is not uncommon to see parents who are responsible themselves but put up with manipulative behavior from their kids. I once saw a pair of hard-working parents whose child refused to comply with the limits they put on his computer game time, telling them, "You can't make me." Rather than move the computer, they had just given up. They didn't see this as part of their son's larger problem with authority at school and in sports.

15   Parents have two serious responsibilities. The first is to love their children without worshipping them. Such adoration is a big danger in today's smaller families where parents' pride and dreams are divided among fewer children. The second responsibility is to discipline children—to hold their feet to the fire. Parents must be able to tolerate the distress that real discipline causes their offspring.

16   To do so, they have to quit worrying so much about damaging their children's self-esteem. When I asked one set of parents why they let their daughter call them obscene names, they looked at me blankly. Later the father told me, "We want to understand her. And we don't want her to feel worse about herself than she already does." Incredible. Especially since it has been my experience that it's behavior like gratuitous disrespect toward parents that actually makes kids feel bad.

17   Recently, I spoke with a grandmother who remarked that her grown children, who were doing very well financially, had lives that revolved around their kids. She said, "They spend

every waking moment giving, giving, giving to their children. They are living for their kids." Another grandmother told me that there is nothing she can give her grandchildren that they don't already have. "Manicures and pedicures are old hat to these kids."

Parents can stop the indulgence—or at least put some limits   18 on it. They also have the power as well as the responsibility to insist that their children see the dark as well as the light side of themselves—the capacity for evil as well as for good that we all have. The last thing our children need is to internalize the sense that they are victims who are not responsible for their actions, echoing the powerlessness that Zevon parodied:

I'm an innocent bystander
Somehow I got stuck
Between a rock and a hard place
And I'm down on my luck.
Yes I'm down on my luck.

Allowing children to evade responsibility may cost parents   19 a lot. But it's nothing compared with the cost to their kids: misery that lasts a lifetime.

Expanding Vocabulary

Study the definitions for any of the following words that you do not know. Then select five of the words and use each one in a separate sentence. The number in parentheses is the number of the paragraph in which the word appears.

shirk (4)	infuse (10)
permeates (4)	confiscated (12)
debacle (4)	coddle (13)
entangled (4)	gratuitous (16)
rescinded (9)	

Understanding Content

1. How did some parents react to their children's cheating on their SATs?
2. What are some parents having trouble doing today?
3. What happens when parents always support their children against authorities? Or when they don't enforce their own rules at home?
4. What are the two responsibilities parents have?

Drawing Inferences about Thesis and Purpose

1. What is Dalton's purpose in writing? What does she want her readers to understand?
2. How serious is the current parenting problem, in the author's view? How do you know?

Analyzing Strategies and Style

1. Dalton presents several extended examples from her experiences. What is effective about these examples? Would you rather have statistics? Explain.
2. What does the author accomplish by including the Zevon song?
3. At times Dalton uses quite short sentences. Find several and explain what they accomplish.

Thinking Critically

1. Dalton asserts that "evasive attitudes" learned at home result in youngsters who are unable to grasp how their behavior affects others. Does this make sense to you? Do you accept the power of early lessons to shape future behaviors? Explain.
2. Would you agree that today's parents—in general—indulge their children excessively? Why or why not?
3. What can we do, as a society, to try to change the current culture of victimhood—the attitude that "I'm not responsible for my actions"? What do you recommend?

Cos and Effect

RAY FISMAN

The Lambert Family Professor of Social Enterprise at the Columbia University Business School, Ray Fisman holds a Ph.D. in business economics from Harvard. He has published numerous articles in business and economics journals and received two National Science Foundation grants. He is at work on *Economic Gangsters* with coauthor Ted Miguel. In his Slate.com article of January 11, 2008, Fisman explains why African Americans buy expensive sneakers.

Questions to Guide Your Reading and Reflection

1. What has been Bill Cosby's complaint about African American spending habits?
2. Do you like to buy status clothes and jewelry? Why or why not?

A few years ago, Bill Cosby set off a firestorm with a speech   1
excoriating his fellow African-Americans for, among other things, buying $500 sneakers instead of educational toys for their children. In a recent book, *Come On People,* he repeats his argument that black Americans spend too much money on designer clothes and fancy cars, and don't invest sufficiently in their futures.

Many in the black community have been critical of Cosby   2
for blaming poor people rather than poor public policies. Others have defended Cosby's comments as an honest expression of uncomfortable truths. But notably absent from the Cosby affair have been the underlying economic facts. Do blacks actually spend more on consumerist indulgences than whites? And if so, what, exactly, makes black Americans more vulnerable to the allure of these luxury goods?

Economists Kerwin Charles, Erik Hurst, and Nikolai   3
Roussanov have taken up this rather sensitive question in a recent unpublished study, "Conspicuous Consumption and Race." Using data from the Consumer Expenditure Survey for 1986–2002, they find that blacks and Hispanics indeed spend more than whites with comparable incomes on what the authors classify as "visible goods" (clothes, cars, and jewelry). A lot more, in fact—up to an additional 30 percent. The authors provide evidence, however, that this is not because of some inherent weakness on the part of blacks and Hispanics. The disparity, they suggest, is related to the way that *all* people— black, Hispanic, and white—strive for social status within their respective communities.

Every society has had its equivalent of the $150 Zoom   4
LeBron IV basketball sneaker, and thanks to Thorstein Veblen, we have a pretty good idea why. As the Gilded Age economist famously put it, "conspicuous consumption of valuable goods

is a means of reputability to the gentleman of leisure," and "failure to consume a mark of demerit." To consume is to flaunt our financial success; it's how we keep score in life.

5   Economists refer to items that we purchase in order to reveal our prosperity to others as wealth *signals*. But why use sneakers, as opposed to phonics toys, as a wealth signal? First off, for a signal to be effective, it needs to be easily observed by the people we're trying to impress. This includes not just those near and dear to us, but also the person we pass on the street, who sees our sneakers but would have a harder time inferring how much we're spending teaching our kids to read. For a wealth signal to be credible, it also needs to be hard to imitate—if everyone in your community can afford $150 sneakers, those Zoom Lebron IVs would lose their signal value.

6   In general, the poorest people in any group are forced to opt out of the conspicuous consumption arms race—if you can't afford the signal, even by stretching your finances, you can't play the game. I, a humble economics professor, don't try to compete in a wealth-signaling game with the Wall Street traders whom I see on the streets of Manhattan. But this still leaves us with the question of why a black person would spend so much more in trying to signal wealth than a white person. The Cosby explanation—that there is simply a culture of consumption among black Americans—doesn't quite cut it for economists. We prefer to account for differences in behavior by looking to see if there are differing incentives.

7   Why would otherwise-similar black and white households have different incentives to signal their wealth? Charles, Hurst, and Roussanov argue that it's because blacks and whites are seeking status in different communities. In the racially divided society we live in, whites are trying to impress other whites, and blacks are trying to impress other blacks. But because poor blacks are more likely to live among other poor blacks than poor whites are to live among other poor whites, poor black families are more susceptible to being pulled into a signaling game with their neighbors.

8   Consider, for example, a black family and a white family each earning $42,500 a year, the median income for a black household during the 1990s. This black family sees that other black families are buying cars, clothes, and other wealth signals

that, while stretching this black family's financial resources thin, are technically affordable for a family making $42,500. So, this family decides to buy them, too, in order to keep up with the conspicuous consumers that they compare themselves with.

Now take the white family making $42,500. The average   9
household income among whites in the 1990s was much higher—$66,800. This white family looks around the neighborhood and is more likely to see white families spending on luxuries that are simply beyond their financial reach. The white family making $42,500 is thus too poor to participate in a signaling game with its neighbors, so they don't. As a result, they're spared the cost of competing, just as I am spared the expense of trying to compete with the Wall Street traders I see driving around Manhattan in their Mercedes sedans.

To test their theory, the authors look at how much a white   10
family spends on conspicuous consumption when it is surrounded by white families making a similar amount of money. They find that this white family spends the same portion of its income on visible goods as a black family surrounded by other black families with similar incomes. They also find that the further a family of either race slips behind the average income of nearby households of the same race (becoming too poor to compete in the signaling game), the less it spends on these visible goods.

Once these effects are accounted for, racial disparities in   11
visible consumption disappear. It's not that black Americans are more inclined to signal wealth; rather, poor blacks are more likely than poor whites to be a part of communities where they are relatively rich enough to participate in the signaling game.

If signaling is just part of a deeper human impulse to seek   12
status in our communities, what's wrong with that, anyway? If a household chooses to spend a lot on visible consumption because it gets happiness from achieving high standing among its neighbors, why should we care? To return to Cosby's concerns, if blacks are spending more on shoes and cars and jewelry, they must be spending less on something else. And that something else turns out to be mostly health and education. According to the study, black households spend more than 50 percent less on health care than whites of comparable incomes

and 20 percent less on education. Unfortunately, these are exactly the investments that the black families need to make in order to close the black-white income gap.

13   In his controversial speech, Bill Cosby appealed to the African-American community to start investing in their futures. What's troubling about the message of this study is that Cosby and others may not be battling against a black culture of consumption, but a more deeply seated human pursuit of status. In this sense, Cosby's critics may be right—only when black incomes catch up to white incomes will the apparent black-white gap in spending on visible goods disappear.

Expanding Vocabulary

Examine each of the following words in their contexts and then write a brief definition or synonym for each one. Do not use a dictionary. Try to guess the word's meaning from its context. The number in parentheses is the number of the paragraph in which the word appears.

excoriating (1)	disparity (3)
vulnerable (2)	incentives (6)
allure (2)	

Understanding Content

1. What is the occasion for Fisman's article? What are the two key questions to be answered about the spending habits of African Americans?
2. What is the answer to the first question: Do blacks spend more than whites on status items?
3. What is it that most people are seeking through some of their purchases? Why do sneakers make a "better" purchase choice than educational toys?
4. What is the problem with status-buying by blacks? What are they not spending money on?

Drawing Inferences about Thesis and Purpose

1. Some people may avoid status purchases because they are "above it all." Why, according to Fisman, are some "spared the expense of trying to compete"?
2. What is Fisman's purpose in writing? Is his primary goal to explain causes of black conspicuous consumption? Does he have another purpose as well?

Analyzing Strategies and Style

1. Why does Bill Cosby's complaint provide a good frame for Fisman's discussion?
2. What is the primary source of evidence for the author's analysis? Why is this important?

Thinking Critically

1. Fisman describes his topic as a sensitive one; why? What's a good way to deal with sensitive subjects—besides using a calm and cool tone?
2. Had it occurred to you that some people do not purchase status symbols for the simple reason that they cannot compete with the group they are closest to—neighbors and colleagues? Does this make sense to you?
3. Many Americans today are losing their homes to foreclosure or are paying mortgages greater than the value of their homes. How did this happen? Is this status-buying by people who really could not afford to compete? Do we always make smart economic choices? Be ready to discuss these issues.

The Overlooked Victims of AIDS

JUDITH D. AUERBACH

A sociologist and former college professor, Judith Auerbach is now vice president for public policy at the American Foundation for AIDS Research. Auerbach has published and presented in a variety of areas of research interest, including AIDS, health research, and family policy and gender. The following column, published in the *Washington Post* during the 2004 presidential campaign, deplores our lack of awareness of who is suffering from AIDS.

Questions to Guide Your Reading and Reflection

1. Who, now, is most often becoming infected with HIV-AIDS?
2. Do you know how most women become infected with AIDS?

In last week's vice presidential debate, moderator Gwen Ifill   1 talked about the disproportionate impact of HIV-AIDS on

African American women and asked what role the government should play in slowing the growth of this domestic epidemic. Both candidates displayed an alarming ignorance of the reality of the crisis in the United States, choosing instead to focus their comments on AIDS in Africa, which Ifill had explicitly asked them not to do.

2   What is inexcusable among the nation's top policymakers is a persistent problem in the general public as well: a failure to recognize that AIDS now disproportionately affects women.

3   According to the Centers for Disease Control and Prevention, the proportion of all AIDS cases reported among adolescent and adult women in the United States has more than tripled since 1986. AIDS is the fourth-leading cause of death among women in this country between the ages of 25 and 44, and is the *leading* cause of death among African American women ages 25 to 34. Black women represent about two-thirds of all new HIV infections among adult and adolescent females.

4   Globally, about half of the 12,000 people ages 15 to 49 infected every day are women. Sixty-two percent of those ages 15 to 24 living with HIV-AIDS are girls and women. In South Africa, that figure climbs to 77 percent. Most women worldwide, including in the United States, acquire HIV infection through heterosexual intercourse.

5   Why is this "feminization of AIDS" occurring? The answer lies in the complex ways that sex and gender intersect, conferring increased vulnerability to HIV infection on women and girls. Biological, sociological and political factors interact differently for women and men, leaving women more susceptible to viral transmission, more distant from prevention and care services, farther away from accurate information, and far more vulnerable to human rights violations. Here are some of the specifics:

6   • Women are more vulnerable to HIV infection than men. The physiology of the female genital tract makes women twice as likely to acquire HIV from men as vice versa. Among adolescent girls, this effect is even more pronounced.

7   • Poverty is correlated with higher rates of HIV infection all over the world. Globally, more than half of the people living in poverty are women. In the United States, nearly 30 percent are African American women.

- Lack of education is associated with higher HIV infection rates.   8
  Girls in developing countries are less likely to complete secondary
  education than boys, and almost twice as likely to be illiterate.
- Early marriage is a significant risk factor for HIV among women and   9
  girls. In developing countries, a majority of sexually active girls ages
  15 to 19 are married. Married adolescent girls tend to have higher
  HIV infection rates than their sexually active unmarried peers.
- A significant risk factor for HIV infection is violence, to which   10
  women are more susceptible in virtually all societies. In a South
  African study, for example, women who were beaten or dominated
  by their partners were 48 percent more likely to become infected
  than women who lived in nonviolent households.
- Rape of women has been used as a tool for subjugation and   11
  so-called ethnic cleansing in war and conflict situations. Of the
  250,000 women raped during the Rwandan genocide, about 70
  percent of the survivors are HIV-positive.

The experience of women and girls in the HIV-AIDS   12
epidemic in the United States and around the world highlights
how social arrangements, cultural norms, laws, policies and
institutions contribute to the unequal status of women in society and to the spread of disease. Together they undermine the
capacity of women and girls to exercise power over their own
lives and to control the circumstances that increase their vulnerability to HIV infection, particularly in the context of sexual
relationships. For African American women, gender inequali-
ties are exacerbated by persistent racism.

It is only when this unhealthy mix is acknowledged and   13
addressed—particularly by the highest levels of government—
that we will be able to stem the alarming increase of HIV-AIDS
among more than half the world's population.

Expanding Vocabulary

Match each word in column A with its definition in column B. When
in doubt, first find the word in the essay and look for context clues to
aid your understanding of the word's meaning. Then, if necessary, use
a dictionary to complete the matching exercise. The number in parentheses is the number of the paragraph in which the word appears.

Column A	Column B
disproportionate (1)	brought into a parallel relationship
intersect (5)	easily attacked or hurt

vulnerability (5)	under control of
correlated (7)	increased in difficulty or harshness
subjugation (11)	lacking proper balance
genocide (11)	cross through, interact
exacerbated (12)	planned killing of a specific group of people

Understanding Content

1. What do politicians, and Americans generally, seem not to know about AIDS?
2. How do most women become infected?
3. For what group of Americans is AIDS the leading cause of death?
4. What are six specifics about women's experiences that make them more vulnerable to HIV infection? Explain in your own words.

Drawing Inferences about Thesis and Purpose

1. What is Auerbach's purpose in writing? How does she want to affect her readers?
2. What is the author's thesis?

Analyzing Strategies and Style

1. How would you describe Auerbach's style—her sentence structures and word choice?
2. Is her style effective for her subject and purpose? Explain.
3. What is effective about the use of bullets in this essay?

Thinking Critically

1. Were you aware of the "feminization of AIDS"? Does this surprise? Shock? Make you wonder how this shift in infected group has happened?
2. Which statistic in the essay is most shocking to you? Why?
3. Which one of the six experiences correlating with increased risk for AIDS is most surprising to you? Why?
4. What should be done to address this serious world health problem? If you were the president's "AIDS czar," what specific programs would you seek to put into place in this country? Explain your cause and effect reasoning.

Dream Deferred

LANGSTON HUGHES

Like many American writers, Langston Hughes (1902–1967) came from the Middle West to New York City, lived in Europe, and then returned to the United States to a career of writing. He was a journalist, fiction writer, and poet, and author of more than sixty books. Hughes was also the first African American to support himself as a professional writer. Known as "the bard of Harlem," Hughes became an important public figure and voice for black writers. "Dream Deferred," one of Hughes's best-loved poems, which comes from *The Panther and the Lash: Poems of Our Time* (1951), illustrates the effective use of metaphor to convey the poet's attitudes and emotions.

What happens to a dream deferred?

Does it dry up
like a raisin in the sun?
Or fester like a sore—
And then run?   5
Does it stink like rotten meat?
Or crust and sugar over—
like a syrupy sweet?

Maybe it just sags
like a heavy load.   10

Or does it explode?

Understanding Content and Strategies

1. How is the poem structured; that is, what is it a series of?
2. The "answers" to the poem's first question are all similes except one. Which line is a metaphor? Explain the metaphor. Why is the one metaphor an effective strategy?
3. What does Hughes mean by a "deferred" dream?
4. Explain each simile. How does each one present a response to, or the effect of, a deferred dream?
5. What do the similes and metaphor have in common?

Drawing Inferences about Theme

1. What, then, is Hughes's attitude toward his subject? What does he want us to understand about deferred dreams?
2. Might the poem also be making a social comment? If so, what?

Thinking Critically

1. Which simile do you find most effective? Why?
2. Has Hughes included most of the responses to deferred dreams? Is there any response you would add? If so, can you state it as a simile?

MAKING CONNECTIONS

---

1. Could one describe the breakdown of family as a loss of a sense of duty? Will an obsession with the self bring happiness? Consider what Ciardi (see Chapter 8) has to say about happiness, along with Patricia Dalton's discussion of self-absorbed young people.
2. Linda Waite thinks that, generally, people's lives are improved by marriage. Keith Ablow is concerned with the deviance of parents that leads to abused children. Apparently not all marriages result in happier adults and children. Should we encourage marriage for everyone? Should there be testing of some kind leading to a marriage license? A parenting license?
3. Have we, in this society, chosen the search for affluence over family commitments and family joys? Does this search divide us by gender or class? Does it affect our compassion for those less fortunate? If the answer is yes to these questions, should we be concerned? Are these problems for society? If so, what can we do to change?
4. Perhaps one indicator of how successfully families today are coping is the rate and types of crimes committed by juveniles. Go online to gather some statistics on juvenile crime. You can look for trends (the last ten years, for example) or look at arrest figures for one type of crime. There are many Websites with statistical information on juvenile crime. Pick a search engine and type in "juvenile crime statistics."

5. AIDS is not a gay problem; it is a family problem and a global scourge. Go online for the latest facts. What groups are most at risk? In what countries is HIV-AIDS spreading the most?

6. We are now living in what seems a scarier world. We read about terrorism, war, the spread of AIDS, the abuse of children by parents, teachers, priests. What are we most at risk for? Find some data on the risks associated with these problems. Be prepared to discuss your findings.

TOPICS FOR WRITING

---

1. In your prereading exercise, you reflected on your decision to attend college. Now reflect on your reasons for selecting the particular college you are attending. In an essay, explain the causes for your choice of school. You can organize according to the decision process you went through, or you can organize from least to most important causes. You might think of writing this essay as a feature article in your college newspaper.

2. Have you ever done something that you did not think you ought to do? If so, why did you do it? And what were the consequences of your actions? In an essay, examine the causes and effects of your action. Be sure that you have a point to make. You might want to show that you should have listened to the warning voice inside you, or you might want to show that one effect of such a situation is that we do learn something about ourselves.

3. Are you "addicted" to something? To chocolate or beer or cigarettes? To television soaps, video games, bridge, or something else? If so, reflect on why you and others like you are addicted to whatever it is that absorbs you. Drawing on your personal experience, your knowledge of others, and perhaps some reading on the topic, develop an analysis of the causes of your addiction. If you use ideas from your reading, give proper credit by stating author and title.

4. Linda Waite brings up some of the problems we face with today's redefining and redesigning of the family. Drawing

on your reading and your own experiences, develop an essay on one (or two related) problems that many face because of changes in family structures or lifestyles today. Give appropriate credit to any of the authors from whose essays you draw material. You may want to focus only on explaining the problems, or you may want to conclude with one or more possible solutions to the problem.

5. Do you get along well (or poorly) with a parent? If so, reflect on why you have a good (or bad) relationship with that parent. What are the causes? Are your experiences similar to those of friends? What do some of the experts say about parent/children relationships? Drawing on your personal situation, your knowledge of others, and perhaps some reading, develop an analysis of the causes for good (or bad) parent/child relationships. If you use ideas from your reading, give proper credit.

6. Have you experienced divorce either as a once-married person or as a child of divorced parents? If so, reflect on the effects of divorce. Drawing on your own experience, your knowledge of the experiences of others, and perhaps some reading, develop an analysis of the effects of divorce on divorced persons or their children. Follow the guidelines for crediting your reading given in topic 4.

7. Is there a current social or political problem that you are especially interested in? If so, think about the causes and effects of this problem. Then write an essay on the problem. Focus on the causes of the problem, the effects of the problem, or both causes and effects. You might want to conclude with one or more proposed solutions to the problem.

A CHECKLIST FOR CAUSAL ANALYSIS ESSAYS

Inventing

☐ Have I selected a topic consistent with the instructor's guidelines for this assignment?

☐ Have I chosen among the possible topics one that fits my knowledge and experience?

☐ Have I reflected on my topic to sort through the various influences and causes that are necessary to my analysis?

☐ Have I reflected on my topic to write a tentative thesis that makes clear my purpose to analyze cause?

☐ Have I "tested" my initial analysis of cause against experience and logic?

☐ Have I generated specifics from my thinking and, if appropriate, reading to illustrate and support my analysis?

☐ Have I thought about the most effective organization?

Drafting

☐ Have I succeeded in completing a first draft at one sitting so that I can "see" the whole?

☐ Do I have enough—enough to meet assignment demands and enough to explain and support my causal analysis?

☐ Does the order work?

Revising

☐ Have I made any needed additions, deletions, or changes in order based on answering the questions about my draft?

☐ Have I revised my draft to produce coherent paragraphs, using transitions and connecting words that reveal my causal analysis?

Polishing

☐ Have I eliminated wordiness and clichés?

☐ Have I avoided or removed any discriminatory language?

☐ Have I used my word processor's spell check and proofread a printed copy with great care?

☐ Do I have an appropriate and interesting title?

Using Argument and Persuasion

Supporting a Fair and Safe World

Losing patience with two friends, you finally moan, "Will you two *please* stop arguing! You've been bickering all evening; you're ruining the party." How often many of us have said, or wanted to say, something similar to parents, children, colleagues, or friends who seem unable to stop yelling or name calling, or quibbling over some insignificant point. In this context, the term *argument* has a negative connotation. In a classroom debate, a courtroom, a business conference, or writing, however, a sound argument is highly valued.

The Characteristics of Argument

Understanding the characteristics of good argument will help you to think critically about the arguments of others and to write better arguments of your own. Some of these characteristics may surprise you, so read thoughtfully and reflect on the following points.

- *An argument makes a point.* Sound reasons and relevant evidence are presented to support a claim, a main idea that the arguer keeps in focus. Collecting data on a particular topic may produce an interesting report, but unless the specifics support a point, there is no argument.
- *Argument assumes an audience.* The purpose of argument is not just to provide information but to change the way listeners or readers think about an issue, to move them to agree with you. Once you accept that argument implies an audience, you have to accept the

possibility of counterarguments, of listeners or readers who will not agree with you and will challenge your thinking. You have not defended your argument by simply asserting that it is *your opinion*. If you have not based your opinion on good evidence and reasons, your opinion will be challenged, and you will lose the respect of your audience.

- *Good argument is based on a recognition of the complexities of most issues and the reality of opposing views.* One of the greatest dangers to good argument lies in oversimplifying complex issues, or in oversimplifying reality by assuming that our claim is "clearly right" and that therefore everyone agrees with us.

- *Good argument makes clear the values and beliefs that we consider relevant to the issue.* Argument is not just an intellectual game. We need to recognize the values that are a part of our reasoning, our way of approaching a particular issue. For example, if you argue that abortion is wrong because it is murder, you *believe* that the fetus is a human being at the moment of conception. Your argument is convincing only to those who share your *belief*. Wanting no uncertainty about the values upon which his claim was founded, Thomas Jefferson wrote: "We hold these truths to be self-evident" and then listed such values as "all men are created equal" and "governments are instituted among men."

- *In argument, we present evidence to support a claim on the assumption that there is a valid or logical connection between evidence and claim,* what British philosopher Stephen Toulmin calls a *warrant*. When you argue that abortion is wrong because it is murder, you assume or warrant that the fetus is a human being who can be murdered. Arguments can be challenged not only on the evidence or stated reasons but also on the assumptions or warrants that support the argument's structure. Therefore, you must know what your assumptions are because you may need to defend them as part of the support for your argument.

- *Argument includes the use of persuasive strategies.* When you write an argumentative essay, you want to convince readers to share your views, or at least to reconsider theirs in the light of your discussion. Of course you are involved in your topic and want to affect readers. Indeed, you will write more persuasively if you write about issues that concern you. In good argument, however, emotions are tempered by logic and channeled into the energy needed to think through the topic, to gather evidence, to consider audience, and to plan the paper. Remember that one of the best *persuasive* strategies is to present yourself to readers as a reasonable person who has done your homework on the topic and who wants to find some common ground with those who disagree.

How to Use Argument and Persuasion

How can you put together a good argumentative essay? Accepting that writing an effective argument is a challenging task, you may want to give appropriate time and thought to *preparing to write* before you actually draft your essay. Use the following guidelines to aid your writing.

1. **Think about audience and purpose**. Unless you are writing about a most unusual topic, expect your readers to be aware of the issue. This does not mean that you can skip an appropriate introduction or necessary background information. It does mean that you can expect readers to know (and perhaps be a part of) the opposition, so be prepared to challenge counterarguments and consider the advantages of pointing out common ground. Also define your purpose in writing; that is, recognize the *type* of argument you are planning. Are you presenting the results of a study, perhaps the results of a questionnaire you prepared? (For example, you could do a survey of attitudes toward campus security, or proposals to eliminate the school newspaper.) Are you writing to state your position on a value-laden issue, such as euthanasia or capital punishment? Are you writing on a public-policy issue, such as whether to restrict smoking in all restaurants? Each of these types of arguments needs somewhat different support and development, so as you work on your argument's thesis or claim, think about the type of argument as well.

2. **Brainstorm about your topic to develop a tentative thesis and think about the kinds of support your thesis (claim) will need**. If you have done an investigation, you need to study your evidence to see what appropriate conclusions can be drawn. (For example, if 51 percent of the students you polled want more security on campus at night, you could say that a majority of students think that increased security is needed. But, it is more accurate to say that about half of the students polled expressed that view.) If you are writing an argument based primarily on values rather than facts, decide on your position and then begin to list your reasons. Suppose you support euthanasia. What, exactly, are you in favor of? Physician-assisted suicide? A patient's right

to refuse all life-support systems? A family-member's right to make that decision? Be sure that you state your claim so that it clearly represents your position, a position you believe you can support. Then consider why: To eliminate unnecessary suffering? To give individuals control over their deaths? If you are examining a problem in education or arguing for restricting smoking in restaurants, you may need to do some reading to locate appropriate facts and statistics. You may also need to consider the feasibility of putting your proposal into place. Will it cost money? Where will the money come from? Who may be hurt or inconvenienced? How can you bring these people to your side?

3. **Plan the organization of your essay**. Remember that any plan is just a guide so that you can get started. As you draft or when you revise, you may find that you want to switch parts around or add new ideas and examples that have come to you while writing. But remember as well that usually some plan is better than no plan. If you are writing an argument based on values, consider these steps:

 a. **Begin with an introduction to get your reader's attention**. If you are writing on euthanasia, you can mention the news coverage of Dr. Kevorkian.

 b. **Decide where to place your thesis**. Although typically a thesis or claim comes early in the essay, you may want to experiment with placing it at the end, after you have presented support for that claim.

 c. **Organize reasons in a purposeful way**. One strategy is to move from less important to most important reasons. Another approach is to organize around counterarguments, explaining why each of the opposition's arguments does not hold up. Consider using some of the methods of development discussed throughout this text. Draw on your reading for statistical details, on your own experience for examples.

 d. **Provide support for each reason**. You have not written an effective argument just by stating your reasons. You need to argue for them, to show why they are reasonable, or better than the opposition's reasons, or have the support of good evidence.

 e. **Conclude by effectively stating or restating your claim**. As a part of your conclusion, you may want to explain to readers how this issue affects them, how they could benefit from embracing your position or your proposal for change.

4. **Revise, revise, revise.** After completing a draft based on your tentative plan, study the draft carefully both for readability and effective argument. Examine reasons and support to be sure you have avoided logical fallacies. See where you may need to qualify statements or control your language. Be certain that you have maintained an appropriate level of seriousness so that you retain the respect of readers. As the writers in this chapter illustrate, you want to write movingly about issues that concern you without forsaking good sense and relevant evidence.

WRITING FOCUS
LOGICAL FALLACIES

When you ignore the complexities of issues or choose emotional appeals over logic, you risk producing an essay filled with *logical fallacies*. Many arguments that could be won are ruined by those who leave reasoned debate for emotional appeals or who oversimplify the issues. Here are some fallacies to avoid in your writing and to watch out for in the arguments of others.

- *ad hominem* Attacking the opponents instead of defending your position is not an effective strategy with intelligent readers. You have not supported an anti-abortion position, for example, by calling prochoice advocates "murderers" or labeling them "proabortion."
- **Straw Man** The straw man fallacy seeks to defend one's position by accusing opponents of holding a position that is easier to attack but is not actually what the opponents believe. To "argue" that those seeking gun registration just want to take guns away from good people and leave them in the hands of criminals is an example. Those who want gun registration certainly do not want criminals to have guns.

- **Bandwagon** Another substitute for good argument is the appeal to join in, or join the majority, often without providing evidence that a majority holds the view of the arguer or, even more important, that the view is a sound one. Appeals to national interest or the good of the country often contain the bandwagon fallacy. For example: All good Americans want respect shown for the flag, so we need a law banning flag burning. Some good Americans also value free speech and see flag burning as an example of free speech.

- **Common Practice** Similar to the bandwagon fallacy, the appeal to common practice is the false logic that "everyone is doing it, so it must be a good thing." However, cheating on tests or on one's income taxes, for example, cannot be logically defended by "arguing" that everybody does it. First, it is not true that everybody does it, and second, even if that were true, it would not make cheating right.

- **Hasty Generalization or Overstatement** When drawing on your own experiences for evidence, you need to judge if your experiences are representative. For example, you may be having difficulty in calculus, but it would be illogical to conclude that the instructor is inept or that the course is too hard. These could be explanations, but they are not the only possible ones. How are other students doing in the course is a key question to ask. Even when you gather extensive evidence from reading, be cautious about generalizing. It is not true that all people on welfare are lazy or that lawyers only want to make piles of money. Qualify assertions; avoid such words as *always, never, everybody,* and *none.* (These words entice readers to find the one exception that will disprove your sweeping generalization.)

- **False Dilemma** The false dilemma is often called either/or thinking. It is the illogic of asserting that only two possibilities are available when there may be several. The effectiveness of this strategy (if you have readers who are not thinking critically) is that you can make one possibility seem a terrible choice, thereby making your choice sound good by contrast. For example: Either we pay more taxes or we will have to cut educational programs. Now these are clearly not the only two possibilities. First, there are other programs that could be cut. Second, we could find ways to save money in the running of government. Third, we can have a growing economy that brings in more government revenues without increasing taxes. Those are just three additional possibilities; there are probably others.

- **Slippery Slope** The slippery slope fallacy makes the argument that we cannot allow A to take place because if we do, then we will head down a slope all the way to Z, a place where no one wants to be. The strategy here is to make Z so awful that readers will agree with you that we should not do A. The error in logic is the unsupported assumption that if A takes place, Z will follow. For example: If the government is allowed to register guns, then before you know it they will ban handguns and then take away all guns, even hunting rifles. But, there is no evidence that registration will lead to confiscation. We register cars and planes and boats; the government has not confiscated any of these items.

Getting Started: Reflections on the Challenges Facing Ourselves, Our Society, Our World

What do you consider the greatest challenge facing you in your personal life? Is it completing school? Giving up cigarettes or junk food? Reestablishing a relationship with a parent or friend? What do you consider the greatest challenge facing society? Is it reestablishing a sense of community? Improving schools? Improving race relations? Finding deterrents to crime? What do you consider the greatest challenge facing the world? Is it saving the environment? Establishing world peace? Eliminating hunger and injustice? Decide on the challenge, in one of the categories, that most troubles you and brainstorm about the reasons for the problem and possible solutions to the problem. Be prepared to discuss your reasons and proposed solutions with classmates.

King Cartoon

JACK OHMAN

Jack Ohman created this cartoon during the presidential primary campaigns in South Carolina, January 19, 2008.

1. Who are the figures in the cartoon? What is the situation? Who is speaking the lines?
2. What idea is expressed by the drawing?
3. What makes the cartoon clever?

Declaration of Sentiments

ELIZABETH CADY STANTON

Elizabeth Cady Stanton (1815–1902) was one of the most important leaders of the women's rights movement. Educated at a
local academy and then the Emma Willard Seminary in Troy,
NY, Stanton studied law with her father before her marriage. An
active reformer in the abolition and temperance movements,
she later focused her attention on women's issues. At the Seneca
Falls Convention in 1848, Stanton gave the opening speech and
read her "Declaration of Sentiments." She founded and became
president of the National Women's Suffrage Association in 1869.
"The Declaration of Sentiments" lists the grievances of women
suffering under the tyranny of men.

Questions to Guide Your Reading and Reflection

1. How is Stanton's speech similar to the Declaration of
   Independence?
2. How does it differ?

1   When, in the course of human events, it becomes necessary
for one portion of the family of man to assume among the people of the earth a position different from that which they have
hitherto occupied, but one to which the laws of nature and of
nature's God entitle them, a decent respect to the opinions of
mankind requires that they should declare the causes that
impel them to such a course.

2   We hold these truths to be self-evident: that all men and
women are created equal; that they are endowed by their
Creator with certain inalienable rights; that among these are life,
liberty, and the pursuit of happiness; that to secure these rights
governments are instituted, deriving their just powers from the
consent of the governed. Whenever any form of government
becomes destructive of these ends, it is the right of those who
suffer from it to refuse allegiance to it, and to insist upon the
institution of a new government, laying its foundation on such
principles, and organizing its powers in such form, as to them
shall seem most likely to effect their safety and happiness. Pru-
dence, indeed, will dictate that governments long established

should not be changed for light and transient causes; and accordingly all experience hath shown that mankind are more disposed to suffer, while evils are sufferable, than to right themselves by abolishing the forms to which they were accustomed. But when a long train of abuses and usurpations, pursuing invariably the same object evinces a design to reduce them under absolute despotism, it is their duty to throw off such government, and to provide new guards for their future security. Such has been the patient sufferance of the women under this government, and such is now the necessity which constrains them to demand the equal station to which they are entitled.

The history of mankind is a history of repeated injuries and 3 usurpations on the part of man toward woman, having in direct object the establishment of an absolute tyranny over her. To prove this, let facts be submitted to a candid world.

He has never permitted her to exercise her inalienable right 4 to the elective franchise.

He has compelled her to submit to laws, in the formation of 5 which she had no voice.

He has withheld from her rights which are given to the most 6 ignorant and degraded men—both natives and foreigners.

Having deprived her of this first right of a citizen, the elec- 7 tive franchise, thereby leaving her without representation in the halls of legislation, he has oppressed her on all sides.

He has made her, if married, in the eye of the law, civilly 8 dead.

He has taken from her all right in property, even to the 9 wages she earns.

He has made her, morally, an irresponsible being, as she can 10 commit many crimes with impunity, provided they be done in the presence of her husband. In the covenant of marriage, she is compelled to promise obedience to her husband, he becoming, to all intents and purposes, her master—the law giving him power to deprive her of her liberty, and to administer chastisement.

He has so framed the laws of divorce, as to what shall be the 11 proper causes, and in case of separation, to whom the guardianship of the children shall be given, as to be wholly regardless of the happiness of women—the law, in all cases, going upon a false supposition of the supremacy of man, and giving all power into his hands.

12   After depriving her of all rights as a married woman, if single, and the owner of property, he has taxed her to support a government which recognizes her only when her property can be made profitable to it.

13   He has monopolized nearly all the profitable employments, and from those she is permitted to follow, she receives but a scanty remuneration. He closes against her all the avenues to wealth and distinction which he considers most honorable to himself. As a teacher of theology, medicine, or law, she is not known.

14   He has denied her the facilities for obtaining a thorough education, all colleges being closed against her.

15   He allows her in Church, as well as State, but a subordinate position, claiming Apostolic authority for her exclusion from the ministry, and, with some exceptions, from any public participation in the affairs of the Church.

16   He has created a false public sentiment by giving the world a different code of morals for men and women, by which moral delinquencies which exclude women from society, are not only tolerated, but deemed of little account in man.

17   He has usurped the prerogative of Jehovah himself, claiming it as his right to assign for her a sphere of action, when that belongs to her conscience and to her God.

18   He has endeavored, in every way that he could, to destroy her confidence in her own powers, to lessen her self-respect, and to make her willing to lead a dependent and abject life.

19   Now, in view of this entire disfranchisement of one-half the people of this country, their social and religious degradation— in view of the unjust laws above mentioned, and because women do feel themselves aggrieved, oppressed, and fraudulently deprived of their most sacred rights, we insist that they have immediate admission to all the rights and privileges which belong to them as citizens of the United States.

20   In entering upon the great work before us, we anticipate no small amount of misconception, misrepresentation, and ridicule; but we shall use every instrumentality within our power to effect our object. We shall employ agents, circulate tracts, petition the State and National legislatures, and endeavor to enlist the pulpit and the press in our behalf. We hope this Convention will be followed by a series of Conventions embracing every part of the country.

Expanding Vocabulary

Match each word in column A with its definition in column B. When in doubt, first find the word in the essay and look for context clues to aid your understanding of the word's meaning. Then, if necessary, use your dictionary to complete the matching exercise. The number in parentheses is the number of the paragraph in which the word appears.

Column A	*Column B*
impel (1)	clearly shows
usurpations (2)	constitutional right to vote
evinces (2)	exemption from punishment
candid (3)	payment
franchise (4)	seize and hold illegally
impunity (10)	right
chastisement (10)	miserable
remuneration (13)	urge to action
prerogative (17)	punishment
abject (18)	deceptively and illegally
fraudulently (19)	impartial

Understanding Content

1. What, in general, do the women at Seneca Falls want? How do they plan to achieve their goals?
2. How have women been restricted in education, in work, if married, and psychologically?

Drawing Inferences about Thesis and Purpose

1. What charges made by Stanton continue to be legitimate, in whole or in part?
2. What is the author's key justification for the demands of women?

Analyzing Strategies and Style

1. Obviously, the key strategy is Stanton's use of the Declaration structure and approach. What does she gain by doing this?

Thinking Critically

1. Do we need a new declaration of sentiments for women? If so, what specific changes would you make?
2. Do we need a new declaration of sentiments for other groups? If so, who? For what reasons?

3. What are the best strategies for generating major social/political changes? Marches? A court case? Civil disobedience? Explain and defend your views.

Adult Crime, Adult Time

LINDA J. COLLIER

An attorney, Linda J. Collier is currently dean of public services and social sciences at Delaware County Community College in Pennsylvania. She has been the director of student legal services at Penn State University and special assistant for legal affairs to two college presidents in addition to teaching courses in sociology and criminal justice. The following essay, published in the *Washington Post* in 1998, is written in response to the case of a 11-year-old and a 13-year-old shooting four students and a teacher at their school in Jonesboro, Arkansas, that same year.

Questions to Guide Your Reading and Reflection

1. What is the trend in juvenile crime?
2. Why do you think we have a juvenile court system?

1 When prosecutor Brent Davis said he wasn't sure if he could charge 11-year-old Andrew Golden and 13-year-old Mitchell Johnson as adults after Tuesday afternoon's slaughter in Jonesboro, Ark., I cringed. But not for the reasons you might think.

2 I knew he was formulating a judgment based on laws that have not had a major overhaul for more than 100 years. I knew his hands were tied by the longstanding creed that juvenile offenders, generally defined as those under the age of 18, are to be treated rather than punished. I knew he would have to do legal cartwheels to get the case out of the juvenile system. But most of all, I cringed because today's juvenile suspects—even those who are accused of committing the most violent crimes—are still regarded by the law as children first and criminals second.

3 As astonishing as the Jonesboro events were, this is hardly the first time that children with access to guns and other weapons have brought tragedy to a school. Only weeks before

the Jonesboro shootings, three girls in Paducah, Ky., were killed in their school lobby when a 14-year-old classmate allegedly opened fire on them. Authorities said he had several guns with him, and the alleged murder weapon was one of seven stolen from a neighbor's garage. And the day after the Jonesboro shootings, a 14-year-old in Daly City, Calif., was charged as a juvenile after he allegedly fired at his middle-school principal with a semiautomatic handgun.

It's not a new or unusual phenomenon for children to   4 commit violent crimes at younger and younger ages, but it often takes a shocking incident to draw our attention to a trend already in progress. According to the U.S. Department of Justice, crimes committed by juveniles have increased by 60 percent since 1984. Where juvenile delinquency was once limited to truancy or vandalism, juveniles now are more likely to be the perpetrators of serious and deadly crimes such as arson, aggravated assault, rape and murder. And these violent offenders increasingly include those as young as the Jonesboro suspects. Since 1965, the number of 12-year-olds arrested for violent crimes has doubled and the number of 13- and 14-year-olds has tripled, according to government statistics.

Those statistics are a major reason why we need to revamp   5 our antiquated juvenile justice system. Nearly every state, including Arkansas, has laws that send most youthful violent offenders to the juvenile courts, where they can only be found "delinquent" and confined in a juvenile facility (typically not past age 21). In recent years, many states have enacted changes in their juvenile crime laws, and some have lowered the age at which a juvenile can be tried as an adult for certain violent crimes. Virginia, for example, has reduced its minimum age to 14, and suspects accused of murder and aggravated malicious wounding are automatically waived to adult court. Illinois is now sending some 13-year-olds to adult court after a hearing in juvenile court. In Kansas, a 1996 law allows juveniles as young as 10 to be prosecuted as adults in some cases. These are steps in the right direction, but too many states still treat violent offenders under 16 as juveniles who belong in the juvenile system.

My views are not those of a frustrated prosecutor. I have   6 represented children as a court-appointed guardian *ad litem*, or temporary guardian, in the Philadelphia juvenile justice system. Loosely defined, a guardian *ad litem* is responsible for looking after the best interest of a neglected or rebellious child who has come into the juvenile courts. It is often a humbling experience as I try to help children whose lives have gone awry, sometimes because of circumstances beyond their control.

7   My experience has made me believe that the system is doing a poor job at treatment as well as punishment. One of my "girls," a chronic truant, was a foster child who longed to be adopted. She often talked of how she wanted a pink room, a frilly bunk bed and sisters with whom she could share her dreams. She languished in foster care from ages 2 to 13 because her drug-ravaged mother would not relinquish her parental rights. Initially, the girl refused to tolerate the half-life that the state had maintained was in her best interest. But as it became clear that we would never convince her mother to give up her rights, the girl became a frequent runaway. Eventually she ended up pregnant, wandering from place to place and committing adult crimes to survive. No longer a child, not quite a woman, she is the kind of teenage offender for whom the juvenile system has little or nothing to offer.

8   A brief history: Proceedings in juvenile justice began in 1890 in Chicago, where the original mandate was to save wayward children and protect them from the ravages of society. The system called for children to be processed through an appendage of the family court. By design, juveniles were to be kept away from the court's criminal side, the district attorney and adult correctional institutions.

9   Typically, initial procedures are informal, non-threatening and not open to public scrutiny. A juvenile suspect is interviewed by an "intake" officer who determines the child's fate. The intake officer may issue a warning, lecture and release; he may detain the suspect; or, he may decide to file a petition, subjecting the child to juvenile "adjudication" proceedings. If the law allows, the intake officer may make a recommendation that the juvenile be transferred to adult criminal court.

10   An adjudication is similar to a hearing, rather than a trial, although the juvenile may be represented by counsel and a juvenile prosecutor will represent the interests of the

community. It is important to note that throughout the proceedings, no matter which side of the fence the parties are on, the operating principle is that everyone is working in the best interests of the child. Juvenile court judges do not issue findings of guilt, but decide whether a child is delinquent. If delinquency is found, the judge must decide the child's fate. Should the child be sent back to the family—assuming there is one? Declare him or her "in need of supervision," which brings in the intense help of social services? Remove the child from the family and place him or her in foster care? Confine the child to a state institution for juvenile offenders?

This system was developed with truants, vandals and   11
petty thieves in mind. But this model is not appropriate for the violent juvenile offender of today. Detaining a rapist or murderer in a juvenile facility until the age of 18 or 21 isn't even a slap on the hand. If a juvenile is accused of murdering, raping or assaulting someone with a deadly weapon, the suspect should automatically be sent to adult criminal court. What's to ponder?

With violent crime becoming more prevalent among the   12
junior set, it's a mystery why there hasn't been a major overhaul of juvenile justice laws long before now. Will the Jonesboro shootings be the incident that makes us take a hard look at the current system? When it became evident that the early release of Jesse Timmendequas—whose murder of 7-year-old Megan Kanka in New Jersey sparked national outrage—had caused unwarranted tragedy, legislative action was swift. Now New Jersey has Megan's Law, which requires the advance notification of a sexual predator's release into a neighborhood. Other states have followed suit.

It is unequivocally clear that the same type of mandate is   13
needed to establish a uniform minimum age for trying juveniles as adults. As it stands now, there is no consistency in state laws governing waivers to adult court. One reason for this lack of uniformity is the absence of direction from the federal government or Congress. The Bureau of Justice Statistics reports that adjacent states such as New York and Pennsylvania respond differently to 16-year-old criminals, with New York tending to treat offenders of that age as adults and Pennsylvania handling them in the juvenile justice system.

14   Federal prosecution of juveniles is not totally unheard of, but it is uncommon. The Bureau of Justice Statistics estimates that during 1994, at least 65 juveniles were referred to the attorney general for transfer to adult status. In such cases, the U.S. attorney's office must certify a substantial federal interest in the case and show that one of the following is true: The state does not have jurisdiction; the state refuses to assume jurisdiction or the state does not have adequate services for juvenile offenders; the offense is a violent felony, drug trafficking or firearm offense as defined by the U.S. Code.

15   Exacting hurdles, but not insurmountable. In the Jonesboro case, prosecutor Davis has been exploring ways to enlist the federal court's jurisdiction. Whatever happens, federal prosecutions of young offenders are clearly not the long-term answer. The states must act. So as far as I can see, the next step is clear: Children who knowingly engage in adult conduct and adult crimes should automatically be subject to adult rules and adult prison time.

Expanding Vocabulary

Match each word in column A with its definition in column B. When in doubt, first find the word in the essay and look for context clues to aid your understanding of the word's meaning. Then, if necessary, use your dictionary to complete the matching exercise. The number in parentheses is the number of the paragraph in which the word appears.

Column A	Column B
cringed (1)	occurrence
formulating (2)	those who are responsible for what has happened
allegedly (3)	obsolete, outdated
phenomenon (4)	revise, make over
truancy (4)	existed in miserable conditions
perpetrators (4)	claim or right given up
revamp (5)	damages
antiquated (5)	preparing in an organized way
malicious (5)	hear a judicial proceeding
waived (5)	give up
awry (6)	clear examination
languished (7)	pulled back in fear
relinquish (7)	

ravages (8)   absence without permission
scrutiny (9)   clearly, without question
adjudication (9)   presumably, unproven
unequivocally (13)   amiss, wrong
                                desire to hurt someone

Understanding Content

1. Summarize the author's examples of recent violent juvenile crime.
2. What are some of the problems with current state laws governing juvenile crimes?
3. Briefly summarize the author's history of the juvenile justice system.
4. In addition to failing to punish properly, in the author's view, what else do juvenile court systems fail to do?
5. Where does Collier look for help in correcting the juvenile justice system?

Drawing Inferences about Thesis and Purpose

1. What is Collier's thesis? Where does she state it?
2. In paragraph 11, when she writes "What's to ponder?" what response does she want from readers?

Analyzing Strategies and Style

1. Although Collier is writing in response to the Jonesboro murders, she refers to other juvenile murders in paragraph 3. What does she seek to gain by this?
2. Collier asserts that she is not writing as a "frustrated prosecutor" and describes her experience as a court-appointed guardian. What does she gain by her discussion in paragraphs 6 and 7?

Thinking Critically

1. What are the main points of Collier's argument? Make a list of the key steps in her argument and then evaluate the argument. Has she supported her thesis convincingly?
2. Could the example of one of Collier's court-appointed "girls" be used to argue *for*, rather than against, the juvenile justice system? Explain your answer.
3. Do you think that juveniles should be tried as adults? If so, in what situations?

Kids Who Kill Are Still Kids

RICHARD COHEN

Richard Cohen, a *Washington Post* columnist who has been syndicated since 1976, writes about both political issues and contemporary culture. The following column appeared in newspapers on August 3, 2001.

Questions to Guide Your Reading and Reflection

1. How many juveniles have been tried as adults in U.S. courts?
2. What assumption is contained in Cohen's title?

1   When I was about 12, I heaved a cinder block over my neighbor's fence and nearly killed her. I didn't know she was there. When I was about the same age, I started a small fire in a nearby field that spread until it threatened some nearby houses. I didn't mean to do it. When I was even younger, I climbed on top of a toolshed, threw a brick in the general direction of my sister and sent her, bleeding profusely and crying so that I can still hear her, to the hospital. I didn't mean to do that, either.

2   I tell these stories to remind us all that kids are kids and to suggest that even the worst of them—even the ones who commit murder—are still kids. I would be lying if I said that I knew what to do with them—how long they should be jailed and where—but I do know that something awful has come over this country. It seems the more incomprehensible the crime, the more likely it is that a child will be treated as an adult.

3   This is what happened to Nathaniel Brazill, 14, who was recently sentenced to 28 years in prison for the murder of a teacher, Barry Grunow. Brazill was only 13 when he shot the teacher on the final day of school. Grunow, a much-beloved teacher, had stopped Brazill from talking to two girls and disrupting the class. Earlier in the day, the boy had been suspended for throwing water balloons. He had gone home, gotten a gun and returned to school. Grunow was Brazill's favorite teacher.

I always feel in columns of this sort the necessity to say 4
something about the victim and how his life was taken from
him. I feel a particular need to do so in this case because
Grunow seemed to be an exceptional teacher, a good person.
Anyway—and this is only me talking—I feel a certain awe, a
humility, toward people who dedicate their lives to teaching
kids instead of, say, peddling tech stocks or mouthing off on
television about Gary Condit.[1]

But Grunow is gone and nothing can be done to bring him 5
back. That is not merely a cliché but also an important point.
Because always in these cases when it comes time to justify
why a minor was treated as an adult, someone says something
about sending a message to other kids. This is absurd.

Consider what Brazill did. He shot his teacher before oodles 6
of witnesses. He shot a man he liked. He shot someone without any chance of his getting away. He shot someone for almost
no reason at all. He shot someone not in the course of a robbery
or a sex crime or because he put a move on his girlfriend but
because he is a screwed-up kid, damaged, full of anger and
with not much self-control. He shot someone without fully
comprehending the consequences. He shot someone because,
among other things, he was just 13 years old.

And yet, he was prosecuted—and sentenced to three years 7
more than the mandatory minimum—as an adult. If there is
one thing he is not, it is an adult. But Brazill and, earlier,
13-year-old Lionel Tate were sentenced as if they were button
men for some crime family. Tate was given life without parole
for the killing of a 6-year-old girl he maintained died in a
wrestling accident. These boys were tried as adults but, I'd
guess, their ability to participate in their own defense would be
labeled juvenile.

Amnesty International says about 200,000 children have 8
been tried as adults by American courts. Florida alone reports
that 3,300 kids were prosecuted as adults in fiscal 1999–2000.
This sends a message—but it's to the adult community: We're
getting tough. Kids, however, are unlikely to get the message.
I mean, you know how kids are.

[1]Former Californian member of Congress—Ed.

9   Where is the deterrence in this policy? Will other 13-year-olds now hesitate before killing their teacher? Hardly. Who is being punished? The child at first, but later the adult he becomes.

10   Brazill will be over 40 when he gets out of jail. When he's, say, 35, will he have anything in common with the child who pulled the trigger? No more, I'd say, than I do with the jerk who nearly killed Richie Miller's mother with a cinder block. I didn't set out to hurt anyone, it's true. But neither did Brazill, he says. He just pulled the trigger and the man, somehow, died. It is, when you think about it, a childish explanation.

Expanding Vocabulary

Study definitions of each of the following words and then use each one in a separate sentence. The number in parentheses is the number of the paragraph in which the word appears.

    heaved (1)
    profusely (1)
    incomprehensible (2)
    prosecuted (7)
    deterrence (9)

Understanding Content

1. What is Cohen's primary example?
2. What was Brazill's sentence?
3. What is Cohen's explanation for Brazill's behavior?
4. When we try juveniles as adults, who, in Cohen's view, is being sent a message?

Drawing Inferences about Thesis and Purpose

1. Why does Cohen doubt that punishing children as adults acts as a deterrent to crime?
2. What is Cohen's thesis?

Analyzing Strategies and Style

1. Cohen begins by recounting stories of his childhood. Why? What point does he want to make?
2. Look at the author's concluding paragraph. What makes it effective? What is clever about the last sentence?

Thinking Critically

1. When you were young, did you do anything that could have resulted in a court case? If so, what were the consequences and how do you feel about the incident now?
2. Evaluate Cohen's argument. Are his reasons and evidence convincing? Why or why not?
3. How should the two boys used as examples by Cohen have been tried and sentenced? Take a stand.

An Elastic Institution

JOHN BORNEMAN
AND LAURIE KAIN HART

The two authors are both anthropologists. John Borneman is professor of anthropology at Princeton University and the author of books and articles, including *Settling Accounts: Violence, Justice, and Accountability in Postsocialist Europe* (1997). Laurie Kain Hart is chair of the anthropology department at Haverford College and author of *Time, Religion, and Social Experience in Rural Greece* (1992). Their discussion of marriage, from a historical and sociological perspective, was originally published April 14, 2004, in the *Washington Post*.

Questions to Guide Your Reading and Reflection

1. What do the authors suggest about marriage in their title?
2. What do you know about marriage from a historical and cross-cultural perspective?

Since its origins in the late 19th century, anthropology—more   1
than any other field of knowledge—has made the understanding of marriage across human societies one of its central tasks. Today the question arises: Can a scientific understanding inform current debates about the meaning of marriage? Would homosexual marriage destroy the principle of marriage as a social institution?

In the 1860s New York lawyer and anthropologist Louis   2
Henry Morgan attempted a systematic cross-cultural study of the institution of marriage. Morgan's data were imperfect, but

he was able to demonstrate that the record of human societies showed a startling diversity of socially approved forms of marriage. All societies had some form of regularized partnership, but no single standard human form could be identified. Generally, even within a society, there was a certain elasticity of marriage forms.

3   The most famous of these unions were the ones most foreign to Western Victorian society: marriage between a woman and several men; marriage between a man and several women; forms of "visiting" marriage, whereby a man might visit his wife but not live with her. As anthropologists assembled more reliable data, they found it difficult to produce a definition of human marriage that would hold true for all its socially legitimate forms.

4   Marriage generally functioned to provide a "legitimate" identity to children—a kind of "last name." Yet, the structure of these arrangements was extraordinarily diverse: Biological paternity was not universally the basis of identity—as, indeed, it is not in the case of adoption in America. In many cases, the biological father (the Latin term is genitor) was distinct from the legal father (pater) produced by the marriage contract and ceremony. Alternatively, it could be the mother's family and not the father that bestowed identity on a child.

5   As for sex, rarely if ever has marriage been able to restrict its varied practice to the relation of man and wife. In most cases, anthropologists agreed, what counted was that some socially approved form of marriage provided a secure place for the child in the social order.

6   But marriage has not been solely about children. In most societies known to us, everyone marries; it is an expected rite of passage and part of the normal life course of all adults. Only in post-classical Western societies do we find high numbers of unmarried people. Unlike other peoples, we consider marriage—however desirable or undesirable—optional.

7   Claude Levi-Strauss, the father of French structural anthropology, argued that it is only the "division of labor between the sexes that makes marriage indispensable." It follows that if men and women are granted equal access to jobs of similar worth—as is often the case today—the meaning of marriage will change.

8   The cult of romantic love in a companionate marriage is a recent innovation in the history of marriage. While romantic

passion has existed in all societies, only in a few has this unstable emotion been elaborated and intensified culturally and con- sidered the basis for the social institution of marriage. Indeed, marriage has traditionally been more concerned with—and successful in—regulating property relations and determining lineage or inheritance rights than with confining passion and sexual behavior.

Marriage, in other words, is not only diverse across cultures   9 but also dynamic and changing in America's own history. We live in a pluralist society, where marriage is not the only form of union or of mutual care in our society. When individuals and groups can, under certain conditions, choose their patterns of self-expression—their intimacy, child-care arrangements, sex- ual practices, place of residence, partnership forms—there will be increased variability. The meaning of marriage—and the value of marriage—changes when it becomes one of several options in a society of self-determining individuals.

This said, it is not the case that "anything goes." Every soci-   10 ety favors forms of union that conform to its ethical standards and its needs.

Our society no longer approves of treating women as incom-   11 petent minors and the wards of their husbands within the structure of a patriarchal union. We do not approve, generally, of plural marriages—the basis of our disapproval being that they abrogate the rights of women and especially of young girls. We no longer generally feel that the sole function of women in society is to produce children and serve men as domestic labor. In other words, when we censure certain types of marriage, the basis on which we do so is our defense of indi- vidual human rights. This is our ethical standard.

Marriage is, then, foundational because it provides a recog-   12 nized form of identity and security for children in society. Its function is not universally to produce children but to provide legitimate forms for their care. And marriage's primary accom- plishment is not to regulate sex (as a quick glance at American society would tell us). The institution survives despite infi- delity, and sex does not by itself create marriage.

In addition, it is a system of exchange whereby families "give   13 up" their own offspring to make new alliances with others, and to enter into broad networks of relationships, including and especially with one's "enemies." Without such arrangements, we would have a world of isolated, incestuous, biological clans—and endemic warfare.

14   What, then, about restriction of the legal bond of marriage to a man and a woman? Does marriage have to be heterosexual? The human record tells us otherwise. While the model of marriage is arguably heterosexual, the practice of marriage is not. In a broad spectrum of societies in Africa, for example, when a woman's husband dies, she may take on his legal role in the family, and acquire a legal "wife" to help manage the domestic establishment. This role of wife is above all social, and not contingent on her sexual relations. These societies, which practice heterosexuality, take this woman-woman marriage as commonsensical; they recognize that above all marriage functions socially to extend and stabilize the network of care.

15   As for marriage as a legal institution, the ethnographic record makes clear that law expresses the dominant ethics of the group. Our history reflects the evolution of our values, and we as Americans are most proud of our deepening tradition of civil rights. To deny marriage to same-sex couples, as President Bush proposes, expresses a rejection of this civil rights tradition and a regression to a politics of exclusion.

Expanding Vocabulary

Match each word in column A with its definition in column B. When in doubt, first find the word in the essay and look for context clues to aid your understanding of the word's meaning. Then, if necessary, use your dictionary to complete the matching exercise. The number in parentheses is the number of the paragraph in which the word appears.

Column A	Column B
diverse (4)	dependent on
paternity (4)	rebuke, official disapproval
lineage (8)	having distinct groups coexisting within a society
pluralist (9)	
patriarchal (11)	a system in which the father is head of the family
abrogate (11)	
censure (11)	close, formal associations
alliances (13)	constant, widespread
endemic (13)	having variety, differences
contingent (14)	abolish

ethnographic (15)   study comparing human cultures
                           direct descent from a particular
                              ancestor
                           fatherhood

Understanding Content

1. What did Morgan's 1860s study of marriage reveal?
2. Why is it difficult to define marriage?
3. What has been the primary, traditional function of marriage? What has marriage not been able to restrict or control?
4. How has the thinking about marriage changed today in Western societies?
5. By what ethical standard do we object to some attitudes and practices within marriages in the past in our culture?
6. By the same ethics, what position on same-sex marriage follows, in the authors' view?

Drawing Inferences about Thesis and Purpose

1. What is the authors' purpose in writing? Do they have more than one purpose?
2. What is their thesis? Where is it stated?

Analyzing Strategies and Style

1. What approach do the authors take to their topic? Think about the essay as an argument. What is the nature of their evidence to support their claim?
2. How would you describe the tone of the essay? How is this an important element in their argument?

Thinking Critically

1. Were you aware that only in contemporary Western societies has marriage now become just one option for structuring one's social life? What is your reaction to this reality? What may be the causes for this change?
2. The authors largely dismiss romantic love as having much influence on marriage as a social institution. Does this surprise you? If so, why? On reflection, do the authors make sense to you on this point?
3. Evaluate the argument.

Abolish Marriage

MICHAEL KINSLEY

A member of the bar with a law degree from Harvard, Michael Kinsley is a former editor of both *Harper's* and *The New Republic*. He is the founding editor (in 1996) of *Slate*, the online magazine, and has been a co-host of CNN's *Crossfire*. The following column appeared in the *Post* July 3, 2003.

Questions to Guide Your Reading and Reflection

1. What are gay marriage proponents seeking? What are social conservatives seeking?
2. Should state governments control marriages?

1   Critics and enthusiasts of *Lawrence v. Texas*, last week's Supreme Court decision invalidating state anti-sodomy laws, agree on one thing: The next argument is going to be about gay marriage. As Justice Scalia noted in his tart dissent, it follows from the logic of *Lawrence*. Mutually consenting sex with the person of your choice in the privacy of your own home is now a basic right of American citizenship under the Constitution. This does not mean that the government must supply it or guarantee it. But the government cannot forbid it, and the government also should not discriminate against you for choosing to exercise a basic right of citizenship. Offering an institution as important as marriage to male-female couples only is exactly this kind of discrimination. Or so the gay rights movement will now argue. Persuasively, I think.

2   Opponents of gay rights will resist mightily, although they have been in retreat for a couple of decades. General anti-gay sentiments are now considered a serious breach of civic etiquette, even in anti-gay circles. The current line of defense, which probably won't hold either, is between social toleration of homosexuals and social approval of homosexuality. Or between accepting the reality that people are gay, even accepting that gays are people, and endorsing something called "the gay agenda." Gay marriage, the opponents will argue, would

cross this line. It would make homosexuality respectable and, worse, normal. Gays are welcome to exist all they want, and to do their inexplicable thing if they must, but they shouldn't expect a government stamp of approval.

It's going to get ugly. And then it's going to get boring. So, we have two options here. We can add gay marriage to the short list of controversies—abortion, affirmative action, the death penalty—that are so frozen and ritualistic that debates about them are more like Kabuki performances than intellectual exercises. Or we can think outside the box. There is a solution that ought to satisfy both camps and may not be a bad idea even apart from the gay-marriage controversy.

That solution is to end the institution of marriage. Or rather (he hastens to clarify, Dear) the solution is to end the institution of government-sanctioned marriage. Or, framed to appeal to conservatives: End the government monopoly on marriage. Wait, I've got it: Privatize marriage. These slogans all mean the same thing. Let churches and other religious institutions continue to offer marriage ceremonies. Let department stores and casinos get into the act if they want. Let each organization decide for itself what kinds of couples it wants to offer marriage to. Let couples celebrate their union in any way they choose and consider themselves married whenever they want. Let others be free to consider them not married, under rules these others may prefer. And, yes, if three people want to get married, or one person wants to marry herself, and someone else wants to conduct a ceremony and declare them married, let'em. If you and your government aren't implicated, what do you care?

In fact, there is nothing to stop any of this from happening now. And a lot of it does happen. But only certain marriages get certified by the government. So, in the United States we are about to find ourselves in a strange situation where the principal demand of a liberation movement is to be included in the red tape of a government bureaucracy. Having just gotten state governments out of their bedrooms, gays now want these governments back in. Meanwhile, social-conservative anti-gays, many of them Southerners, are calling on the government in Washington to trample states' rights and nationalize the rules of marriage, if necessary, to prevent gays from getting what they want. The Senate Majority Leader, Bill Frist of Tennessee, responded to the Supreme Court's *Lawrence* decision by endorsing a constitutional amendment, no less, against gay marriage.

6   If marriage were an entirely private affair, all the disputes over gay marriage would become irrelevant. Gay marriage would not have the official sanction of government, but neither would straight marriage. There would be official equality between the two, which is the essence of what gays want and are entitled to. And if the other side is sincere in saying that its concern is not what people do in private, but government endorsement of a gay "lifestyle" or "agenda," that problem goes away, too.

7   Yes, yes, marriage is about more than sleeping arrangements. There are children, there are finances, there are spousal job benefits like health insurance and pensions. In all these areas, marriage is used as a substitute for other factors that are harder to measure, such as financial dependence or devotion to offspring. It would be possible to write rules that measure the real factors at stake and leave marriage out of the matter. Regarding children and finances, people can set their own rules, as many already do. None of this would be easy. Marriage functions as what lawyers call a "bright line," which saves the trouble of trying to measure a lot of amorphous factors. You're either married or you're not. Once marriage itself becomes amorphous, who-gets-the-kids and who-gets-health-care become trickier questions.

8   So, sure, there are some legitimate objections to the idea of privatizing marriage. But they don't add up to a fatal objection. Especially when you consider that the alternative is arguing about gay marriage until death do us part.

Expanding Vocabulary

Write a definition for each of the following words. Then select five of the words and use each one of those in a separate sentence of your own. The number in parentheses is the number of the paragraph in which the word appears.

tart (1)	government-sanctioned (4)
breach (2)	implicated (4)

ritualistic (3)   trample (5)
Kabuki (3)   amorphous (7)

Understanding Content

1. What has just happened that is the occasion for Kinsley's column? What argument does he think the event will lead to?
2. Who will win the argument, in Kinsley's view?
3. What is the author's solution to end the argument?
4. What is ironic about gays fighting for the right to marry? What is ironic about conservatives seeking a constitutional amendment against gay marriage?
5. What problems would we have if governments stopped sanctioning marriage? Can the problems be solved?

Drawing Inferences about Thesis and Purpose

1. When Kinsley writes that the argument over gay marriage will "get boring," what does he mean? How does his comparison to Kabuki performances or to debates over abortion illustrate his point?
2. What is the author's thesis, the claim of his argument? Where does he state it?

Analyzing Strategies and Style

1. What is clever about the last sentence of the essay?
2. When Kinsley writes "Or rather (he hastens to clarify, Dear) . . ." who is the "Dear" in this sentence? What makes this line amusing?
3. Analyze the essay's tone. How serious is Kinsley in presenting his solution to the argument over gay marriage? If he is not entirely serious, why is he proposing his solution? What seems to be his purpose in writing?

Thinking Critically

1. Do you agree with Kinsley—whether you like it or not—that gay marriage will be sanctioned? If you disagree, what evidence do you have to support your view?
2. What is your reaction to Kinsley's proposal?
3. Is there any hope of finding common ground on this issue, or are we doomed to live with another issue that generates only ritualistic "debates"? Do you have any new suggestions for thinking outside the box on any social issues that are currently divisive?

Waterboarding: A Clarification

MARK BOWDEN

A reporter for the *Philadelphia Inquirer*, Mark Bowden is the author of a number of books, including *Guests of the Ayatollah: The First Battle in America's War with Militant Islam* (2006) and *Black Hawk Down* (2002), which was made into a movie. The following essay appeared in the *Inquirer* on January 2, 2008.

Questions to Guide Your Reading and Reflection

1. What does Bowden want to clarify in this column?
2. Is torture ever justified?

1   Few subjects I have written about in this column provoked such an outpouring of response as the one last week about the waterboarding of al-Qaeda leader Abu Zubaydah.

2   In a nutshell, I argued that torture in all its forms should be banned, but that in some instances, as with the waterboarding of Zubaydah, it is defensible. The trial and punishment of those who break the law is always subject to the discretion of prosecutors, juries and judges. In rare cases, such as Zubaydah's, in which a coercive method is employed to prevent a greater wrong, the interrogators involved should not be prosecuted.

3   Many readers found this outrageous. I received the usual cascade of comment from the Sandbox School of Argument, the name-callers and those whose idea of persuasion is to state their own opinion loudly—lots of capital letters, bold type and underlinings. Several responders belong to the Ostrich School; they won't be reading this because they have forsworn reading anything I ever write again, presumably on the assumption that if you ignore opinions you don't like, they go away.

4   Most of the responses were polite and thoughtful, and some actually agreed with me. The biggest confusion stemmed from my apparent failure to state the argument above clearly, because many were outraged by my presumed willingness to "allow" torture. So I will try to approach the same point in a different way.

When researching this topic in 2003 for an essay in the 5
Atlantic, I met an impressive young woman in Tel Aviv named
Jessica Montell. She headed a human-rights organization
called B'Tselem, which had successfully sued the Israeli
Defense Forces to ban all forms of coercive interrogation.

Here is how Montell framed the same point: 6

"If I as an interrogator feel that the person in front of me has 7
information that can prevent a catastrophe from happening, I
imagine I would do what I would have to do in order to prevent that catastrophe from happening. The state's obligation is
then to put me on trial for breaking the law. Then I can come
and say: 'These are the facts that I had at my disposal. This is
what I believed at the time. This is what I thought it was necessary to do.' I can evoke the defense of necessity, and then the
court decides whether or not it's reasonable that I broke the
law. . . . But it has to be that I broke the law. It can't be that
there's some prior license for me to abuse people."

I suspect Montell would prefer to see the interrogators of 8
Zubaydah prosecuted, at which point they could raise the
defense of necessity. I argued that if official accounts of Zubaydah's history of mass murder, and of his handling during questioning, are true (and various investigations are under way),
then his interrogators should not even be charged.

Another school of thought took me to task for placing 9
such a risky burden on interrogators. One former military
interrogator wrote that the ban I proposed "would put brave
men and women who are charged with protecting us in the
untenable situation of breaking the law for doing what's
right and necessary."

But placing interrogators in such legal jeopardy is the only 10
way to prevent large-scale abuses. In a perfect world, one
where military interrogators were all scrupulously responsible
and bright, you could prescribe certain rules governing the use
of coercive methods and could feel confident that they would
be employed only where appropriate, and only to the extent
necessary. We don't live in that world. As anyone who has ever
worked in a large organization knows, there are many people
with responsibility who will seize upon any opportunity to
abuse it. I believe something very much like this has happened
with the Bush administration's effort to authorize "aggressive

methods." It had the same effect such efforts always have had: It unleashed the sadists at Abu Ghraib and elsewhere.

11   There is a good passage in E.L. Doctorow's novel *The March*, about Sherman's march through Georgia, that speaks directly to the difference between soldiering in the abstract vs. soldiering in the real world. As the huge Union Army approaches Atlanta, a young woman is forced to choose between abandoning her bedridden father and fleeing the advancing troops or staying and trying to protect her home. She bravely stays. Her fears are allayed when an officer with an advance guard announces that she has nothing to fear, and even positions a private at her gate to protect the house from invasion. Then the noble officer leaves—all is right with the world in his mind. Hours later, as the vast army flows past, the private tires of his mission. He sees friends among the passing troops and goes off with them. The marauding troops that follow invade the house and trash it.

12   This is fiction, but apt. Armies are not perfect engines. Certain rules, no matter how well-considered and intended, are impossible to enforce. Conscientious leaders must consider not just the abstract, but also the real. In an army where hundreds, if not thousands of men and women will be interrogating prisoners, there will be those who given the slightest opportunity will abuse their power. Human nature being what it is, there is a natural tendency for abuses to occur when one man is given complete authority over another, and when men are at war, dealing with prisoners they dislike or even hate (and who hate them in turn), whose languages and customs are foreign, the abuses will be widespread and severe.

13   There is ample historical precedence for this tendency, and even fascinating psychological experiments that have demonstrated it. The only practical way to curb abuses in prisons is for guards and interrogators to have strict, clear, rigorously enforced limits. That's why I believe that any interrogator who employs coercive methods ought to be mindful that his actions are crossing a serious line, and that he had better have compelling reasons for doing so.

14   One of the best arguments against mine did not fault either my reasoning or my blackened soul. It questioned the wisdom of allowing any exceptions, even defensible ones, because of the impact it has on the moral stature of the United States.

There is no question that something important is lost when   15
we as a nation accede to tactics considered reprehensible. One
correspondent asked: "What is the harm done to the citizens of
the country whose agents have a policy that allows torture?,"
and argued that we ought to accept impending tragedy in the
name of honoring a high-minded policy.

In my column I raised the example of the German police   16
chief who threatened a captured kidnapper with torture
because he refused to reveal where he had buried alive
his 12-year-old victim. The kidnapper promptly gave the
location. The German police chief lost his job for making
the threat.

It may well have been more noble on some level for him not   17
to have made the threat, but I prefer a less rigid concept of
morality. I would not have fired the police chief, or prosecuted
him. I agree completely with his actions, even though torture
is repulsive. The boy's life matters more than my rectitude or
peace of mind.

Expanding Vocabulary

Find definitions for each of the following words and then select five
and use each of them in a separate sentence. The number in parentheses is the number of the paragraph in which the word appears.

discretion (2)	sadists (10)
coercive (2)	allayed (11)
forsworn (3)	marauding (11)
untenable (9)	accede (15)
scrupulously (10)	rectitude (17)

Understanding Content

1. What was Bowden's claim in his first column on torture?
2. What kinds of responses did he receive?
3. What is the key reason for making torture illegal?
4. Why should some torture be "defensible"?

Drawing Inferences about Thesis and Purpose

1. What sentence in paragraph 17 contains an inconsistency? How
   does Bowden justify this inconsistency?
2. What is Bowden's claim?

Analyzing Strategies and Style

1. In describing responses to his previous column, Bowden gives names to two types of responses. Explain the "Sandbox School of Argument" and the "Ostrich School."
2. In paragraph 11, the author provides an example from the novel *The March*. What point does the example illustrate?

Thinking Critically

1. Bowden refers in general to psychological studies and to "human nature" as evidence that some people will abuse power. Bowden expects readers to agree with him. Do you? Why or why not?
2. If you disagree with Bowden's position on torture, how would you challenge his claim?

The Torture Myth

ANNE APPLEBAUM

A graduate of Yale and the London School of Economics, Anne Applebaum is a *Washington Post* columnist and editorial board member. She has been published in many newspapers and magazines and is the author of *Gulag: A History* (2003). Her contribution to the torture debate appeared on January 12, 2005.

Questions to Guide Your Reading and Reflection

1. What is the question about torture that Applebaum raises for debate?
2. Should the debate be practical or moral—or both?

1   Just for a moment, let's pretend that there is no moral, legal or constitutional problem with torture. Let's also imagine a clear-cut case: a terrorist who knows where bombs are about to explode in Iraq. To stop him, it seems that a wide range of Americans would be prepared to endorse "cruel and unusual" methods. In advance of confirmation hearings for Attorney General-designate Alberto Gonzales last week, the *Wall Street Journal* argued that such scenarios must be debated, since

"what's at stake in this controversy is nothing less than the ability of U.S. forces to interrogate enemies who want to murder innocent civilians." Alan Dershowitz, the liberal legal scholar, has argued in the past that interrogators in such a case should get a "torture warrant" from a judge. Both of these arguments rest on an assumption: that torture—defined as physical pressure during interrogation—can be used to extract useful information.

But does torture work? The question has been asked many times since Sept. 11, 2001. I'm repeating it, however, because the Gonzales hearings inspired more articles about our lax methods ("Too Nice for Our Own Good" was one headline), because similar comments may follow this week's trial of Spec. Charles Graner, the alleged Abu Ghraib ringleader, and because I still cannot find a positive answer. I've heard it said that the Syrians and the Egyptians "really know how to get these things done." I've heard the Israelis mentioned, without proof. I've heard Algeria mentioned, too, but Darius Rejali, an academic who recently trolled through French archives, found no clear examples of how torture helped the French in Algeria—and they lost that war anyway. "Liberals," argued an article in the liberal online magazine *Slate* a few months ago, "have a tendency to accept, all too eagerly, the argument that torture is ineffective." But it's also true that "realists," whether liberal or conservative, have a tendency to accept, all too eagerly, fictitious accounts of effective torture carried out by someone else.

By contrast, it is easy to find experienced U.S. officers who argue precisely the opposite. Meet, for example, retired Air Force Col. John Rothrock, who, as a young captain, headed a combat interrogation team in Vietnam. More than once he was faced with a ticking time-bomb scenario: a captured Vietcong guerrilla who knew of plans to kill Americans. What was done in such cases was "not nice," he says. "But we did not physically abuse them." Rothrock used psychology, the shock of capture and of the unexpected. Once, he let a prisoner see a wounded comrade die. Yet—as he remembers saying to the "desperate and honorable officers" who wanted him to move faster—"if I take a Bunsen burner to the guy's genitals, he's going to tell you just about anything," which would be pointless. Rothrock, who is no squishy liberal, says that he doesn't know "any professional intelligence officers of my generation who would think this is a good idea."

4   Or listen to Army Col. Stuart Herrington, a military intelligence specialist who conducted interrogations in Vietnam, Panama and Iraq during Desert Storm, and who was sent by the Pentagon in 2003—long before Abu Ghraib—to assess interrogations in Iraq. Aside from its immorality and its illegality, says Herrington, torture is simply "not a good way to get information." In his experience, nine out of 10 people can be persuaded to talk with no "stress methods" at all, let alone cruel and unusual ones. Asked whether that would be true of religiously motivated fanatics, he says that the "batting average" might be lower: "perhaps six out of ten." And if you beat up the remaining four? "They'll just tell you anything to get you to stop."

5   Worse, you'll have the other side effects of torture. It "endangers our soldiers on the battlefield by encouraging reciprocity." It does "damage to our country's image" and undermines our credibility in Iraq. That, in the long run, outweighs any theoretical benefit. Herrington's confidential Pentagon report, which he won't discuss but which was leaked to *The Post* a month ago, goes farther. In that document, he warned that members of an elite military and CIA task force were abusing detainees in Iraq, that their activities could be "making gratuitous enemies" and that prisoner abuse "is counterproductive to the Coalition's efforts to win the cooperation of the Iraqi citizenry." Far from rescuing Americans, in other words, the use of "special methods" might help explain why the war is going so badly.

6   An up-to-date illustration of the colonel's point appeared in recently released FBI documents from the naval base at Guantanamo Bay, Cuba. These show, among other things, that some military intelligence officers wanted to use harsher interrogation methods than the FBI did. As a result, complained one inspector, "every time the FBI established a rapport with a detainee, the military would step in and the detainee would stop being cooperative." So much for the utility of torture.

7   Given the overwhelmingly negative evidence, the really interesting question is not whether torture works but why so many people in our society want to believe that it works. At the moment, there is a myth in circulation, a fable that goes something like this: Radical terrorists will take advantage of our

fussy legality, so we may have to suspend it to beat them. Radical terrorists mock our namby-pamby prisons, so we must make them tougher. Radical terrorists are nasty, so to defeat them we have to be nastier.

Perhaps it's reassuring to tell ourselves tales about the new   8 forms of "toughness" we need, or to talk about the special rules we will create to defeat this special enemy. Unfortunately, that toughness is self-deceptive and self-destructive. Ultimately it will be self-defeating as well.

Expanding Vocabulary

Examine the following words in their contexts in the essay and then write a brief definition or synonym for each one. Do not use a dictionary. Try to guess the word's meaning from its context.

scenarios (1)	gratuitous (5)
trolled (2)	rapport (6)
reciprocity (5)	fable (7)

Understanding Content

1. What is the occasion for Applebaum's column? What views about torture have been offered by others?
2. What issue does Applebaum choose to examine?
3. Summarize her evidence.
4. What is the author's view of the current thinking in defense of torture?

Drawing Inferences about Thesis and Purpose

1. In paragraph 2, Applebaum presents various "accounts" of torture use. What are we to infer from this paragraph?
2. What is Applebaum's thesis?

Analyzing Strategies and Style

1. In describing the thinking in defense of torture, Applebaum characterizes it as "myth," "fable," and "tales." What do these words tell us about the author's attitude?
2. In paragraph 2, the author writes: "I've heard it said," "I've heard," and "I've heard." What does she accomplish with the repetition of these words?
3. Examine the repetition in the last paragraph. What is effective about her use of this strategy?

Thinking Critically

1. Evaluate Applebaum's evidence. Is her use of military figures convincing? Why or why not?
2. If torture does not work, and if it's morally questionable, is there any way to justify its use? Be prepared to debate this question.

Cartoon on Global Warning

TOM TOLES

Pulitzer-prize winning syndicated cartoonist Tom Toles published this cartoon on November 26, 2007, in the *Washington Post*.

1. Who are the figures in the cartoon? What situation is depicted visually? Who is speaking the lines?
2. What ideas does the cartoon express?
3. What makes the cartoon clever?

When Size Really Mattered

JOEL ACHENBACH

A staff writer for the *Washington Post*, Joel Achenbach is the author of several books, including collections of his formerly syndicated column "Why Things Are." Achenbach maintains a regular blog on the washingtonpost.com website. The following article appeared October 2, 2005.

Questions to Guide Your Reading and Reflection

1. Is Achenbach defending the Gas Age?
2. Do you like big cars? If so, why?

A thousand years from now, if anyone is still alive, they'll   1
call this the Gas Age. The Petroleum Period. The Oil Epoch. We'll be known by what we burned.

These humans of the future, gliding to work on solar-   2
powered plasma beams, won't care about our wars, and they'll have trouble keeping the Napoleons and Lincolns straight, the same way that today we struggle to remember the difference between Attila the Hun and Genghis Khan. Mainly, they'll recall that we were promiscuous with hydrocarbons as we gallivanted all over the place in machines called cars. They'll shake their genetically modified, watermelon-sized heads in disapproval.

What they'll never grasp is what a blast the Gas Age has been.   3

The car may be evil, worse even than the belching, flatulent,   4
carefully bred beast we call the cow, but the car is also the most delightful invention since fire. A car is fire converted to speed. The bad news: A planet is gradually ruined. The good news: The 2006 eight-cylinder Chevy Corvette can go zero-to-60 in 3.8 seconds!

We've all had gas on the brain lately, since it now costs more   5
than milk. Some of us remember gas at 21 cents a gallon, 25 cents for premium, all of it leaded, burned in cars as big as rocket ships. We didn't have global warming back then, or "environmentalists." We had conservationists, who were people who did lots of hiking, fishing and hunting in remote

places they'd driven to in a Pontiac ocean liner, towing an Airstream.

6   The car is a singularly American technology. It is a freedom machine in a freedom-crazed society. It promotes individuality. It laughs at communal living. The HOV lanes are under-subscribed for deep cultural reasons. Rugged individualism in America means never joining a car pool.

7   Whether you're male or female, a car is fundamentally virile. It is sex wrought in metal. Maturity in America comes not at puberty or high school graduation, but with the receipt of a driver's license and the state-sanctioned ability to get in a car, pick up a date, drive somewhere dark, park and make out. *Vroom, vroom*, baby.

8   When you get tired of tooling around town in American Graffiti mode, you light out for the territory, hit Route 66, get in a drag race like James Dean, head to Vegas like Hunter S. Thompson, spend weeks on the road like Jack Kerouac. Our cult heroes were brilliant drivers. You have to put out of your mind that Route 66 has been largely obliterated by freeways, that Dean died young in a car crash, that Thompson burned out and took his own life, and that Kerouac became a drunk and died of internal bleeding in St. Petersburg at the age of 47. Just keep driving.

9   In a car, you can change gears, directions and your destiny. The car is an extension of your body. Here's a Duke University neuroscientist rhapsodizing after an experiment showing how primates manipulate tools: "We're saying that it's not only the brain that is adaptable; it's the whole concept of self. And this concept of self extends to our tools. Everything from cars to clothing that we use in our lives becomes incorporated into our sense of self."

10   It's not just your car—it's your wheeled appendage!

11   This is particularly important if you are a guy and you have appendage issues. As modern society robs us of masculinity, we compensate with bigger, brawnier, more priapic automobiles, those giant SUVs and Hummers and Monster Trucks, some of which we can jack up on hydraulic suspensions so they'll lurch and buck and bounce and make all kinds of *whompa-whompa-whompa* noises and do everything this side of mating with the nearest hatchback. Some cars are sexy, some just plain slutty.

This connection between the car and American society is so   12
intense it's hard to imagine what we'll do if we run out of stuff
to burn. If we can't drive fast, the thing we're driving is not a
car anymore. It's a *cart*. Maybe they'll come up with a new,
magic fuel, renewable and clean, somehow allowing us to
scream down a highway without causing any environmental
damage or violating the Second Law of Thermodynamics.

But, at the moment, we have to assume that our cars, and   13
our individual sense of self, will have to change. Maybe the
laws governing energy are the same as those governing life
itself: We grow up, we get old, we slow down.

And we remember what a great ride we had.   14

Expanding Vocabulary

Study definitions of each of the following words and then use each
one in a separate sentence. The number in parentheses is the number
of the paragraph in which the word appears.

promiscuous (2)   obliterated (8)
gallivanted (2)   appendage (10)
virile (7)

Understanding Content

1. How does Achenbach describe people of the future? What will be
   their reaction to the "Gas Age"?
2. How does the author describe and characterize the car? What can
   you do with a car? How does it connect to American culture?

Drawing Inferences about Thesis and Purpose

1. What is Achenbach's attitude toward cars? Is it appropriate to say
   that he has mixed views?
2. What is the author's thesis?

Analyzing Strategies and Style

1. In paragraph 8, Achenbach refers to three American figures. First,
   learn about any of them unfamiliar to you. Then explain how the
   author uses these figures to develop his essay.
2. Achenbach is known for his use of humor. Find four examples of
   humor in the essay and explain why each one is funny and how
   each one functions in the essay.

Thinking Critically

1. There are many ways to present an argument, including cartoons and humor. How effective is Achenbach's humorous approach to his subject? Explain and support your reaction.
2. What can humor accomplish in argument? Do you think you should try it sometimes? Why or why not?

STUDENT ESSAY—REFUTATION

BLAME IT ON THE MEDIA AND OTHER WAYS TO DRESS A WOLF IN SHEEP'S CLOTHING
David M. Ouellette

If an activity is legal, then people should be free to engage in that activity without fear of defamation. But smokers are being defamed, even persecuted, by a biased media bent on casting smoking as an unmitigated evil. This is Robert J. Samuelson's assertion in his September 24, 1997, <u>Newsweek</u> article "Do Smokers Have Rights." He says the media distort research on passive smoking's effects, demonize tobacco companies into teen-targeting drug pushers, and use these ill-founded claims as justification for punitive cigarette taxes. The result, Samuelson says, is that we "deny, ignore or minimize" the right of smokers to do something that is perfectly legal. He is mistaken on all counts.

Introduction includes author, title, publication place, and date of work to be refuted.

Attention-getter

Thesis

When it comes to the effects of passive smoking, Samuelson does not want to accept what researchers have to say. He cites a ten-year study of non-smoking nurses that reported 25 to 30 percent of their heart attacks were caused by passive smoking. No matter how you look at the figure, it clearly states that passive smoking is dangerous. He says, "the practical significance of this is negligible." Ask any one of those people whose heart attacks were caused by someone else's smoking if what happened to them was "negligible." The practical impact is that if smoking were eliminated, heart attacks among nonsmokers would drop by 25 to 30 percent, according to this study.

Student blends summary and direct quotation to present author's position.

The media, contrary to Samuelson, are not the ones who have painted tobacco companies as purveyors of addiction to teenagers. The tobacco industry has demonized itself. Samuelson himself admits that "the tobacco industry no doubt targets teens," but he excuses this by saying, "the ads may affect brand choices more than the decision to smoke." However, advertising for a brand of cigarettes is, necessarily, at the same time advertising for smoking. If a brand is made to look attractive, then that also

Student analyzes the author's logic.

means smoking itself is made to look attractive, for you cannot have one without the other.

Finally, Samuelson argues that heavy cigarette taxes actually hurt smokers more than help them. In reality, the taxes are intended to deter people from smoking by raising the price. The people who would most likely be deterred are teenagers and the poor, both of whom smoke more than any other age group or economic class. "Sin taxes," such as cigarette taxes, attempt to limit or discourage legal behavior. A high price is not tantamount to unlegislated prohibition; it is society's way of dissuading people from destructive behavior. Samuelson asks whether we have a right to limit legal behaviors, or is this infringing on individuals' rights. There is a middle ground between prohibition and unlimited right. Alcohol consumption is just such an example, a behavior so dangerous that its use is controlled yet still legal. Clearly, society has a right to prohibit or control dangerous behavior. Not only is it society's right to control the danger to which its citizens are exposed, it is its responsibility.

Student uses a comparison with alcohol to challenge the author's argument.

Samuelson's claim that the media are besmirching smokers and tobacco companies with misleading reports is false. It is the media's responsibility to report news, such as the health threat of passive smoking, and how tobacco companies target teenagers. As for the right to smoke, smoking's dangers—both to smokers and nonsmokers alike—demand its control. Conceding fist-pounding demands for unlimited rights, regardless of who gets hurt or what other rights get infringed, would be an abdication of our responsibility to protect the health and welfare of the nation.

Student concludes by restating his thesis and defending it as the responsible one.

MAKING CONNECTIONS

1. Examine the arguments in this chapter for the various strategies that the authors use. Then decide: (a) What particular strategy works consistently well from one essay to the next? And (b) What particular essay is the best argument, overall? Be prepared to defend your decisions.
2. Select one of the pairs of arguments and study the pair for any common ground that you can find. You may find something stated directly in the essays, or you may have to infer some common ground based on what the authors have written in general. Think about how you would explain to the two authors that they do share some common ground in spite of their differences.
3. Select one of the issues debated in this chapter, perhaps the one you know the least about, and get some facts relevant to the issue. For example: What are the statistics regarding gun deaths per year in the U.S.? In other countries? By state

or region of the country? By type of crime—murder of someone known, suicide, armed robbery, gang killing, etc.? Be prepared to discuss how this information may influence the way your classmates should read the relevant essay(s) in the chapter.

TOPICS FOR WRITING

1. Did any one of the writers change your way of thinking on his or her issue? If so, write an essay in which you explain how that writer's argument convinced you to rethink your position and why the writer's argument should convince other readers. Do not assume that your audience knows the essay, so provide the author, title, and publication information in your essay.
2. Select a personal problem that concerns you, perhaps because you have a friend or family member with that problem. In an essay, present and defend your view on this issue. You can write to a general audience or directly to the person involved in a letter format and tone. Possible topics include staying in school, quitting smoking or using drugs or abusing alcohol, controlling starving or binge eating, maintaining relationships with parents, selecting a career, eliminating abusive language, or other bad habits.
3. Select any writer in this chapter whose position you disagree with and prepare a refutation of the writer's argument. Do not assume that your reader has read the article you are refuting. As shown in the student essay, begin by giving author, title, publication information, and the author's position. Then present and support your position. Your argument may be developed in part by showing weaknesses in the opposing view.
4. Reflect on educational issues and problems to select a topic from this area that interests and concerns you. There are many possible topics, including censorship of books in high school libraries, control of high school and college newspapers, discrimination in sororities and fraternities, academic freedom, plagiarism, grading systems, admissions policies, and others. Definitions may play an important role in

developing your argument. Be sure that you understand the arguments on both sides, acknowledge whatever common ground you share with opponents, and write in a restrained, conciliatory manner.

5. Many serious problems face our society—from drugs to taxes (and the deficit) to illegal aliens to homelessness to insider trading and other business and banking crimes to AIDS to ethical concerns such as abortion, euthanasia, and genetic engineering. Select a problem that concerns you and write an argumentative essay that presents and defends your proposed solutions to the problems. Part of your development will probably include challenging other proposed solutions with which you disagree. You may want to do some reading so that you have current facts about the problem. (If you use sources, including Internet sources, be sure to credit them properly.)

6. Serious problems also face our world, for example, depletion of the ozone layer, acid rain, deforestation, polluted water, global warming, and possibly overpopulation. Select a problem that concerns you and prepare an argumentative essay according to the guidelines discussed in topic 5. Give thought to how you can narrow your topic to a manageable length. For example, instead of examining the problem of water pollution, write about the pollution of a lake or river or bay near where you live.

A CHECKLIST FOR ARGUMENT ESSAYS

Inventing

☐ Have I selected a topic consistent with the instructor's guidelines for this assignment?

☐ Have I chosen among possible topics one that fits my knowledge and experience?

☐ Have I thought about reasons and evidence that can be used to support my topic?

☐ Have I reflected on my topic and support to write a tentative thesis, a clear claim for my argument?

☐ Have I "tested" my initial brainstorming of reasons and evidence against experience and logic?

☐ Have I thought about an effective organization, based on my support and the type of argument I am preparing—for example, presenting solutions to a problem, challenging someone else's argument?

Drafting

☐ Have I succeeded in completing a first draft at one sitting so that I can "see" the whole?

☐ Do I have enough—enough to meet assignment demands and enough to provide convincing support for my claim?

☐ Does the order work?

☐ Have I avoided logical fallacies?

Revising

☐ Have I made any needed additions, deletions, or changes in order based on answering questions about my draft?

☐ Have I revised my draft to produce coherent paragraphs, using transitions and connecting words that emphasize my logic and evidence?

Polishing

☐ Have I eliminated wordiness and clichés?

☐ Have I avoided or removed any discriminatory language?

☐ Have I used my word processor's spell check and proofread a printed copy with great care?

☐ Do I have an appropriate and interesting title?

Glossary

Alliteration   Repetition of initial consonant sound in two or more words. For example, the *first frost*.

Allusion   Reference to lines or characters from literature or mythology or to figures or events from history. For example, if someone describes you as "an old *Scrooge*," then, like the character in Charles Dickens's *A Christmas Carol*, you are not generous with money.

Analogy   An extended comparison of two things that are essentially not alike with several points of similarity (or difference) established to support an idea or thesis.

Analysis   The division of a work or a topic into its component parts. To analyze a writer's style is to examine the various elements that compose style, such as word choice, sentence structure, use of figurative language. (See also **Causal analysis**.)

Argumentation   A form of thinking and writing in which reasons and evidence are presented to support a position on an issue. (See Chapter 10.)

Audience   The readers of a piece of writing. Hence, as a writing concept, the expected or anticipated readers to whom a piece of writing is directed. A sense of audience should guide a writer's choice about approach, content, and tone for a piece of writing.

Brainstorm   Prewriting strategy for generating material on a subject by jotting down all ideas and examples or details that come to mind.

Causal analysis   The examination of a situation by division into and study of its several causes, or its pattern of conditions, influences, and remote and immediate causes. (See Chapter 9.)

Character   Any person in narrative and dramatic works; also, the personality traits that together shape a person's "character."

Characterization   The description of a person, either a real person or one from fiction or drama. A detailed characterization includes physical appearance, speech and behavior patterns, personality traits, and values.

Chronology   The arrangement of events in time sequence. A narrative or historical account organizes events in chronological order. A process analysis explains steps in their appropriate chronology.

Classification   A pattern of thinking and writing in which a subject is divided into logical categories, and then elements of the subject are grouped within those categories. (See Chapter 7.)

Cliché   Overused, worn-out expressions, often metaphors, that were once fresh and clever but should now be avoided in writing, except as examples or to reveal character. *I'm fit as a fiddle, hungry as a bear*, and *head over heels in love* are examples of clichés.

Coherence   A quality of good writing marked by a logical ordering of statements and by the use of words and phrases that guide readers through the material and show them how the writing hangs together. Some techniques for obtaining coherence include repetition of key words, use of pronouns, and use of transition words and phrases.

Colloquial language   Language used in conversation but usually avoided in writing, especially in academic and business writing, unless used purposely to create a particular effect.

Comparison   A pattern of writing in which similarities between two subjects (two schools, two jobs, two novels) are examined. (See Chapter 4.)

Complex sentence   Sentence containing at least one dependent or subordinate clause and one independent clause. For example, "When you come to a term about writing that you do not know, [dependent clause] you should look it up in the Glossary [independent clause]."

Compound sentence   Sentence containing at least two independent clauses. For example, "A comparison develops similarities between two like things [first independent clause], but [coordinating conjunction] a metaphor expresses a similarity between two unlike things [second independent clause].

Conclusion   The ending of a piece of writing; it gives the reader a sense of finish and completeness. Many strategies for concluding are available to writers, including restating and emphasizing the significance of the thesis, summarizing main points, and suggesting a course of action. Writing needs to conclude, not just stop.

Connotation   The suggestions and emotional overtones conveyed by a word. Selecting the word with the appropriate connotative significance allows writers to develop subtle shades of meaning and to convey their attitudes.

Context clues   The words or sentences surrounding a word that help readers to understand the meaning of that word.

Contrast   A pattern of writing in which differences between two subjects (e.g., two schools, two jobs, two novels) are examined. (See Chapter 4.)

Purpose   One's reason for writing. General purposes include to inform, to explain, and to persuade.

Refutation   A form of argument in which the primary purpose is to counter, or show weaknesses in, another's argument. (See Chapter 10.)

Reporter's questions   Traditionally the questions *who, what, where, when,* and *why* are considered those a journalist should answer about each story covered. Essay writers can also use these questions in planning a topic's development.

Rhetorical question   A question raised by a writer when the writer believes that readers will see only one possible answer—the answer the writer would give.

Sarcasm   Bitter or cutting expression, often ironic.

Satire   Work that ridicules the vices and follies of humanity, often with the purpose of bringing about change.

Simile   A comparison between two essentially unalike things that is stated explicitly by using connectors such as *like, as,* or *seems.* For example, "I wandered lonely *as* a cloud," written by William Wordsworth.

Simple sentence   A sentence containing only one independent clause. For example, "A simple sentence contains only one independent clause."

Style   A writer's selection and arrangement of language.

Summary   A brief, objective restatement of the main ideas in a work.

Symbol   An object, character, or action that suggests meanings, associations, and emotions beyond what is characteristic of its nature or function. A rose is a flower, but a rose symbolically represents love and beauty.

Theme   The central idea (or ideas) that a work embodies.

Thesis   The main idea of an essay. It is often but not always expressed in a *thesis sentence.*

Tone   The expression of a writer's attitude (e.g., playful, bitter).

Transitions   Words and phrases that show readers how ideas in a work are related or connected. For example, *in addition, for example, however.*

Unity   A characteristic of good writing in which everything included relates to the work's main idea and contributes to its development.

Whole by whole   A structure for comparison or contrast that organizes by the two subjects being compared rather than by their specific points of similarity or difference.

Credits

Andrew Sullivan, "Society Is Dead: We Have Retreated into the IWorld" used with the permission of *The Sunday Times of London*.

Richard Wilbur, "The Writer" from *The Mind Reader*. Copyright © 1971 by Richard Wilbur. Reprinted by permission of Harcourt, Inc.

Gail Godwin, "The Watcher at the Gates," from *The New York Times*, January 9, 1977. Copyright © 1977 by The New York Times Company. Reprinted by permission.

Terry McMillan, "Introduction," copyright © 1990 by Terry McMillan, from *Breaking Ice* by Terry McMillan. Used by permission of Viking Penguin, a division of Penguin Putnam Inc.

Kurt Vonnegut, "How to Write With Style." International Paper Company: *The Power of the Printed Word*. Reprinted by permission of International Paper.

N. Scott Momaday, "The End of My Childhood," from *The Names*. Copyright © 1976. Reprinted by permission of the author.

Luis Rodriguez, from *Always Running*. Curbstone Press, 1993. Reprinted by permission of Curbstone Press.

Sandra Cisneros, "Only Daughter" Copyright © 1990 by Sandra Cisneros First published in *Glamour*, November 1990. Reprinted by permission of Susan Bergholz Literary Services, New York, NY. All rights reserved.

Mansour al-Nogaidian, "Losing My Jihadism" from *The Washington Post*, July 22, 2007. Reprinted with permission of the author.

Bob Kerr, "The Best Story Turned Out to Be No Story At All," *The Providence Sunday Journal*, April 3, 2000. Copyright © 2007 *The Providence Journal*. Reproduced by permission.

Gaye Wagner, "Death of an Officer," from *The American Enterprise*, May 1995. Reprinted with permission from *The American Enterprise*, a magazine of politics, business, and culture.

Keith Ablow, "When Parents Are Toxic to Children," from *The Washington Post*, May 28, 1996. Copyright Keith Russell Ablow, M.D. Reprinted by permission of the author.

Linda J. Waite, "Social Science Finds: 'Marriage Matters,'" from *The Responsive Community*, Vol. 6, issue 3, Summer 1996. Reprinted by permission.

Amitai Etzioni, "Working at McDonald's," from *The Washington Post*, 1986. Reprinted by permission of the author.

Patricia Dalton, "Don't Blame Me Generation," *The Washington Post*, March 5, 2006. Reprinted by permission of the author.

Ray Fisman, "Cos and Effect," from SLATE.COM, January 11, 2008. Reprinted by permission of the author.

Judith D. Auerbach,"The Overlooked Victims of AIDS," from *The Washington Post*, October 14, 2004. Copyright © The American Foundation for AIDS Research, 2004. All rights reserved.

Langston Hughes, "Dream Deferred," from *The Collected Poems of Langston Hughes* by Langston Hughes. Copyright © 1994 by The Estate of Langston Hughes. Used by permission of Alfred A. Knopf, a division of Random House, Inc.

Linda J. Collier, "Adult Crime, Adult Time," from *The Washington Post*, 1998. Reprinted by permission of the author.

Richard Cohen, "Kids Who Kill Are Still Kids," from *The Washington Post*, August 3, 2001. Copyright © 2001, The Washington Post Writers Group. Reprinted with permission.

John W. Borneman and Laurie Hart, "An Elastic Institution" from the April 14, 2004 issue of *The Washington Post*. Copyright © 2004 *The Washington Post*. Reprinted with permission.

Michael Kinsley,"Abolish Marriage" from the July 3, 2003 issue of *The Washington Post*. Used by permission of the author.

Mark Bowden, "Waterboarding: A Clarification," *Mcclatchy-Tribune News Service*. January 2, 2008. Used by permission of the author.

Anne Applebaum, "The Torture Myth," from *The Washington Post*, January 12, 2005. Copyright © 2005 *The Washington Post*. Reprinted with permission.

Joel Achenbach, "When Size Really Mattered," from *The Washington Post*, October 2, 2005. Copyright © 2005 *The Washington Post*. Reprinted with permission.

Photo Credits

page 92: © 1991 Amy Tan
Color insert (following page 94):
Francisco de Goya y Lucientes, *Third of May, 1808*. Museo del Prado, Madrid, Spain. Copyright Erich Lessing/Art Resource.

Index

Albow, Keith, 391–97
"Abolish Marriage," 458–61
Achenbach, Joel, 471–74
"Adult Crime, Adult Time," 444–49
"Africa," 103–10
Aigner, John P., 235–40
Al–Nogaidan, Mansour, 55–60
"Always Running," 47–51
Analysis, 13–15
  Causal, 386–89
  Process, 231–33
Applebaum, Anne, 466–70
Argument, 432–39
Auerbach, Judith D., 423–26

Barras, Jonetta Rose, 195–201
Berger, Garrett, 331–38
"Best Story Turned Out to Be No Story At All, The," 60–66
"Blame It on the Media and Other Ways to Dress a Wolf in Sheep's Clothing," 474–77
Bonilla, Denisse, 165–70
Borneman, John, 453–57
Bowden, Mark, 462–66
"Boys and Girls: Anatomy and Destiny," 136–42
"Bring Back Stinks and Bangs!" 154–160
Brooks, David, 323–26
"Buying Time," 331–38
Bzdek, Vincent P., 210–18

"Camping Out," 267–72
Cassatt, Mary, art insert
Christakis, Dimitri A., 191–95

Ciardi, John, 347–52
Cisneros, Sandra, 51–55
"Class Acts: America's Changing Middle Class," 316–22
Classification, 284–87
Cliches, 345–46
Cohen, Richard, 450–53
Coherence, 129–30
Collier, Linda J., 444–49
Communicating with instructors and peers, 34–35
Comparison, 126–29
Contrast, 126–29
"Conversational Ballgames," 131–36
"Cos and Effect," 418–23
Council for Biotechnology Information, ad, 181
"Curiosity," 375–77

Dali, Salvador, art insert
Dalton, Patricia, 414–18
Dance Class, The, art insert
"Date to Remember, A," 218–22
"Death of an Officer," 66–73
"Declaration of Sentiments," 440–44
Definition, 343–45
Degas, Edgar, art insert
Description, 82–84
"Difference Between 'Sick' and 'Evil,' The," 356–62
"Discrimination Is a Virtue," 352–56
Division and Classification, 284–87
"Dog Ate My Disk, and Other Tales of Woe, The," 326–31
"Don't Blame Me Generation, The," 414–18
"Dream Deferred," 427–28

"Elastic Institution, An," 453–57
Elgin, Suzette H., 241–51
"End of My Childhood, The," 44–47
Ericsson, Stephanie, 305–16
Etzioni, Amitai, 408–13
Examples, 174–76
Expedia.com ad, 182

"Faded Stain, The," 165–70
Fallacies, 436–38
Fila ad, 179
Fischer, David Hackett, 362–67
Fisman, Ray, 418–22
"Five Stages of Crisis Management,
    The,"257–63
"Freedom's Not Just Another
    Word," 362–67

"Gender Games," 150–54
Givhan, Robin, 371–75
"Glamour, That Certain
    Something," 371–75
Global Warming Cartoon, 470
Godwin, Gail, 19–23
Got Milk? ad, 180
Goya, Francisco de, art insert
"Greatness Gap, The," 368–71
"Ground Zero," 114–19

Hart, Laurie Kain, 453–57
Hemingway, Ernest, 267–72
Hopper, Edward, art insert
"Hot Boxes for Ex–Smokers,"
    295–99
"How to Get Unstuck Now!"
    251–56
"How to Write with Style," 29–34
Hughes, Langston, 427–28

"Improving Your Body Language
    Skills," 241–51
"Inconspicuous Consumption,"
    74–77
"Is Everybody Happy?" 347–52

Kerr, Bob, 60–66
Kidder, Tracy, 86–90
"Kids Who Kill Are Still Kids,"
    450–53

King Cartoon, 439
King, Colbert I., 160–63
Kinsley, Michael, 458–61
King, Michael, 222–27
Krauthammer, Charles, 368–71
Krucoff, Carol, 63–67

Laskas, Jeanne Marie, 74–77
"Learning to Love," 272–79
"Losing My Jihadism," 55–60
"Lost Lives of Women," 90–95

"Marks," 164–65
Martin, Judith, 288–94
McGarvey, Jack, 183–91
McKie, Robin, 154–60
McMillan, Terry, 23–29
Metaphor, 129, 345–46
Miller, Robert Keith, 352–56
Momaday, N. Scott, 44–47
Montgomery, David, 110–14
Mora, Pat, 95–99
"More Powerful Than . . . Ever:
    On-Screen and Off,
    Superheroes Are a Force to
    Reckon With," 210–18
Morrow, Lance, 103–10
"Mrs. Zajac," 86–90
Mullins, Laura, 377–81
Mundy, Lisa, 218–22

Narration, 40–42
"Notes from the Hip-Hop
    Underground," 201–06

Ohman, Jack, 439
"Only Daughter," 51–55
"On Reading and Becoming a
    Writer," 23–29
Ouellette, David M., 474–77
"Overlooked Victims of AIDS,
    The," 423–26

"Paragon or Parasite?" 377–81
Pastan, Linda, 164–65
Peer Evaluations, 35–36
Persistence of Memory, The, art insert
Picasso, Pablo, art insert
Prior, Markus, 206–10

"Psst! Human Capital,"
    323–26
Punctuation, 233–34
"Putting Your Job Interview into
    Rehearsal," 235–40

"Rap's Refusal of Injustice," 222–28
Reading
    responses to, 1–4
    steps to active, 4–12
"Real Media Divide, The," 206–10
Reid, Alistair, 375–77
"Remembering Lobo," 95–99
"Restoring Recess," 263–67
Ripley, Amanda, 143–50
Rodriguez, Luis J., 47–51
"Roles of Manners, The,"
    288–94
Room in New York, art insert

Sadker, David, 150–54
Sakamoto, Nancy Masterson,
    131–36
Saltz, Gail, 251–56
Schell, Jonathan, 114–19
"Science and the Secrets of Personal
    Space, The," 299–305
Segal, Carolyn Foster,
    326–31
Sentences, 176–78
    punctuating, 233–34
    varying, 176–78
7 Habits of Highly Successful
    Students, The, 36–37
Sharples, Tiffany, 272–79
Skandar, Alexa, 119–22
"Smarter Kids, Brought to You by
    the Letters T and V," 191–95
"Snow: A Prism of More Than
    Frozen Water," 110–14
"Social Science Finds: 'Marriage
    Matters,'" 397–408
"Society Is Dead: We Have
    Retreated into the IWorld,"
    9–12
Stanton, Elizabeth Cady,
    440–44
Steele, Shelby, 201–6
Sullivan, Andrew, 9–12

Summary, 13–14
Suplee, Curt, 299–305
"Surveying the Damage on Campus
    USA," 160–63
Synthesis, 13–17

Tan, Amy, 90–95
Third of May, 1808, The,
    art insert
Three Dancers, art insert
"Time's Trophy," 119–22
"To Be or Not to Be as Defined by
    TV," 183–91
Toles, Tom, 470
"Torture Myth, The," 466–70
Transitions, 128
"Trouble Woman," 100–03
*Two Women Seated by a Woodland
    Stream,* art insert
Tyrangiel, Josh, 100–03

Vachss, Andrew, 356–62
Viorst, Judith, 136–42
Vonnegut, Kurt, 29–34

Wagner, Gaye, 66–73
Waite, Linda J., 397–408
"Watcher at the Gates, The," 19–23
"Waterboarding: A Clarification,"
    462–67
"Ways We Lie, The," 305–16
"We Are Our Own Worst Imuses,"
    195–201
Welch, Jack, 257–63
"When Parents Are Toxic to
    Children," 391–97
"When Size Really Mattered,"
    471–74
Whitehead, Ralph, Jr., 316–22
"Who Says a Woman Can't Be
    Einstein?" 143–50
Wilbur, Richard, 17–18
"Working at McDonald's," 408–13
"Writer, The," 17–18
Writing
    preparing manuscript, 42–43
    reasons for, 2–4

Zimring, Franklin E., 295–99